The World at War, 1914–1945

Jeremy Black
University of Exeter

ROWMAN & LITTLEFIELD
Lanham • Boulder • New York • London

Executive Editor: Susan McEachern
Editorial Assistant: Katelyn Turner
Senior Marketing Manager: Kim Lyons

Credits and acknowledgments for material borrowed from other sources, and reproduced with permission, appear on the appropriate page within the text.

Published by Rowman & Littlefield
An imprint of The Rowman & Littlefield Publishing Group, Inc.
4501 Forbes Boulevard, Suite 200, Lanham, Maryland 20706
https://rowman.com

6 Tinworth Street, London SE11 5AL, United Kingdom

Copyright © 2019 by The Rowman & Littlefield Publishing Group, Inc.

All rights reserved. No part of this book may be reproduced in any form or by any electronic or mechanical means, including information storage and retrieval systems, without written permission from the publisher, except by a reviewer who may quote passages in a review.

British Library Cataloguing in Publication Information Available

Library of Congress Cataloging-in-Publication Data
Names: Black, Jeremy, 1955- author.
Title: The world at war, 1914-1945 / Jeremy Black.
Description: Lanham : Rowman & Littlefield, [2019] | Includes bibliographical references and index.
Identifiers: LCCN 2018058286 (print) | LCCN 2018060902 (ebook) | ISBN 9781538108369 (ebook) | ISBN 9781538108345 (cloth : alk. paper) | ISBN 9781538108352 (pbk. : alk. paper)
Subjects: LCSH: Military history, Modern—20th century. | World War, 1914-1918. | World War, 1939-1945. | History, Modern—20th century.
Classification: LCC D431 (ebook) | LCC D431 .B539 2019 (print) | DDC 940.4—dc23
LC record available at https://lccn.loc.gov/2018058286

For Laura and Jonathan Westbury

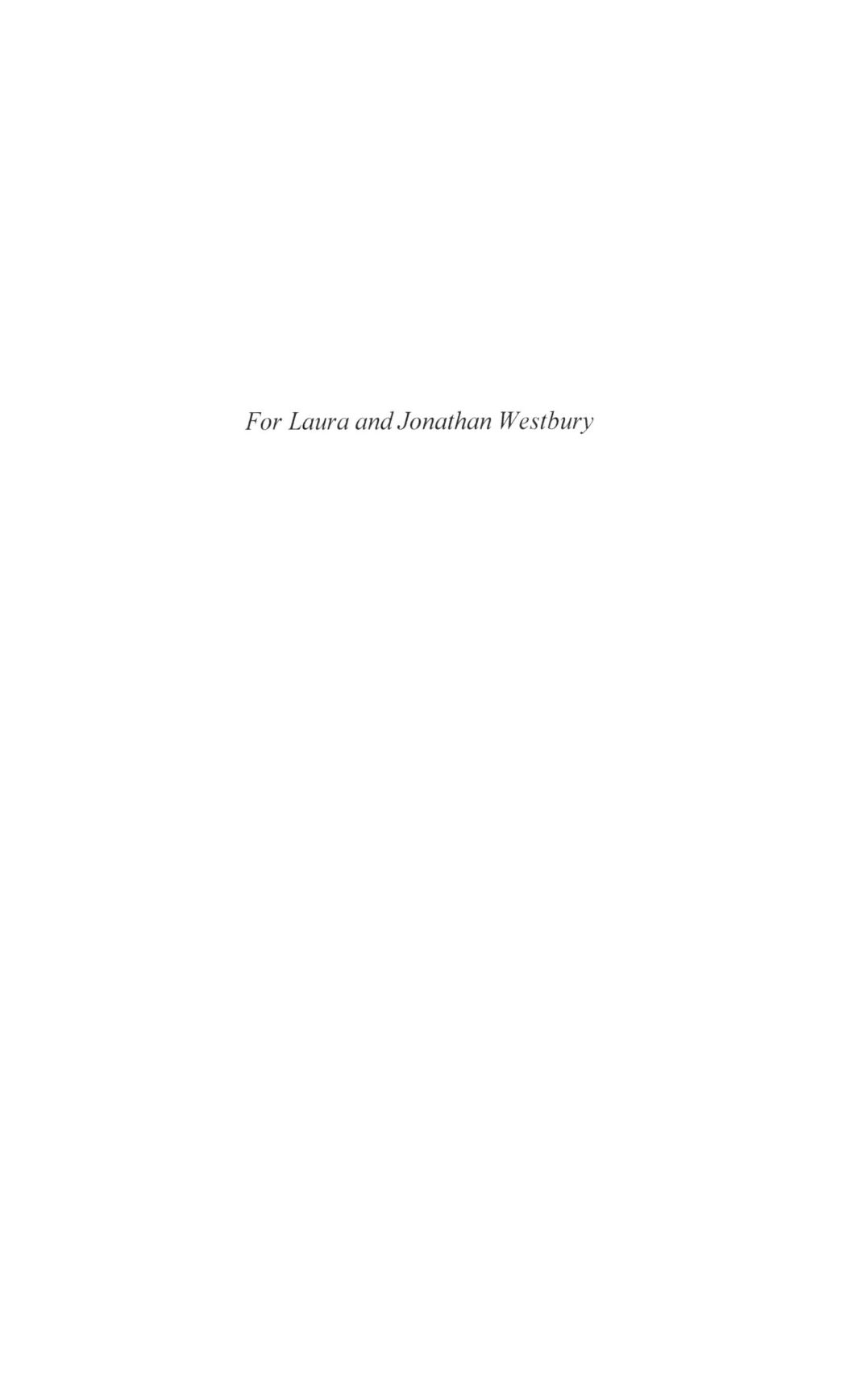

Contents

Preface	vii
Abbreviations	ix
Introduction	1

Part I: The First World War

1	Causes	7
2	The First World War, Land Warfare	29
3	The First World War at Sea	57
4	The First World War in the Air	79

Part II: The Interwar Years

5	The Interwar Years, Land Warfare	95
6	The Interwar Years at Sea	113
7	The Interwar Years in the Air	139

Part III: The Second World War

8	Causes	159
9	The Second World War, Land Warfare	187
10	The Second World War at Sea	227
11	The Second World War in the Air	269

Conclusions	303

Notes	315
Index	337
About the Author	351

Preface

"When one dug in the trenches to try and improve them, one always dug up French bodies, or arms, or legs." In his diary, writing on the Western Front in December 1914, Major Ian Forbes of the British army was in no doubt about the horrors of war. We must remember them also as we try to make sense of them.

Two world wars, being so close together, invite discussion in one book. Their history, important in itself, has also been of great consequence in world history. Focusing on the military history of these wars, this book discusses what happened and explains Allied victory in the two conflicts. The significance and complexity of the latter ensures that analysis has to come alongside narrative. The structure of the book is explained by dividing warfare into land, sea, and air, which are treated in that order for the First World War, the interwar period, and the Second World War. To explain each war, there is a separate chapter on the causes of each of the two world wars. The introduction very briefly sets the scene before we begin with the First World War. The conclusion brings the story together and focuses on several issues of key significance.

It has been a great pleasure to try out new ideas in lectures at the National WWII Museum in New Orleans, the University of Oxford, the American Museum in Bath, the New York Historical Society, the Chalke Valley Historical Festival, Marlborough College, Radley College, and the Torquay Library. Stan Carpenter, Heiko Werner Henning, David Morgan-Owen, Ciro Paoletti, and Frédéric Saffroy kindly commented on an earlier draft. Susan McEachern, as ever, has proved a most helpful publisher. This book is dedicated to Laura and Jonathan Westbury, good friends, kind hosts, and the bringers of much cheer.

Abbreviations

ABCD	America, Britain, China, and the Dutch
AFC	Australian Flying Corps
ASDIC	Anti-Submarine Detection Investigation Committee
AWM	Canberra, Australian War Memorial
BE	British Experimental
BEF	British Expeditionary Force
BL Add.	London, British Library, Department of Western Manuscripts, Additional Manuscripts
CAB	Cabinet Office papers
COIN	counterinsurgency
DRO	Devon Record Office
IRA	Irish Republican Army
LH	London, King's College, Liddell Hart Archive
LMA	London Metropolitan Archives
MS	manuscript
NA	London, National Archives
NAA	Canberra, National Archives
PREM	Prime Minister's Office Records
RAAF	Royal Australian Air Force
RAF	Royal Air Force
RFC	Royal Flying Corps

RNAS	Royal Naval Air Service
RUSI	Royal United Services Institute
VLR	very long range

Introduction

The crisis of the European world order and the rise of American power are the two leading contenders among many in the discussion of the world wars. They are both significant elements when searching for similarities between the two wars; but, in truth, the contrasts between the two conflicts also require discussion and certainly challenge attempts to provide a common analysis.

For example, as a consideration of the two chapters on the causes of the respective world wars (1 and 8) will underline, there were formidable contrasts between them. The most obvious include the very differing roles of China and Japan. Important to the Second World War, they were not substantially so to the causes and course of the First World War, which indeed has much to say about the character of global power and power politics of the 1910s. In this light, the argument, advanced by Michael Howard in a much-cited published lecture,[1] that a new world war began in 1941 with the German invasion of the Soviet Union and that the earlier German campaigns in 1939–41 were really the second stage of the First World War, suffers badly from its failure to consider the significance of the Sino-Japanese War that was already well in progress. Instead, as will be discussed in chapters 1 and 8, each of the world wars, and notably the Second World War, were "umbrella wars" involving a number of interacting, but also at least partially independent, struggles. For example, Japan and the Soviet Union fought a limited conflict in 1938–39 and, very separately, a totally successful full-scale one in 1945.

However interesting for Europe alone, the attempt to provide a common narrative is still deeply flawed. This attempt was particularly associated with Fritz Fischer, a German professor who, in *Griff nach der Weltmacht: Die Kriegzielpolitik des kaiserlichen Deutschland 1914–1918* (1961), held Germany responsible for the First World War. While a reasonable approach, he also suggested, more problematically, that there was continuity in German foreign policy from then to the Second World War, notably in his *Bündnis des Eliten: Zur Kontinuität der Machstrukturen in Deutschland, 1871–1945* (1979) and *Hitler war kein Betriebsunfall: Aufsätze* (1992), which led to a major controversy.

Separately, comparisons may well serve with other conflicts rather than with the other world war. For example, during the American Civil War (1861–65), the role of the Union blockade in creating savage economic pressures for the Confederacy prefigured the British blockade of Germany in the First World War. Both indicated a primacy of the strategic use of sea power in pursuit of total war goals, in this case blockade, over the alternative goal of seeking battle. To this extent, Britain understood the economic dimension of war to a greater extent than Germany.

The flaws in the idea of a common narrative for the two world wars are highly significant for the strategic dimension, the dimension that is generally underplayed in favor of a focus on the fighting, and certainly so for the First World War. Indeed, understanding the differences in goals between powers, including allies, helps to make sense of their priorities and casts light on questions of capabilities and effectiveness. Moreover, the development of strategic goals during the wars represents a dimension that requires underlining. So also, separately, does the need to focus on why one side won, rather than a tendency to explain why the other lost.

The two world wars were unprecedented in scale and casualties, but also in means. These were the first large conflicts waged simultaneously on land, on the sea, under the sea, and in the air, and the following discussion captures these elements, although there were major contrasts, for example in the use of air power in the two world wars. They were also the wars that attracted description as "industrial" and "total." The latter was in fact no novelty. Many conflicts have been "total," and certainly so as far as attacks on civilians were concerned. It is not easy to determine how best to present the element of conflict seen as "total." That is not a term that adequately captures the character of the two world wars, either in terms of the "face of battle" for individual combatants or with reference to the "home front." In practice, the regimented nature of the combatants and the disciplined character of industrial society were important contexts, each of which linked the war to prewar conditions, but the extent of industrial mobilization in the two world wars was certainly unprecedented. This, and other economic and social characteristics of the world wars, should be kept in mind during the assessment of the conflict.

At this point, it is necessary to turn to the causes of the First World War, a conflict that was long prepared and planned for but that certainly did not turn out as generally anticipated. It had that in common with the Second World War.

Part I

The First World War

Chapter One

Causes

The prospect of major war was discussed and planned for by many in the decades that closed for good with the beginning of fighting in 1914; but the probable nature and, still more, consequences of the resulting conflict were understood by few. War seemed likely because both experience and assumptions led in that direction. The experience of the previous century had been that key issues were settled by conflict, whether the two overthrows of Napoleon I of France by a European alliance (1814 and, after his return from exile, 1815), the unification of Italy (1860), the eventual maintenance of the American union in the face of the Civil War (1861–65), the transformation of Prussia into the German Empire thanks to repeated triumphs in the Wars of German Unification (1864, 1866, 1870–71), or the rise of Japan, with victories over China (1894–95) and Russia (1904–5). This process was also true for other, lesser states, such as Italy, Serbia, Greece, Romania, and Ethiopia, all of which traced their independence and expansion to success in recent warfare.

Conversely, states that had failed in such warfare, for example the Ottoman Empire (Turkey for short) or Bulgaria, both of which had been heavily defeated in the conflicts of 1911–13, the Balkan Wars, saw such defeats as an encouragement to reverse failure through subsequent struggles. Movements that lacked statehood, such as Irish and Polish nationalism, also looked to past defeats, notably unsuccessful rebellions against British and Russian rule in 1798 and 1863 respectively, as a call for fresh valor. These movements (correctly) saw war between the major states as an opportunity to press their claims. So also did second-rank states.

War and victories as a measure of national success constituted a key ideological and practical predisposition to struggle. This predisposition had a variety of bases, including the intellectual conviction that such struggle was a central and inevitable feature of natural and human existence and development, as well as a cultural belief that struggle expressed and secured masculinity and thus kept both society and civilization dynamic. Doubt was presented as female and was associated with weak emotions and feelings. Belief in war, as an expression of a martial spirit and an ideology of masculinity, was greatly sustained by popular literature in Europe, the United States, and Japan. In Britain, those who volunteered to fight in 1914–16 were the generation who would have grown up in the 1890s and 1900s reading storybooks like *Union Jack*, *Captain*, and *Chums*, and also the bellicose novels of G. A. Henty. Although Britain was not bellicose as far as other European powers were concerned, these and other publications had promoted popular militarism, especially in an imperial context.[1]

Linked, for some, to these views was a sense of anxiety based on the belief that the present situation was necessarily unstable and also prone to decline, decay, and degeneration. Such a fate apparently could only be avoided by vigilance, effort, and sacrifice. This cultural anxiety was accentuated by concerns about the alleged consequences of industrial society, urban living, and democratic populism. These concerns were focused in some cases, notably Germany, by an opposition to the left-wing politics believed to flow from these developments. Socialism was seen on the political right wing as a threat to Germany's ability and willingness to fight, and a similar view was held elsewhere.

There were also doubts about the strength of masculinity in the face of cultural and social changes. These doubts were related to worries about national degeneration in the context of a belief in Darwinian competition between nations and races, a competition that was seen as inherently violent. This approach in fact rested on a false understanding and a corruption of Darwinian theory from "survival of the fittest," which, as originally conceived, did not apply to states or peoples or groups within society, but to species and adaptations within species, for which the dynamics were different. Thus, Darwin's arguments were misused to justify aggression and domination and to offer a misplaced clarity.

These factors were accentuated by the apparent exigencies of an international system in which the only choice seemed to be between growth or decay, empire or impotence, and standing by allies or showing weakness.[2] To fail to act was, allegedly, to be doomed to failure. Furthermore, the territorial expansionism of the imperialism of the period gave a tone of greater competition to international relations, with alliances of mutual restraint being replaced by alliances focused on securing additional power.[3] Expansionism rose from a belief that there was a simple choice of growth or decline, a belief that encouraged a concern with relative position. Existing pacts, such as the Triple Alliance of Austria, Germany, and Italy, established in 1882, had often restrained allied states by joining together powers with different interests, notably Austria and Italy. However, these alliances appeared inadequate in the 1900s and 1910s as anxieties grew about shifts in international geopolitics and national politics.

The imperial hopes, dreams, anticipations, expectations, anxieties, and nightmares of the great European powers affected, and were affected by, the fate both of the non-European world and that of southeastern Europe, and to a degree not seen before. In particular, anxieties in, and about, the Balkans were to press directly and strongly on competing European alliance systems, ensuring that the limited wars and compromises at the expense of others, seen with large-scale European expansionism outside the Continent, could not eventually be sustained as a system within Europe itself.

These factors encouraged bellicosity, or at least an acceptance that war might be noble and strengthening as well as necessary; but, on a continuing pattern, they did not explain why large-scale conflict seemed more of a risk in the 1900s and early 1910s than earlier, nor why it broke out in 1914 and not earlier. Such explanation in part rests on contrasting assumptions. In particular, there is a tension between a "systemic" account of the outbreak of war, which would trace it to the nature of the competitive international system, and, alternatively, one that places greater weight on the agency (actions) of particular powers. The latter is a more convincing account as it makes greater allowance for the extent to which individual leaders and specific policy-making groups took the key decisions, including the crucial decisions of how, and when, to act. Insofar as a systems approach is adopted, this account is one that offers more for the role of strategic cultures and for the mismatch between them and the disputes and uncertainties that might arise as a result.

In particular, it is apparent that the leading factor was the encouragement provided to Austria (short for Austria-Hungary, the empire ruled by the Habsburgs) by German policy makers, notably the kaiser (emperor of Germany), Wilhelm II (r. 1888–1918), and his military advisers. The nervy kaiser was volatile, arrogant, weak, and highly competitive, not least toward Britain: he was hostile to his British mother.[4] The conservative German elite were worried about domestic changes, including left-wing activism, as well as about international challenges. This elite reflected the atavistic roots of much militarism and imperialism and the prejudices of a traditional ruling group who felt threatened by change and modernization and who used militarism to entrench, as well as to reflect, their privileges. The German regime, like others, was operating in an increasingly volatile situation, in which urbanization, mass literacy, industrialization, secularization, and nationalism were creating an uncertain and unfamiliar world. There was a particular spatial dynamic in that the wealth and political activism of industrial advance was concentrated in the west, notably the heavy industry of the Ruhr valley and the oceanic trading center of Hamburg, but much of the military elite based their position on landholdings in the agrarian east. Their relative value had diminished, both within Germany and, as a result of increased transoceanic trade, globally. Moreover, those who dominated the agrarian east felt threatened by Russian strength in neighboring Poland.

Faced by international and domestic challenges, the temptation, both in Germany and Austria, was to respond with the use of force, to impose order on the flux, or to gain order through coercion. Germany was affected domestically by pressures for welfare and education reform, and also by religious divisions. Militarism, in contrast, appeared to offer a source of unity and agreement. A growing sense of instability both encouraged the use of might to resist or channel it and provided opportunities to do so. In large part, militarism fed itself in Germany, particularly after the failure of the liberal revolutions there in 1848, for, instead, German nationalism was focused on the more authoritarian political culture of Prussia. By means of defeating Austria in 1866 and France in 1870–71, Prussia, which had earlier been one of the weaker and, due to its central position, more vulnerable of the major powers, created the German Empire, and the Hohenzollern kings became emperors.

German strength in a central position in Europe created a new set of geopolitical tensions. In part, tensions arose because the annexation of most of Alsace and part of coal- and iron-rich Lorraine from France as part of the peace settlement in 1871 left, as Otto von Bismarck, the German chancellor and a key figure in German unification, had been warned by the French emissary, a long-term sense of French grievance that posed a lasting security challenge to Germany on its western border.[5] This challenge was greatly mitigated, however, by Germany's far larger population and, therefore, army, and her stronger economy. France, moreover, was weakened by its competition with Britain in imperial expansion, especially, but not only, in sub-Saharan Africa. The two powers nearly went to war over control of Sudan in the Fashoda Crisis of 1898. Bellicosity in that case, however, was lanced by the possibilities of compromise at the expense of the vastness of Africa. In return for France's acceptance of Britain's position in Egypt and Sudan, Britain was to accept French expansion in Morocco.

Instead of fearing France alone, German policy makers saw danger in the possibility of French cooperation with other powers overshadowed by Germany's rise to power, such as Austria and Russia. Bismarck secured his achievement by means, from 1871, of alliance with Russia and Austria, notably the Dreikaiserbund (League of Three Emperors) of 1881. However, this achievement was neglected by Bismarck's successors, notably because Wilhelm II, who parted company with Bismarck in 1890, was scarcely risk averse and, instead, was committed to expansion, not stability. Wilhelm also viewed Russia with suspicion and regarded it as a racial threat, a theme that linked him to Hitler, as did anti-Semitism. The nonrenewal of the German-

Russian Reassurance Treaty represented a clear strategic deviation from Bismarck's foreign policy and his overriding strategy of keeping France isolated, and thus deterring her from seeking to overturn the system. France's failure in 1870–71 convinced French policy makers that they must not fight alone again.

Anxiety was a key element throughout, but the process of anxiety-driven aggression was particularly apparent with both Austria and Germany. The Austrian elite worried that the breakdown of Turkish power, notably as a result of Turkey's heavy defeat by the Balkan powers in the First Balkan War of 1912–13, was leading to a change in the balance of power and a degree of nationalist assertiveness in the Balkans, especially by Serbia, which had made major territorial gains as a result of the war. This assertiveness apparently threatened the cohesion of the Austrian Empire, not least because Serbia encouraged opposition to Austrian rule in neighboring Bosnia, which Austria had occupied in 1878 and annexed in 1908. Whether Austria was itself overstretched in the face of rising nationalism within the empire, which included the modern states of Croatia, Slovenia, Bosnia, Slovakia and the Czech Republic, and parts of Poland, Romania, and Italy, is a matter of controversy. However, political disputes related to this nationalism, some of which was separatist in character, affected the ability to pursue policy initiatives. Moreover, these disputes helped create a destabilizing sense of the enemy within, with these enemies having friends outside the empire.

In Austrian eyes, this enemy would be neutered by reordering the Balkans in a way that served Austria's interests and demonstrated its superiority, specifically by weakening Serbia. Ironically, an equal, or more serious, danger to the Austrian Empire came not from Slav nationalism but from a bellicose nationalism on the part of much of the ruling Austrian elite. There was both a misleading belief in military solutions to internal and external problems and a serious overestimation of their military potential, which accentuated Austrian domestic and international weaknesses. Each prefigured the German situation in 1939.

In Germany in 1914, there was concern about the problems of its Austrian ally and, as a result, about the problems of having Austria as an ally, although not to a sufficient degree. In the event, neither Germany nor Austria was to restrain the other sufficiently in 1914. This proved the key instance of the manner in which, with this war, the geopolitical logic of alliances drew powers into actions that were highly damaging, which was to be Italy's situation in 1940. Austria believed in its own might and capability, and in its German allies in case anything went wrong.

Yet, although Austria helped cause the war, Austria was not the crucial element for Germany, for there was fear of Russians, not Serbs, in Berlin, and not of Russians and Serbs as there was in Vienna. The negotiation of a Franco-Russian military agreement in 1894 had led Germany, fearing, indeed predicting, war on two fronts at once, to plan to achieve by speed the sequential war making (fighting enemies one after another) that had brought victory to Prussia in 1864–71 over Denmark, Austria, and France.

However, it appeared difficult for Germany to achieve a knockout blow against Russia, the frontier of which had moved west to include much of Poland as a result of the major role of the Russians in victory over Napoleon I in 1812–14. This westward movement, a key geopolitical factor, provided the defense-in-depth, which indeed was to enable Russia to survive considerable territorial losses to Germany in the first three years of the Great War and again in 1941. This defense-in-depth led German planners to focus prewar, first, on defeating France before turning against Russia, the course followed in 1940–41. Unlike Moscow, Paris appeared to be within reach of German forces, as had been shown unsuccessfully in 1792, and successfully in 1814 and 1870, and was to be nearly shown again in 1914, 1918, and, finally, successfully, 1940.

German strategy in 1914 depended on a key capability gap, which had uncertain operational results and strategic consequences: the contrast between rapid German mobilization of its forces, particularly reserves, for war, and its slower Russian counterpart. As a result of the significance of this gap, there was German concern as Russian offensive capability improved. This was a capability financed by France, not least in the shape of railway construction in Russian Poland, construction designed to speed the movement of Russian troops westward toward the Austrian and German borders. Each power had benefited from the three partitions of Poland in 1772–95 in order to seize all of the country between them.[6] The Russian military program announced in 1913 caused particular anxiety in Berlin, which gave Count Helmuth von Moltke (Moltke the Younger), chief of the German General Staff from 1906, further motivation to press for war in 1913–14. He feared that Germany would increasingly not be able to win later (a verdict endorsed in very different circumstances by the Second World War), and he thought that by 1916, Russia, with its larger population, would be in a position to start attacking effectively before the Germans had had an opportunity to defeat France. In Moltke's view, Germany's existing plans could not operate after 1916.

Had Moltke been open to other ways of thinking, matters might have been different. Ironically, although the Russians had built up an army superior to that of Austria, against whom they repeatedly did well in 1914–16, and had quickly recovered from defeat by Japan in 1904–5, the Russian attack on Germany was to be defeated easily and rapidly, and by only a small section of the German army, in 1914. That year, the Russians focused on Austria. Moreover, much of Russian Poland was conquered by the Germans in 1915, even though Germany was then fighting a two-front war and under attack on the Western Front.

The Germans, both military and politicians, had consistently overestimated Russia's military potential, in part because they exaggerated the quantitative indices of army strength at the expense of qualitative criteria. This factor indicates the more general problems of assessing strength, which is a major problem with the theory and practice of deterrence. These problems with assessment are more generally true of planning. Numbers are fixed and easily calculated, unlike motivation and other nonmetric factors that in practice play a key role. There is nothing to suggest that the German overestimation of Russian strength was deliberate, but the misperceptions proved very powerful. They owed much to more widespread irrational fears, which overshadowed practicalities and which also satisfied aspirations and concerns focused on promoting war. In 1941, in contrast, Soviet strength was underestimated.

In 1914, the defeat of France was regarded as probable because the Germans, encouraged by the example of victory over France in 1870–71, assumed that their better-prepared forces would win regardless of French actions. Although Moltke knew that the German army was not inherently superior to that of France, German commanders were very much in the shadow of expectations created by the repeated successes of 1864–71, just as British naval commanders were greatly affected by the Nelsonian legacy in their quest for a supposedly decisive, and certainly glorious, victory. Affected by advances in technology and planning methods, German commanders felt that their plan would work even better than those of 1864–71. The majority and, after 1906, all the British service attachés in Berlin reported that the German armed forces were preparing for attack, and 1913–15 was seen as the likeliest period for this aggression.[7]

Moltke's predecessor, Count Alfred von Schlieffen, had changed the General Staff when he was its head from 1891 to 1906, allowing its members to become military specialists at the expense of more general, nonmilitary knowledge. Nonmilitary problems were consciously excluded from General Staff thinking. Military decision makers therefore were allowed to conduct their planning in a vacuum, with scant regard for the political situation around them.[8] In 1914, by stressing future threats and affirming that Germany was still able to defeat likely opponents, the General Staff helped to push civilian policy makers toward war, although, in practice, civilians were not greatly consulted by the military, which had independent access to Wilhelm II. Moltke hoped that the resulting conflict would be the short and manageable war for which the Germans had been planning, but he feared that it could well be a long war, a struggle indeed for which Germany was unprepared. Because Moltke did not develop an alternative plan (instead deciding to scrap one in 1913), the option of deploying troops only in the East against Russia no longer existed in 1914.[9] Planning focused on France, and neither Germany nor Austria prepared adequately for war with Russia, which was an aspect both of how poorly they worked together and of the short-term nature of most military planning.

German intelligence capacity proved erratic, as indeed it also did in the Second World War. In 1941, there was to be inadequate planning by Germany for war with the Soviet Union, and in 1942 for the renewed attack. Inadequate planning was matched by poor preparation. In both world wars, the emphasis on "rational" planning encouraged the setting of goals that appeared viable but were overly ambitious.

German policy makers believed they could control the situation created by their Austrian ally, that if war came they had the necessary plan, and that their army was the best and was capable of executing the plan. Long-range economic planning was completely ignored in Germany, where it was treated as heresy against the confident belief in a short war and the conviction that quick victory was feasible thanks to rapid success on land, whatever threat the British fleet might pose in the long term. This conviction proved totally misplaced.

Alongside anxiety about Russia, there was an ambition on the part of German leaders that was more clearly a case of wishful thinking and strategic overreach, a process also seen in the following world war. This ambition in 1914 was for becoming not simply a great power but a world power, able to match Britain in this and thus to overthrow and replace her imperial position. To do so, Germany sought a navy able to contest that of Britain and in 1914 had the second largest in the world. This drive, in practice, was unnecessary to Germany's goals in Europe. Moreover, naval ambition was likely to alienate Britain seriously, both the government and the public, and therefore to ensure that these goals became unattainable, as indeed was to be the case. The assumptions that Britain's differences with France and Russia would remain insurmountable, and thus would lessen Britain's concern about Germany and make alliance with these powers unlikely, proved greatly mistaken. The Japanese elimination of Russia as a naval power in 1905 undermined Germany's calculations as it helped the British to focus on the German challenge rather than, as in the 1890s, those of France and Russia.

Concern about German intentions, particularly her naval ambitions, encouraged closer British relations with France from 1904. The Anglo-French entente of that year led to military talks between Britain and France, in part because defeat in the Russo-Japanese war of 1904–5 weakened Russia as a balancing element within Europe, thereby exposing France to German diplomatic pressure and also creating British alarm about German intentions, as in the First Moroccan Crisis of 1905–6. This crisis, provoked by Germany and an instance of how a struggle for primacy in a peripheral area could lead to warlike moves, was followed by Anglo-French staff talks aimed at dealing with a German threat. In 1905, a General Staff war game focused on a German violation of Belgian neutrality, while in 1907, British military maneuvers were conducted on the basis that Germany, not France, was the enemy. Moreover, also in 1907, fears of Germany contributed to an Anglo-Russian entente, which eased tensions between the two powers, notably competing ambitions and contrasting anxieties in South Asia. Germany, with its great economic strength, naval ambitions, and search for a "place in the sun," was increasingly seen in Britain as the principal threat. This was not an unreasonable view, as such a drive would certainly have followed German mastery of the Continent, again a situation that anticipated that in the following world war.

Political opinion was divided. There were influential British politicians who sought to maintain good relations with Germany. Moreover, the ententes with France and Russia were not alliances, and Britain failed to make her position clear, thus encouraging Germany to hope that Britain would not act in the event of war, which was also Hitler's mistaken belief when he invaded Poland in 1939.

European tensions rose in the years after 1910, with the respective alliances increasingly concerned about the real actions and supposed intentions of their rivals. The visits of President Raymond Poincaré of France to Russia in 1912 and 1914 seemed to underline the apparent danger to Germany posed by their alliance and therefore the need for protective action. The French increase in army spending in 1912, a response to the German move of the previous year, in turn led to a German rise in expenditure on the army. These increases and other moves encouraged a sense of instability and foreboding and helped drive forward an arms race on land, notably from early 1912.

In turn, this greater military capability, by lessening earlier weaknesses, made armed diplomacy more plausible while, at the same time, increasing a sense of vulnerability to the armed diplomacy of others. As deterrence appeared weaker, so it seemed necessary to identify and grasp windows of opportunity for action, which in turn greatly weakened deterrence.

The Germans obtained further evidence of closer links between Britain, France, and Russia in May 1914, with espionage information on Anglo-Russian talks for a naval agreement. Although in practice there was no joint war plan between France and Russia,[10] the Germans increasingly felt encircled and threatened, but, as a reminder that there were also failings in analysis elsewhere, British strategy was affected by an inability to grasp the consequences of closer diplomatic relations with France and Russia. In the sense that they, together, instead of serving as a deterrent, could make war with Germany more likely, this outcome was appreciated to a degree but not sought.

Russia attempted to recover from its defeat by Japan by building up its military anew with resources that came from economic growth and French loans, notably that of 1905, which gave Russia access to French capital markets. The percentage of total Russian expenditure on the military rose from 23.2 in 1907 to 28.2 in 1913, although the majority of Russian officers remained unable to put men and equipment to good use and, indeed, the Russo-Japanese War led to a conservative reaction in Russian military circles against attempts to reform operational practice.

From 1911, when Prime Minister Peter (Pyotr) Stolypin was assassinated, Russia was under a more interventionist and aggressive government, one that was less willing to subordinate geopolitical goals to domestic issues. Russia became Serbia's protector, although they were not formally allies, as the relationship was based upon Russia's implicit support for the Bulgarian and Serbian alliance of March 1912 and her explicit agreement to settle any ensuing disagreement over the disposition of the region of Macedonia when it was conquered from Turkey. There was a religious dimension, as Russia, Bulgaria, and Serbia were all Orthodox states, opposed alike to Islam and Catholicism, the latter the religion of the Austrian and Hungarian elites. In the autumn of 1912, international tension over Serbian policy led Austria and Russia to deploy troops in mutually threatening positions, but these forces withdrew in the spring of 1913.

The 1914 crisis, however, had a very different outcome. Visiting Sarajevo, the capital of the province of Bosnia, Archduke Franz Ferdinand, the nephew and heir to the very elderly Emperor Franz Joseph of Austria, and his wife Sophie were assassinated on June 28 by Gavrilo Princip, a Bosnian Serb, leaving black-and-white photographs of violence in hot streets. The terrorist group was under the control of the Black Hand, a secret Serbian nationalist organization pledged to the overthrow of Austrian control in South Slav territories, notably Bosnia. "Apis," Colonel Dragutin Dimitrijević, the head of Serbian military intelligence, was a crucial figure, able to ignore his government's efforts to contain the activities of the Black Hand, which he had founded in 1911. Apis sought both to create a Greater Serbia and to overthrow the Serbian prime minister, Nikola Pašić.

When the news of the killings in Sarajevo reached Vienna, there was shock and the customary response, not least by a militaristic state, to an unexpected and dramatic event, a sense that a display of action and power was required. This sense interacted with an already powerful view that war with Serbia was necessary, and this new situation apparently provided the excuse to take care of Serbia, a policy already discussed in 1912 and 1913. Believing that German backing would deter Russia, an inaccurate assessment, the Austrians sought not agreement with the Serbs, who in fact were willing to make important concessions and were prepared to accept binding arbitration on the points to which they objected, but a limited war with Serbia.

This policy was pushed by a key advocate of the value of force and the necessity of war, Franz Conrad von Hötzendorf (referred to as Conrad), the self-absorbed and seriously flawed head of the Austrian General Staff. In addition, aside from the conversion of Leopold Berchtold, the foreign minister, to a military solution to the challenge apparently posed by Serbia to Austrian rule, the aristocratic culture of the Austrian diplomatic corps did not favor compromise. Instead, prefiguring German attitudes to Slavs during the Second World War, the South Slavs were generally viewed with contempt, and there was a strong cultural preference supporting the alliance with Germany. At the same time, military decision makers, not diplomats, played the vital role in pushing for conflict with Serbia.[11] Alongside a number of other Austrian policy makers, Conrad believed that war was the best way to stabilize the Habsburg monarchy in the face of serious nationalist challenges from both within, notably Czechs and Poles, and without, especially Italy and Serbia. The killings at Sarajevo provided him with the opportunity to carry out his belief in preventive war.

German support to Austria meant crucial encouragement. This support reflected the belief in Berlin that a forceful response was necessary, appropriate, and likely to profit Austrian and German interests at a time when an opportunity for success existed. The Serb response of July 25 to a deliberately unacceptable Austrian ultimatum of July 23 was deemed inadequate and, on July 28, without pursuing the option of further negotiations, the Austrians declared war. The Russians, meanwhile, responded to the ultimatum to Serbia by beginning military preparations on the 26th. They were confident of French support and believed it necessary to act formally in order to protect Serbia.

On July 30, Russia declared general mobilization, a step that the Germans had already been preparing to take. Erich von Falkenhayn, the war minister, wanted to mobilize the previous day. As a result of Russia acting first, the Germans were able to present their step, in a misleading fashion, as defensive. Doing so helped to lessen potential domestic opposition, notably in the Reichstag (German Parliament), to the voting of necessary credits for war. German mobilization was, in part, a question of timing in the knowledge that Russia was about to mobilize.

In line with its planning, but also with a paranoia about encirclement, the German military was convinced that it must win the race to mobilize effectively and use the resulting strength, notably before the Russians could act against both Germany and its ally Austria. This concern encouraged the Germans, if they could not use the crisis to divide France and Russia, to attack both.[12] In part, they were led by their strategic concepts and operational concerns, notably how best to ensure victory in any war that broke out, but, throughout, German leaders opportunistically sought to use the Balkan crisis to change the balance of power in their favor. They were willing to risk a war because no other crisis was as likely or could be planned to produce a constellation of circumstances guaranteeing them the commitment of their main ally, Austria, and the support of the German public.

Thus, it is too much to say, as has been argued for Germany, that the war plans of 1914, with their dynamic interaction of mobilization and deployment, made "war by timetable" (a reference to the railway timetables that guided and registered the pace of mobilization) difficult to stop once a crisis occurred. Instead, such an argument both exaggerates the role of one particular factor and underplays the extent to which rulers, generals, and politicians were not trapped by circumstances. In fact, as was understood, their own roles, preferences, and choices were important. An underplaying of the importance of choice reflects an anachronistic, later sense that no one could have chosen to begin the war; but, in fact, in 1914, decision makers believed that war was necessary and could lead to a quick victory. So also with Hitler in 1941 when he attacked the Soviet Union.

The role of choice is illustrated by the extent to which an awareness of likely risks had helped prevent earlier crises since 1871 from leading to war. Moreover, alliances did not dictate participation: despite being their ally, Italy chose not to join Germany and Austria, instead declaring neutrality on August 3, prefiguring its choice in 1939. Again doing the same, the United States, which was not allied to any of the combatants, also opted for neutrality, President Woodrow Wilson ignoring pressure from Theodore Roosevelt, a former president, to go to war in response to the German violation of Belgian neutrality. In Europe, the Scandinavian states, the Netherlands, Portugal, Spain, Switzerland, Greece, Romania, and Bulgaria, all declared neutrality.[13] Reasons varied. Some powers, such as Italy, Romania, and Bulgaria, had territorial goals but did not think the situation sufficiently clear and propitious yet to encourage them to take sides in order to pursue them. Italy had made clear to its allies that it would not fight Britain.

In 1914, the key element in leading to war was that Austria and Germany chose to fight, and Russia to respond. All three were empires with their constitutionalism held in check by practices of imperial direction, the latter providing characteristics that were autocratic and that ensured that small coteries of decision makers had great influence. As with Japan, these states were happy to see war with other major powers as a tool of policy, rather than as a means of distant overseas colonial expansionism that had only limited consequences for their societies, the position of the British, French, and American elites.[14] Foreign offices and diplomats played only a secondary part in the policies of the autocracies, as the prospect of war led military considerations to come to the fore, while the rulers and their advisers took the key role in arbitrating between contrasting attitudes and policies.

The aggressive and ambitious views of Wilhelm II were certainly important to the serious deterioration in Anglo-German relations.[15] There was a clear contrast between the commitment of the British elite, including the monarchs, Edward VII (r. 1901–10) and George V (r. 1910–36), to parliamentary democracy and Wilhelm's antipathy to liberalism and parliamentary government, both of which were seen as weak. Edward's statue in Hobart, Tasmania, carries with it the inscription "The Peacemaker," which his personal diplomacy in furthering Anglo-French relations justified. The right-wing nationalists who looked to Wilhelm also despised parliamentary limitations, while Wilhelm's authoritarian position in the governmental system ensured that the extent to which such right-wing views were not, in fact, held by the bulk of the public could not determine policy. The moves to war were not taken by the elected representatives of the German populace.

For the Germans, Russian mobilization increased the imminent danger of war and provided an opportunity to advance their interests by demanding its cancellation, a step that would have identified Russia as an inadequate ally, and thus have wrecked the Franco-Russian alliance.[16] When this demand was refused, war on Russia was declared on August 1. Russia's ally, France, then became the key element for the Germans. They issued an ultimatum, one that France could not accept, that France declare neutrality and provide guarantees for this neutrality, steps that would have destroyed the alliance with Russia and made France appear a worthless ally for any other power. The guarantees included its forts at Toul, Verdun, and elsewhere, which would have left France highly vulnerable. These forts provided France with protection from German attack across their common frontier and also provided bases from which to anchor any French attack on German-held Lorraine. France's refusal to accept the ultimatum led the Germans to declare war on August 3.

This declaration did not exhaust the bellicosity of those early August days. Operational factors dictated strategy for the Germans: the heavily defended nature of the Franco-German frontier and the German need for speedy advances if sequential victory was to be obtained, with France overcome before Russia was defeated, led to a decision to attack France via Belgium. The flat terrain of much of Belgium north of the River Meuse was more appropriate for a rapid German advance than the more hilly terrain of eastern France, while the Franco-Belgian frontier was poorly fortified. Belgium, however, rejected a German ultimatum to provide passage. This step ensured that the Germans would launch a violent invasion, instead of mounting an occupation, and that entailed commitments and delays that helped derange the German plan.

Belgian neutrality was guaranteed under the 1839 Treaty of London by the major powers, including Britain as well as Prussia, now Germany. The Germans hoped that Britain would not respond to the invasion of Belgium and were inclined to discount or minimize the risk. Theobald von Bethmann-Hollweg was surprised by the British decision to go to war over what he termed "a scrap of paper," while Britain, with its small army, which had done conspicuously badly in 1899–1900 in the early stages of the Second Boer War (1899–1902) against the Afrikaners of South Africa, anyway was a minor concern to German army planners. This view proved very foolish. There was no concern about the possibility of American intervention, which, indeed, could have had no immediate military effect. "Necessity knows no law," declared Bethmann-Hollweg when speaking in the Reichstag on August 4 about the invasion of Belgium. "Necessity" had ensured that the German army had equipped itself with heavy howitzers and mortars before the war specifically to deal with the Belgian forts, especially around Liège.

The British government was far from keen on war, and, due to longstanding competing interests in Asia, there were serious tensions in Anglo-Russian relations despite an agreement of 1907 over spheres of influence in Persia. Nevertheless, the government was unwilling to see France's position in the balance of power overthrown and was concerned about the implications, if so, for Britain, while Germany's naval buildup had left the British profoundly distrustful of her expansionism. Indeed, this aggressive expansionism was regarded as more threatening than any particular calculations of the balance of power.

That concern did not necessarily mean war with Germany on behalf of France, which, in fact, was distrusted by many British strategists, as the debates in the Committee of Imperial Defence on a projected tunnel to France under the English Channel made clear. However, British military planners had long been concerned that war between France and Germany would lead to a German invasion of the Low Countries that had to be stopped.[17] In 1914, it was unclear until late whether Britain would join the conflict, but the invasion of Belgium united most British political opinion behind the war. National honor was an important factor in the political culture and international realities of British politics.[18]

As in other states, different British political groups had particular views, with the governing Liberal cabinet focused on the issue of Belgian neutrality, as was public opinion, while the leadership of the Conservative opposition was particularly concerned about maintaining the Anglo-French entente. The Liberals felt compelled to enter the war in part due to the knowledge that if they did not and the government fell (as it would), the Conservatives would gain power and would certainly become involved in support of France. On August 4, an ultimatum demanding the German evacuation of Belgium was issued. Prefiguring the outbreak of war with Germany in 1939, it was unanswered, leading to British entry into the war, which thereby became a more wide-ranging conflict and one that was to be far longer than the Germans had envisaged.

The flawed expectation of how Britain would react, and the longer-term mishandling of British sensitivities, anticipated the total German misjudgment of Britain in both 1939 and 1940 and were aspects of the wider German failure to address the political aspects of any conflict. As the Germans, overestimating their military capabilities and competence, sought, planned in great detail for, and anticipated a swift and decisive victory in order to avoid the military, political, economic, and social complexities of a large-scale and lengthy war between peoples, the political dimension was not significant for their military planners, who, in any case, seriously underestimated their opponents' power and resolve. An absence of rational assessment in the context of much wishful thinking, as well as calculations that in fact suggested to some that the planned short war was improbable, resulted, in Germany, in a countervailing attempt to control anxiety as well as risk. This attempt led to a focus on planning that deteriorated into both dogma and failure to note wider strategic and political parameters.[19]

The war therefore arose from a breakdown of deterrence accompanied by a willingness of key figures to turn to war. If the latter was combined with a strategic confusion at the heart of decision making, then the combination was deadly. Alongside this was the extent to which the dynamics of the crisis meant that constructive ambiguity was no longer credible. While planning for a war is not simple proof of intent, pressure from the military was highly significant. The decision makers had lost the sense of the fragility of peace and order. The politicians used the threat of war to put the other side (notably internationally but sometimes also domestically) at a disadvantage with the aim of increasing their own leverage, and, in so doing, they miscalculated.

In 1914, the British sought to rely on the traditional means of addressing an international crisis, that of negotiations by the leading powers, the Concert of Europe, seen from the seventeenth century and, more particularly, the nineteenth. This approach indeed had succeeded in the case of the First Balkan War (1912–13) in preventing a wider war. However, in 1914, operating to different purposes and on other timetables, Austria and Germany were unwilling to subordinate themselves to this approach. Their policies and attitudes caused the war, not the varied errors of the statesmen struggling with the developing crisis. It is also of course necessary to locate this German preference in the political and cultural bellicosity that was so strong in Germany, particularly in the early 1910s. A fervent national patriotism, a belief that war was a natural state, and a conviction that it was honorable to die for one's country were linked to a strong fear of falling behind and a sense that the opportunity that existed to attack might not continue.

Across Europe, cultural factors, such as national pride and a powerful sense of duty to fight, helped support the willingness of governments to declare war. Fatalism encouraged the resort to conflict, as did the potent cult of honor of the period[20] and a militarism seen even, in its widest sense, in Britain, which did not have conscription but which was a proud and confident nation at that time.

British participation in the war helped ensure that Germany would not win. This participation was not itself responsible for the serious failures to achieve victory in 1914 at the operational level, notably that of Germany, but was of strategic significance from the outset. That the attempt at victory was continued nevertheless, with a degree of success against weaker states, until it finally led to the defeat of all the German-led Central Powers in 1918 is a dimension that deserves attention. There is an obvious contrast in duration with the Franco-Prussian and Russo-Japanese Wars, but this was due not to a change in weapons technology but to the scale of conflict. The key scale was strategic, not operational, notably the extent to which alliance systems made it difficult to isolate a conflict and, instead, ensured that a military-political outcome involved the overthrow of an entire alliance. The involvement of an alliance made the First World War, and, indeed, the Second World War, very different from any major war since the Napoleonic Wars; and in the latter the alliance system had essentially been one-sided in that it was the case of Napoleon's opponents.

The primacy of the political dimension of strategy was demonstrated by the failure of the German alternative of dictating victory by means of pushing military factors to the fore. Germany subordinated political to military considerations in bringing Britain and the United States into the war against her in 1914 and 1917, respectively. In each case, although policies were justified on military grounds, respectively those of advancing more easily via Belgium and of trying to knock out British trade by submarine attack, this was a serious strategic mistake and one that contributed greatly to eventual German failure.

The German campaign had failed already in 1914 before the Allied counterattack in the Battle of the Marne and the subsequent stabilization of what became a Western Front in France and Belgium. This failure was because Britain's entry into the war, an entry that ultimately rested on the Belgian question, promised that what was already, due to Russian involvement, a two-front war would become a longer and more difficult struggle. This was so as long as France did not collapse, as it was to do in 1940 when, thanks to its alignment with the Soviet Union, Germany only faced a one-front war. In 1864–71, there had been no two-front wars for Prussia/Germany. Moreover, British involvement meant that German resources would be diverted to the navy.

The likely nature of a major war was one that had long attracted commentary, with correspondence in *The Times* of London about the industrialization of warfare as early as 1870. Initially, a small number of European thinkers had anticipated the horrific casualties that developments in military methods and the expansion of army size were likely to produce. Frederick Engels had argued that the American Civil War (1861–65) indicated the likely destructiveness of future conflict between European powers, and he thought that this destructiveness would undermine existing state and class hegemonies and make revolution possible. In his *War of the Future in Its Technical, Economic and Political Aspects* (1897), part of which was published in English as *Is*

War Now Impossible? (1899), the Polish financier Ivan Bloch suggested that the combination of modern military technology and industrial strength had made great-power warfare too destructive to be feasible, and that, if it occurred, it would resemble a great siege and would be won when one of the combatants succumbed to famine and revolution. Bloch argued that the stalemate on the battlefield that came from defensive firepower would translate into collapse on the home front.

The elder Moltke, the chief of the Prussian General Staff in the Wars of German Unification, himself had become increasingly skeptical about the potential of the strategic offensive after 1871, and, presciently, he was fearful that any major war would be a long one.[21] However, concerns about the consequent impact on casualty figures and military morale, and emphasis on the dangers of battlefield stalemate and of breakdown on the home front, only encouraged a focus on preventing the stalemate by winning the initial offensive and thus ensuring a short war. Indeed, in 1914, the dominance of thinking about the attack, rather than anything else, persuaded armies that the war could be won quickly.

That view suggests a degree of folly that was apparently to be underlined by the subsequent conduct of the war; but, in practice, military planners were well aware of the possibilities of defensive firepower, and some of the remedies that were to be employed during the conflict were already in evidence. For example, German planners emphasized infantry-artillery coordination in the attack, as well as minimizing exposure to artillery fire by advancing in dispersed formations that coalesced for a final assault. Furthermore, it was observed that defensive strength could be challenged by field artillery operating in support of the attacking force.

However, a major problem with the German military maneuvers and war games was posed by the need to satisfy the expectations of Wilhelm II, so that the defensive effect of machine guns, for example, was often underplayed, while the effect of the assault was overplayed. The maneuvers were contrived to show the strength of cavalry against infantry or machine guns.

On land and at sea, nevertheless, all powers sought to integrate new weapons, as well as improved weaponry, such as new artillery, and organizational means and systems, into their militaries, their maneuvers, and their plans, as part of the process by which they responded to advances and to apparent deficiencies.

The major war in the decade prior to the First World War was that between Russia and Japan, and it was followed carefully by foreign observers who saw the war as a triumph for Europeanization in the form of Western military organization: the Japanese, whose army was modeled on the German and navy on the British, won by employing European military systems and technology more effectively than the Russians. Yet the Japanese victory also came as a shock, in part because of Western racialist assumptions. Advocates of the offensive argued that the Russians stood on the defensive in Manchuria and lost, while the Japanese took the initiative, launched frontal assaults on entrenched forces strengthened by machine guns and quick-firing artillery, and prevailed, despite horrific casualties.

Most commentators focused on tactical and operational factors and overlooked the strategic dimension, notably the extent to which the land battles had not been decisive but only caused the Russians to fall back in Manchuria, while the Japanese, like the Germans in France in the winter of 1870–71, had been put under great pressure by the continuation of the war, which they could not afford. Japanese victory in practice owed much to political weakness in St. Petersburg in 1905, notably a revolution there, in part fostered by Japanese military intelligence, rather as German sponsoring of the Bolsheviks played a role in 1917. However, this strategic dimension behind Japanese victory was neglected, while Japanese success on the battlefield and in the war ensured that the tactical superiority of the defense was further underplayed. Given contemporary racist attitudes, European experts concluded that the infantry of the superior races of Europe would be capable of at least similar deeds, albeit at heavy cost, maybe a third of the army.[22]

European army leaders assumed that troop morale and discipline would enable them to bear such losses, but the expectation of them provided the impetus for programs to expand the army's size, including discussion in Britain about the need for conscription or more volunteering. The expansion in army size across much of Europe took forward the example created by the German army in the Wars of Unification and also drew on the major growth in the population of the West and Japan. The military, however, failed to anticipate how long a major conflict might last; or anticipated it, but omitted to tell civilian politicians, for fear that, if they knew, they would never contemplate war as an option. In Austria, the army leadership, which believed that war would be socially rejuvenating, failed to inform civilian ministers about the reality of the military situation.[23]

SUBSEQUENT ENTRIES

With subsequent entries into the war in Europe, nationalism and power politics interacted in the prism of individual and group hopes and fears.[24] Control over territory was a key bargaining basis. In 1914, Italy had not come to the aid of Germany and Austria, its allies since 1882. This enabled France to redeploy the nine divisions left to cover the border. Instead, Italy was won over by the Treaty of London, signed on April 26, 1915, by which Britain, France, and Russia promised Italy extensive gains from Austria: the Trentino, South Tyrol, Trieste, Gorizia, Istria, and northern Dalmatia. This meant that those territories, presented to the public in Italy as the last stage of the war for independence from Austria, had to be conquered. Germany had bullied Austria into offering the Trentino to Italy, but Austria was not willing to match the Allied offer elsewhere.

Only the Socialist Party opposed the war when it was voted on by the Italian Parliament on May 20. The remainder of the political world wished to see Italy become a great power, and Antonio Salandra, the conservative prime minister, presented Italy's policy as "sacred selfishness." Benito Mussolini, the editor of the Socialist Party newspaper *Avanti*, was expelled from the party because of his support for the war, which he saw as a reconciliation of patriotism and socialism. Instead, with support from Italian and French industrialists, Mussolini launched the interventionist paper *Il Populo d'Italia*. Italy declared war on Austria on May 23 and on Turkey on August 21, although not on Germany until August 27, 1916, as the government did not wish to provoke the Germans to send more troops to the Italian front.

Bulgaria, in turn, joined the German alliance in 1915. This was part of the equations of territorial offers. The entry was related to the position of Romania. Bulgaria's entry into the war had been pressed for by the Hungarian political establishment, which had resisted support from Wilhelm II and Franz Josef for the Romanian offer of continued neutrality in return for autonomy for Transylvania. It was the part of the Habsburg Empire with a Romanian majority, a part within the kingdom of Hungary. Instead, the Hungarian leadership argued that Bulgarian entry would isolate and neutralize Romania. The Bulgarians were promised Serbian Macedonian and Serbian territory on the left bank of the River Morava by Germany and Austria, who also successfully pressed Turkey to offer Bulgaria territory. In contrast, Russia had supported Serbia in opposing promised gains for Bulgaria in Macedonia if it joined the Allies.

The entry of Bulgaria and Italy into the war did not reflect a commitment to particular alliances but, rather, the continued determination and perceived need for second-rank powers to make assessments of opportunity. Far from the perceived ideology of either alliance playing a role, the key element was the possibility of gaining territories. They were small in themselves but were made important as a result of nationalist public myths. Their gain was seen as a sign of national success, one that justified the regime.

In turn, Romania entered the war in 1916. Its government sought Transylvania and Bukovina from Austria and was encouraged to enter the war by Russian success that year. By going to war, the Romanians hoped to benefit as a victor in what might be an imminent peace. On August 27, Romania declared war on Austria, but Germany declared war on Romania the following day and was rapidly followed by Bulgaria and Turkey. Most of Romania was swiftly overrun.

AMERICA ENTERS THE WAR, 1917

The German decision to turn to unrestricted submarine warfare reflected not a rationalist balance of risks and opportunities but an ideology of total war and a powerful Anglophobia based on nationalist right-wing circles, for example the Pan-German League, that saw British liberalism and capitalism as a threat to German culture. These ideas were given political bite by the argument that the German government, notably the chancellor, Bethmann-Hollweg, was defeatist and interested in a compromise peace, which he indeed hoped for in late 1916 via American mediation. Instead, support for unrestricted warfare was presented as a sign of, and security for, nationalist commitment, a view later to be taken by the Nazis when they pressed for total war.

On January 31, 1917, despite Bethmann-Hollweg's opposition, Germany announced, and on February 2 resumed, unconditional submarine warfare, which led to America breaking diplomatic links the next day and declaring war on Germany (but not its allies) on April 6. The German military leadership, increasingly politically influential, was unsympathetic to American moralizing, while, as in 1941, there was also the view that America was already helping the British and French war effort as much as it could commercially, which was the case to a considerable extent. Moreover, there was a conviction that Britain could be driven out of the war rapidly by heavy sinkings of merchantmen: a belief that the submarines could achieve much and that this achievement would have an obvious consequence. It was claimed that the British would sue for peace on August 1, 1917. Furthermore, many German submarine enthusiasts assumed that their force would be able to impede the movement of American troops to Europe very seriously and, more generally, there was a failure (shared by the Allies) to appreciate American strength.[25] Thus, Germany in 1917 prefigured the situation of Germany and Japan in 1941, and with similar dire consequences.

In 1914, there was active hostility in America to the idea of participation in the European war. It was seen as alien to American interests and antipathetic to her ideology, although the liberal credentials of American policy were rather tarnished by interventions in Mexico in 1914 and 1916, Haiti in 1915, and the Dominican Republic in 1916. These interventions reflected and camouflaged imperialist assumptions, but not a drive for territorial expansion, which, indeed, was not pursued. The unrestricted submarine warfare that sank American ships (and also violated international law) led to a major shift in attitudes in which Americans became persuaded of the dangerous consequences of German strength and ambitions, and did so in a highly moralized form that encouraged large-scale commitment. Thus, the United States constructed national interest in terms of the freedom of international trade from unrestricted submarine warfare.

Germany's crass wartime diplomacy and mishandled propaganda efforts exacerbated the situation, notably an apparent willingness to divert American strength by encouraging Mexican opposition, including revanche for the major losses suffered in the Mexican-American War of 1846–48. The Americans were made aware of this when the British intercepted a telegram to the German ambassador in Mexico from Arthur Zimmermann, the foreign minister. The logic of this apparently bizarre move was preemptive: the Germans wished to distract American energies from war in Europe. Yet again, strategic factors were ignored in favor of operational considerations. American sensitivity about German links with unstable Mexico was acute: later that year, the *San Francisco Chronicle* claimed that German submarines were being constructed at a secret base in Mexico, an aspect of a more varied sensitivity to real and alleged German military plans.[26]

The United States had given neutrality added legitimacy to other states.[27] In turn, after she broke off diplomatic relations with Germany in February, she invited all neutral countries to do the same, and this appeal had some success. Aside from Latin American states breaking off diplomatic relations with Germany, others followed the United States in declaring war, including Cuba and Panama, both American client states, on August 7, and Brazil, which also suffered from the unrestricted submarine warfare, on October 26, 1917. However, the Brazilian contribution was more modest than in the Second World War, when about twenty-five thousand troops were sent to fight. In the First World War, in contrast, only a small Brazilian naval squadron was eventually dispatched, and it did not see active service. Nevertheless, the Brazilian declaration of war contributed to Allied commercial warfare against Germany. Guatemala, Nicaragua, Costa Rica, Honduras, and Haiti followed in declaring war in 1918.[28] The United States had declared war on Austria on December 7, 1917, but did not follow suit against Bulgaria or Turkey.

Seeking an opportunity to enter the conflict, China broke off diplomatic relations with Germany on March 14, 1917, and declared war on Germany and Austria on August 14: Siam (Thailand) had done so on July 22. The French proved receptive to the Chinese idea of an expeditionary force, but, although laborers in the "Chinese Labour Corps," active since 1916, were acceptable, the other Allies were opposed to the dispatch of Chinese troops, for political reasons and because of concerns about fighting quality and the transportation burden, and the plan failed.[29] Japan was determined to retain its political position in China and was unwilling to see the latter contribute to the war effort. Although important, the war was far less central for East Asia than was to be the Second World War.

Chapter Two

The First World War, Land Warfare

> On the 14th [April 1918] about 6.30 am the Germans attacked our right in two lines, but were quickly stopped by our fire. This attack was supported by an armoured car, which though inflicting two casualties would not face the music from our Lewis Guns. A tree was later felled across the road to block any further attempt. At about 8.00 am there was a heavy bombardment on the battalion on our left, against whom they advanced in waves presenting excellent targets for cross-fire. . . . This attack quietened down about noon, and at this time the battalion on our right was attacked, heavily shelled and machine-gunned and withdrew, but No. 2 Company at once restored the situation by a gallant charge, some going through up to their waists in water. . . . Battalion headquarters was shelled about 5.00 pm and we evacuated it. A formation in front of the centre company was dispersed by artillery fire, and no attack materialised.[1]

The dominant image for this cataclysmic conflict is that of the apparent bloody stasis and senseless slaughter of trench warfare. That view is endlessly repeated and became the leitmotif of public commemoration during the anniversary occasions from 2014 to 2018. Indeed, many public myths invest in this account of the First World War. In particular, it serves as a way to discredit the ancien régimes of Europe; to provide a counterpoint to military conduct subsequently, notably in the Second World War, which is presented as a "good war" in comparison; and as an allegedly key background to the foundation in 1958 of what became the European Union. The last was symbolized in 1984 by President François Mitterrand of France and Chancellor Helmut Kohl of West Germany holding hands when visiting the deadly battlefield of Verdun, the site of a major and sustained Franco-German clash in 1916. Family narrative and influential literary constructions of the novels and poems deemed worthy of attention both also look back to these views of the war. Explanations of the Russian Revolution, the postwar development of

Fascism, the rise of the United States to great-power status, the origins of instability in the Middle East, the foundation of Israel, and much else all focus on the conflict.

The situation was in fact far more complex. The impressions of tactical stasis, operational failure, strategic nullity, and indecisive conflict are not well founded if the war as a whole is considered, as opposed to many of its individual offensives, while certain offensives were indeed successful, decisive, and effective. From the perspectives of Eastern Europe, the Balkans, the Middle East, and Germany's overseas colonies, the war saw much movement. Moreover, Serbia and Romania were in effect knocked out of the war in 1915 and 1916 respectively, while, in 1917, Russia was knocked out, and Italy nearly was. In 1918, Bulgaria, Turkey, Austria (i.e., Austro-Hungary), and Germany were all defeated to the point of surrender.

Even if attention is shifted solely to the Western Front, that in France and Belgium, the concentration of so much force and resources there, in defense as well as attack, did not prevent near victories for Germany in 1914 and 1918, and victory for its opponents (principally Britain, France, and the United States) in 1918. Moreover, as part of this process, the major tactical problems posed by trench warfare were overcome, and at the tactical, operational, and strategic levels. The Western Front was never in stasis, although it did appear to be static. In a relatively rapid learning process, the Allies worked out how to direct unprecedented firepower with effect, German trench systems were broken into and through, and fresh advances were made. It proved possible in 1918 for the Allies (although not earlier in the year for the Germans) to coincide and sustain attacks along a broad front in order to prevent the sealing of any breakthrough by means of concentrating reserves. This situation prefigured Allied success against Germany in 1945. In that respect, the two wars were not too different.

Problems that had confronted perceptive commentators in the prewar decades were overcome, as were longer-lasting command issues, notably that of the combination of firepower and mobility. Technology played a role. This was not so much with the invention and deployment of the tank, as its potential, at once undoubted and problematic, was not yet brought to fruition. Instead, the key element, among many aspects of developing technology, was the use of effective aerial reconnaissance in order to map opposing trench systems so that large-scale heavy artillery fire, eventually supported by a plentiful supply of shells, could be accurately directed and monitored. The net effect was a conflict that, despite its being between advanced economies deploying unprecedented resources, was, nevertheless, able to deliver a decisive military and political result, and in fewer campaigning seasons than in the Second World War.

STRATEGIES

It is instructive to consider the First World War in the light of the other conflicts of that decade, because the key element that emerges is that the campaigns of movement in that war were not, as it were, falling away from the "true state" of the conflict, that on the Western Front, but, instead, were more consistent with those elsewhere. The major contrast is that of the political dimension, in that the conflicts in Mexico, China, and, from 1917, Russia were civil wars, whereas the different aspect of the First World War was that it did not involve much civil warfare, and, indeed, less than that in the Second World War.

This contrast serves to remind us of the varied strands of war in terms of their political context. Wars between states necessarily focused on frontier zones, unless there was a collapse of one state and occupation became a key means through which the continuing conflict was pursued. In contrast, the capture of the capital and of other major cities was the central means in civil warfare of any scale, as opposed to simply regional insurrections defying state authority. As a result, capitals were the crucial settings for the Irish rising in 1916, the Bolshevik takeover of Russia in 1917, and the nationalist movements in the Austro-Hungarian Empire at the close of the war.

In 1914, Germany sought to adapt the Franco-Prussian War of 1870–71 for the exigencies of a two-front conflict also involving Russia. As a first stage, Germany envisaged a repeat of the Franco-Prussian War, with France collapsing, having suffered similar serious command failures to those in 1870. Austria similarly believed that a war would be quick and decisive and therefore worth taking the risk.

Nothing really played out according to the script, as their opponents proved to be tougher to break than anticipated, which led to exhaustion as well as very high casualties. Austria failed badly in an attempt to conquer Serbia, whose army was less well resourced but much better commanded,[2] and Austria was also put under heavy pressure by Russia. The 1914 campaign showed, moreover, that German war making, with its emphasis on surprise, speed, and overwhelming and dynamic force at the chosen point of contact, was not effective against a French defense that retained the capacity to use reserves by redeploying troops by rail during the course of operations.

German troops were well trained, and their morale may have been better than that of the French and British, although that is both far from clear and, anyway, as in the Second World War, something that is difficult to assess in aggregate. Nevertheless, aside from serious faults in German planning and execution, notably the lack of coordination between the moves on the German left flank and overall German strategy, as well as serious operational incoherence on the right flank, there were also problems with German equipment and discipline that qualify the usual picture of German competence.[3]

This is a point that is also valid for the Second World War, and one that, because it is widely underrated, raises questions about how armies are assessed, both in scholarly terms and by the public.[4]

The Germans had also failed to appreciate the exhaustion their troops would experience on their rapid and lengthy advance, and the difficulties their logistical tail would face in keeping up with a rapidly advancing assault force. This was an aspect of the German failure to understand the weakness of plans and that Germany, as well as France, would suffer from "friction." This was key to the ineptness of the German plan in 1914. It required faultless execution in order to outflank the French and catch them in a sort of vice in northeast France and allowed for little friction. In addition, a dangerous overconfidence was apparent. The Germans were apt to consider the enemy a "constant" instead of an "opposing variable." So also for other powers, such that it was a question of which among the armies, all of whom had grave structural, logistical, and leadership problems, would manage most successfully.

The "fog of war" discerned by Clausewitz—the distorting impact of circumstances and events on plans—was much in evidence, as it was again to be with the German offensives in the West in 1916 and 1918. Initially, however, the war appeared to demonstrate the vulnerability of fortresses to German attack. The Belgian fortress complexes all fell in 1914 after bombardment by Austrian 305 mm and German 420 mm heavy howitzers, designed before the war specifically for this purpose. The latter fired high-explosive shells able to penetrate ten feet of concrete, which were devastating. Nevertheless, Liège, the most important complex for the German advance, took far longer to fall than the Germans had anticipated and planned: eleven days instead of two. This dramatic failure of the schedule of conquest hit the carefully planned, sequential character of the German advance, more specifically because Liège was a major crossing point over the River Meuse and an important rail junction. The significance of railways ensured that the control of rail junctions was more important than in earlier conflicts, notably in the logistical requirements posed by the very large armies that were available, in particular their artillery.

As a result, the defense of Liège delayed the provision of an adequate supply system to support the German advance across Belgium. The initial attacks on Liège were driven back on August 5, but the fortification system depended on a powerful force to fill the gaps between the twelve armored forts. In its absence, the Germans were able to move through these gaps, although the forts continued to resist, some until August 16. The Germans thus gained mobility and were not subsequently held up by fortifications in their advance on Paris. Namur and Antwerp also fell, the first, another Meuse crossing point, after only four days' bombardment, and the Germans were able to advance into France without worrying much about fortresses, although Maubeuge put up a good resistance.

Compared to the time taken to capture these fortresses on earlier occasions, the speed in 1914 indicated a greater potential against prepared defenses. Conversely, there had also been speedy captures earlier. One difference in 1914 was that of the greater geographical extent of a fortress and, therefore, the scale of the effort potentially required to capture it, notably the deployment of huge masses of artillery, including large-caliber artillery with their heavy shells.

As in 1941 against the Soviet Union, the German army did not measure up to its aspirations or match its leading sectors. The training of German reserves was much less developed than that of the regular units, and this problem helped explain the failures of 1914, for German war planning counted on the reserves to do much more than they were trained to do. Reserve units were placed straightaway into the front line without the benefit of a few weeks of intense preparation and training to bring them up to full combat readiness, which is the modern practice. There was a tendency to believe that the "German soldier" could, and would, do whatever was planned.

During their gaming for an invasion of France, the Germans at times encountered armies in the "entrenched camps" at Paris or elsewhere. In almost every game, the German officers playing the French put up a stout defense but did not attack the forces moving past their positions, apart from in a 1911 war game when the "French" player made some spoiling attacks from Paris. All senior German commanders appear to have been convinced that entrenched camps need only be bypassed after being screened, a task for which they made inadequate preparations.

Their neglect of the ability of French troops to attack out of their defenses contributed to the German failure of 1914 when the French Sixth Army attacked out of Paris, initiating the Battle of the Marne. In this battle, the overextended, exhausted, badly commanded, and poorly deployed Germans, who had successfully advanced through Belgium, were stopped and driven to pull back from near Paris. Operating on interior lines and using rail, trucks, buses, and taxis, the French could redeploy in a way that the Germans, operating on exterior lines and walking, could not. Earlier in the campaign, the Germans had been surprised by the ability of the British Expeditionary Force (BEF) to put up a good defensive fight against the German advance in the Battle of Mons.

By September 1914, therefore, the carefully prepared German prewar strategic planning appeared precarious and overoptimistic, not least because two corps had been transferred to the Eastern Front to oppose an initially successful Russian invasion of East Prussia. The absence of a German plan B became a readily apparent issue as the Germans did not know how to deal with the check at the Marne, either operationally or strategically. Moltke, the chief of the General Staff, was then replaced.[5]

After the Battle of the Marne, both sides, in the "Race to the Sea," then sought to turn their opponent's flank toward the English Channel in a new version of envelopment. Each failed. The result left a front line now extending from the Alps to the Channel, the Western Front. Initially not continuous and poorly fortified, this line was soon consolidated. That bland remark scarcely gives due weight to the nature of the fighting. On November 12, 1914, Lieutenant John Dimmer of the British army, in command of four machine guns at Klein Zillebeke, Belgium, was exposed to heavy German attack, subsequently writing to his mother,

> They shelled us unmercifully, and poured in a perfect hail of bullets at a range of about 100 yards. I got my guns going, but they smashed one up almost immediately, and then turned all their attention on the gun I was with, and succeeded in smashing that too, but before they completed the job I had been twice grounded, and was finally knocked out with the gun. My face is spattered with pieces of my gun and pieces of shell, and I have a bullet in my face and four small holes in my right shoulder. It made rather a nasty mess of me at first, but now that I am washed and my wounds dressed I look quite all right.[6]

Dimmer was to be killed in action in 1918. His account is instructive for the fortitude he displayed, a factor that does not tend to be emphasized in the modern treatment of the contemporary British literature of the war selected for consideration, which, instead, focuses on criticism of the conduct of the war and the despair of the writers. In 1914–15 and 1941–42, there was a similar consolidation of the German front line on the Eastern Front, but the lower density of troops there made the consolidation far less pronounced.

In late 1914, the Germans were now committed to the two-front war they had launched. Fixed in the West, they could not switch all their forces eastward in order to knock Russia out of the war, as had been initially planned for the aftermath of a rapid victory in the West. However, in 1914, the German victory, in battles at Tannenberg and the Masurian Lakes, over invading Russian forces in East Prussia, as well as the defeat of the large-scale French offensive in Lorraine, ensured that Germany's problems were not those of having to defend itself from sustained major land offensives, as was to be the case in the Second World War in 1944–45.

German strategy was also affected by the extent to which the rate of change in military technology outstripped strategy because the tactics employed did not match the power of the technology. This was a problem more particularly in the stalemate following the opening battles of the war. The tactics, and indeed the operational doctrine and methods, simply did not take account of the capabilities of the technology, largely because no one fully appreciated what these capabilities were. The shortness of European wars from the 1860s did not help. Easy victories against less able opponents proved misleading.

The failure of the 1914 plans of all the powers bar Serbia, which had mounted a successful defense against Austrian attack, led not to a strategic impasse but to a struggle with a very different timescale from that which had been anticipated. What has been presented as the tactical impasse of the trenches was in reality subordinate to this situation. As a consequence, there were very different requirements for manpower and supplies than those assumed at the outset.

Moreover, the strategic situation was inherently volatile as each side made major efforts to alter the equations of alliance strength, either by bringing down the alliance structure of the other side or by expanding their own alliance system. Thus, the entry of Italy (1915) and the United States (1917) and the loss of Russia (1917) in the system of the Allies were all crucial events for land warfare, as they affected the number of fronts and the forces available, sometimes greatly so. Won by promises of territorial gain, Italy's entry put pressure on Germany's leading ally, Austria, although less than the British and French had hoped. The entry of the United States greatly enlarged the Allied forces available for the Western Front, although, unlike in the Second World War, it did not mean an increase in the number of fronts on which the war was contested. The loss of Russia gave Germany the prospect of a one-front war, albeit against far worse odds than in 1870–71: by late 1917, Britain, the United States, and Italy were all allied with France. Japan's participation in the war on the Allied side from 1914 was mostly significant at sea but also greatly lessened the number of strategic challenges the Allies had to face.

Returning strategic considerations to their due place, and within a conflict characterized, like other wide-ranging ones, by simultaneity and interactions,[7] particular offensives should be seen in the light of these issues and opportunities. The Allied Gallipoli expedition of 1915 would, it was hoped, knock Turkey out of the war, help keep Serbia in it, and maybe also lead to Greek entry. It failed. Similarly, Romania's entry on the Allied side in 1916 did not produce the hoped-for results, for an invasion by Austria, Bulgaria, and Germany rapidly defeated Romania. Nevertheless, this was another instance of strategic enhancement by alliance building, and one that tied down some German forces that year.

THE WESTERN FRONT

On the Western Front, the stalemate, threatened by the turn to trench warfare in late 1914 arising from the failure of Germany's war plan, was eventually overcome by France, Britain, and their allies, particularly the United States.

However, this success, which was necessary in order to regain territory conquered by the Germans, gains that they were not willing to negotiate away, was achieved only after a very costly learning curve.

In contradiction to what might appear today to be the obvious danger of advancing against defensive positions, both sides believed that they would be more successful if they took the initiative. By doing so, they would be able to choose the terrain for attack—as well as a battlefield where they had amassed artillery and, if possible, undermined some of the opponents' defenses—and the timing of the attack, the last calculated for time of day, the element of surprise, and also likely weather conditions. These factors, it was assumed, would lead to success by countering the advantages the defenders enjoyed.

In practice, however, repeated attacks revealed the difficulties of breaking through an opposing front line, as opposed to breaking into it, costly as the latter was. The scale of operations, even early in the war, and its linkage to the struggle to produce goods on the "home front," were apparent in the account by the journalist Philip Gibbs, published in the *Daily Telegraph* of September 29, 1915, about the major British assault on German lines at Loos five days before, an assault that was poorly conceived.[8] Of the preliminary bombardment, he wrote,

> All the batteries from the Yser to the Somme seemed to fire together, as though at some signal in the heavens, in one great salvo. The earth and the air shook with it in a great trembling, which never ceased for a single minute during many hours. A vast tumult of explosive force pounded through the night with sledge-hammer strokes, thundering through the deeper monotone of the continual reverberation. . . . This was the work of all those thousands of men in the factories at home who have been toiling through the months at furnace and forge. They had sent us guns, and there seemed to be shells enough to blast the enemy out of his trenches.

The physicality of the combat was described by Gibbs: "The battalions disappeared into a fog of smoke from shells and bombs of every kind . . . our soldiers, digging themselves into the ground they had gained, were clogged with mud." In practice, the German lines were breached at Loos, but, as on other occasions in both world wars, the exploitation of this success was mishandled, a situation that is made easier to understand by the parlous nature of the communications available. The British reserves were fed in too late, and they could make no impact on the German second position, which provided a crucial defense-in-depth. The British suffered sixty-two thousand casualties at Loos, and Germany twenty-six thousand.

From Loos, the British took the lesson of the need to increase the intensity and duration of the preparatory bombardment, which led to the massive (although inadequate) preparatory bombardment at the Somme in 1916. The British had adopted a policy of systematic and sustained destruction, but the

Germans had already abandoned such an approach in their attack at Verdun in 1916 where they went for neutralization with a hurricane bombardment of great intensity but short duration. They had realized that a bigger *and* longer bombardment was governed by diminishing returns. The British and French had yet to reach the same realization.

The Germans took the lesson from Loos of the value of defenses in greater depth in order to contain any break-in and to prevent the breakthrough that nearly happened at Loos. This helped ensure that, on a greater scale than at Loos and with far heavier casualties, the British failed in their Somme offensive in 1916, although they also inflicted heavy losses on the Germans.

In early 1915, having failed on the Western Front in 1914, the Germans, under Moltke's replacement, Erick von Falkenhayn, sought to attack again, breaking through and driving Britain or France, or both, out of the war, and thus splitting the opposing alliance. However, the serious problems facing Austria as a result of Russian pressure, notably the capture in March of the major fortress of Przemyśl, led instead, in April, to a shift to the Eastern Front, where the Germans sought, successfully, to turn to their advantage victories won over Russia in 1914. Nevertheless, although a significant amount of territory was gained by repeated attacks in Russian Poland in 1915, it did not lead to any decisive military or political breakthrough. Moreover, troops were taken from the Western Front.

In practice, that conclusion underplayed the success that had been obtained by the Germans and, as a key strategic point, the serious strains already present in Russia and in the Russian war effort. Indeed, these strains encouraged the Western Allies to launch attacks in an attempt to take pressure off Russia. This helped explain both the Gallipoli offensive against Turkey in 1915 and the large-scale Anglo-French attack on the Somme on the Western Front in 1916.

Having failed to force the Russians into a separate peace, the Germans, in 1916, sought in effect to do so to the French by inflicting a serious defeat in the Verdun offensive. This was at once operational, strategic, and political. Falkenhayn felt that a breakthrough attack was not easy given the nature of warfare on the Western Front. On the pattern of Moltke the Elder in 1866 and 1870 against Austria and France respectively, Falkenhayn planned to gain the advantages of the strategic and operational offensives and the tactical defensive. He aimed to do this by advancing rapidly, on the front of his choice, to capture territory, which the French would then suffer heavy losses seeking to regain.

More generally, this approach represented an attempt to get within the French strategy by causing losses of territory and manpower that would sap the French will to persist, let alone win. Thus, strategic effect was to be achieved by tactical means. The approach, which was similar to that of Japan toward the United States in 1941–42, was flawed in its understanding of French willpower and political cohesion, and also rested on an assumption that the opposing alliance could readily be disassembled.

In practice, there were operational as well as strategic flaws with this plan: German effectiveness was less than had been assumed. Falkenhayn attacked on too narrow a front, and initially with too few troops. He also exposed the German troops to French artillery fire from the other bank of the River Meuse. As the offensive developed, it served no strategic purpose and cost the Germans, as well as the French, very heavily.

Verdun had great symbolic significance for the French, notably for politicians who resolutely linked national glory to their presentation of the self-sacrificing dedication of the troops. Verdun was also seen as important to the defense of Paris against attack from the east. It was protected by a series of detached forts, notably Douaumont and Vaux, and their concrete casements and steel cupolas. Although field defenses played the key role in the protection of Verdun, the struggle over these forts was important to the progress of the campaign, not least the sense of success. Thus, a strategic offensive became a matter of tactical struggle, with the defenses eventually blocking the Germans, although not stopping them from inflicting damage on the French by attrition, which became the German goal. The Germans captured both Douaumont (February 25) and Vaux (June 7), but their impetus was lost as units were moved to oppose the British Somme and Russian Brusilov offensives, and the French were able to regain the forts, on October 24 and November 2, respectively. Moreover, the French had been able to maintain the movement of supplies into Verdun, with the *voie sacrée* from Bar-le-Duc becoming a route for trucks (lorries).

Falkenhayn also hoped to make the British attack before they were ready, and thus prepare the ground for a successful German counterattack.[9] The Verdun offensive certainly ensured that the British would take a bigger role in the Somme offensive later that year: a campaign originally planned in order to take German pressure off the Russians instead became one designed to help France. In that, the strategy succeeded, with the Germans having to deploy reserves accordingly and therefore losing the initiative, or at least the ability to apply significant pressure, on the Verdun front. This point is lost sight of due to the focus on the heavy British casualties in the Somme offensive, especially in its first day.

This focus also detracts from the learning curve seen with British attacking techniques in 1915–16 and during the 1916 campaign. The experience of war on the Western Front was very different from that on the Eastern Front. In the former, defenders fought in fixed positions and were heavily exposed to the power of artillery. Whereas, in 1915, France and Germany focused on the production of field artillery, the British concentrated on adding heavy guns, which were designed to destroy the opponent, a contrast that prefigured that in the Second World War when the Germans deployed a tactical rather than a strategic air force. Although the British were unable to produce sufficient artillery by the summer of 1916, which helped ensure that their Somme offensive was inadequately supported, the ability to sustain their attack put the Germans under great pressure that year.[10] In response, the German High Command, as part of a rapid German learning process,[11] pressed for an increase in the production of guns and shells. Moreover, the Allies sought to produce the numbers of troops and artillery necessary to win on the Western Front.

Alongside criticism of the Allied attacks, there is a tendency to underplay the heavy casualties inflicted on the Germans and the psychological impact of the Allied offensives. The German line did not break, but, as with the naval Battle of Jutland in 1916, German confidence in existing arrangements was hit hard. Heavy casualties, and the strains resulting from the Somme offensive, helped ensure that the Germans did not mount a major attack on the Western Front in 1917, while their 1918 offensives there were dependent on troops transferred from Russia and on the prospect of more transfers.

Indeed, in 1917, as part of a strategy that emphasized success in the East and not the West, the Germans fell back to a stronger and shorter line in the West. This Siegfried Line, known to the Allies as the Hindenburg Line, replaced the earlier system—deep dugouts and continuous trench lines packed with infantry—with one of mutually supporting concrete bunkers surrounded by obstacle belts. This system provided a more potent and relevant fortification system that included a flexible defense-in-depth, a defense that challenges traditional notions of siegecraft. Reverse-slope positions were used to reduce vulnerability to artillery, while, with its three defense lines, the "Line" was up to fifteen miles deep.

This was a way to resist the Allies, but, as a key strategic element, not one with which to impose a settlement on them. Indeed, barring Russia's collapse, which gave her an opportunity in 1918 to try again for a military verdict, Germany, not least due to America's entry into the war, had lost in the West, but was unwilling to accept this.

This was a situation that was to recur in 1944–45. In 1917, the Germans beat off the Allies' attacks in the West, but the Germans were pressed very hard by the British at Passchendaele (Third Ypres). Germany's decision to attack in 1918 reflected America's entry into the war, because that suggested a closure of any window of opportunity the Germans might enjoy. The Americans had already made a great contribution to the Allies in the shape of industrial production and credit, but the prospect of a major addition in manpower was important.

As so often with warfare, the hypotheticals of conflict come into play when assessing power. The Americans were constrained by the small size of their prewar army and were affected by inadequate and inappropriate doctrine, by their army's lack of training for trench warfare, and by an overconfident failure to appreciate the nature of the conflict and to learn from British and French experience, one seen in particular with General John J. Pershing. This led to outdated tactics and heavy American casualties on the Western Front in 1918. However, the Americans still played a significant part in Allied operations, notably in the Meuse-Argonne offensive,[12] although this role was not instrumental to victory.

Yet, the American role would have been more important had the war continued into 1919, as was widely anticipated. Large numbers of trained American troops would have provided the Allies with an important advantage in manpower. Moreover, such an advantage was necessary given the reliance of both sides on infantry in large quantities and the prospect of Germany redeploying more troops from Eastern Europe. Thanks to the Americans, the German superiority of three hundred thousand troops on the Western Front in March 1918, a superiority in part due to Russia's collapse, was transformed into an Allied superiority of two hundred thousand troops four months later. Nearly two million American troops were in Europe by the armistice by November 1918. Their arrival greatly affected German resolve. It was more significant in terms of relative power than the impact of American support at sea, important as that was. Had the war continued, American productive capability would have offered the Allies an avalanche of heavy equipment in the shape of tanks and heavy artillery.

FACE OF BATTLE

Placing the strategic dimension first offers a way to provide meaning to the nature of the fighting. This is necessary because the costly trench warfare that most characterizes the First World War on land, both for public discussion and for the academic approach described as "face of battle," can make the struggle seem not only worthless but also pointless. Neither is a fair view unless it is assumed that aggression should not be resisted and that international agreements, notably the guarantee of Belgian neutrality, should be ignored. That strategies, or indeed individual operations, failed, or only succeeded after very many problems, did not make them pointless.

Tactics were in many respects a response to the opportunities offered by artillery and the problems it correspondingly caused. The greatest killer on the battlefield was artillery, followed by machine guns and rifles. In the opening battles of 1914, artillery firing by line of sight was more than capable of breaking up an attack. Thanks to the French invention in 1897 of a reliable hydraulic recoil system, the French 75 mm field gun could fire over fifteen rounds a minute,[13] while German 150 mm field howitzers could fire five rounds a minute. Air-burst shrapnel shells increased the deadly nature of artillery fire and encouraged the use of steel helmets to reduce head injuries. Fifty-nine percent of the casualties of the British Expeditionary Force on the Western Front were caused by high explosives, which included trench mortars, while 39 percent were caused by small-arms fire, including machine guns, which could scythe through attacking waves like no other weapon and could do so in minutes. As a reminder of the problems posed by statistical analysis, however, notably the assumption that a single classification is possible, grenades might be used to force the enemy out of cover and into the killing zone of a light mortar or rifle. The static nature of defenses increased the lethality of artillery, while the close ranges in trench warfare led to the development of the submachine gun.

Poison gas was first used in this war by the Germans in the Second Battle of Ypres in April–May 1915, and to considerable effect against surprised and unprepared Allied troops.[14] Gas greatly shocked the Allies. However, it was the British, in the form of the Special Brigade, who subsequently became the biggest user and indeed the most effective user of gas, developing new techniques such as the hundreds of Livens projectiles fired simultaneously on a small area (although the Germans learned about the projector as a piece of equipment, and even copied it, they never caught on to the fact that its success lay in simultaneous firing) and the successful use, late in the war, of specially built railway tracks, in an arc, for goods trucks carrying gas cylinders. France also developed chemical weapons, while the United States established a Chemical Warfare Service. Gas was responsible for ninety thousand military deaths and 1.29 million military injuries, as well as much psychological strain.

The stress in much discussion of the war is on impasse and indecisiveness. There are frequent complaints about incompetent commanders and foolish command cultures, and the abiding image is of machine guns sweeping away lines of attackers. Battles such as Verdun (1916), the Somme (1916), and, in particular, Passchendaele (1917) are presented as indictments of a particular way of war. On September 21, 1917, the *Times* of London, writing about the British offensive at Passchendaele, captured the reduction of campaigning to fighting over small areas at great cost, as well as the horrors of the battleground:

> The extreme depth to which we sought to penetrate [today] was about one mile, but that mile we have overrun, and grasped, and hold. Already the enemy has been counter-attacking. . . . We in these last seven weeks have made no, or very little, progress. . . . All shell-holes are full of water. Every man I saw was coated with mud, some only to the knees, but many to their very throats, and it is to be feared that some wounded must slip into the holes and never get out again.

Similarly, Italian attacks in 1915–17 were greatly hit by a lack of room to maneuver. Successive Italian attacks on the Austrians in the harsh, rocky terrain on the Isonzo front, designed to open the way to Gorizia, Trieste, and Istria, were unsuccessful. Thanks in large part to the advantages offered by the terrain, Austrian defensive positions were strong. On a concentrated front, where there was no way to outflank the Austrians and few opportunities to vary the axis of attack, Austrian defensive firepower prevailed, and, advancing uphill, the Italians in 1915 suffered about 250,000 casualties (compared to about 160,000 for the Austrians) for very few gains. The Italians were also affected by shortages of artillery.

There was, indeed, an attritional character to particular battles as they developed without breakthroughs, but that does not mean that combatants simply set out to wear down opponents. Instead, there were attempts to develop the handling necessary for offensives by very large forces taking part in theater-wide campaigns and with combined-arms methods.[15] These attempts succeeded. Like the Confederates in the American Civil War and the Germans in the Second World War, the Germans were, in 1918, eventually outfought and defeated, both in offensive and defensive warfare.

In terms of casualty rates, the war was one of a number of conflicts in which rates were very heavy, as again notably on the Eastern Front and in the Normandy campaign in the Second World War. To give an example, Canada, which provided important sections of the British (i.e., British Empire) army on the Western Front, had 65,000 dead and over 100,000 wounded out of a population of just over eight million, of whom 620,000 enrolled. New Zealand lost more men on October 12, 1917, at Passchendaele than on any other date in its history.[16] The modern tendency to regard casualties as avoidable, however, does not match the reality of the consequences of engagements between large forces, a point readily apparent from the Iran-Iraq War of 1980–88.

The heavy casualties of the First World War, for example 1.4 million dead in the French army and nearly 3 million Germans with permanent disabilities, owed much to its being waged by well-armed and populous industrial powers that were willing and able to deploy much of their young male populations. It is reasonable to focus on the repeated failure and heavy costs of operations, but also necessary to note the adaptability of militaries, economies, and governments so that they could sustain a large-scale, long-term war and increase their effectiveness.

THE STRENGTH OF THE DEFENSE

In many respects, the war was about fortifications far more than other major conflicts over the previous century, for the large-scale trench systems that were constructed at the end of 1914 marked an effective form of fortification and one that was new on this scale. Moreover, tactically effective, this form was also operationally, and thereby strategically, appropriate. Large-scale trench systems were not only designed to repel frontal attack but also, by their length, to prevent outflanking and a campaign of encirclement. Furthermore, the speed with which a new trench line could be dug meant that a breakthrough by opponents, or their creation of a new axis of operations, could be thwarted, as Anglo-French amphibious forces, admittedly poorly commanded, discovered when they landed at Gallipoli in 1915 and Salonica in 1916, and would probably have also done had they landed elsewhere.

The strength of defensive positions did not mean that there was no progress in developing techniques for the attack. As with other siege systems, there was interest, at the strategic level, in the contradictory methods of breaking through, attacking elsewhere, and blockade, and, at the tactical level, in both bombardment and storming. Indeed, while, as the Germans showed in 1917, fortifications were developed to deal with changing tactics of attack, each, in practice, grew out of the other, and to a degree that had not happened in any previous war, nor since. The evolution of artillery tactics made linear defensive lines unworkable during the latter part of 1916 and into 1917, and this led to the globular defensive plans in which mutually supporting strongpoints with all-round defense interacted to make many square miles of territory dangerous to an attacker. When the Germans built the Hindenburg Line in 1917, not only did they shorten the line, but they made the area between it and their old line into a vast killing zone. They cleared the civilian population and leveled villages and other obstacles in order to create clear fields of fire, and they utilized vast amounts of concertina barbed wire in order to funnel an attacker into zones covered by machine guns, artillery, and mortars.

By 1917, the Germans no longer manned "frontline" trenches, because such trenches no longer existed as such. Instead, the first line was a series of thinly manned outposts, because the Germans knew that, in the event of an assault, the front line would be hit hard. The British were in the process of constructing these sorts of defensive structures when the Germans launched their spring offensives in 1918. Thus, from the autumn of 1914, defenses had evolved from a single trench line, often broken rather than continuous, to several lines by 1916, and to multiple lines many miles in depth by 1917, with the purpose of containing break-ins and preventing them from becoming breakthroughs.

The use of steel-reinforced concrete for defensive structures also developed, being used by the French at Verdun in particular. A big advantage of ferroconcrete was the speed of construction. The modern method was patented by François Hennebique in 1892. Ferroconcrete is very strong and tough, as it has high tensile and compressive strengths, unlike unreinforced concrete, which meant that high-explosive shells have little impact on it. While artillery and mortars found it difficult to penetrate the deep-dug defenses, such defenses were not invulnerable. In particular, Livens gas attacks on them were very effective because the gas cloud was so dense and could penetrate everywhere.

And once infantry got among the defenses, no matter how deep they were, they were vulnerable to demolition by sappers, who had large explosive charges ready for the purpose, made in facilities such as the British First Army Workshop. These charges were used mostly in raids. Infantry tactics, devised specifically for overcoming strong posts, were made more effective by 1917 by the development of the all-arms infantrymen, skilled with rifle, bayonet, Lewis gun (light machine gun), and hand and rifle grenade, and accustomed to working in cooperation with artillery and mortars, notably the Stokes light mortar. Thus, during the war, the evolution of infantry tactics, toward more mobile firepower, and of artillery tactics was instrumental in reducing the utility of fortifications and defenses[17] and in increasing uncertainty about outcomes.

TRENCH WARFARE

Trench warfare is frequently held up for much of the blame for the costly stasis, but, had the campaigns been waged in a different manner—for example, had they been more maneuverist and less static, which was implausible given the limited mobility of the infantry—there is no reason to assume that casualties would have been lower. Instead, in the open, troops would have been more exposed to both offensive and defensive fire. Indeed, trenches served to protect troops as well as to stabilize the line.[18]

However, once the trenches had been constructed, it proved difficult to regain mobility, despite the combatants seeking to launch attacks that would enable them to do so. These attacks were both a measured response to the political and military issues posed by the war and a reflection of the aggressive spirit and attacking ideas that were inculcated prewar.[19]

The problem was not so much posed by the inherent strength of trench systems, significant as they became, because these could be broken into and even through, as with the German Hindenburg Line in 1918. Instead, problems were posed by the force-space ratios of the war, notably, but not only, on the Western Front. The available manpower made it possible to hold the front line with strength and to provide reserves. Moreover, although frontline trenches were not held in strength by the Germans from 1916 onward, this was part of the defense-in-depth around strongholds that was designed to counter artillery bombardments and break-ins, and to facilitate counterattacks.

The scale of warfare was matched by grim determination[20] and organizational sophistication. Brigadier John Monash of the Australian army wrote to his wife in 1915,

> We have got our battle procedure now thoroughly well organized. To a stranger it would probably look like a disturbed anti-heap with everybody running a different way, but the thing is really a triumph of organization. There are orderlies carrying messages, staff officers with orders, lines of ammunition carriers, water carriers, bomb carriers, stretcher bearers, burial parties, first-aid men, reserves, supports, signalers, telephonists, engineers, digging parties, sandbag parties, periscope hands, pioneers, quartermaster's parties, and reinforcing troops, running about all over the place, apparently in confusion, but yet everything works as smoothly as on a peace parade, although the air is thick with clamour and bullets and bursting shells, and bombs and flares.[21]

Although generals planning attacks had plentiful troops, and the supplies to sustain them, they faced the difficulties of handling large formations in battle and of devising an effective tactical system that would not only achieve the breakthrough of the opposing trench line but then be able to sustain and develop it. This problem was greatly accentuated by facing defenses-in-depth, such as those developed by the Germans in 1917. This task was far from easy, not least because of the problem of advancing across terrain badly damaged by shell fire, as well as the difficulties of providing reserves in the correct place. It was difficult to maintain the availability of shells for the all-crucial artillery, which had a very heavy usage, and to provide adequate information to commanders about developments. Deficiencies in communications fed directly into command: the potential of radio was inadequately grasped, although that is also a view that reflects the strength of hindsight. This helped underline the significance of able and determined junior leadership, as with the defending Germans on the Somme in 1916.

Individual battles had wider strategic consequences. In the major British offensive of 1917, which subsequently became known as Passchendaele, the planned breakthrough battle, designed in part to threaten German submarine bases on the Belgian coast, did not occur. In part, this was due to the inherent difficulties of the task and to appalling and unseasonal wet weather, which made the low-lying Flanders countryside particularly boggy. The British commander, Douglas Haig, subsequently justified the heavy casualties in the very different terms of attritional calculations. The Germans, indeed, also suffered debilitating casualties, but Haig seriously underrated the strategic problems arising from manpower shortages caused by British losses.[22] Moreover, the long term appeared increasingly precarious for the Allies in late 1917 as Russia slipped away.

The theory of artillery dominance over trench fortifications had been expressed in the report in the *Times* of London on April 13, 1917, about the

British attack on the Germans in the Battle of Arras on the Western Front and the value of knowledge gained from earlier offensives on that front:

> The chief lesson learnt is that against strong defensive positions the pace of a sustained attack is the pace of the heavy artillery. To attempt to force the pace is to neglect the searching preparation which alone can make assaults in force successful without overwhelming sacrifice. . . . If time is given for the guns to get into position and to prepare the way for the infantry, then the strength of the defensive lines crumbles to chaos. . . . The role of the guns must be taken up again, and when they have played their part again, then the storming lines will go forward.

EASTERN FRONT

Where, in contrast, the force-space ratio was lower, weaker defenses, and notably less developed defenses-in-depth, ensured that it proved possible to achieve breakthroughs, make major gains, and obtain decisive results. This was particularly the case on the Eastern and Balkan fronts, on which, in 1915–17, the Germans, Austrians, and Bulgarians captured large swathes of territory and defeated enemy armies in impressive campaigns of maneuver that were frequently aided by a geography that was easier for such advances than the Western or Italian fronts. Serbia was conquered by overwhelming Bulgarian, German, and Austrian forces in 1915,[23] while Romania was largely overrun in 1916.[24] Russian Poland was conquered by the Germans in 1915, countering multiple failures[25] by the badly commanded Austrians. The Germans proved particularly successful in employing heavy artillery barrages against the primitive Russian trench systems.[26] In 1916, the Russian Brusilov offensive made major gains against the Austrians, but, unlike with the Soviet offensive in 1944, it was starved of backup support to sustain it, while German reinforcements helped stabilize the line.

In 1917 in Russia, a crisis in political and popular support for Tsar Nicholas II, due to failure in the war and its management, with which he was closely associated, led to his abdication. The new Russian government continued the war, but with only limited control over the army and without success, and was overthrown in a Bolshevik coup in November 1917. The new leadership, under Lenin, negotiated the Peace of Brest-Litovsk with Germany the following spring, accepting major territorial cessions. This hardly demonstrated the indecisiveness of conflict in this war, and it contrasted with Russian resilience during the Napoleonic Wars and the Second World War. The Germans pressed on into Russia to try to confirm additional gains.

ITALY

Nor did the fate of Italy, nearly knocked out of the war by the surprise Austro-German Caporetto offensive of October 1917, demonstrate indecisiveness in campaigning. Launched on October 24, 1917, the rapid Austro-German advance, using infiltration tactics and gas, broke into and through the Italian line and greatly disrupted Italian communications and cohesion, leading to an enforced withdrawal. Withdrawing eighty miles, the Italians lost 20,000 dead, 40,000 wounded, and 350,000 prisoners, as well as 3,152 pieces of artillery, one-third of their firearms, ordnance, and supply depots, as well as airfields. Nevertheless, in December the Italians were able to return to the front line most of the troops who had lost cohesion in the retreat. Meanwhile, the Austrians and Germans were able to advance to the River Piave, but their exhaustion, combined with the stiffening of the Italian line, in part by Allied contingents, resulted in a stabilization of the line. It was important to Britain, France, and the United States to keep Italy in the war. Doing so kept up the pressure on Austria and also obliged Germany to divert attention from the Western Front.

In June 1918, the Austrians attempted to resume their offensive but totally failed. On June 12, Italian artillery silenced the Austrians with counterbattery fire, and on June 13 the attack by the Austrian infantry was wrecked by the Italian artillery.[27]

MIDDLE EAST

In far more difficult circumstances, notably in terms of terrain, climate, infrastructure, logistics, and disease, Britain and the Turks fought in the Middle East, with Palestine and Mesopotamia, to use the contemporary British terms, the major areas of operation. This was after a knockout blow against Constantinople, the poorly prepared and conducted Gallipoli campaign of 1915, failed.

The British hoped that they would cause the Turkish Empire to collapse, providing opportunities for pressure on the opposing coalition and for postwar territorial gains. The deployment and sustaining of forces were key elements requiring effective staff work and organization as well as resources.[28] Although their army had been improved by German advisers, the Turks faced major problems, not least because they were deploying larger numbers of troops in these areas than hitherto and being obliged to move resources for a period of time greater than in recent wars. Moreover, the heavy costs in manpower to the Turks, even of victorious campaigns, notably Gallipoli (1915), Kut (1915–16), and Gaza (1917), exacerbated these problems, as well as helping to ensure that the Turks derived scant strategic success from these operational victories, each of which was defensive. The pressures on the Turkish home front were particularly acute.[29]

As on other fronts, the British faced problems of developing capabilities and pursuing learning curves, but in harsh circumstances, notably of logistics, including water supply, and with the additional problems created by a tendency to disparage and underestimate their opponent. Racism played a role in this tendency. Failure in Mesopotamia in 1916, however, was followed by improvement, and the British were able, as a result, to capture Baghdad (1917) and Mosul (1918). Similarly, defeats at Gaza were followed by the breaking of the Turkish defensive line and the conquest of Palestine and, eventually, Syria.[30] Yet again, a learning curve was in evidence.

1917–18 ON THE WESTERN FRONT

Germany was not just fighting on. It had a strategy. In 1917, this entailed going onto the defensive on the Western Front, indeed retreating to the straighter and better-fortified Hindenburg Line, thus freeing up some forces; knocking out Russia; using unrestricted submarine warfare, as well as bombing, to weaken Britain; and testing new infantry tactics of surprise attack and infiltrating opposing defenses against Italy. Having beaten Russia, the Germans planned to transfer forces to the Western Front so as to defeat Britain and France before the United States could make a key contribution. It also hoped to use submarine attacks to limit the number of American troops crossing the Atlantic. Thus, the United States posed strategic issues that had implications on land and at sea, but the Germans thought they could counter them, rather as Japan did in 1941–42.

By 1917–18, the nature of fighting on the Western Front was very different from 1915, let alone 1914. What were to be called storm-trooper techniques or infiltration tactics had been developed by the Germans, and notably so in raids against the French from October 1915. These storm-trooper techniques, for which the Germans get the credit because of the term *Stosstruppen* (storm troops), relied on carefully planned surprise assaults employing infiltration and focusing on opponents' strongpoints in order to destroy the cohesion of their defense. The Germans used these techniques on a wider scale at Verdun and in Romania in 1916, and at the operational level in 1917 and 1918. For the Germans, these tactics were those of specialists. They helped ensure the defeat of the Italian army at Caporetto. In the winter of 1917–18, an attempt was made to train German units so as to inculcate the need for appropriate action at the level of individual soldiers. Training was now done near the front line.

The British and the French developed similar tactics at much the same time, with Captain André Laffargue of the French army possibly launching the idea in print in August 1915 with his pamphlet *Étude sur l'attaque dans la période actuelle de la guerre* (*Study of the Attack in the Current Period of the War*), which called for mobile firepower and infiltration. An English version was published that December.[31] The British made the tactics widespread across the BEF, on a pattern also to be seen in the Second World War. As a result, the "ordinary" German infantry was not necessarily better trained in the latter stages of the war compared to their British or French counterparts. Training took place near the front line as a way to incorporate field experience. The British gained a lot of tactical experience from raids, which often encouraged infiltration and artillery-box barrages, as well as mortars and machine guns operating in fire-suppression roles, before these tactics became widespread among the infantry during larger-scale operations. The Canadians developed raid-like tactics for major operations in 1916–17.

Thus, the idea that the Germans alone invented so-called storm-troop tactics is misleading. More generally, tactics developed continuously, often in response to what the enemy was doing. Generals approved tactics, rather than devising them, and, as also in the next world war, these tactics evolved from experience. For example, British grenade and mortar tactics came from experience, which was taught in infantry schools set up from mid-1915 onward. With both grenades and mortars, inventors improved on what had existed hitherto. Their inventiveness led to the proliferation of grenades and light mortars, and manufacturing systems were put in place to manufacture them in quantity. Without these inventions in 1914 and 1915, the fighting on the Western Front would have been very different. The report of operations by the British Fifty-Sixth Division in January 1917 noted a frequent use of Lewis guns, Stokes mortars, and rifle grenades.[32] A battalion report of September 1918 noted that No. 2 Company advanced under considerable machine gun fire by dribbling men across open spaces under covering fire from massed company Lewis guns.[33]

The Germans used their techniques with considerable success in their spring 1918 offensives. However, the Germans won tactical breakthrough only to lose the advantage because, owing to very poor military leadership, they had not thought out how to exploit success, militarily or politically. Instead, focused on the tactical level and, due to the tacticalization and operationalization of strategy, with no adequate operational or, even more, strategic understanding, the Germans assumed they could use shock to force an Allied collapse, a situation that prefigured the German offensive in the Battle of the Bulge in December 1944. In practice, Allied defenses-in-depth, and the use of reserves by an integrated command structure, helped thwart the Germans, who failed to persist on any individual axis of attack or to capture the key rail junctions. American forces played a significant role in the defense, notably in mid-July alongside the French in thwarting the German advance on Rheims. The Germans also suffered greatly from failing to keep their logistical tail up with their advancing assault force. The offensive led to heavy German losses, close to a million casualties, which could not be replaced, and to a new extended front line that left them vulnerable to attack.[34]

The British had greatly improved their fighting methods in 1917.[35] In particular, alongside improvements in infantry tactics and firepower, they successfully focused in 1917–18 on improving artillery firepower and accuracy so that they could dominate the three-dimensional battlefield and apply firepower more effectively than in earlier attacks. The number of heavy guns increased greatly. For example, in preparation for the Canadian attack on Vimy Ridge in 1917, more than 125,000 shells were fired by the Canadians, who engaged in successful counterbattery work to suppress German fire.[36] In addition, a better scientific approach to gunnery and ranging calculations had a major impact, as it changed how artillery was, and is still, used. By late 1917, gunners could calibrate their guns for every shot and, in doing so, take account of air temperature, barrel wear, and propellant power. This process did not so much need new technology, but new devices were invented to help, ensuring that what had not been feasible in 1914 was now practical. The more scientific approach saw meteorology become increasingly important and led to advance weather forecasting. Wind speed and air temperature were given to artillery batteries several times daily.[37] Information was integrated and rapidly transmitted in a process, responding to the greater complexity of war and the more sophisticated understanding of capability, which was also to be seen in the Second World War.

With these advances, more sophisticated barrages could be fired, which was not possible earlier in the war. A creeping barrage that could match the trace of the enemy trenches meant that the entire length was hit at the same time, which was not possible if each gun was not calibrated according to its own requirements. Artillery-infantry coordination was also significant. In place of generalized firepower, there was systematic coordination, reflecting precise control of both infantry and massive artillery support, plus improved communications. Effective counterbattery fire was developed. The key to converting a break-in into a breakthrough was artillery that neutralized the German ability to mount counterattacks. And the key to breaking in was infiltration rather than wave assaults. Infantry infiltration, taking advantage of skillfully applied artillery firepower, neutralized the German defenses-in-depth, whereas sheer firepower alone could not do that. The Allied learning curve in offensive battle beat that of the Germans in defensive battle.

The Allies' 1918 campaign on the Western Front, a counterattack to the recent German offensives, was eventually a major success in the shape of the "Hundred Days Offensive." The successful Allied assault on the Hindenburg Line near Cambrai on September 27, 1918, led the German generals to move rapidly toward an armistice. This assault reflected the development of appropriate artillery and infantry tactics, including "deep battle," in which targets beyond the front, such as headquarters, were being bombarded. Trench warfare had evolved into deep battle, with important help from aerial reconnaissance, which provided guidance for the artillery. The Allies had also developed the mechanisms, notably greatly improved logistics, and deployed the resources, particularly large numbers of heavy guns, necessary to sustain their advance and offensive in the face of continual German resistance, and to do so across a broad front. Thomas Blamey, the chief of staff to the Australian Corps, noted that the campaign differed from earlier operations in that there was an emplacement of a large proportion of artillery within two thousand yards of the front line, which enabled the advance to be covered by an effective barrage to a depth of four thousand yards into enemy country.[38] The tactics for deep battle overcame the new-style German defenses.

The German defenses were breached; the German counterattack divisions, which had been so effective in 1917, failed; and German military morale faced a serious crisis at every level.[39] In contrast to poor German leadership, the Allies were ably led by Ferdinand Foch, who provided effective coordination of the often bickering coalition. In fighting quality and combat effectiveness, the Allies benefited from their marked capacity for improvement.[40] Heavy casualties put a continued strain on Allied manpower,[41] but the Germans were in greater manpower difficulties, and repeated successes were delivered in the closing weeks of the war.[42] Under the pressure of defeat, the German delegates signed the Allied armistice terms, which took effect on November 11, 1918. The German military leadership had also been greatly influenced by the Austrian collapse, which opened the way for an Italian advance into Bavaria, and by Bulgaria's decision to seek an armistice, which threatened the unraveling of the alliance. It was agreed on September 29. On November 3, Austria agreed to the Allied terms for an armistice, and Germany on November 11.

The resolution of stalemate on the Western Front might appear a vindication of the prewar belief in the triumph of attack over defense, but it was not on the timetable envisaged. Moreover, the scale of the conflict proved very different, leading to a vocabulary of total war. The French minister Georges Clemenceau pressed for "La guerre intégrale" when he took office in 1917, and the German general Erich Ludendorff used the term in his postwar memoirs, eventually writing a book on *Der Totale Krieg* (1935).

In pursuit of higher morale and in response to concerns raised about the impact of the Somme offensive, Ludendorff in 1917 had instituted political instruction for the German army in order to explain to the soldiers what they were fighting for. The British did the same. There is little evidence of this method proving successful. Many soldiers slept in the classes. Nevertheless, the effort was instructive, as, more generally, was the greater concern with morale in 1917–18 as a consequence of the problems that had faced the French, Italians, and Russian armies in 1917. This was one of the many ways in which the war was different in its last section from the opening campaigns. British morale held up well, and the soldiers continued resilient and confident that success would be soon.[43]

TANKS

The unexpectedly early end to the war left unclear the consequences of the development of the tank. Plans for armored land vehicles were pushed forward as a result of the outbreak of the war and the urgent helter-skelter of inventiveness it encouraged. This inventiveness was furthered by the existence of well-developed social and industrial bases for innovation and manufacture. Invented independently by Britain and France in 1915, tanks were used in combat from September 1916. The use spread from the Western Front. Indeed, the British employed them against the Turks at Gaza in Palestine the following April, although there was no Turkish collapse.

In contrast, in the case of the tank, German inventiveness and application proved deficient, and few were built. The German AV7 tank was huge and required a lot of armor plate, but Germany was affected by metal shortages and had other priorities for metal use. As a reminder of the extent to which a number of explanations may be pertinent, the success of the German counterattack at the Battle of Cambrai in 1917, sealing the British tank breakthrough, ensured that the Germans saw less need for developing tanks.

From the perspective of just over a century later, the invention and deployment of tanks provides a development that looks to the modern situation. Furthermore, the tank acts as an exemplar of the more general point that the armies went into the First World War looking backward and ended looking forward. The plentiful presence of cavalry and bright (and uncamouflaged) infantry uniforms (notably those of the French) in 1914 is held to encapsulate the former, while mechanization in 1918 apparently represents the latter. This interpretation, however, faces problems, not least an overly pat, even rigid notion of modernization and a teleology of development. More significantly, there is a misleading tendency to primitivize the situation running up to (and including) the first campaign of the war and, correspondingly, a misreading of the situation in 1918.

The usage of tanks provides a good instance of this misreading. The war did see a development from fluid to static warfare, such that the idea of a front line took hold. As the means of, and to, maneuverability, tanks were to be seen as the antithesis of the front line. That, however, underplayed the problems involved in sustaining mobility in the late 1910s. Indeed, tanks—essentially, as both designed and used, a tool for operating on the front line—were suited in 1918 more for assisting in transforming static into maneuver warfare, rather than for the latter itself. In providing, like light mortars, moving firepower, tanks helped overcome the problems that trenches posed to attackers. They offered precise tactical fire to exploit the consequences of the massed bombardments that preceded attacks. A memorandum of June 1918 from the British Tank Corps Headquarters claimed, "Trench warfare has given way to field and semi-open fighting. . . . The more the mobility of tanks is increased, the greater must be the elasticity of the co-operation between them and the other arms." The following month, Sir Henry Wilson, the chief of the Imperial General Staff, proposed that the Allies coordinate plans for tank warfare.[44]

In practice, however, durability, firepower, protection, speed, range, mobility, command and control, and reliability were all major problems with tanks. These problems were accentuated by the rapid development by the Germans of antitank techniques and weaponry, particularly guns and mines, a process already seen on both sides in countering airships and aircraft. There was also the problem posed by the use of tanks in small numbers in order to help the infantry, instead of in large formations that were better able to achieve goals. The combination of tank losses and slow tank production ensured that from the close of August 1918, there was a reaction against tank warfare.[45]

ENHANCED CAPABILITIES

Tanks were most successful if part of a combined-arms force, a point that directs attention to the more general value of the Allied development of effective artillery-infantry tactics and the provision of the necessary equipment. In particular, well-aimed, heavy indirect artillery fire, ably coordinated with rushes by infantry who did not move forward in vulnerable lines, was important in 1918 in overcoming the German defense-in-depth. Some commentators have seen this as ushering in the "modern system," one requiring initiative and leadership way down the command hierarchy, so that technology and tactics are brought into appropriate harmony.[46] In specific terms, this is a questionable definition, however, as, in practice, it describes most combat.

Instead, 1917–18 saw an effective response to the particular tactical and operational issues of the moment. As such, it demonstrated the continual process of assessing and implementing fitness for purpose, rather than establishing a more general condition of industrial warfare or, indeed, modernity. Fitness-for-purpose was part of a more general process of learning, one in which training and improved staff work played a major role. J. F. C. Fuller was to present the war as a development from mass toward machine fighting.[47]

MAPS

For example, air-artillery coordination greatly enhanced the potential of maps. A report in the *Times* of London on December 27, 1914, noted of the Western Front,

> The chief use of aeroplanes is to direct the fire of the artillery. Sometimes they "circle and dive" just over the position of the place which they want shelled. The observers with the artillery then inform the battery commanders—and a few seconds later shells come hurtling on to, or jolly near to, the spot indicated. They also observe for the gunners and signal back to them to tell where their shots are going to, whether over or short, or to right or left.

However, with time came more static positions, as well as a need for heavier and more precise artillery fire in order to inflict damage on better-prepared trench systems in an attempt to renew mobility. The invention of cameras able to take photographs with constant overlap proved to be a technique that was very important for aerial reconnaissance, and thus surveying, notably with the development of three-dimensional photographic interpretation. Maps worked to record positions as well as to permit the dissemination of the information. In May 1917, the standard message form on British maps included "Am held up by a) M.G. [machine gun] b) wire at . . ."[48] The ability to build up accurate models of opposing trench lines was part of the equation.

It was also necessary to locate the position of artillery in a precisely measured triangulation network. This network and location permitted directionally accurate long-range artillery by means of firing on particular coordinates. Responding to a German attack, Lieutenant Colonel Percy Worrall noted of the Western Front in April 1918, a period in which the British were under great strain: "The artillery and machine-gun corps did excellent work in close co-operation. . . . It was seldom longer than 2 minutes after I have 'X-2 minutes intense' when one gunner responded with a crash on the right spot."[49] In turn, the intensity of reconnaissance photography was such that the Germans were able to produce a new image of the entire Western Front every two weeks and thus rapidly produce maps that responded to changes on the ground.

CONCLUSION

During the war, the need to rethink combined-arms operations in order to suppress defenses that were stronger than those generally anticipated prior to the conflict gave urgent point to widespread interest in new technology and new tactics, each drawing on a mobilization of resources, both human and economic. The costs were formidable. In 1917, the British public was informed that the daily cost of the war to Britain was nearly £7 million.[50]

Eventually, on all the surviving fronts in 1918, the Allies developed the mechanisms necessary to sustain their advance and offensive in the face of continued opposition, and thus to acquire an operational dynamic that gave effect to their strategy. The large numbers of troops involved posed particular problems of logistical support. Filling the many gaps created by heavy casualties meant that there was a continual need for the mobilization of manpower, and this need posed organizational, political, and social issues, as well as meaning that training proved a continued demand.

The effort of war, a conflict waged on land in Africa,[51] as well as in Europe and the Middle East, entailed a mobilization of resources and a militarization of societies. The latter was especially apparent in countries, such as Britain and Canada, that had not hitherto had conscription. There was some opposition, as in Quebec City in April 1918, when four rioters were shot dead, but surprisingly little. So also with the general pattern of loyal service among the military, despite harsh and unprecedented circumstances. The situation varied by individual and state but was generally more positive than later critical literary accounts would suggest.[52] Despite serious issues with morale in 1917, the French and Italian armies rallied and fought on. In contrast, the Russian army in 1917, and its Austrian counterpart in 1918, essentially collapsed due to opposition to the government.

The political issues involved in raising support overlapped with another aspect of the war that tends to be underplayed, that of the war as an imposition of control in the domestic sphere. This was more frequently a matter of force than tends to be appreciated. Force played a role in the maintenance of control in occupied areas and also in controlling domestic discontent, notably in multinational empires such as, very differently, those of Turkey, Russia, and Britain. Britain suppressed an Irish nationalist rising in Dublin in 1916 and Russia a larger-scale rebellion in Central Asia.

The war also saw considerable novelty, especially in the use of new weaponry, particularly tanks, submarines, gas, and aircraft, but also less prominent weapons that were improved, such as grenades and mortars. Lessons learned in the war were to affect the subsequent specifications of weapons. The industrial scale of manufacturing weaponry also increased greatly. Vast and unprecedented quantities of munitions were produced. Combined with improvements in fighting quality and skill, these helped deliver the military decisiveness that swept aside or dislocated the old order across much of the world.

In 1917, the Romanov dynasty was overthrown in Russia,[53] followed in 1918 by the Habsburg, Hohenzollern, and Ottoman Empires of Austria, Germany, and Turkey, respectively. The earlier failure of the powers to negotiate a peaceful end to the conflict was a key feature of the war, as it also was to be of the Second World War. This failure ensured that the destructiveness of the conflict did not lead to its end but, instead, to a determination to devote even more effort to it. This effort proved politically traumatic but militarily conclusive.

Chapter Three

The First World War at Sea

Germany's failure to knock France rapidly out of the war in 1914 made the First World War a conflict in which naval power was crucial, even if there were no decisive naval battles in the sense of overwhelming victories. As in 1870, when France's navy had been larger than that of Germany, the German military leadership in 1914 sought a campaign and a victory on land before the equations of naval power could kick in. The territorial gains pursued by Germany were mostly in Europe, although there was interest in a larger African empire. This attempt to direct the strategy of the war assumed that British entry on the side of France and Russia would not matter, as Britain would be isolated by French and Russian defeat. In the event, although the bulk of the fighting was on land, the war in part became that of continental versus oceanic power. This dynamic was important, both to the basic strategic situation and to the outcome of the war.

1914

Thanks to the strength of the Royal Navy, which remained the largest and most powerful navy in the world throughout the conflict and the leading force in the foremost naval alliance, the British retained essential control of their home waters. They were able to avoid blockade and serious attack, although German warships bombarded English east coast towns, notably Hartlepool, Scarborough, and Whitby on December 16, 1914, causing great popular outrage by doing so. These were only raids. In contrast, Britain was able to maintain the flow of men and munitions to the army in France unmolested, to retain trade links that permitted the mobilization of British and imperial resources, and to use stop and search to impede the flow of contraband to Germany. The last, the blockade, was the crucial aspect of economic warfare.

On November 3, 1914, Britain declared that the North Sea would be a military area with shipping subject to Admiralty control. Germany, however, continued to receive imports at the beginning of the war through neutral ports, notably the leading Dutch port, Rotterdam. This access to trade was gradually reduced as the Allies steadily increased pressure on neutral powers to stop the lucrative practice of reexporting their imports to Germany, with particular pressure on the Dutch not to reexport food to neighboring Germany. British actions breached the Paris (1856) and London (1909) agreements on wartime trade but appeared necessary if economic warfare with Germany was to work. This indicated the fragility of attempts to restrain the operations of international powers, a fragility also seen in prewar regulations on war on land that were ignored. British actions were justified, on a legal basis, as reprisals for Germany's equally unlawful submarine campaign.

Economic warfare was supported by a system of preemptive purchasing, for example of Norwegian fish and pyrites, that was important to the international control of raw materials, as well as greatly influencing neutral economies. In particular, cutting off trade with Germany lessened American economic and financial interest in its success. Intelligence about shipping and commercial movements was also crucial to the blockade.[1]

Economic warfare made it difficult for planners in Berlin to realize schemes for increased production and contributed greatly to the sense of frustration and anger that increasingly affected German strategy and, along with German failure to win on land, led toward unrestricted submarine warfare. In turn, the economic warfare only really became effective once the United States, hitherto the leading neutral, entered the war. The Germans failed adequately to appreciate the nature of the strategic situation, in particular the fact that Britain was a key part of a global maritime system, and one with considerable resilience.

Alongside resources, geography was a crucial factor, with the Germans bottled up in the North Sea by Britain's location athwart their routes to the oceans. To contemporaries, this helped underline the significance of geopolitics and geostrategy. There was periodical German interest in sending cruisers out into the Atlantic, and further afield, in order to harry British trade. However, aside from the issue of coaling such ships once they were at sea (problems that could be overcome), the location of British bases was a key problem. The German route to the Atlantic was threatened by the major base of Scapa Flow in the Orkneys, although the base lacked necessary infrastructure in 1914. Moreover, in 1909, a new base at Rosyth on the Firth of Forth, in east Scotland, had been begun in order to help the British Grand Fleet contest the North Sea. Work there was much more extensive than at Scapa Flow.

While economic warfare threatened the German productive system and affected German military options, Britain's supply system was that of a country that could not feed itself: nearly two-thirds of British food consumption was imported. Britain also had an imperial economy that relied on global trade, and a military system that required troop movements within the vast empire. For example, during the war, 1.3 million men were sent to serve outside India, while 332,000 Australian troops served overseas. Canada's ability to contribute was very important to the British war effort in France. The sea constituted Britain's interior lines.

All this, and the capacity for ready responsiveness it indicated, was challenged by German warships. However, those outside Europe were hunted down by Britain and its allies in the early stages of the war. The East Asia squadron, under Vice Admiral Maximilian Graf von Spee, was the leading German naval force outside Europe at the outset of the war. It sailed to Chile where, off Coronel on November 1, a weaker and heavily outgunned British force was defeated with the loss of two cruisers. Spee then sailed on to attack the Falkland Islands, a British colony in the South Atlantic which had, at Port Stanley, a naval base including crucial coaling facilities. Britain had already sent two battle cruisers and six light cruisers there to hunt Spee down. Spee, surprised, was defeated off the Falklands on December 8, with all but one of his ships sunk.

Thereafter, outside Europe, the Germans only had individual warships, including armed merchant cruisers, at large, and these were eventually hunted down. As a result, the threat to the Allies from German surface raiders was essentially restricted to the opening months of the war. Indeed, Allied success in blockading the North Sea, the English Channel, and the Adriatic (where Germany's ally Austria had a coastline in modern Croatia and Slovenia), and in capturing Germany's overseas colonies, ensured that, after the initial stages of the war, and despite the use of submarines and new surface raiders, the range of effective German naval operations was smaller than those of American and French warships when attacking British interests between 1775 and 1815. Germany would need to change its maritime geography for the situation to be different, as occurred in 1940 with the conquests of Norway and France.

Allied sea power was crucial in supporting operations against German colonies and, in particular, wireless stations and ports, with the Japanese capturing undefended German island possessions in the northwest Pacific, as well as Germany's base of Tsingtao on the coast of China. Other Allied forces conquered German colonies in the southwest Pacific: Samoa and German New Guinea. At a very different scale, the British and French conquered Germany's colonies in Africa, although the British encountered great difficulties in German East Africa (modern Tanzania).[2] In 1915, exploiting their control of the Persian Gulf, British forces were landed in southern Iraq and Iran in order to oppose Turkish moves.

On August 6, 1914, following on from an informal agreement in 1912, Britain and France signed a naval convention under which the French navy was responsible for much of the Mediterranean and the British for the remainder of the world. As a result, there were no French warships in the North Sea, the key area of conflict between the British and German surface fleets. Aside from providing the bulk of Allied troops on the Western Front, the French role was more than might appear as it helped provide the Royal Navy with a sufficient margin of power over the Germans to survive losses. With British as well as French warships present, German and Austrian naval power was outnumbered and outclassed in the Mediterranean, which enabled France to move troops from North Africa safely and also greatly affected the military and political options for Italy, which was a background to Italy's entry into the war on the Allied side in 1915.[3]

The small German squadron in the Mediterranean, the battle cruiser *Goeben* and the light cruiser *Breslau*, shelled the ports of Philippeville and Bona in the French colony of Algeria on August 4, 1914; evaded British attempts to intercept them; and took shelter with the Turks later in August. The ships entered Turkish service, and their actions against the Russians in the Black Sea helped bring Turkey into the war against the Allies at the end of October.

In the North Sea, there were surface actions in 1914, but no battle between battleships and nothing to match the struggle on land. The British had decided to rely on a distant, not a close, blockade, and this strategy denied the Germans the major struggle they sought, although the British were also determined to limit German operations in the North Sea.[4] In the Battle of Heligoland Bight on August 28, British battle cruisers played the decisive role in an engagement that started as a clash between British and German squadrons of light cruisers and destroyers. The Germans lost three light cruisers and one destroyer. In contrast, although one British light cruiser and two destroyers were badly damaged, the fact that none were lost helped ensure that the battle was presented to the Allied public as a striking victory. In practice, it was not so much a coherent, highly structured battle but rather a series of individual ship engagements conducted in the poor visibility caused by dense fog. The British were hindered by the general lack of coordination in the Admiralty; the force composition for the raid; the limitations of, and constraints on, gunnery and torpedo skills (which ensured that the heavy use of ammunition and torpedoes brought few successes); and the quality of the British shells: many failed to explode. British torpedoes also faced problems.

Given these and other deficiencies, it is unsurprising that the British did not inflict heavier losses on the Germans in this battle. Nevertheless, all the latter's warships were outgunned by their British counterparts, while the

German torpedo boats were outclassed. The Germans were also affected by serious tactical problems, and communications were an issue. In addition, there was a poor command response to the British raid and, in particular, a lack of coordination and an inaccurate assessment of likely and actual developments. Most significantly, the battle reflected, and strengthened, a sense of psychological inferiority on the German part. This confirmed their cautious use of the fleet. The belief that the British would not send heavy units into the Bight had proved misplaced, while the Germans were both properly, and yet overly, anxious about risking their better ships, which greatly affected their response to the raid. Wilhelm II felt justified in his instructions that battle was to be sought only under the most favorable circumstances. These restrictions were now underlined.[5]

In 1914, the loss of ships to German submarines and mines cost the British more men and major ships than the Germans lost in battle, but the impact of these British losses was less dramatic in terms of the perhaps crucial sense of relative advantage. Indeed, submarines and mines appeared to be a means only to snipe at the British naval advantage rather than an effective counter to it, let alone a strategic tool. Moreover, Wilhelm's restrictions helped ensure that the surface war at sea would probably be lost by Germany through limited contest. Wilhelm's tight rein was no way to challenge the British blockade, although the fleet in being remained a threat to Britain. The British naval war effort had suffered from an inadequate war staff, but it proved able to adapt to the strategic circumstances of 1914. Moreover, by the end of 1914, foreshadowing events in the Second World War, the Allies, working in unusual concert, had cracked the three German naval codes. While the Germans appeared oblivious to this, the Royal Navy repeatedly, through slovenliness or mistrust, arguably failed to exploit this advantage to its full potential.[6]

1915

In 1915, although the Germans attacked at sea, their bold plan, to fall upon part of the British Grand Fleet with their entire High Seas Fleet and thus achieve a superiority that would enable them to inflict serious casualties that affected the overall situation at sea, was not pursued. Instead, on January 23, a German force of four battle cruisers and four light cruisers under Admiral Franz von Hipper put to sea in order to lay mines in the Firth of Forth, threatening the British base at Rosyth, and also to attack the British fishing boats on Dogger Bank in the North Sea, boats which were correctly seen as an intelligence asset. The interception of a German naval signal led to a loss of surprise, but the British missed the opportunity to deploy their navy so as to cut off the German force and instead relied on battle cruisers, which were not inherently designed for this role.

On the morning of January 24, in the Battle of Dogger Bank, five British battle cruisers under Vice Admiral David Beatty engaged the Germans, although in a stern chase it proved inherently time consuming to close, and this problem enabled the German ships to concentrate on his leading ship, *Lion*, the flagship, which took serious damage. By contrast, confused signaling by Beatty, the fear of submarine attack, and a lack of initiative by subordinate commanders ensured that the British force focused on the *Blücher*, an armored cruiser with medium guns. This was sunk, but the other German ships were able to escape and the Germans had learned valuable lessons in the deficiencies of their own ships and in how to fight the British. Firing their shells at long range, the British had few hits, while heavy smoke affected the optical range finding crucial to gunnery. The Germans had better optics.[7] Yet, alongside these disadvantages, the Grand Fleet was becoming both absolutely and relatively stronger, with five newly operational dreadnoughts added to it in the winter of 1914–15.

There was no other battle in the North Sea in 1915, and even less surface naval warfare elsewhere. Italy's decision to abandon Germany and Austria, with which it had agreed to a naval convention in 1913, and instead to join Britain and France ensured that the Mediterranean was controlled by this alliance. A French squadron at Corfu off northwest Greece, and most of the Italian fleet at Taranto supported by British, including Australian, warships, confined Austrian surface ships to the Adriatic and sought to stop submarines from getting into the Mediterranean. Italian success with torpedo boats led to the sinking of Austrian battleships, a clear instance of asymmetric naval warfare. In the Black Sea, the Russians had more warships than the Turks and were able to blockade the Bosporus, but no decisive blows were struck.[8]

In the Baltic, the Russian fleet was weaker than the forces the Germans could deploy if they moved in some of their High Seas Fleet units from the North Sea via the Kiel Canal. Although there were clashes off Riga in 1915 and 1917, this German capability encouraged Russian caution, which was also in keeping with a stress on the Russian army, with long-established Russian naval doctrine, and with the Russian emphasis in the Baltic on local naval operations. Defeat by the Japanese navy in 1905 was scarcely an encouragement for bolder operations. The Russians laid extensive minefields to protect the Gulf of Finland and staged raids into the southern Baltic in order to mine German shipping routes, while the Germans, in turn, also laid mines.

Although the British, prior to the war, had considered sending a fleet into the Baltic in order to help Russia, threaten an attack on northern Germany, force battle on the Germans, and cut German trade with Scandinavia, no such expedition was mounted, just as none was to be mounted in 1939–40, when Winston Churchill was again First Lord of the Admiralty. The idea was both risky in itself and a diversionary challenge to the numbers necessary for British naval superiority in the North Sea. The Germans had sufficient mines and submarines to make Baltic plans so unrealistic that more prudent Admiralty and War Department planners ignored or blocked the schemes, encouraging the emphasis on the blockade. There was also little mileage in the idea that naval power could make a material difference to operations in Flanders, an idea pushed by Churchill. Aside from the serious naval problem of operating inshore against a protected coast, there was also the difficulty posed by the strength of German forces with the mobility offered them by the railway. Once the British warships appeared off the Belgian coast, they discovered that the Germans had erected ever-heavier shore batteries that could outrange them and had the advantage in terms of ship-versus-shore accuracy. More generally, naval operations in the Adriatic, Baltic, and Black Seas made little difference to the course of the First World War on adjoining land masses.

An Anglo-French fleet was given a major role in 1915, being sent to force the Dardanelles en route to threatening Constantinople, the Turkish capital. However, this poorly planned attempt was stopped by minefields, shore batteries, and an unwillingness, in the face of the loss of ships, to accept the risk of further naval operations. There had been a misplaced belief that naval power alone could force a passage through the Dardanelles because of a serious underestimation of the Turkish minefields and the mobile shore batteries protecting them, and of the Turkish ability and willingness to resist attack. Moreover, the viability of any strategy of knocking Turkey out of the war by this means, and thus helping Russia and affecting Balkan developments, was dubious. As an instance of new vulnerabilities, a British officer recorded a German aircraft flying low and machine-gunning a sailor on a destroyer.[9]

At the same time, the scheme, which owed much to Churchill, showed the extent of British naval power, as the naval force sent—mostly older capital ships—did not endanger the situation in the North Sea.[10] In place of the unsuccessful naval attempt, the Allies switched to an attempt to take control of the eastern side of the Dardanelles, but the amphibious capability revealed was not matched by success on the part of the forces once landed. However, Allied naval power was such that it was possible to supply these forces and, eventually, to withdraw them successfully.[11]

SUBMARINE WARFARE

The Atlantic trading system on which the British economy rested, and which was a core component of its maritime position and power, was the prime target for German naval warfare by 1915. Trade played the key role in accumulating and mobilizing the capital and securing the matériel on which

Allied war making depended. Neither Britain nor France had an industrial system to match that of Germany, which by 1914 had forged ahead of Britain in iron and steel production. As a result, the Allies were dependent on America for machine tools and much else, including the parts of shells. American industrial output was equivalent to that of the whole of Europe by 1914, and the British ability to keep Atlantic sea-lanes open ensured that America made a vital contribution to the Allied war effort before its formal entry into the war in 1917. This was a key strategic capability and outcome. Transoceanic trade and naval dominance also allowed Britain and France to draw on the resources of their far-flung colonial empires. Canadian help proved especially significant.[12]

Submarines had not featured prominently in naval operations over the previous decade, and their potential had been greatly underestimated by most commentators. Britain, which had only launched its first submarine in 1901, had the largest number—eighty-nine—at the outbreak of the war, many intended for harbor defense, but had not found answers to the problems of the defense of warships and merchantmen against submarines.

Once war had begun, the Germans stepped up the production of submarines, but relatively few were ordered and most were delivered late. In part, this was because of problems with organizing and supplying construction. Germany, as in 1939, also started war at what turned out to be the wrong time for the navy. Crucially, alongside the dominance of strategy by the army, a dominance Wilhelm II did not challenge, there was a long-standing concentration of industrial resources on the army, a pattern that was to be repeated in the Second World War. A lack of commitment from within the German navy to submarine warfare was also important. Instead, its preference was for surface warships, which required more maintenance in wartime. As a result, although submarines swiftly affected the conduct of operations, the Germans did not have the numbers to match their aspirations. In early 1915, only twenty-nine German submarines were available, and by the end of the year, only fifty-nine. The number on patrol at any given time was insufficient for an effective maritime interdiction campaign.

Aside from using scarce resources, the submarine also faced serious deficiencies as a weapons system. To move submerged, submarines were dependent on battery motors that had to be recharged on the surface where the submarines were highly vulnerable to attack. In addition, submarines, particularly when submerged, were slow, and this lessened their chance of maintaining contact and of hitting a warship moving under full steam. The low silhouette of a submarine provided an advantage, as it made it harder to locate, but also, without radar, it limited the area it could oversee. Even with radar, the problem of low height limited the range of any line-of-sight instrument. Using a highly placed radar, a destroyer could survey a much greater area than a submarine could with its much lower-placed radar.

Submarines, however, benefited over time from an increase in their range, seaworthiness, speed, and comfort; from improvements in the accuracy, range, and speed of torpedoes (which, by 1914, could travel seven thousand yards at forty-five knots); and from the limited effectiveness of antisubmarine weaponry. These improvements reflected the possibilities for war making of a modern industrial society, with its ability to plan, design, manufacture, and introduce better specifications for instruments and processes.

In time, submarines came to play a significant role in naval planning, both tactically and operationally, in terms of trying to deny bodies of water to opponents and sinking warships. In practice, however, merchant shipping, not warships, proved the most important target for German submarines and ensured that they were given a role in strategic planning. Indeed, by attacking merchantmen, the Germans were demonstrating that the sea, far from being a source of protection for Britain, could in fact be a serious barrier to safe resupply.

Operating commerce raiding by the well-established prize rules was restricted submarine warfare, and, without regard to these rules, unrestricted. The prize rules were essentially to stop suspected vessels, search them for contraband, and, if contraband was found, take them into port where the ship could be condemned by a court as a prize. If it was impossible to get the vessel into port, the prize rules stipulated that it was to be scuttled after provision had been made for the crew and passengers by allowing them into the lifeboats or by holding them on board the submarine. This approach entailed the submarine coming to the surface to stop the vessel and subsequently sinking it, usually by gunfire: submarines carried a deck artillery piece as well as torpedoes, and the former used less bulky and less expensive ordnance and was more accurate. Moreover, U-boats carried very few torpedoes. For example, the U-31-41s of 1915 carried six torpedoes, so U-boat commanders preferred to use their gun wherever possible. In one cruise in 1916, the submarine ace Arnaud de la Perière sank fifty-four ships in a U-boat armed with only six torpedoes. Even the boats of 1917–18 carried only twelve to sixteen torpedoes, so that if they were to sink enough merchant shipping to win the war, they still needed to use their guns on the surface.

However, coming to the surface entailed the risks of being detected and sunk, not least by Q-ships, converted merchant ships designed to look vulnerable but equipped with hidden guns. The effect of the Q-ships was less in the actual number of submarines sunk than in the possible threat of sinking, which forced a change in the behavior of the submarines.

In 1915, Germany increased the threat and tempo of their assault on Allied shipping by declaring, on February 4, unrestricted submarine warfare, which began on February 18. This policy entailed attacking all shipping, Allied and neutral, and without warning, within the designated zone. The British *Lusitania*, the largest liner on the transatlantic run, was sunk off

Ireland by *U-20* on May 7. Among the 1,192 passengers and crew lost, there were 128 Americans, and there was savage criticism in America. In response, Germany offered concessions over unrestricted warfare, and on September 18 it was canceled altogether in order to avoid provoking American intervention. Aside from the impact on neutrals, Germany anyway was unprepared for such a war, as it lacked sufficient submarines, trained crew, or bases to mount an effective blockade of Britain. The Germans sunk 748,000 tons of British shipping in 1915, only for Britain to launch 1.3 million tons. Moreover, although a heavy burden, the British could afford to take the loss of trained crew.

1916

In 1916, the Germans sought again to implement their plan to fall upon part of the British Grand Fleet with their entire High Seas Fleet. Having been attempted in three sorties earlier in 1916 that did not result in a battle, the plan, tried again, led to the Battle of Jutland of May 31 to June 1. With a reasonable grasp of the operational as well as strategic situation, the British did not fall for the German plan. Nevertheless, despite having the larger fleet at Jutland, they failed to achieve the sweeping victory hoped for by naval planners and the public, whether their reference was to Trafalgar (1805) or Tsushima (1905).[13]

Instead, in the battle, the British suffered seriously from problems with fire control; inadequate armor protection, especially on the battle cruisers; the unsafe handling of powder in dangerous magazine practices that were an effort to compensate for the poor gunnery of the battle cruisers; poor signaling; and inadequate training, for example in destroyer torpedo attacks and in night fighting. For the Royal Navy, there was a general problem of underperformance. German gunnery at Jutland was superior (more accurate) to that of the Royal Navy, partly because of better optics and better fusing of the shells, and partly because of the advantages of position, notably the direction of light. The Germans were far less visible to opposing fire, and their range firing was therefore easier.

Command decisions were important. Admiral Sir John Jellicoe's caution, not least about night action, possibly denied the British the victory they might have obtained had the bolder Beatty, commander of the battle-cruiser squadron, been in overall command. As an aspect of the manner in which the politics of command, personality, and faction affected current, as well as subsequent, assessments, this was an assessment encouraged by Beatty when he was First Sea Lord from 1919 to 1927. However, as Churchill was to point out, Jellicoe only needed to avoid losing. Moreover, from before the war, Jellicoe was concerned about how best to protect the fleet from German torpedoes, and at Jutland he used the tactic of turning away from destroyers and torpedo boats that had been considered prewar. Indeed, the German torpedo attack had little impact. Jellicoe's tactic, however, lessened the options for sustained British battleship fire.

As with American commanders at Midway (1942) and Leyte Gulf (1944), Jellicoe was also faced with the problems of managing and winning a naval encounter of unprecedented scale and complexity. Jellicoe confronted an incomplete picture of the battle, not only of the Germans but also of the British fleet because subordinates failed to report expeditiously. The technological possibilities of radio communications, let alone aerial reconnaissance, were not matched by operational practice and tactical implementation. The latter was also true with spotting for naval bombardments in amphibious operations, notably that of the British at the Dardanelles in 1915. At Jutland, in bad weather, the commanders and captains on both sides lacked adequate spatial knowledge of where everything was.[14]

In the equations of loss and casualties, the British lost more ships and men at Jutland than the Germans: fourteen ships, including three battle cruisers, and 6,097 men, compared with eleven ships, including one battle cruiser, and 2,551 men. The British ship tonnage lost was about twice that of the Germans. In addition, there was much damage to ships and many wounded, including, on *Warspite*, Walter Yeo, who was the first to receive plastic surgery. Beatty's rash performance at Jutland suggests that, had he been in overall command, there might have been more serious losses.

Wilhelm II announced at the North Sea naval base of Wilhelmshaven on June 5, "The English were beaten. The spell of Trafalgar has been broken." The British mistakes had certainly ensured that they had not gotten what they wanted. Nevertheless, the German fleet had been badly damaged in the big-gun exchange. Its confidence had been seriously affected by the experience of the power of the Grand Fleet, which had superior gunnery. Moreover, the strategic situation prior to the battle still pertained. Thereafter in the war, the High Seas Fleet sailed beyond the defensive minefields of the Heligoland Bight on only three occasions, the first on August 18, 1916. On each occasion, it took care to avoid conflict with the Grand Fleet. In turn, the High Seas Fleet and the fact that it was not confined to port posed a major threat as a fleet in being, and this threat acted as a restraint on British naval operations by containing the Grand Fleet's activities. Their losses at Jutland made both Jellicoe and the Admiralty more cautious.

Yet the British employed their fleet by deterring the Germans from acting and thus challenging the British blockade or use of the sea. This deterrence thwarted the optimistic German plan of combining surface sorties with submarine ambushes in order to reduce the British advantage in warship numbers, a plan for attrition that was difficult to implement. This advantage was supplemented by British superiority in the intelligence war, especially the use of signals intelligence. The location of German warships was generally known by the British. Moreover, Jutland acted as a catalyst for change for the Royal Navy, encouraging intense activity for the remainder of the war and into the postwar period. This activity involved new tactics, as well as new types of shells, guns, and armor for new battleships.

Jutland, furthermore, was decisive in that it demonstrated to the Germans that a gradual degradation of the Grand Fleet was unlikely to be possible. While, therefore, the High Seas Fleet always posed a threat and was active on occasion, it left Germany without a clear fleet strategy. On July 4, 1916, recognizing that Jutland had left the British still dominant in the North Sea, the German commander there, Vice Admiral Reinhard Scheer, the commander of the High Seas Fleet, suggested to Wilhelm II that Germany could only win at sea by means of using submarines.

That October, Jellicoe, who was to become First Sea Lord in December, observed that the greater size and range of submarines and their increased use of the torpedo, so that they did not need to come to the surface to sink their target by gunfire, meant that the submarine menace was getting worse. Indeed, during the war, most vessels sunk were due to mines or torpedoes. In November, Arthur J. Balfour, the First Lord of the Admiralty, wrote, "The submarine has already profoundly modified naval tactics. . . . It was a very evil day for this country [Britain] when this engine of naval warfare was discovered."[15]

The greater emphasis on submarines altered the nature of the war at sea, as submarine warfare did not offer the prospect of a decisive victory in a climactic engagement. Instead, the submarine conflict helped to ensure that the attritional dimension of naval warfare became more pronounced. Combined with the British blockade of Germany, the submarine conflict ensured that the war was more clearly one between societies, with an attempt to break the resolve of peoples by challenging not only economic strength but also social stability and, indeed, demographic health. In Germany, rickets was known as "the English disease" due to the blockade. The role of food shortages in weakening resistance to disease was well understood. As such, this means of war led to a sense that extreme means were already at play. As yet, aerial attacks were not on a scale that could offer this "total war" character, while land warfare had a limited effect on the home front.

1917

In 1917, having failed in 1916 to drive France from the war at the Battle of Verdun (on land) and the British at Jutland, and having in turn experienced the lengthy and damaging British attack in the Somme offensive (on land), the Germans sought to force Britain from the war by resuming attempts to destroy its supply system. There was a parallel with the invasion of France via Belgium in 1914, in that the strong risk that a major power would enter the war as a result, Britain in 1914 and American in 1917, was disregarded on the grounds that success could be obtained as a result of the German attack and the resulting broadening out of the war. In 1917, however, the Germans, unlike in 1914, had had plentiful warnings as a result of their earlier use of unrestricted submarine warfare in 1915.

There was also a serious failure of planning, as anticipated outcomes from the submarine assault did not arise, and the timetables of projected success totally miscarried. This situation reflected confusion about submarine capabilities—mirroring German strategic overconfidence in 1914—and also overconfidence in technology-based solutions to problems.

Ironically, America's entry into the war increased the importance of submarines to German capability as it further shaped the balance of surface warships against Germany. This prefigured the situation in 1941, when the United States entered the Second World War against Germany, although then the German surface fleet was weaker in relative terms. In 1917, America had the third-largest navy in the world after Britain and Germany, and the Navy Act of 1916 had increased the shipbuilding program, although it had not yet come to fruition.

Moreover, in part due to the dominance of the army's needs, and certainly compared to the grip of the British Admiralty over wartime procurement, the Germans added fewer battleships and battle cruisers during the war than the British (four and three compared to fourteen and five). This contrast ensured that the pronounced British numerical superiority of 1914 was greatly expanded. Victory in the prewar naval race was followed by victory in a wartime naval race, which is not surprising given that prewar building rates prefigured the outcome. Thus, the Germans did not have the margin of success in a large-scale shipbuilding program on which to fall back.

Nor, more seriously, did the Germans have the prospect of support from the warships of new allies that the Allies gained with the alliance of Italy (1915) and, even more, America (1917). Italy was the European neutral with the largest fleet. Portugal, which also joined the Allies in 1916, had a modest fleet. Brazil, which also suffered from unrestricted German submarine warfare, followed America by declaring war in October 1917, but the small squadron it eventually dispatched did not see active service. Furthermore, in late 1916, in accordance with a British request, four Japanese warships were sent to the Mediterranean. Based in Malta, they added to escort capacity, as well as strengthening the Allied position in the equation of naval power. These additions more than nullified the success of German submarines in sinking Allied warships. Moreover, in 1917, the British lost only one predreadnought battleship and one armored cruiser this way. The Allies lost the support of Russia in 1917, but of no Atlantic naval power, unlike with France in 1940.

These factors affecting surface warship strength accentuated the importance of the submarine war on British trade. Indeed, the initial rate of Allied shipping losses was sufficiently high to threaten defeat. Serious losses were inflicted on Allied, especially British, commerce, in large part due to British inexperience in confronting submarine attacks. The limited effectiveness of antisubmarine weaponry was also an issue, as depth charges, another new technology, were effective only if they exploded close to the hull of the submarine. This was also a period when effective artillery techniques on land were having to be worked out. It took time to establish and disseminate such techniques. In February to April 1917, 1,945,240 tons of British shipping were sunk, with only nine German submarines lost. The Germans calculated that if they could sink six hundred thousand tons of British shipping per month for six months, it would drive Britain out of the war. This calculation was also based on the assumption that 40 percent of neutral trade would not enter the war zone due to the threat and, especially, the high maritime insurance rates.

In the event, as later in the Second World War, Britain survived the onslaught, and, as in the later conflict, this was thanks to both outfighting the submarines and success on the home front. The introduction, from May 10, of a system of escorted convoys cut shipping losses dramatically and helped lead to an increase in the sinking of submarines. Convoys, which were introduced first in February to protect ships carrying vital coal to France, in response to calls from the French government, might appear such an obvious solution that it is surprising they were not adopted earlier and that they were introduced in a piecemeal fashion. Initially, the British patrolled the sea while the French escorted their merchantmen. Then, seeing the bad results of the former, the Allies began patrolling the routes and convoying merchantmen.

Nevertheless, there were counterarguments to convoys. These included the number of escorts required, the delays that would be forced on shipping, congestion in harbors as a result of convoys, the lack of a dedicated bureaucracy, and the possibility that convoys would simply offer a bigger and slower target to submarines. Convoys were also resisted by certain naval circles as not sufficiently in touch with the bold "Nelson touch" they believed necessary and appropriate. To look after convoys did not appear the role of warriors. Nineteenth-century Royal Navy culture had obfuscated the success of convoys in the French Revolutionary and Napoleonic Wars from 1793 to 1815.[16]

However, against a background of resource superiority and a degree of naval control that enabled them to choose options, the Admiralty, under pressure from the new prime minister, David Lloyd George, eventually took the necessary steps. The Naval Staff had already created a dedicated antisubmarine section, and it became better organized in 1917. Convoying proved effective: only 393 of the 95,000 ships that were convoyed across the Atlantic were sunk. Convoys facilitated the transport of over two million American troops to Europe aboard thousands of ships and thus provided a vital new force for the Allies on the Western Front. Only three transports, one of which managed to limp to the French Atlantic port of Brest after being torpedoed, were lost, and only sixty-eight soldiers drowned. Another two million troops were ready to sail to France when the war ended.

Despite uncertainties at the outset about how best to deploy warships, notably destroyers, against German U-boats,[17] this convoying was the priority for the American navy, and convoying owed much to American support. Although they lacked experience in antisubmarine warfare, the Americans at once deployed their fleet to help protect communication routes across the Atlantic. From May, American warships took part in antisubmarine patrols in European waters, initially with six destroyers based in Queenstown in southern Ireland where Admiral Sir Lewis Bayly, the British commander, was a key figure in fostering Anglo-American cooperation. The resourceful Vice Admiral William Sims, commander of American naval forces in European waters, was important in encouraging convoying. To assist convoying in the Mediterranean, American warships were based in Gibraltar. American escort vessels rapidly contributed to the effectiveness of convoying, the key help being in destroyers. They were fast enough to track submarines and keep them submerged, which reduced their effectiveness. The Americans proved proficient in antisubmarine warfare.

More generally, convoying was an aspect of the Allies' direction, on a global scale, of most of the world's shipping, trade, and troop flows. The Allied Maritime Transport Council oversaw an impressive system of international cooperation at sea, allocating shipping resources so that they could be employed most efficiently. This was important as an aspect of economic warfare and also in lessening targets for German submarines. British merchant shipping provided close to half of France's imports, which was a key aspect of the British maritime contribution to the war effort. Allied cooperation, organized through meetings such as the naval conference held in London in mid-November 1917, prefigured the situation during the Second World War.[18] British control of the substantial shipping of neutral Norway, which was unable to protect its shipping itself, increased greatly as a result of the new German policy, and Norway's ships were transferred to the British flag.[19] Neutral shipping and shipbuilding were important to the Allies, including in the cases of the Netherlands, Spain, and Sweden. There was a measure of imposition in the form of effective confiscation in this support.

Convoys not only reduced the targets for submarines but ensured that, when they found the convoys, the submarines could be attacked by escorts, and by escorts with appropriate goals and weaponry. In providing sufficient numbers of the latter, the British were helped by their wartime shipbuilding program, which included fifty-six destroyers and fifty antisubmarine motor launches. The tonnage of merchant shipping lost fell below half a million in August.

Convoys also benefited from the "shoal" factor: submarines, when they found a convoy, only had time to sink a limited number of ships. In coastal waters, convoys were supported by aircraft and airships. Viewing submerged objects is far easier from above than from sea level. This support forced the submarines to remain submerged.

Aside from convoying, there was a major effort to employ intelligence, especially the use of radio and the possibilities it offered, in defeating the submarines. Command and control was a key area of naval operations that benefited greatly from technological improvement. Developments with radio made it easier to retain detailed operational control. Directional wireless equipment aided location and navigation and was employed to hunt German submarines by triangulation, while radio transmissions changed from a spark method to a continuous wave system. Submarines had an inherent operational disadvantage in that it was not necessary to sink the submarine, but only to have shipping come safely home, a key strategic achievement. This was a weakness appreciated during the next war when air cover forced U-boats to submerge and allowed convoys to outrun them. Nevertheless, it was also important to weaken the submarine force by sinking boats, killing crew, and weakening morale. Thanks to the tracking of submarine movements, the British acquired an edge. However, there was not yet any equivalent to the sonar used in the Second World War in order to provide a local tactical advantage, and this absence affected the level of submarine losses.

Mine laying, generally an underrated activity and one treated as unheroic (rather like mine laying on land and antiaircraft guns), was very significant in the war with U-boats and indicated the degree to which antisubmarine warfare displayed the complex relationships between technological advance, industrial capacity, organizational capability, operational experience, and tactics. Although convoys definitely limited the potency of German attack, mines sank more submarines than other weapons, while mine barrages limited their options. Intelligence information was important in the planning of mine laying. The Allies laid massive barrages across the English Channel at Dover in late 1916, which limited the movement of German submarines into the English Channel, and across the Straits of Otranto, at the entrance to the Adriatic. The largest, containing seventy-five thousand mines, was across the far greater distance of the North Sea between the Orkneys and Norway, from March 1918, with the Americans playing a major role. Drawing in part on German mines, there were also important improvements in mine technology during the war: magnetic mines were developed and were laid by the British.

There were also improvements in navigational skills, such that it was possible to cross one's own minefields more successfully. The British also made valuable advances in firing depth charges.

Yet, alongside incremental improvement, there were limitations. Aircraft were not yet able to make a fundamental contribution to antisubmarine operations because key specifications they had by the Second World War were lacking during the First World War. Moreover, the antisubmarine weapons dropped by aircraft were fairly unsophisticated compared to those of the Second.

The strategic limitations of submarine warfare were underlined by the success of the British government, helped by better weather, in greatly improving cereal/grain production. In part, this improvement came from converting land from the production of meat and milk by plowing it up. In addition, coal and food were rationed in Britain from 1917, which both controlled and directed demand. Thus, submarine warfare helped greatly in moving Britain toward a total war mobilization of the resources of society and the capabilities of government. Again, this anticipated the situation during the Second World War.

1918

By 1918, the rate of Allied tonnage sunk per German submarine lost had fallen. Nevertheless, the Germans continued to inflict considerable damage, with at least 268,000 tons of British shipping sunk each month from January to August, and heavy concentrations of losses in the Western Approaches and the Irish Sea. The hard work of convoying under persistent threat of submarine attack continued until the end of the war. The threat from submarines led to a bold and partly successful attack on April 22–23 on the Zeebrugge entrance to the canal to Bruges from which German submarines based in Belgium sortied. A similar attack on Ostend followed on May 9. Falling German effectiveness ensured that only 288,000 tons of British shipping were sunk in September and October combined.

German surface ships made far less of an impact other than in diverting Allied resources. However, in January, the *Goeben* and *Breslau* sortied from the Black Sea into the Aegean, sinking Allied shipping until the *Breslau* hit a mine and the *Goeben* returned to the Black Sea. British aircraft and submarines had failed to sink it.

The arrival in France of American troops and matériel made the strategic irrelevance of the German navy abundantly clear, although it always remained a fleet in being, fixing the British Grand Fleet. Moreover, American entry into the war made any idea of a decisive German naval sortie less credible and thus paralleled the buildup of American troops in France, which also helped limit German options. Five American dreadnoughts, the Sixth Battle Squadron, a formidable force, joined the Grand Fleet in December 1917 and took over escort for the vital Norwegian convoy twice. Four of these dreadnoughts sailed with the Grand Fleet on April 24, 1918, when it failed to intercept an ultimately unsuccessful German sortie into the North Sea aimed at a Scandinavian convoy.[20]

In the face of clear Allied superiority, a decisive German naval sortie was less credible. The German surface fleet languished, while its men became seriously discontented, leading to their mutiny at the end of the war. This matched the breakdown in the Russian and Austrian fleets in 1917 and 1918, respectively. The mutiny of the sailors in the German High Seas Fleet on October 27 proved a key precipitant for rebellion across the country, as well as thwarting the German naval command's plan for a final sortie that was designed to justify postwar political support for the navy. The fleet had also been sent to sea in 1917 to campaign in the eastern Baltic against Russia, in part to quell unrest. In 1918, the idea of a glorious last sortie proved unacceptable to the sailors.[21]

In the event, the fleet sailed forth only to surrender, nine battleships and five battle cruisers entering the Firth of Forth to do so on November 21, escorted by the Grand Fleet in an impressive display of British naval power. In addition, 176 German submarines were handed over after the war. German naval power had been totally destroyed.

NAVAL AIR POWER

The impression of naval potency had been amplified during the war. The battleship remained the key currency of naval power and its most potent demonstration. However, aside from submarines, naval air power suggested another future. Air power developed at sea in a number of directions. Airships were much used for reconnaissance, Jellicoe warning, "the German airships will be of the greatest possible advantage to their fleet as scouts."[22] Although their range was shorter than that of airships, aircraft proved less exposed to the weather. Prior to the conflict, Britain and France had converted ships to provide seaplane tenders. Seaplanes, generally operated from naval bases but also able to perform sea takeoffs and landings and to be catapulted from ships, as well as aircraft operated from coastal air stations, were more important at sea during the war than airships.

Britain took a lead in the use of aircraft for reconnaissance, spotting naval gunfire (in order to improve accuracy), patrols against submarines, and attacks on shipping, although the French also played a role. On December 5, 1914, a French squadron of seaplanes was deployed at Port Said, with French pilots and British observers, in order to protect the Suez Canal and to observe

Turkish naval and land moves. In April 1916, the squadron was moved to Greece.[23] In 1915, British seaplanes employed torpedoes against Turkish supply ships. In August 1918, British seaplanes eliminated an entire naval force: six German coastal motorboats. Visibility was a key element. In 1916, both the British and German fleets failed at Jutland in the North Sea, in poor visibility, to use their air reconnaissance adequately.

In July 1918, Britain conducted the first raid by aircraft flown off an improvised aircraft carrier, a technique not used by any other power. In September 1918, *Argus*, an aircraft carrier capable of carrying twenty aircraft, with a flush deck unobstructed by superstructure and funnels—in short, the first clear-deck carrier—was commissioned by the British, although she did not undergo sea trials until October. At the end of the war, the British were planning an air attack, with torpedo bombers designed for the purpose, on the German High Seas Fleet in harbor at Wilhelmshaven on the North Sea, an attack that had been postponed to 1919. The plans look toward the successful British attack on the Italian fleet at Taranto in 1940.

Naval air power was also introduced elsewhere. For example, the antecedents of Australian naval air power began during the war, with seaplanes flown off the major ships of the Royal Australian Navy and with Australian personnel in the British Royal Naval Air Service. There was also a short-lived Royal Canadian Naval Air Service, which served from Nova Scotia hunting for German submarines.[24] America did not take any aircraft to sea.

CONCLUSION

Naval power played a key role in the conflict and with far fewer casualties than in the war on land. However, many of the bolder hopes of such power on the attacking side were not fulfilled. This was not only the case with the absence of a decisive battle. The navalist emphasis on ship-to-ship engagement overshadowed amphibious operations, but these also proved a disappointment. Winning dominance of the sea had to come before its use for force projection, but this led to a neglect of planning for the latter. This relative neglect was accentuated by the greater prominence of commerce raiding and protection that arose from the development of the submarine and from the relative unimportance of amphibious operations in the 1890s and in the first four decades of the twentieth century. The course of the First World War did not really bear out the claim in Charles Callwell's *Military Operations and Maritime Preponderance: Their Relations and Interdependence* (1905) that there was a close connection between command of the sea and control of the shore.

Already, prior to the war, the British had concluded that amphibious operations against Germany were not practical. Plans in 1914–15 for an attack on Schleswig, the part of Germany south of Denmark, a part exposed to British naval power in the North Sea, were not pursued. Moreover, in 1915, the attempt to use naval power to force a way to Constantinople failed. Plans for coordinated operations in Flanders were vitiated by the strength of the German resistance.

There were fewer amphibious operations than in the Second World War, when need, opportunity, and capability were all greater. In part, this was a reflection of the greater extent of campaigning in the Second World War, notably in the Pacific and Mediterranean; in part of the opportunities presented for hitting at opponents by these means; and in part of the capabilities provided by carrier-borne aircraft and large numbers of powered landing craft.

In both May 1915 and December 1916, the British Admiralty leadership changed as a consequence of perceptions of failure. Yet much was achieved.[25] Naval dominance had been achieved and ensured that the Allied war effort could be mobilized, applied, and sustained. The hopes that commerce could continue in war had been fulfilled.

The submarine was future potential turned into present reality and appeared much more relevant than aircraft. It created a very distinctive and troubling image of naval conflict, one that answered to a different analysis of modernization and potential than that of the battleship.[26] A fictional echo was provided in 1917 when Arthur Conan Doyle, the British author, in *The Last Bow*, published "The Bruce-Partington Plans," a short story set in 1895. In this, Mycroft Holmes, the fictional intellectual panjandrum of the British government, told his brother Sherlock about

> the plans of the Bruce-Partington submarine. . . . Its importance can hardly be exaggerated. It has been the most jealously guarded of all government secrets. You may take it from me that naval warfare becomes impossible within the radius of a Bruce-Partington operation.

Alongside technology, the global dimensions of the struggle deserve attention. The war very much indicated the value of maritime links. For example, the British effort to resist the German and Turkish presence in Iran was mounted by sea, whereas German and Turkish forces moved overland. The Russian presence in northern Iran was supported by ships operating across the Caspian Sea.

These global dimensions related not only to the major states but also to others. Some gained experience in coalition warfare that looked toward a later pattern of multilateral global naval operations. Expertise was spread. Argentina sent a naval mission to the United States in 1917 to obtain training in naval aviation and submarines. Returning to Argentina, these officers were the promoters of the naval air arm and the submarine force.

At one level, the war had served primarily to show that battle fleets were of defensive value, with Britain and France successfully defending their control of the oceans,[27] rather than being an effective offensive tool that had the capability to deliver victory. At the same time, this defensive value was a key aspect of the durability of an alliance that was able to mobilize and deploy its forces for victory. The railway gave Germany and its allies valuable interior lines in Europe, facilitating the application of the resources of a continent and for moving troops within it, but the sea did so for those of the world.

Chapter Four

The First World War in the Air

"Flying Men: The Chivalry of the Air" was the title of a piece in the *Times* of London on March 20, 1917. This article suggested that air battles represented the "chivalries" of the past, whereas the "desolation" of conflict on the ground threatened to destroy traditional values. Pilots were presented as a "race apart" and as "air-warriors" taking part in one-to-one fighting, "wing to wing."[1] The advent of flight indeed led young men to do something "different and exciting," but the reality was much bleaker. Conflict in the air was brutal as well as dangerous, and death there was as unpleasant as that among the "desolation" on the ground. Pilots lacked parachutes. Aircraft, once hit, disintegrated or burned up.

The scale of change in air power really escalated from 1914, because, in the existing situation, change was bound to be radical and impressive. In part a matter of new types of aircraft and new weapon technologies, change also involved the rapid and significant development of doctrine and production. Most important was a sense of air power as an integral aspect of other branches of conflict, including its use for reconnaissance, artillery spotting, bombing, and action against submarines. The flexibility of air power, its use for land and sea conflict, and its potential for tactical, operational, and strategic ends all emerged clearly. These factors were important in their own right and looked to the future. They encouraged an interest in such concepts as air superiority, command of the air, and strategic air warfare.

BACKGROUND AND 1914

Air power played a role from the opening campaigns in 1914, developing the potential already glimpsed prior to the war. Reconnaissance was a key capability, with aircraft more flexible and less vulnerable than tethered balloons, and far better and more responsive than the cavalry widely used by all armies. Despite the serious operating constraints posed by the weather, aircraft came to supplement and then replace the reconnaissance functions of cavalry, although the pace of change varied. Over land, French aircraft reported the significant change of direction of the German advance near Paris, creating the opportunity for the successful Allied counterattack in the Battle of the Marne. Aircraft reconnaissance also helped the Germans in the Tannenberg campaign as they responded victoriously to the Russian invasion of East Prussia. In contrast, German aircraft saw and reported the crucial French redeployment of forces from Lorraine to Paris but were not believed.

From the outset, bombing was one of the most modern and terrifying aspects of the war. In 1910, Colonel Frederick Trench, the British military attaché in Berlin, reported that Germany was aiming to build "large airships of great speed, endurance and gas-retaining capacity."[2] Supporting the German invasion of Belgium, a zeppelin (airship) raid bombed Liège on August 6. German airship raids on Antwerp, Paris, and Warsaw soon followed. In response, and indicating what was to be a key element in the employment of air power, its use against other air forces, the aircraft of the British Royal Naval Air Service (RNAS) conducted effective raids from Antwerp in September and October 1914. Twenty-pound bombs were dropped on zeppelin sheds at Düsseldorf on October 8, destroying one airship. The zeppelin base at Friedrichshafen on Lake Constance was attacked on November 21. Nothing was hit, but the success consisted of reaching the target and coming back. As a result, the British Admiralty developed an interest in strategic bombing.

As yet, the scale of activity was still modest. At the start of the war, the British Royal Aircraft Factory at Farnborough could produce only two airframes per month, but its artisanal methods (which encouraged the dependence on French aircraft) were swiftly swept aside by mass production. The first important aircraft built at Farnborough was the BE (British Experimental) aircraft, which was designed for reconnaissance and observation. Entering service in 1912, it was a very stable aircraft, making it ideal for reconnaissance. About 3,500 were built between 1912 and 1918. Existing factories were rapidly converted to war uses. The Birmingham and Midland Carriage Company built Handley Page bombers, while Sunbeam, Wolverhampton's carmakers, manufactured aero-engines.[3]

Drawing on the experimentation of Igor Sikorsky, who had built and flown the first four-engined aircraft in 1913, the Russians developed four-engined bombers capable of a considerable range and bombed East Prussia, but Russian air power suffered from the limitations of its industrial base. Austria, which was relatively late in appreciating and deploying aircraft, had only five aircraft on the Eastern Front, and only two worked. Cavalry, not aircraft, was used by the Austrians to locate the Russian armies in the vast space of western Ukraine in August.

1915

Air warfare became bolder in conception as the war continued, with the strategic impasse, mounting casualties, and attritional character of the war on the ground providing the impetus for a search for added capability and alternative means, as well as the time necessary in order to develop innovations. From January 19, 1915, zeppelins attacked Britain, while they continued to bomb French cities, being joined by aircraft. The material damage was relatively modest. A total of fifty-one zeppelin attacks on Britain (involving 208 sorties) during the war dropped 196 tons of bombs that killed 556 people and caused £1.5 million worth of property damage. These air attacks, which continued on Britain until 1918, had considerable impact in terrorizing civilian populations, with up to a million people decamping into the countryside, and inflamed British and French opinion.[4] These attacks also affected troops at the front, collapsing the distance between it and the home front. Lieutenant Colonel Alan Thomson, a gunner, was worried about his wife in London and referred to the zeppelins as "those infernal devils."[5]

Bombing raids on civilians were both an application of new technology for the established goal of targeting civilians and a preparation for a new type of total war, in which the centers of opposing states could be attacked with increasing speed and scale. While the sense of what air power might achieve expanded rapidly, many ideas were not feasible, as when the British Committee of Imperial Defence considered using long-range aircraft based in Russia to drop incendiary bombs that would destroy German wheat and rye crops.[6] Although overrating the vulnerability of agriculture, the impracticable idea indicated how quickly military planners began to envisage that this form of conflict should be a war virtually without limits. That was not the same as air power itself being novel as a new war without limits, because antisocietal goals and means were long established, a point that some discussion underplays. Instead, air power represented a new delivery system. Other ideas were considered unacceptable, as when Major Lord Tiverton recommended the use of potato blight, which would also have provided a more pointed instance of the food shortages that naval blockade was intended to produce. This would also have been the first use of biological warfare.

While there were only limited changes in airships, the capabilities of aircraft swiftly improved, and tactics for the effective use of aircraft were worked out. That zeppelins impressed contemporaries as a bomber, tended to attack at night, could fly at a great height, and could climb rapidly created challenging requirements for the intercepting fighters; but they were expensive compared to aircraft, and their vulnerability to aircraft firing newly developed explosive and incendiary bullets became apparent.

Meanwhile, the ability of aircraft to act in aerial combat with other aircraft was enhanced thanks to increases in aircraft speed, maneuverability, and ceiling. Engine power increased, and engine size fell, while the rate of an aircraft's climb rose. The air-combat capability of an aircraft was helped by improved structural designs.

The need to shoot down reconnaissance aircraft, the first shot down on October 5, 1914,[7] resulted in the development of the fighter as well as an emphasis on antiaircraft guns fired from the ground. Initially reliant on small arms, generally revolvers and carbines fired by the observer, rather than on fixed arms, the fighter soon carried machine guns. Because of the ballistic complexities of firing off axis, it soon became clear that firing along the aircraft's flight path was far more accurate. In trials, the British fired Lewis guns through the propeller, merely binding the blades with tape to prevent splintering. Adding deflector plates or wedges to propeller blades permitted the firing of machine guns ahead and thus on the axis of attack. Adopting this device enabled the French to establish *escadrilles de chasse* (hunting squadrons). Roland Garros was the first French pilot to use deflector plates or wedges on propeller blades. He shot down three German aircraft with the system in April 1915.[8]

In turn, the interrupter gear ensured that the machine gun would not fire when the gun muzzle and the propeller were aligned. Interrupter and synchronizing mechanisms work by allowing a pulse to be sent from the engine to the firing mechanism to fire the gun, which effectively fires on semiautomatic. Effective synchronizing gear, which enabled bullets to pass through the arc of a propeller without hitting the propeller, was developed by a Dutchman, Anthony Fokker. Utilized by the Germans from April 1915, this enabled aircraft to fire repeatedly in the direction of flight, which made aiming far easier. The Fokker Eindecker aircraft, a speedy and nimble monoplane the Germans deployed from mid-1915, gave them a distinct advantage for the rest of the year; hence the "Fokker Scourge." The first British interrupter gear went into production in December 1915. Whereas on the eve of the war there had been no armed aircraft designed to attack other armed aircraft, now the situation was different, although emerging air power did not as yet affect the planning of campaigns and the pursuit of strategy.

Meanwhile in 1915, specialized bombing developed using adapted aircraft. Both Britain and France made significant advances, with Britain using bombers against German rail links in the Battle of Neuve Chapelle in March. Accuracy, however, was a major problem, as was vulnerability to fighters. Hugh Trenchard, who became the head of the Royal Flying Corps (RFC) in France in August, keenly fostered a sense of aggression and persistent attack for his aircraft, but this attitude led to high casualties. The following month, the French offensive launched in Champagne was accompanied by a large-scale air assault, leading to an aero-terrestrial battle. The bombing of Germany was relegated to the second rank, in part also because of the losses suffered by the French in bombing the Rhineland that November. The Champagne offensive led, on November 21, 1915, to the adoption by France of a program of large-scale expansion. An air force of 1,310 aircraft was planned.

Moreover, the use of aircraft in distant areas increased. In 1915, an exchange program began, with some German pilots serving in the Turkish army and some Turkish pilots under advanced training in Germany. The Turks used aircraft more than they had done in the Balkan Wars of 1912–13. More aircraft were purchased by Turkey, and they were organized as air companies. In Iraq, the Turks faced the first Australian Flying Corps (AFC) unit to see active service.

1916

The distinct benefit the Germans had gained from their use of Fokker Eindecker aircraft enabled them to seek the aerial advantage over Verdun in the key battle on the Western Front in early 1916. French vulnerability to German fighters was swiftly demonstrated. In addition, troops on the ground increasingly had to be mindful of the risk of air attack. The order of October 26 for the British 169th Infantry Brigade noted, "When hostile aeroplanes are in sight, troops will halt and clear the road as far as possible."[9] The effectiveness of aircraft machine guns, and their psychological impact, was underscored by the use of the German verb for such an attack, *strafen*, to punish. In just one pass, an aircraft could kill or wound twenty to thirty soldiers.

Nevertheless, in an abrupt demonstration of the action-reaction cycle that was so significant, the French, who sought what they termed air superiority, were eventually able to drive off German reconnaissance aircraft from Verdun because they succeeded in contesting the German Fokker fighters through their employment of large groups of aircraft and because they now had the agile "Bébé" Nieuport fighter. The first French fighter with a synchronized forward-firing machine gun, the Spad VII, became effective at the end of the year. Thus, war accelerated technological development but, with equal speed, resulted in another stalemate of sorts.

Over Verdun, each side complained about the other's aircraft and pursued a battle for air superiority with large-scale air-to-air conflict, but neither side had control of the air. In contrast, in the Battle of the Somme in the second half of the year, air power came to the fore. The German infantry and artillery complained bitterly about the way the British used aircraft for spotting and ground attack, and about the lack of a German response. Although the British were limited by bad weather, the Germans were impressed during the Somme offensive by the skill the British brought to coordinating the action of artillery, aircraft, and infantry. Because the long arm of the British artillery and aircraft reached well into the German rear, units out of the front line lacked restorative time. This was a key aspect of Trenchard's insistence on taking the war to the enemy, a stance the Germans were to copy in 1917 to good effect. In their zone, the French also gained air superiority and launched effective air attacks on the German artillery. Aircraft proved a particular problem for the Germans due to the exposed nature of the terrain.[10] This situation caused a real change in how the Germans thought about air power and control of the air, and they poured resources into developing their own air power, while also bringing aircraft and antiaircraft guns under the same corps. Now a key goal, air superiority required technological proficiency as well as the mass expressed in large formations.

1917

In turn, the Germans gained the advantage in the air in the winter of 1916–17 thanks in part to their Albatross D-1 with its top ceiling of eighteen thousand feet. Aerodynamically efficient, faster than the Nieuport, maneuverable, and armed with two synchronized machine guns, the Albatross entered service in September 1916. The advantage was apparent on the ground, the report on the operations of the British Fifty-Sixth Division noting for January 21, "The hostile bombardment was very accurate, evidently as a result of aerial reconnaissance carried out the previous day."[11]

The Germans lost their aerial advantage from mid-1917 as more and better Allied aircraft were deployed, especially the French Spad VII and Spad XIII and the British Bristol Fighter, with its forward- and rearward-bearing armament, and the extremely nimble Sopwith Camel. These aircraft, in turn, offered the Allies qualitative superiority. At the same time, this process was one of experimentation and with people's lives, the Sopwith Camel proving highly dangerous to its pilots, who joked that it offered the choice of "a wooden cross, a Red Cross, or a Victoria Cross."

The British abandoned mechanical synchronizing gears and, in 1917, adopted the superior synchronizing gear (the CC gear) invented by a Romanian engineer, George Constantinesco. This gear employed no mechanical linkages but a column of fluid in which wave pulses were generated and transmitted. This was not a hydraulic system because of the use of the pulse, but the process produced the hydraulic equivalent of an alternating current in electricity. It was more reliable than mechanical systems and allowed for a faster rate of fire. The CC gear was fitted to British fighters from March 1917 (Bristol Fighters, DH-4s and SE-5s) until the Gloster Gladiator of 1934 (it entered squadron service in 1937). Because Constantinesco's theory of sonics was kept secret, the Germans failed to copy the gear from shot-down aircraft (a regular source of technical intelligence) because they wrongly assumed the device to be purely hydraulic and could not make it work. They still used synchronizing gears in the Me-109 and FW-190 of the Second World War.

On the Western Front, the use of air power increased in 1917, both in scale and in type, not least with an increase in ground attack. This could be seen in the Allied Third Ypres Offensive, although the weather did not permit much flying in August, while in September dust often prevented accurate spotting. Nevertheless, in late September and early October, when the weather improved, the spotters helped the successful "bite and hold" limited offensives of Second Army under Herbert Plumer. In the Battle of Cambrai, from November 20 to December 5, the British made a large-scale use of tanks for the first time, and both they and the Germans first used ground attack extensively. Already on May 23, the Italians had used 109 aircraft in an attack on Austrian positions in advance of an offensive, a mass use of aircraft for ground support. Aircraft use was therefore part of a more general embrace of the new. In contrast, during the April Chemin des Dames offensive, the French air force concentrated on trying to win a separate victory in the air.

In 1917, paralleling the turn to unrestricted submarine warfare, the Germans launched an air assault on Britain because they believed, possibly due to reports from Dutch intelligence, that the British were on the edge of rebellion, which was very much not the case. As a result of this belief, the attacks were intended not so much to serve attritional goals but rather to be a decisive, war-winning, strategic tool. This, the first attempt to use air power as a truly strategic weapon, rather than simply a renewal of the zeppelin offensive, was a form of war that was novel. The use of bombers—the twin-engined Gotha—from May 25 reflected the rapid improvement of bombing capability during the war. The Germans imitated the design of the Russian Ilya Mourometz four-engined bomber, a development of the prewar Sikorsky model, which made over four hundred raids on Germany. The Gotha MK IV could fly for six hours, had an effective range of 520 miles, could carry 1,100 pounds (500 kg) of bombs, and could fly at an altitude of 21,000 feet (6,400 meters or four miles), which made interception difficult. As in the following world wars, the need for bombers to be able to outperform fighters was crucial. A rear machine gun that could depress to fire below was designed to thwart fighters firing up from below where aircraft were vulnerable to a surprise attack. Furthermore, the crews were supplied with oxygen and with electric power to heat their flying suits.

The first (and deadliest) raid on London, a surprise daylight one on June 13, led to a public outcry in Britain. Fourteen aircraft (six had dropped out), approaching at 16,500 feet and each carrying six 110-pound bombs, killed 162 people and injured 432, not least as a result of a direct hit on the North Street School in Poplar that killed sixteen children. In the characteristic action-reaction cycle, the raids resulted in the speedy development of a defensive system involving high-altitude fighters based on airfields linked by telephone to observers. This led to heavy losses among the Gothas and to the abandonment of daylight raids. Britain's early detection and response system, which was effective, provided the model for that used in 1940 when the Germans launched a deadlier air assault.

Moreover, the rationale of the 1917 German air campaign was misplaced because, as with the air attacks on France, those on Britain, far from hitting British morale, led to a hostile political, media, and public response. This remained the case in the winter of 1917–18, when the Germans unleashed large, four-engined Riesenflugzeug, or R-series, bombers, difficult to control but able to fly for eight hours and to drop 4,400 pounds (2,000 kg) of bombs. These aircraft, which themselves required a major logistical support system and thus represented a significant opportunity cost, failed to inflict sustained serious damage, and this did not set an encouraging example for strategic bombing.[12] The same was the case with the German rocket program in the Second World War.

1918

New weapon systems developed rapidly during the war. However, in 1918, aircraft remained particularly significant for reconnaissance, notably in spotting for artillery, the key weapon on the Western Front. This spotting was fundamental to the effectiveness of the earlier aerial reconnaissance work, which had produced the photography necessary for the accurate mapping of opposing positions, as well as for identifying targets. Thanks to spotting by aircraft such as the French Breguet XIV A2, the German Albatross C3, and the British RE-8, the accuracy of artillery fire could be assessed and fresh targets of opportunity found. As a reminder of the cumulative character of technological change in developing capabilities, radio permitted air-ground communication. British ground stations were operated by RFC personnel attached to artillery batteries. The radio communication, however, was one way: the operators had to take down and interpret the signals from the aircraft but could only reply by laying out cloth strips. By the end of the war, about six hundred reconnaissance aircraft were fitted with the Tuner Mark III, and there were one thousand ground stations and eighteen thousand wireless operators.

Air spotting aided counterbattery work and deep shelling: targeted fire on opposing positions that were within range behind the front. Haig and Trenchard both saw artillery-aircraft cooperation as crucial. Enhanced accuracy, which transformed the nature of range, was central to a modernization of artillery effectiveness, one, paradoxically, that, while dependent on air power, nevertheless ensured that ground-based fire remained far more significant as the essential form of firepower. Although limited by the range of the guns, artillery could deliver far heavier weights of firepower than aircraft alone. This modernization has been seen as akin to a revolution in military affairs.[13]

The capability and range of ground-support operations expanded. There was also a development in low-level ground attack, including trench strafing by machine gun, while there was also ground support in the form of interdiction: isolating the battlefield through attacking targets, notably supply links such as bridges, to the rear of the front line. In 1918, the Germans used specially organized ground-attack squadrons, coordinated in what became known in the Second World War as blitzkrieg attacks, to saturate and overrun Allied defenses on the Western Front. This forced the Allies to focus on repelling the German air assault, while, in turn, frequent Allied air attacks on their supply links inhibited German advances.

The Fokker D7 fighter, which entered German service in April, suffered problems at first, such as rib failure, shedding fabric on the upper wing, fuel tank splits at the seams, and engine heat igniting phosphorous in the ammunition. However, the D7 provided the Germans with a highly maneuverable and effective aircraft able to outclimb its British opponents, and British ground attacks on the Western Front that August were affected by German air power: "During the whole of these operations, enemy low flying aircraft were extraordinarily active, bombing and machine gunning our troops."[14] The Allies also had some good aircraft, notably the British SE-5, a fast, durable fighter that played a major role in the closing stages of the war. The French Spad XIII was well armed, agile, and robust and was used by the British and Americans as well. The French Breguet XIV, which entered service in June 1917, proved very successful in both reconnaissance and tactical bombing versions.

The impact of Allied fighters on the Western Front, not least in challenging the advantages the Germans won on the ground with their Spring Offensive, led the Germans to call off their Gotha attacks on London and, instead, to use these aircraft to take part in the air war over France. This involved both interdiction, in the shape of attacking railway stations, and the pursuit of air supremacy by means of raiding Allied airfields. The bombing of Paris, however, continued.

The range and scale of air activity increased in 1918, notably with the Allies carrying the fight to the enemy. The diaries of German corps and army commanders, such as Oskar von Hutier of Eighteenth Army, reported that strafing had replaced artillery as the greatest threat to German troops, who, as a result, could only move by night.[15] Despite serious problems with recognition and accuracy (which led to "friendly fire" losses), as well as the limited time aircraft could stay in the air, aircraft, tanks, artillery, and infantry were combined by the British and French to provide mobile firepower. German aircraft destroyed moving French tanks in Champagne, while the British used air strikes in their advances on the Western Front and in Palestine and Macedonia. However, the casualty rate among aircrew was high, not least due to the deployment of more fighters, and, moreover, in larger groupings.

Numerical superiority was a key element in Allied success. By the end of the war, Germany had a frontline strength of 2,500, but France had 3,700 and Britain 2,600. Moreover, the combined Franco-American-British force of 1,481 aircraft employed to support the American attack on the St. Mihiel salient on September 12 was not only the largest deployment so far but also gained air control, which was not usually possible during the war. The French had done so with six hundred aircraft, the "Division Aérienne," in support of a counteroffensive launched south of Montdidier on June 11. The French bombers participated in the ground battle, attacking German artillery positions and lines of communication and helping to stop the German forces. Prefiguring the situation in the Second World War for all powers, there was a major problem with providing French fighters with a range able to escort the bombers, including the Italian-built Caproni used by the French to raid German targets including Friedrichshafen. This was not settled until the Caudron R-XI entered service and was integrated with the bomber units. The French had played a major role in providing the US Army Air Service with aircraft and training. Massed offensive tactics were employed by the Americans under Colonel Billy Mitchell in support of the Meuse-Argonne offensive at the end of September. This was an instance of the so-called American Way of War, namely the use of massed force at the decisive point for victory. In 1918, these tactics were also employed by the French and the British.

The big dogfight philosophy gave fighters an apparently enhanced role comparable to that of bombing to victory. This role was detached from the need to protect bombers and from the realities of the difficulties of managing large-scale clashes. Nevertheless, scale on a level inconceivable before the war was now on offer. On October 7, Haig recorded being impressed by the promise from the RAF that it could provide three hundred aircraft practically at once to attack the Germans if their position collapsed around Busigny. He had good relations with Trenchard.

The aircraft and techniques used by the British on the Western Front were also employed successfully in Palestine. There, the British defeated their German and Turkish opponents in the air and then used this advantage to great effect in the Battle of Megiddo that September. Australian and British aircraft inflicted great damage by strafing on retreating Turkish forces, notably at Wadi el Fara, and made it difficult for them to rally.

The British established the Royal Air Force (RAF) as a separate force on April 1, 1918. This independence from the army, which anticipated service rivalries and tensions in other states, was not only a testimony to the argument that such an organization would make it easier to pursue control of the air, both for offense and defense, but also a reaction to the demand for retribution for the German raids on Britain. Envisaging a strategic potential and outcome, air power was designed to surmount the deadlock of the trenches by permitting the destruction of the enemy where vulnerable.[16] The German cities of Cologne, Frankfurt, and Mannheim were all attacked in 1918, but the purpose of degrading industrial and logistical capability proved difficult in practice. Moreover, there were civilian casualties, which underlined popular bitterness. At any rate, in a pattern later familiar with the RAF and other air forces, notably the American, the British exaggerated what their bombers had achieved. This greatly affected interwar (1919–38) discussion of strategic bombing, leading to a misrepresentation of its potential.[17]

The Italians launched a bomber offensive against Austria, which included dropping leaflets on Vienna on August 8, 1918, just as Britain directed one against Germany. Austrian aircraft had bombed Italian targets including Venice. The French preferred to focus on ground attack, not on distant bombing, but they produced nine hundred Voisin Renault Type X, capable of dropping 660 pounds (300 kg) of bombs, and had 245 of them in service in August: they specialized in night attacks.

Although they had already used with success the Handley-Page 0/100 and 0/400, the war ended before the British could use the large Handley-Page V/1500 bombers they had built to bomb Berlin, but, had the war continued, bombing would have become more important. These aircraft could carry 7,500 pounds of bombs and fly for over twelve hours, but large bombers faced many problems in performance and handling, not least unreliable engines. Moreover, the Germans had deployed fighters, including the Fokker D8, a high-wing parasol monoplane with excellent visibility and a tubular-steel fuselage structure, that could have posed a major problem for any bomber offensive.

The Italians had an effective bomber in the shape of the Caproni biplane and then, in 1918, triplane, which was also used by the British, French, Italians, and Americans. The first Caproni was ready in 1914, the second improved version following in 1916. Its maximum speed was eighty-five miles per hour (137 kmh), its range 372 miles (599 kilometers), and its service ceiling 15,892 feet (4,844 meters); it had two machine guns and carried 1,764 pounds (800 kg) of bombs. The triplane, the Ca4, could carry 3,200 pounds (1,450 kg) of bombs.

At the same time, antiaircraft capability increased considerably. It was particularly dangerous for low-flying ground-attack aircraft. In 1918, the antiaircraft guns of the German air service shot down 748 Allied aircraft. Aside from such guns, which had to be rapid firing and able to elevate to a high angle, there were specialized spotting and communication troops, as well as relevant training, manuals, and firing tables. In September 1918, Arthur Child-Villiers, a British officer on the Western Front, noted greater success "in bringing down the night-flying [German] aeroplanes."[18]

CONCLUSION

The extension of air power to the sea made scant impact on the course of the war, while on land many of the hopes of air power were based on a misleading sense of operational and technological possibilities. In practice, the prime value of air power remained aerial reconnaissance throughout the war. This was not the lesson taken by those in command. Indeed, leading air-power advocates of the interwar years took command positions in the war. These included Giulio Douhet, author of *Il Dominio dell'Aria* (*The Command of the Air*, 1921), who, despite insubordination, had been appointed head of the Italian Central Aeronautical Bureau in 1917; Billy Mitchell, the senior American air commander in the war; and Hugh Trenchard, who commanded the British Royal Flying Corps in France during the war and was the first chief of the Air Staff in 1918 and from 1919 to 1929. Hermann Göring, Hitler's head of the Luftwaffe, served in the German air force throughout the First World War, eventually as a squadron leader. Ernst Udet, who served under Göring in the war, was put in charge of the Luftwaffe's technical office in 1936.

Artisanal methods in aircraft production had been swept aside by mass production so that France was able to manufacture over fifty-two thousand aircraft during the war, Germany forty-eight thousand, and Britain forty-three thousand. This mass production was a response to the high rate at which aircraft (as well as pilots) were lost, as well as to the need to invest in new generations of aircraft. Wear and tear was also a major problem, and the life expectancy of aircraft remained below a year in 1925.

Air power also exemplified the growing role of scientific research in military capability: wind tunnels were constructed for the purpose of research. Strutless wings and aircraft made entirely from metal were developed. Huge improvements in design, construction, engines, and armaments, as well as effective systems of procurement,[19] had turned the unsophisticated machine of 1914, such as the German Taube and the French Blériot 9, into a more potent weapon. There was a marked specialization in aircraft type, with bombers very different from reconnaissance aircraft and fighters, and separate units for the particular functions. Parachutists on operational missions were first used in 1918 by the Italians. The war also saw the development of aeronautical medicine, a branch established to study people's suitability as pilots and to assess pilots' fitness.

However, as yet, air superiority did not have the same effect that was to be seen in the Second World War and certainly did not lead to air supremacy in the sense of an ability to command the air. For example, on November 8 and 9, 1918, on the Western Front, Alan Thomson benefited from information from an aircraft about the situation ahead, and, on November 9, he watched British aircraft dropping ration boxes by parachute as the cratered roads had made it impossible to bring up supplies. Yet he was bombed that night and, on the last night of the war, a German aircraft flew over.[20] Moreover, the tactical and operational effectiveness of air power remained heavily dependent on the weather. There were also serious technological issues, notably with engine development.

The limitations of air power did not prevent a marked spread in familiarity with it, not least because of the articulation of powers into alliance systems. For example, in 1917, Portuguese pilots acquired combat experience in France, while the Portuguese navy established its Aviation Service and School. In the Portuguese colony of Mozambique in 1917–18, there were Portuguese air operations against German forces invading from neighboring German East Africa (now Tanzania).

The extension of the use of air power in Africa had particularly unpleasant aspects, notably in September 1916, when, in reprisal for Senussi tribal attacks on a French border position in southern Tunisia, the French on one occasion bombed the Libyan town of Nalut with gas bombs.[21] The more general French use of air power in North Africa from 1916, notably in southern Tunisia, southern Algeria, and Morocco, in part prefigured the policy of "Air Control" that was to be associated with the RAF. The British used aircraft in Egypt in 1916 against Senussi tribesmen raiding from Libya; the tribesmen were encouraged by the Turks.

It was the potential for the future that was most striking, not the amount of damage air attack had already inflicted, nor its integration with war on land or at sea, nor the range and scale of operations. Instead, the image of a different world was chilling. Blackouts to make targeting by bombers harder demonstrated both the consequences of the war for civilian life and the range of government. In July 1916, John Monash wrote from London to his wife in Australia, "You can hardly imagine what the place is like. The zeppelin scare is just like as if the whole place was in imminent fear of an earthquake. At night, the whole of London is in *absolute darkness*."[22]

A year later, the fear reached Australia. There were claims that a seaplane from a German merchant raider had flown over Sydney harbor. In 1918, Australians began to see mystery aircraft everywhere. The navy and the army fruitlessly searched for hidden German bases or raiders from where these aircraft could be flying. This was an impetus for the creation of the Royal Australian Air Force (RAAF). There was a similar scare in New Zealand at the same time.[23]

In a reaction to the misery in the trenches, the image of the war in the air that was widely propagated was that of individual heroism personified by fighter aces, such as Manfred von Richthofen (German), Charles Guynemer (French), René Fonck (French), and Eddie Rickenbacker (American), and their duels with each other. This image, which reflected the novelty of aerial combat and served as a contrast to the intractable nature of land warfare, did not, however, capture the reality of this warfare. Instead, this reality was of aircraft that could be difficult to fly, exposure to the elements, deadly combat, very high casualties, and extraordinary mental strain.[24] The latter two elements were captured in *Winged Victory* (1934), a semiautobiographical novel by Victor Maslin Yeates. Joining the Royal Flying Corps in 1917, he crashed four times and was shot down twice during his 248 hours of combat flying. In the novel, the pilots loathe war, seeing it as boredom interspersed with horror, they drink heavily, and all the pilot friends of the protagonist die, while he is left a broken man. This was a reality of air warfare, as was the plight of bombed civilians.

Part II

The Interwar Years

Chapter Five

The Interwar Years, Land Warfare

The interwar period is generally presented in terms of digesting the lessons of the First World War and preparing for the Second. This, traditionally, is a tale of tanks, aircraft, and new military doctrine, with this doctrine being tested out, notably by the Germans in the Spanish Civil War (1936–39). The assessment of this period was conventionally presented in terms of the varied degree to which militaries responded to the possibilities of the new, notably mechanization and, in particular, the development of doctrine, operations, and tactics, such that tanks were used *en masse* and for bold attacking maneuvers, rather than being split up among the infantry and employed as a form of mobile artillery.[1]

Mobility was also a theme for the infantry. In 1920, in a memorandum titled "Explanations of the Theory of the Application of the Essential Principles of Strategy to Infantry Tactics," Basil Liddell Hart, a British army officer turned commentator, sought to turn his perspectives into rules given credence by recent history:

> The improvements in weapons and the wide extensions enforced by them have created new conditions in the infantry fight. It has developed into what may be termed group combats; the defenders realising that a self-contained group based on a tactical point is more effective than a trench line, the breaking of which results in the whole line falling back; the attackers countering this method of defence by endeavouring to penetrate between the centres of resistance and turn their flanks.[2]

It is understandable that, if a period is delimited in terms of the end of one world war and the start of another, and is defined as an interwar period, there is a tendency to look for the consequences of the former war and the anticipation of the latter one. These indeed are part of the story, and, in the public eye, there was a focus on the Western Front and thus on the possibility of another such war. However, land warfare in these years also included much else. Moreover, the combination of the two provided an opportunity not only for different narratives at the time (and subsequently), but also for some major powers to decide how best to prioritize between clashing commitments and the differing requirements they posed.

The immediacy of the conflicts that occurred after the First World War will take precedence here, to be followed by the working through of the supposed lessons of the war. This distinction can be complicated by pointing out that one lesson was that war could cause the total overthrow of a political system, as happened with the Russian, Austro-Hungarian, German, and Turkish Empires. Moreover, the significance of conflict within China and Mexico in the 1910s provides a way to assess similar patterns of civil warfare in the 1920s and 1930s. The range of wars after the First World War in part arose from its consequences, both in terms of the Russian Revolution of 1917 and with regard to the peace settlement, which is generally referred to as the Peace of Versailles. Each was disputed, and some of the conflicts were large scale, notably the Russian Civil War, the Russian invasion of Poland,[3] and the Greco-Turkish War. Fourteen foreign powers sent troops to help the anticommunist side in Russia, but only limited resources were committed, not least thanks to the general unpopularity at home of intervention.

A separate but related series of conflicts, stretching from Morocco to Afghanistan, reflected the unease across the Islamic world at the extension of Western power that in part arose from the peace settlement, but which also had separate, specific causes, as in both resistance to the extension of Spanish control in northern Morocco and the Third Anglo-Afghan War.

As also with conflict in both Mexico and China in the late 1910s and 1920s, war should be seen not as the breakdown of systems of peace and practices of deterrence, but rather as a product of the willingness, indeed eagerness, to fight, together with the additional encouragements offered by the large numbers of men habituated to fighting by the recent war and the plentiful supplies of armaments. Ideology was very much to the fore in the conflicts focused on communism, which included the Romanian overthrow of a communist regime in Hungary in 1919, as well as those relating to the Islamic rejection of Western control, as in Iraq in 1919 and Syria in 1925–26. Ideology was far less present in the struggles between Chinese generals (and their Mexican counterparts) over who would dominate government. Indeed, those struggles, which in the case of China were civil wars in the 1920s on a major scale, were a form of politics in the absence of the legitimation provided by governmental systems that had been overthrown in the early 1910s.

The explicitly anti-Christian nature of Russian communism pushed religion to the fore in the reaction to it, as in Poland. Indeed, it would not be fanciful to see a new period of religious warfare as breaking out in the late

1910s. The key characteristic of ideological conflict that was readily apparent was that of the interrelationship of international and domestic warfare. This was very much the communist thesis and rested on a concept of continuous class conflict directed by a higher power (the Politburo) seeking to implement an all-encompassing plan. In that approach, the "system" came first, a system of never-ending conflict. This was the "Cold War," which, in its opening stages, was far from limited or "cold."

The focus on preparing for great-power war, however, led, and leads, as with the Cold War, to an underrating of other political and military tasks, particularly the defense of imperial possessions, authority, and claims from insurrections and disturbances, as against British rule in Egypt, Iraq, and India; French rule in Morocco and Syria; and Spanish rule in Spanish Morocco. In particular, the overthrow of the Ottoman Empire (Turkey) in 1918 had resulted in an unprecedented advance of the Western empires into the Islamic world, but this, alongside the new volatility in the Middle East, led to a number of conflicts that tested new imperial pretensions and patterns of control. In response, the imperial powers, as well as regional states struggling to enforce their rule, notably Persia (Iran) and Saudi Arabia, used established means of operations, especially rapidly advancing columns of infantry and also cavalry, as well as new means, notably aircraft and lorries mounting machine guns. By the end of the 1930s, a series of revolts had been suppressed in Persia (Iran), Iraq, Saudi Arabia, and Turkey.

The biggest wars of the period 1919–36 were the civil wars in Russia and then China. As with the struggles over imperial control, these brought together traditional and new elements, and did so in states made volatile by the end of monarchical rule and by the related introduction of new governmental systems and ideologies. Control over troops played a major role, as they also did in Mexico, which was convulsed by revolution. However, whereas in China and Mexico the resulting dominance of generals or warlords remained significant in the governmental structures that were established, in Russia, the Soviet Union after the First World War, the warlord generals, who were indeed fundamental to the counterrevolutionary "White" side, were rapidly defeated. Thus, they were unable to ground themselves in regional power bases and, crucially, were not brought over to the new ruling system.

In turn, the Soviet army abandoned and avoided many of the regime's initial revolutionary ideas about military organization, but it was under civilian control. This control was brutally demonstrated in the purges carried out by the order of Josef Stalin, dictator from 1924 to 1953, who suspected a military-Fascist plot. Begun in 1937, these purges led to the slaughter of most of the leadership, notably Marshal Tukhachevsky, and part of the officer corps.[4] That resulted in a loss of experience, cohesion, and operational skill and encouraged a marked degree of caution on the part of most of the survivors. This led to an avoidance of risk and an obedience to orders that helped result in devastating losses at German hands in 1941, although overly rapid expansion and a crucial weakness in junior officers and noncommissioned officers (NCOs) may well have been more significant.[5]

DIFFERING GOALS AND MEANS

The interactions of politics, ideology, and warfare frequently encouraged antisocietal practices, notably the determination to isolate and destroy what were presented as internal enemies. This was very much seen in the warfare in Europe that followed the First World War, and notably so in the Russian Civil War. In part, this situation can be treated as a simple product of civil wars and also of the projection into Europe of the small-wars techniques hitherto employed as an aspect of imperial conquest. However, there was an added element of political terror directed against those presented as social enemies. This was not new and had been clearly seen with wars of religion in the past, but it certainly contrasted with the situation during the First World War. In Europe, there was relatively little deliberate slaughter of civilians by armies during that conflict, and certainly not as compared with German military conduct on the Eastern Front during the Second World War.

After the First World War, however, military necessity contributed to the internal violence because the mobilization of society had to operate in an inchoate political context. Tensions were not only ethnic-nationalist, but also ideological, with the Bolsheviks (a communist faction) seeking to use class identity to bridge ethnic divides and, instead, in a warfare they actively wanted,[6] to isolate and destroy what were seen, and presented, as internal enemies. The consequences were brutal, with the mass killing of those regarded as social enemies and, therefore, political traitors. Soviet attempts to build support ultimately relied on violence, and this violence was social warfare. This violence and warfare were on a massive scale, for example the killing of up to one hundred thousand in Crimea in 1920–21 after the fighting had ended, with over twenty thousand executed in the city of Simferopol alone.

Moreover, the conflict continued. Although the Russian Civil War is conventionally dated 1918–21, it can be extended to 1926, when the Red Army finally suppressed active resistance on the Turkestan front in Central Asia.[7] In addition, opposition then, and later, to the Soviet regime, and to its brutal and uncompromising policy of farm collectivization, can be regarded as part of the continuance, or at least aftermath, of the extremely violent civil wars and of the inability of the Bolsheviks to treat opposition as anything less than a foe.[8]

The fighting, both in the Russian Civil War and in other conflicts of the period, was far more confused than that during the First World War. In place of clear-cut adversaries came shifting alignments and uncertain interventions, both international and domestic. The coalitions that had waged the First World War were more coherent.

Also, instead of regular forces, readily apparent command structures, and clearly demarcated front lines, there were irregulars, complex relations between civil and military agencies and goals, and fluid spheres of operations. Guerrilla groups played a significant role.[9] The emphasis was on activity (albeit small scale compared with the world war), on raids, and on the seizure of key political centers, rather than on sieges or on staging battles from prepared positions, as in 1918, when the newly established communist government in Tashkent sent a small force that rapidly seized Kokand, overthrowing the Muslim government that had been established there. The difficulty of sustaining operations, a difficulty that stemmed from the lack of an organized logistical support system, encouraged this emphasis. As a result, the focus was very much on the offensive, not least in order to seize resources.

The wars of the period indicated the difficulties both of sustaining a revolutionary struggle and, conversely, of mounting effective counterinsurgency action. The force-space ratios of conflict in Eastern Europe were different from those in Western Europe during the recent world war; but, far more, the problems of political and, to a lesser degree, military control were greater. The need that both revolutionaries and their opponents faced to create new armies put a premium on overcoming problems in recruitment and in resisting desertion. The creation and implementation of government structures were important in providing the context for harnessing resources.

Remedies were often brutal, notably in Russia. Recruitment was enforced with violence and the threat of violence, and desertion, a major problem in some armies, was punished savagely, often with executions. Faced with major logistical problems, armies raised supplies through force. There was much destruction, both in order to deny resources to opponents and to punish those judged disloyal.

The defensive remained important at the tactical level, in some respects more so than in the First World War, in part because the artillery necessary to suppress fire was in limited supply and not really useful for fast-moving operations over large areas. At the same time, defensive positions could be stormed, while the absence of continuous fronts made it easier to outflank such positions. This encouraged the stress on maneuver, one very much seen in the Russian Civil War, in which large-scale battles were few, as opposed to small-scale clashes.

The stress on maneuver was also encouraged by the need to establish control rapidly in contested areas in order to present peacemakers and other powers with faits accomplis. This was a response to such action by others, and also to the international context. The latter included both the failure of peacemakers to accept the complexity of situations on the ground and a rejection, in the latter, of the attempt by outside bodies to dictate developments. Moreover, the presence of German forces in the western parts of the former Russian Empire, and their active role in political struggles, notably in Latvia, ensured that there was no clear divide between the First World War and postwar struggles.

"Institutions will curl up like burnt paper" was the closing phrase in the poem "Escape" (1929) by the innovative British writer D. H. Lawrence (1885–1930). The early decades of the twentieth century were important not simply for the insurrections that occurred, but also for the development of an ideology of insurrectionary warfare, one very much linked to the political Left, and for a sense that there would be a more general dissolution of authority. Although seizures of power were also mounted from the Right, there was not generally in their presentation a comparable theme of social transformation, although, in practice, such a transformation was indeed sometimes intended. In terms of change, nationalism, on the Left, was given a particular direction toward peoples' wars or, at least, what could be presented as such. Moreover, as with the French Revolution, this led, at least for a while, to an accompanying rejection of conventional military structures and doctrine, first with the Russian Revolution of 1917 and then with Maoist thought and practice in the 1930s and again in the 1960s.

The emphasis on peoples' wars cut across the attempt in the years prior to the First World War, which began in 1914, to develop legal restrictions on warfare by defining, and thus separating, combatants and noncombatants. This was a process that directly related to the alleged legality of irregular warfare.[10] So also with the clash between peoples' wars and subsequent discussion of such legal regulation and restrictions. Regulatory attempts were treated by critics as a bourgeois affectation. Instead, there was a call and pressure by radicals for a total social mobilization for war that was, theoretically, different in kind from "the bosses' wars" of industrial society. More generally, by opting out of "traditional" combat, most likely because of clear disadvantages, insurgents flew in the face of attempts to regulate war and make it more humane.

Aside from the theoretical development of the idea of peoples' war, the pattern of insurgencies was also different because of the pronounced ideological division involved in many insurgencies, certainly as compared to the late nineteenth century. As a result, the insurgency that attracted, and still attracts, greatest attention is the Russian Revolution of 1917. Internal conflict began in Europe, with the Bolsheviks successfully imposing their order, but spread as the Austro-Hungarian Empire collapsed in 1918, leading to struggles over the existence, boundaries, and government of states. By the end of the year, Germans and Czechs were clashing in the Sudetenland, as were Carinthians and Slovenes in what became the Austrian-Yugoslav border area. Prewar disputes became postwar clashes. The Czechs fought with the Hungarians to get Slovakia and against the Poles to get Upper Silesia.

Civil war ensured that the number of sides and participants in conflict rose, and, with this, notions of a clear-cut definition of military forces, and of war as the prerogative of the state, were both put under severe strain. As a result, regular armies, some newly formed as states were created, were obliged to confront situations in which goals and opponents were far from clear, and atrocities, terrorism, and terror became more than the small change of war. Paramilitary forces took a significant part.[11] In November 1918, Foch only permitted the Germans one modification to the armistice terms: they were allowed to keep some of their machine guns in order to help against a Bolshevik rising.[12]

Ideology and nationalism both played a role. In the former case, Romanians and Czechs suppressed a communist regime in Hungary in 1919, a conflict that involved relatively large forces. Nationalism was to the fore in the occupation of the town of Fiume by an Italian volunteer force in 1919, the Polish seizure of Vilnius from Lithuania in 1920, and the Lithuanian seizure of Memel (Klaipeda) in 1923. There was also considerable overlap between ideology and nationalism. While this wave of conflict was largely over by 1923,[13] there was no guarantee that it would not revive. Territorial claims, for example by Hungary on Romanian-held Transylvania, remained an issue.

The shadow of the First World War, although powerful at the political level, was less pronounced in terms of military lessons than is generally believed, and certainly if the focus for the latter is on a small number of commentators. In part, this was because the postwar concerns for most states were not those of large-scale conflict. Moreover, the First World War, although different in scale from what had gone before, was part of a sequence of conflicts for many states and areas. It was less novel, for example, for Bulgaria, Romania, and Greece than it was for Britain.

Similarly, in Latin America, the years after the First World War saw a continuation of earlier patterns of conflict, as in Mexico where Venustiano Carranza, who had a base as governor of Coahuila and who was the *primer jefe* (first chief) of the Constitutional Army, seized power in 1915 until 1920. As in China, the provinces splintered under the control of various generals in 1914, but Carranza benefited from control over the major ports and oil production and enjoyed more revenue. In 1920, General Álvaro Obregón and allied generals turned against Carranza, driving him from Mexico City, and the former president was killed soon after. Obregón was president until 1924, overcoming a rebellion in 1923–24 by Adolfo de la Huerta, a former supporter. Obregón won the 1928 election but was assassinated soon after by a Catholic radical.

Much of the warfare in Latin America was insurrectionary in character—for example, the failed invasion of Costa Rica in 1919 by exiles based in

Nicaragua, the Liberal revolt in Nicaragua in 1925, and the Cristero rebellion in central-western Mexico in 1926–29, a Catholic rising against the secularizing policies of the government. Estimates of the dead in the last focused on the figure of ninety thousand. The rebels were effective against the local militia but found the well-armed federal forces more difficult. A conciliatory governmental approach led to a settlement in 1929.[14]

Another element of continuity was provided by the struggle against banditry. By 1931, most of Corsica was under the effective control of bandits who charged for transit through their zones of control. In 1931, France deployed troops, armored cars, and aircraft from the French mainland under General Fournier, the commander in chief in Corsica, in order to provide mobile columns to advance into the mountains and seize bandit leaders. Benito Mussolini, the Fascist dictator of Italy, used force to try to suppress the Mafia in Sicily and also against banditry in Sardinia.

In the Western colonial empires, policies designed to ensure control did not change in the 1920s, with the major exception of the addition of air power.[15] Japan (in China) and the United States (in the Caribbean and Central America[16]) continued their power projection in what they sought to define as their areas of control. These elements of continuity provide an important aspect of the military history of these years, and one that should not be treated as eccentric to the legacy of the First World War.

The complex interrelationships of ethnic and religious rivalries, and the interaction of ideologies, were such that it could be very difficult for outsiders to understand the dynamics of any situation. Force proved one way to seek to contain and control the situation, but force was generally only a panacea. Indeed, the most successful policy, one that overlapped with force, was the alliance with local groups. This was a process facilitated by the extent to which the military strength of Western empires relied on local forces, as with the French in Lebanon, and notably so if policing was concerned. The British sought to lessen this issue by using Indian units in the Middle East, as in Iraq in 1919, but it was still a factor of consequence, especially as policing was essentially paramilitary.[17]

In the case of the conflict between Greece and Turkey from 1919 to 1922, the war was a struggle between two independent states. Although not on the scale of the Russian Civil War, this was a major conflict, and one that in 1921, when the Greeks were checked at the Battle of Sakarya, and, far more, 1922, delivered a clear verdict, that of total Greek defeat. The fighting had elements of the First World War, with commanders and troops experienced from that conflict and using similar weaponry and tactics. The contrast with the Western Front was apparent in the maneuverability shown by the forces and in the search for open flanks and encirclement. This entailed considerable overlap with the campaigning in Eastern Europe and, more particularly, the Balkans during the First World War.

The Greek-Turkish War was also significant for the antisocietal elements of ethnic brutalization seen with the Turkish treatment of those of Greek origin living in Turkey, notably at Smyrna/Izmir when it was captured in 1922. This was a long-standing and large group, but it was treated as unacceptable by the Turks, who sought a monoglot definition of nationalism, one that took forward pre–First World War ethnic violence and the mass murder of Armenians during that conflict. This violence looked toward German and Japanese policy during the Second World War.

Secondly, the Greek-Turkish War very much involved international tensions. It was the key element of the Turkish attempt to reverse the treaty settlement that had followed the First World War, notably the establishment of British, French, Greek, and Italian spheres of influence. This came to be intertwined with the Cold War between the Soviet Union and its opponents. The Soviets backed the Turks as part of a more general and successful process of encouraging anti-Western nationalism, one also seen in China, Persia (Iran), and Afghanistan. At the same time, the alliance against the Turks disintegrated, with the Italians backing the Turks against the French, and the Greeks, who followed their own course, making themselves the focus of Turkish attack.

The war in Turkey, like the Russian Civil War, showed the difficulty of ensuring international cooperation against a determined adversary. In each case, the international coalition suffered from a lack of strong support within the country in which it was intervening. This was far more the case in Turkey, where nationalism was a greater factor than in Russia. Kemal Atatürk, in practice, overthrew local opponents, notably those who had agreed to accept the Allied terms, but this element was not one that the Allies could turn to their advantage.

The Russian Civil War also entailed efforts by the Bolshevik government, thwarted in its hopes of world revolution, to regain control by force of regions where non-Russian ethnic groups had sought to win independence. Russian control was reimposed in the Caucasus, Central Asia, and Ukraine, but not in the Baltic states (Estonia, Latvia, and Lithuania), Finland, or Poland. The Russo-Polish War in 1920 demonstrated the characteristics of the warfare of the period. It was very mobile, both militarily and politically. This type of warfare, which was typical of many of the conflicts after 1945, was also important earlier. Attacking in April–May 1920, the Poles overran western Ukraine, capturing Kiev. In turn, a Soviet counterattack in late May led to an advance to close to Warsaw, only for a well-executed Polish counterattack to drive the Soviets back in August. The advancing Soviet forces were poorly coordinated, overextended, and failed to understand Polish intentions. The Red Army lost about 150,000 troops. The campaigning in this region in the Second World War was not so rapid but could also be swift.

Lenin had had a clear strategy, one in which military operations sat within a political prospectus. He hoped that the Polish working class would support the cause of the working class in the shape of the Red Army and lead to an advance of the latter that would secure revolution in Germany. However, this proved wishful thinking.[18] Stalin did not pursue this illusion during the Second World War.

Nationalism as an opponent of Western control was seen not only in Turkey but also in Persia (Iran), China, Iraq, and Arabia and, less successfully, in Afghanistan. In Turkey, Persia, China, and Iraq, the nationalist movement, having overthrown local rivals, established a militarized regime, for example, the Jiang Jieshi government in China. The conflicts that led to these outcomes, and that stemmed from them, were an important part of the military history of the 1920s and, to a degree, 1930s. Moreover, much of this warfare was sustained because the sole means of registering opposition and securing control was through violence or through a politics of patronage that was negotiated by means of violence.

Again, when space is at a premium, such conflicts tend to be downplayed or ignored in the rush to get from one world war to another. This is mistaken, not least as the military verdicts of the period were often lasting, and more so than some of those of the world wars. Moreover, the experience of the period remained significant in the subsequent and current attitudes of governing groups, notably with the ruling house of Saud in Arabia. These conflicts are again resonant of those at present, in that nationalism was frequently imposed with brutal force at the expense of ethnic and religious groups, whose difference and autonomy appeared unwelcome, as with Assyrian Christians in Iraq and Arabs in southwest Persia.[19] These issues provided a continuity that has lasted to the present. In the fighting, battle was less significant than the "small war" methods of smaller-scale clashes and raids. This was a warfare of rapid advances, not of front lines, and the tactics used in fighting accorded with this dynamic. The nearest equivalent in the Second World War was the conflict between German occupiers and Yugoslav partisans.

IRELAND

In contrast to the determination shown in Iraq (although not in Iran, Afghanistan, or Russia), the British made only a modest effort to maintain control in Ireland. This provided an instructive instance of the difficulties of suppressing an insurrection, and in the part of the empire longest under British control, the sole part, moreover, that was represented in the London Parliament. The Irish Republican Army (IRA), a violent nationalist force, drawing its support from much (but by no means all) of the Catholic majority, organized its active service units into flying columns that staged raids and ambushes in order to undermine the stability of the British government. Assassinations and sabotage were also employed. The IRA was short of arms and gained many by raids on the British. The Thompson submachine gun came from the United States. The IRA was outnumbered by the army and the police but was able to take the initiative, to profit from its willingness to use murder and intimidation, and to benefit from the limited options available to those trying to restore control. The murder of about one hundred Protestants in the south helped terrorize the bulk of the Protestant community, many of whom fled.[20] British reprisals against Catholic civilians, though limited, sapped support for British rule within Ireland among the Catholic majority.

Nevertheless, the British were not clearly failing, and it is worth noting that earlier Irish rebellions, from the sixteenth century to 1916, had failed, as did later IRA campaigns, including in 1939, 1956–62, and 1969–97. Indeed, the IRA, in the summer of 1921, was under severe pressure from the British army. Over the previous two years, the government and army had developed a series of responses, including internment (detention without trials), the employment of active-service platoons, wireless telegraphy, and air power. The introduction of these measures meant that the IRA had ceased to provide a significant military threat, and, by 1921, as in 1971 in Northern Ireland, their operations had been reduced to a terrorist rather than military threat. The ability of the British army to respond flexibly is clear.[21]

Crucially, however, the British government, in part because of the range of its international commitments, was unwilling to take the firm steps advised by military leaders and instead favored negotiation. Most of the island was then granted independence in the Anglo-Irish Treaty of December 1921, although the Protestant-dominated region in the north, most of the historic province of Ulster, remained with Britain.

Ironically, the IRA then divided, leading to a civil war in the new Irish Free State. This was won by the pro-treaty forces, in part because the government was willing to take a firmer line than the British had done, not least with the trial and execution of prisoners. To critics, British influence in the new state was being maintained by the forces of local allies. A key contrast was provided between the new National Army, which had an effective logistical system, with all the subsequent advantages for morale and capability, and the anti-treaty IRA. The latter could not provide the supplies to support a large force in the field or to resupply smaller groups. These groups turned to guerrilla warfare but also commandeered supplies, which hit their local backing.[22]

Chapter 5
CHINA

In China, the major form of conflict in the early 1920s was that between warlords, but, from the mid-1920s, that between the Guomindang (Nationalists) and the warlords became more important, while a rift developed between the communists and the Guomindang, leading to significant conflict. There were elements similar to the Russian Civil War in terms of a conflict of maneuver and presence, rather than necessarily of battle or siege.

The warlords who ruled much of China were aligned by means of leagues. This was scarcely a stable system, as there were serious personal rivalries, no experience of making the new system work, and no institutional context to provide cohesion. The similar difficulties of getting the "White" generals in Russia to cooperate was also notable, as was the situation in Mexico. The 1920s in China are characterized as the warlord era. However, this was a judgmental, indeed polemical, term, one introduced from the Japanese *gunbatsu*, meaning the militarist interest. Those referred to were generals, mostly members of a fissiparous, but internationally recognized, government in Beijing. As an instructive instance of a more general situation in military history—the vote for the winner—the warlords are treated as anachronistic and in a pejorative fashion. This is because they lost to the Guomindang, which, in practice, was an insurgent movement. In contrast, in the 1920s alone, as Kemal Atatürk showed in Turkey, Ibn Saud in Arabia, and Riza Khan in Persia, success can provide a very different gloss. There were warlord elements in the Japanese military in the 1930s and early 1940s. There is also the problem of semantics, as the term "warlord" wrongly suggests that warlord warfare was somehow qualitatively different from the other warfare waged before and after.[23]

In the case of China, long-standing regionalism, including strong historical tensions between north and south, as well as political and military developments prior to, during, and after the 1911 revolution, were all of significance. The collapse in 1916 of the presidency of Yuan Shikai, commander of the Beiyang army, helped discredit the central government based there. Subsequent rivalries among the now leaderless northern generals were a key element in the breakdown of order. Large-scale conflict began in 1920, with the overthrow of General Duan Qirui, the prime minister, by the forces of two leading generals, Wu Peifu and Zhang Zuolin. This step brought the power of the warlords to fruition.

The local commanders were essentially regional figures, but the leading generals used territorial bases to contend for power over all China. Zhang Zuolin, the Manchurian warlord from 1916 to 1928 and head of the Fengtian Clique, was the leading figure in northern China, and in 1928 he and his allies were able to deploy four hundred thousand troops. In Central China, the major figure, Wu Peifu, was head of the Zhili Clique. In 1922, in the First

Zhili-Fengtian War, Wu defeated Zhang in a struggle for control of Beijing, whereupon Zhang declared Manchurian autonomy. The pressure of conflict caused a military modernization in China that was fit-for-purpose as far as circumstances permitted, a situation seen more generally in the 1920s. In contrast, this process was less apparent in states that were not involved in large-scale conflict. Reorganizing and retraining his army, Zhang brought forward younger officers.[24] In the Second Zhili-Fengtian War, Zhang moved south, occupying Beijing in 1926–28.

Large infantry armies were the situation in China, with scant mechanization. The lack of significant mechanization was the norm across much of the world, although trucks in Arabia demonstrated the place for variety. The Guomindang under Jiang Jieshi came, in part, to operate as a military faction of its own, indeed as the faction that came, with the Northern Expedition of 1926–28, to dominate most of China, with the significant exception of Manchuria. Jiang succeeded by fighting his opponents sequentially,[25] and by an aggressive, attacking fighting style, notably using columns, as in the Battle of Longtan in 1927.

The result of this cohesion was to be challenged in the 1930s by Japanese expansion, and to be overthrown in 1946–49 by eventual communist success. On another timescale, however, this result was to be lasting, as it left China as a coherent state and not as, in effect, a series of states, which had been the pattern during periods of Chinese history, for example the eleventh and early twelfth centuries, with no reason to believe that it would not recur. The Turkish and Austro-Hungarian Empires had totally collapsed. That China did not is part of the military history of the period that does not attract attention because, however significant, Chinese military history tends to be underplayed in Western military history, and there is a lack of attention to what would have had important outcomes had it occurred, and notably so at the political level.

At the Gutian Conference in December 1929, the Chinese communists decided that the Red Army was both a "mass propaganda" organ as well as a fighting force, and under the total control of the Communist Party. In China, the nature of military struggle changed in the 1930s, first with the rise of large-scale hostilities between the Guomindang and the communists in the early 1930s, which led to the deployment of significant forces in search-and-destroy operations in marginal areas, and second, from 1937, with full-scale Japanese invasion.

Initially very successful with the capture of Beijing, Shanghai, and Nanjing in 1937, and of Guangzhou and Wuhan in 1938, the Japanese invasion of China did not bring Japan the victorious closure it had anticipated. The Japanese invasion at first saw Japanese forces attack Chinese regular units in the major settled areas of the country, notably in the difficult and lengthy battle for control of Shanghai in 1937. Although outnumbered, the Japanese had better air support and artillery, profited from amphibious capability, and faced poor command by Jiang Jieshi. The military methods the Guomindang had used so successfully in 1925–30 no longer proved appropriate. Thus, it suffered from continuity in what was a changing context.[26]

Despite, however, inflicting many casualties, including the destruction of the best-trained Chinese divisions,[27] as well as numerous civilian casualties, the Japanese could not drive the Chinese to surrender. This situation prefigured the German invasion of the Soviet Union in 1941. Instead, by late 1938, the Japanese found that much of their effort was tied up in a fruitless attempt to enforce control in occupied areas, while it proved impossible to maintain the dynamic of advance. The resulting sense of frustration affected Japan's response to the international situation in 1939–41, notably with the developing conviction that supply routes to China had to be cut, notably via Vietnam and Burma (Myanmar), respectively French and British colonies.[28]

Each type of military struggle indicates the range of land warfare in the period, but they also captured the dependence of this warfare on the ability to persuade defeated opponents that they had lost. Because this did not occur, the ability to win success in the field did not lead to an outcome. The British chiefs of staff noted in December 1939,

> Japanese authority in China is limited to certain main centers and to lines of communication, and Chinese guerrilla forces continue to take a considerable toll of Japanese garrison posts. . . . The Japanese army is heavily committed in China, where 30 out of a total of 48 divisions are engaged. . . . Little, if any, economic return is being obtained from the territories overrun. . . . Japan is living on her capital.[29]

THE PURPOSES OF FORCE

In the aftermath of the First World War, the so-called war to end all wars, the understanding of success varied greatly. One purpose of military capability was to create a deterrent that would ensure that no future wars were attempted. This was seen in particular with ideas of air warfare, the probable extreme destructiveness of which was regarded as a deterrent to future hostilities or as likely to cause a rapid outcome to any war.

International cooperation, even agreements, appeared as other means of deterrence. If the former had not led to success in overthrowing Russian communism, it had better fortune in blocking communist/Russian expansion in Hungary and Poland and in confining Russia. Indeed, in the 1920s, there were not, as there were to be from the late 1940s to the end of the 1980s, two competing alliance systems, with the military strength of both affecting the equations of deterrence.

This situation changed in the 1930s, helping to cause the outbreak of the Second World War in 1939. That shifting international context centered on the rise, expansionism, and aggressiveness of Germany under Adolf Hitler, its ruler from 1933, notably at the expense of Czechoslovakia in 1938 and Poland in 1939. This process became more important because of his ability to align with other powers, notably Italy, Japan, and, eventually, in 1939, the Soviet Union, and, more specifically, to prompt the backing of lesser states, such as Hungary, Bulgaria, Romania, and Finland.

THE MEANS OF WAGING WAR

Changes in the means of waging war were less significant than political developments. The period is generally seen in terms of the rise of mechanization, more specifically the development of armored warfare, and the bringing forward of ideas that were subsequently to be labeled (and simplified) as blitzkrieg (lightning war), the term that is applied to the methods employed in German offensives in 1939–41. In practice, that was not the obvious narrative in the 1920s and 1930s. Even if attention is restricted to Europe, the emphasis on infantry, artillery, and fortifications is readily apparent. This was the case with doctrine, force structure, procurement, training, and command patterns. Indeed, the "froth" created by some of the protagonists for armored warfare reflected their desire for attention in what they felt was a largely indifferent, even hostile, environment. More positively, there was an engagement with armor on the part of military leaderships, but as part of a process of devising a range of capabilities in response to a variety of commitments. For example, there was much investment in systems of fortifications, notably with the French Maginot Line, but also the Finnish Mannerheim Line, the Dutch Water Line, the German West Wall, the Italian Vallo Alpino, and the American fortifications to protect Manila Bay, particularly on the island of Corregidor, which was overoptimistically termed the "Gibraltar of the Pacific." The British fortified their new naval base at Singapore. Their record was mixed: none of the fortification systems mentioned above prevented failure during the Second World War, but that does not exhaust the subject.

The lack of an appropriate, or at least (and differently) successful, plan was seen with the French Maginot Line, named after André Maginot, the minister of defense from 1928 to 1930. Begun in 1930 to offset Germany's larger population, and therefore capacity for a larger army, this was an economy-of-force measure and a means to create jobs. The fortifications covered the Franco-German frontier from Switzerland to Luxemburg, although more densely in particular areas, and were regarded by the French as an aspect of a force structure that could support an offensive or a defensive strategy. The fortifications were intended to constrain the options of any attacker,[30] as they indeed did in 1940. In 1935, Sir Archibald Montgomery-Massingberd, the perceptive chief of the British Imperial General Staff from 1933, saw the Maginot Line as providing support for operational mobility, which is frequently an aspect of the strategic and operational value of fortifications. Referring back to the First World War, he wrote,

> My recollections of our attacks against strong lines during the war, even with masses of heavy guns and tanks, is that this frontier, in three or four years will be practically impregnable, always provided of course that the French keep up their present garrison and maintain everything at the standard they are doing at present. Here again the underlying idea of economy in men so as to set free as many troops as possible for the mobile army.

He also commented on the strength of the French fortifications facing Italy—"tunnelled as they are under 40 or 50 feet of rock, with embrasures for guns and machine guns covering every approach."[31] In turn, the Italians refurbished their Alpine fortresses, while the French developed their coastal defenses in Provence to provide protection against Italian attack, especially to protect the naval base of Toulon. Similarly, in southern Tunisia, the French built the Mareth Line against invasion from the neighboring Italian colony of Libya. There were also fortifications on Corsica against possible Italian invasion.

Opposing the Maginot Line, the Germans constructed the three-hundred-mile-long Western Wall in 1936–40, and mostly from 1938. This was not designed to be as strong as the Maginot Line but, instead, to delay attackers so that reserves could be moved up, a facet of defensive systems that can be too easy to overlook. The focus was on mutually supporting pillboxes and concrete antitank defenses. In addition, in what is now western Poland but was then eastern Germany, between the Rivers Oder and Warta, a fortified system, the Ostwall or Festungsfront im Oder-Warthe Bogen, was built between 1934 and 1944 to protect Germany's eastern border and thus also to create greater flexibility in the event of a German attack on Poland. The line in part relied on lakes as an integral part of the system. However, in January 1945, the fortifications were relatively easily captured by Soviet forces.

Other states also invested heavily in fortifications. The Finnish Mannerheim Line was constructed across the Karelian Isthmus, the most vulnerable point to Soviet attack. Forty miles long, it comprised fieldworks strengthened by forty-four concrete bunkers, and the main line was backed by two rear lines of fieldworks. Poland began to build fortifications in the early 1920s. The priority was to provide protection against the Soviet Union, which had invaded in 1920. This remained the priority, but fortifications against Germany were also built from 1934. Most started too late to provide protection when Poland was invaded by both Germany and the Soviet Union in 1939.

The lengthy nature of the Polish frontier created a major strategic problem, one that was accentuated when Germany took over Czechoslovakia in 1939. Similarly, in 1938, the viability of French-designed Czech defenses in the Sudetenland against German attack was in part compromised when, earlier in the year, the Germans took over Austria, making the Czechs vulnerable to invasion from the south.

Debates over capabilities and procurement were an aspect of the analysis of the First World War during the 1920s, and of the linkage of what became the 1930s' arms race to the distinctive strategic culture of particular states. This arms race was unprecedented, as it involved not only what had been conventional weaponry prior to the First World War but also a novel race in air power over both land and sea. The arms race was largely not a case of matching like for like, for much of it involved trying to develop particular capabilities or deploying antiweaponry to cope with such capabilities on the part of others. As a result, there were major contrasts between militaries. Equipment, however, was obtained from other states by means of purchase and gift, as with the important arms relationship between Germany and the Soviet Union, which helped each to rearm despite the treaty limitations on Germany.

At the same time, the large size of most militaries made the cost of improving them especially high. Indeed, the burden of sustaining forces that were so numerous, in particular, feeding, clothing, housing, and arming such numbers, was a serious problem. This problem accentuated the tendency to focus on key sectors, which in turn helped encourage debate about their identity. In contrast, the bulk of the military lacked comparable investment and improvement. This bulk provided the mass that appeared necessary to many, notably most army commanders. In 1936, Montgomery-Massingberd, a general, like many, from an artillery background, wrote at the end of his period in post,

> I feel that the biggest battle that I have had to fight in the last three years is against the idea that on account of the arrival of air forces as a new arm, the Low Countries are of little value to us and that, therefore, we need not maintain a military force to assist in holding them ... the elimination of any army commitment on the Continent sounds such a comfortable and cheap policy ... especially among the air mad.[32]

The emphasis by many on the leading sectors of mass militaries, including air power, was an attempt to reconcile the need for both quality and mass in modern warfare, and the apparent requirements of individual states in each case. This was seen in the French army, where the development of mechanized and motorized divisions was intended to provide a mobility capable of countering the German advance in Belgium as a prelude to an engagement by the mass army with its infantry and artillery.

The taskings related to strategy and the politics of prioritization had implications for industry capacity and policy, and for politics. Josef Stalin moved to support a major Soviet military buildup because of the emerging threat of war with Japan from 1931.[33] However, Tukhachevsky was a danger to Stalin because he had displayed an unhealthy habit of elevating military necessity to the point of demanding the subordination of the whole economy to the army. The Soviet Terror overlapped with, and was related to, the acceleration of the arms race.[34] Tukhachevsky was associated with an emphasis on armor designed to give force to doctrines of "deep battle" focused on taking and sustaining the offensive. The Soviet Union, which was investing heavily in equipment, had as many as seven thousand tanks in 1935, but the 1936 maneuvers revealed design flaws as well as serious tactical and operational problems in their use. Thus, even before the large-scale 1937–38 purges, there were major problems with the Soviet army. At the same time, Soviet successes against Japan in border conflict in 1938–39 led Japan to prefer peace with the Soviet Union.

CONCLUSION

In hindsight, as with the protagonists of aircraft carriers as opposed to battleships, the pattern of finding good and bad, progress and reactionary failure, in the discussion of force structure, doctrine, and procurement is seriously misguided, and anyway requires a measured assessment of conflict in the Second World War. Turning, instead, to the situation prior to the war, it is readily understandable that powers confronted with a range of commitments did not invest heavily in unproven technologies, such as large tank forces, that could not fulfill all their needs. This point helps to ensure that doctrinal arguments have to be put in the context of the greater urgencies of current concerns. At the same time, the reliance of rearmament on economic strength was readily understood. Yet, as a new world war neared, so preparations were both stepped up and focused. The lessons of the First World War were assessed in terms of new weapons systems and new doctrine.[35]

Chapter Six

The Interwar Years at Sea

In many senses, the naval situation in the 1920s was similar to that in the modern world. After a period (the First World War for then, the Cold War for now) that had defined naval superiority, there was no large-scale conflict to chart subsequent shifts in capability or the impact of technology. The First World War defined naval superiority in terms of Allied, especially British, predominance, with the Americans now taking a key role. However, the issue of submarine versus battleship was partly unresolved, while the role of naval air forces remained completely undefined. Heavily dependent on their navy, the British worked hard to learn all the lessons they could from the war.

In the interwar period (1919–38), shifts in capability and the impact of technology were both important, as was the key role of political concerns in shaping strategic tasking and plans. From the outset, the growth of Japanese naval power proved a threatening and unpredictable challenge for Britain and the United States, rather as that of China has been for the United States over the last decade, although China today lacks the aggressive military culture and potent naval commitment Japan had in the interwar years, or, rather, does not have it to the same extent. China is a continental power able to enter the maritime environment because it is currently not threatened on the landward frontier by Russia.

NAVAL LIMITATIONS

The war was followed by the removal of the naval strength of the defeated, by a degree of demobilization among the victors, and by an attempt to prevent any future naval races. There was to be no return to the situation in 1914, when Germany was the world's number-two naval power. The Germans scuttled their interned ships at Scapa Flow on June 21, 1919, which greatly increased the relative size of the Royal Navy. The Peace of Versailles of that year denied Germany permission to build a replacement fleet, limiting both the number and type of warships it might have. As German air forces were prohibited, there was no fleet air arm, and therefore no buildup of the relevant talent. Moreover, as part of the 1919 peace settlement, the merchant ships seized from Germany were allocated to the victors in proportion to their wartime maritime losses.

Austria had had the world's eighth-largest navy in 1914. This disappeared with the collapse of the Habsburg monarchy and the loss of an Adriatic coastline now divided between Italy and, to a larger degree, Yugoslavia.

Russia had a different fate as a result of the Bolshevik revolution in 1917, in which the sailors in the Baltic Fleet played a particularly revolutionary role,[1] and of the subsequent large-scale civil war and foreign intervention. Its navy and shipbuilding capacity were badly affected by both. The Bolsheviks also focused on the army. In 1926, the navy was reduced to a section of the army, and it did not regain an independent status until December 1937. Even then, there was no return to prewar Russian priorities. For example, no attempt was made to rebuild a Far East fleet. Instead, war plans with Japan were to center on long-range bombers and on the army.

Naval power politics were transformed after the First World War. The naval challenge to Britain now came from the increased naval power of two of her wartime allies: the United States and Japan. This competition was to be played out after the war in the diplomacy of naval limitation that, in accordance with the disarmament provisions of the Treaty of Versailles, led to the Washington Naval Conference of 1921–22, the Washington Naval Treaty of 1922, and the later London Conference of 1930. It is possible to emphasize suspicions and rivalries, and this is understandable in light of Japan's attack on the United States and Britain in 1941. However, in the 1920s, wartime alliance followed by these negotiations ensured that naval competition ceased to be the key theme that it had been prior to the outbreak of the First World War with the Anglo-German naval race.

In the Washington Naval Treaty, Britain accepted naval parity with the United States, voluntarily relinquishing its traditional superiority at sea while maintaining sufficient naval strength nonetheless to protect its vital interests.[2] This was a marked departure from the two-power naval standard, a navy equal in size to the next two naval powers—which, having been developed against France and Spain in the eighteenth century, had been pursued by Britain in the late nineteenth century—and the "one plus 60 percent" standard pursued before the First World War. This development, however, did not represent a straightforward case of decline. In each case, the British maintained a standard that best provided security against the potential threats it faced.

The world order, nevertheless, had changed. America was the leading industrial and financial power, while Britain was under pressure from economic problems, harsh fiscal circumstances, demands for social welfare, and extensive postwar military commitments, especially in India, Iraq, Ireland, and Russia. In addition, the British were in the shadow of the buildup of the American navy ordered in 1916, which, had it happened postwar, Britain could not have matched. In the event, despite continuing rivalry for primacy,[3] Congress did not vote the money for what was proclaimed as the "Navy Second to None" until 1940, when the situation was very different.

The Washington Naval Treaty fixed the ratios for the major naval powers, and did so with a focus on battleships, reflecting the lessons learned from the First World War about what was seen as the decisive arm. War-gaming at the American Naval War College in 1921 led to a measure of skepticism about the value of battleships, and there was interest in vulnerability to air attack. Nevertheless, the battleship remained key. A 5:5:3 ratio in capital ship tonnage for Britain, the United States, and Japan was agreed to in the Washington Naval Treaty, with 525,000 the total battleship tonnage for each of the first two. The quotas for France and Italy were 35 percent of the capital ship tonnage of Britain. Russia was left out of the Washington Naval Treaty. It was still ostracized as a consequence of the Russian Revolution, but it also lacked a strong oceangoing navy and had been unable to counter British, French, Japanese, and American naval power during the Russian Civil War. As a result, the major powers were able to decide on preferable levels of naval strength without worrying about any Soviet naval threat.

Limitations as well as ratios were a key element. The treaty involved an agreement to scrap many battleships, in service or under construction, and to stop most new construction for ten years: the three major navies were allowed to complete two new battleships each, and America and Japan were permitted to complete two incomplete ships as carriers. By fixing ratios, the Washington Naval Treaty appeared to end the prospect of expensive and destabilizing naval races between the major powers and to fix the character of battleship size and technology. The treaty limited warships other than battleships and carriers to ten thousand tons and eight-inch guns but placed no treaty limits on the number of warships displacing fewer than ten thousand tons. As a result, the great naval powers could build and maintain as many cruisers and destroyers as they wanted to afford. A competition started in the so-called treaty cruisers, heavy cruisers displacing ten thousand tons and carrying eight-inch guns, rather than in the battleships built prior to 1914. Although *Nelson* and *Rodney*, two battleships (with sixteen-inch guns) were completed in 1927, Britain did not lay down any battleships between January 1923 and December 1936. While on paper the Americans had parity with Britain, and a comfortable superiority over Japan in the number of battleships, it had, in practice, a decided superiority, as American battleships on average had more heavy guns.[4] This reflected a focus on winning war by battle, and on battle by battleships.

The limitations on battleships under the treaty, and the consequences of postwar downsizing and fiscal retrenchment, helped ensure in the 1920s that carriers, as yet largely untested, could be more rapidly produced by converting existing warships than by building new ones. As a result, and in a largely unexpected fashion, the cost of investing in new technology, in the shape of carriers, was cut. The conversion of battle cruisers (which were less armored and faster than battleships) helped ensure that carriers were faster than the standard battle fleet, centered as it was on the battleship. This basis was to be important to a key characteristic of carrier warfare, the relatively high speed of the carriers, which reduced the consequences of their vulnerability to surface fire and interception.

Despite British efforts in 1922 and 1930, there were no limitations on submarines, although the Peace of Versailles had banned Germany from using them. The French were keen to prevent limits on submarine warfare and built the most in the 1920s, in part in response to the limitations on their fleet under the Washington Naval Treaty, and in part in response to an emphasis on a defensive fleet: some of the submarines were for coastal defense. In particular, this was a French response to Italian naval expansion. The 1930 London Conference's decision that submarines should only sink noncombatant ships after giving fair warning did not represent a practical limitation on what submarines might do in the future and, indeed, was not to be heeded, being already redundant before the Second World War, as the warlike conduct of Italian submarines during the Spanish Civil War (1936–39) showed.

The role of Japan in the treaty clauses reflected its improved relative position as a result of the First World War, having been an active member of the Allies. Moreover, Japan's postwar position as one of the leading states to intervene in the Russian Civil War further affirmed both its significance and the importance of its cooperation with America and Britain. Japanese naval power in the Pacific was recognized in the Washington ratios, while the 1922 treaty also included a clause stopping the military development of American colonies in the western Pacific, the British base of Hong Kong, and also many of Japan's island possessions in the region. This clause greatly affected the American ability to exercise sea power against Japan, as it meant that naval bases in the western Pacific, notably Guam, could not be improved. However, America's relative position was enhanced because the Anglo-Japanese Alliance of 1902, which was up for renewal, was replaced instead by a Four-Power (Britain, United States, Japan, and France) Treaty committing the powers to respect each other's Pacific possessions and to consult in the event of conflict. As a result, there was no specific agreement between Britain and Japan, which lessened American vulnerability in the western Pacific.

FORCE STRUCTURES

Alongside the commitment to battleships, the combined impact of submarines and air power in the First World War, and their likely future role, suggested to some a fundamental change, both in naval capability and in the tactical, operational, and strategic aspects of naval power. As a consequence, many commentators argued, naval methods and goals had to be rapidly rethought.

At the same time, the specific strengths and character of weapons' systems had to be understood. For example, for submarines, there was a contrast in roles between the emphasis on stealth, which enabled a submarine to mount surprise attacks and thus to counter the greater firepower advantage of surface warships, and, on the other side, the need, if action was to be more effective, to come close to, or to, the surface—in the former case to periscope depth, and in the latter to make more speed. However, in doing so, submarines compromised stealth as, even if not on the surface, periscope and torpedo wakes could be tracked. Moreover, close to the surface, submarines were visible to, and detectable by, aircraft and vulnerable to air attack.

Submarine warfare emphasized a major difference between naval and land capability. The resources to build and maintain naval units was restricted to relatively few powers, and thus the options to be considered by contemporaries in terms of strategic goals and doctrine were relatively limited. Echoing earlier fears of torpedo boats, Jellicoe, the former British First Sea Lord, argued that submarines destroyed the feasibility of close blockades of opposing harbors for the purpose of preventing hostile warships from sailing out, and instead led to a reliance for trade protection on convoys protected by cruisers, which required a large number of the latter. Jellicoe was worried that Britain had insufficient cruisers both to do this and to work with the battle fleet in a future war.

Cruisers were regarded as a protection of imperial maritime routes, but, between *Enterprise* in 1918 and *Berwick* in 1924, the British laid down no new cruiser. Nor did any other European state. Only the Americans and the Japanese laid down new cruisers. British Admiralty concern about the impact of naval limitations on the size and number of ships was expressed by Admiral Sir Charles Madden, the First Sea Lord, in a meeting of the Cabinet Committee preparing for the 1930 London Naval Conference, where he

> explained that it was not possible to build a battleship of less than 25,000 tons with the necessary quantities of armament, speed and protection, which would include an armored deck of 5" [thick armor] and 6", to keep out bombs and plunging shell, and have sufficient protection under water against mines, torpedoes and bombs. . . . The Admiralty required a sufficient number of cruisers to give security to the overseas trade of the Empire against raiding forces of the enemy and a battle fleet to give cover to the trade-protecting cruisers.[5]

This dual need reflected a long-standing pattern that was not dependent on the technological parameters that affected its particular manifestations and that had clear implications as far as doctrine was concerned and with regard to strategy, operations, and tactics. The variety in warships ensured an asymmetrical quality to naval conflict itself, even while this quality frequently arose inherently from fundamental asymmetries in goals and related capabilities.

In the 1920s and 1930s, the problem with negotiating arms-control agreements, whether or not in the shape of parity or percentages, was that every naval power had different force requirements to meet its strategic needs. For example, with less long-range trade to protect, the Americans needed far fewer cruisers than the British and also sought to limit the number of British cruisers so that Britain would find it harder in wartime to blockade neutral commerce, which had been a long-standing point of tension in Anglo-American relations. This difference led to a serious Anglo-American dispute over cruiser numbers at, and after, the Geneva Naval Conference of 1927. The Americans wanted bigger cruisers with longer cruising ranges because they lacked Britain's first-rate network of bases at which their ships could refuel. Since disarmament agreements worked on the basis of total tonnage, the Americans preferred fewer (but bigger) cruisers, and the British, in contrast, preferred more (but smaller) cruisers. However, again as a reminder of the complex factors affecting force structures, for the Royal Navy, if American-style bigger cruisers were built by Japan, then the smaller British cruisers would be outgunned. Therefore, the British Admiralty wanted qualitative arms limitations rather than quantitative ones. The 1927 conference failed to reach an agreement.

At the 1930 London Naval Conference, quantitative limits (overall tonnage restrictions on each class of warship) were placed on the great naval powers in addition to the 1922 restrictions. The British government agreed to a limit of fifty cruisers, as opposed to the seventy the Admiralty sought. In practice, the financial cuts enforced in the late 1920s anyway ensured that the British cruiser program was not sustainable.

In many respects, the type of cruiser was an easy topic to debate, for, in contrast, as had been the case prior to the First World War, efforts to develop naval strength and weaponry were complicated by acute controversy over the potential of different weapons systems in any future naval war. The respective merits of air power (both from aircraft carriers and shore based), of surface gunnery (especially from battleships), and of submarines were all extensively discussed, as well as their likely tactical and operational combinations and strategic consequences. Some theorists argued that battleships were now obsolete in the face of air power and submarines. Nevertheless, big surface warships had a continued appeal, and there was considerable opposition to making carriers the key capital ship. Instead, in the 1930s, the

Americans, British, and Japanese put a major emphasis on battle-fleet tactics based on battleships. Given the serious weakness of naval aviation, this emphasis was not simply a sign of conservatism, as was to be suggested at the time and, even more, subsequently. For example, as commander in chief of Britain's Mediterranean fleet from 1930 to 1933, Admiral Alfred Chatfield, later First Sea Lord from 1933 to 1938, sought to introduce an effective tactical doctrine for the use of aircraft in naval battle, albeit with limited success. Conservatism played a role in support for battleships, but the British, who, with the largest fleet, had the greatest interest in maintaining existing systems, also displayed adaptability in their tactics, not least in training captains to act on their own initiative, conducting maneuvers at night and in bad weather, and introducing a highly effective long-range fire-control system. The Germans, French, Soviets, and Italians were also greatly interested in developing an effective battleship capability.

It was argued that, thanks to the antiaircraft guns on them and on supporting warships, battleships could be protected against air attack. Moreover, carriers (correctly) appeared vulnerable to gunnery and could not operate at night or in poor weather, and the First World War had shown that submarine campaigns could be beaten. Carriers lacked artillery and carried fragile biplanes. Indeed, to many contemporaries, they were more like civilian ships than true warships. Carrier decks were a large and vulnerable target. Moreover, once badly damaged, the carrier became useless. The individual aircraft could carry the equivalent of one battleship shell; indeed, at Pearl Harbor, Japanese bombers used modified fifteen-inch shells. As a result, with all aircraft active, they could only deliver a few minutes of fire. Carriers, therefore, had serious weaknesses. Pre-1939 navies, the Japanese providing an especially good example, conceived of carriers and submarines as a subordinate part of fleets that emphasized battleships, indeed, in part as anti-battleship aids to their own battleships, only to find in the Second World War that, while battleships were important, carriers proved more useful in many circumstances.

Gunnery experts were particularly keen on battleships, and these experts were important in senior ranks. There was no comparable lobby for carriers or submarines. The continuing role of battleships was enhanced by the absence of a major change in battleship design comparable to those in the late nineteenth century and the 1900s. Indeed, with the arrival of the dreadnoughts in the 1900s, battleship architecture had reached a new period of relative stability in which existing battleships remained effective. For example, the USS *New York* of 1914, *Texas* of 1914, and *Nevada* (BB-36) of 1916 participated in the D-day bombardment of 1944, while, although refitted in 1937, four of Italy's battleships in 1941 had been launched in 1913–14. The ten fourteen-inch guns of the *Texas* (which can be visited near Galveston) could fire one and a half rounds per minute, each armor-piercing shell weighing 1,500 pounds. There was still great interest in such weaponry, both for ship destruction, of comparable as well as of different ships, and for shore bombardment, including the destruction of harbors and the covering of amphibious attacks. No other system, including bombers, could provide such firepower. Given the problems posed by defensive gunfire, entrenchments, and concrete fortifications, battleships, despite the low trajectory of their main guns limiting their value against modern coastal defenses, appeared to be the best means available to engage with coastal positions and to maintain an amphibious capability.

Moreover, there were considerable efforts to strengthen battleships, as well as other ships, in order to increase their resistance to air attack. Brigadier General Billy Mitchell, the top American combat air commander and assistant chief of the American air service in 1919–25, argued that aircraft could sink any ship afloat. The latter assertion, which resulted in the test sinking of a seized German battleship, the *Ostfriesland*, in twenty-one and a half minutes of bombing in 1921, led Mitchell to furious rows with the American navy. The value of the test sinking was compromised because the battleship was stationary and unable to fight back. Moreover, Mitchell violated the rules of the test. For example, he claimed he could hit ships from high altitude, but, during the test, the bombers came in at almost mast height and would have been highly vulnerable even to the primitive antiaircraft capability of the day. The success of Mitchell's tests led to prominent calls, especially in the *New York Herald*, to convert incomplete capital ships into carriers and resulted in the navy creating a Bureau of Aeronautics and improving the air defenses of its warships. Mitchell, however, was critical of carriers, as he feared they would make it harder to wage a unified air war under a single air command. He preferred shore-based aircraft.[6] The carrier aircraft of the time were not very rugged and lacked range. Also, the communication between aircraft and carriers was unreliable.

On battleships, armor was enhanced to resist bombs; outer hulls added to protect against torpedo attack from aircraft, submarines, or surface ships; and antiaircraft guns and tactics were developed, not least with improved fire control. Furthermore, following developments prior to the First World War, more accurate fire with the main battleship guns was achieved through the addition of primitive computer-like calculators to integrate course and speed calculations into fire-control systems. Air spotting for naval gunfire also developed in the 1920s and 1930s with better communications between aircraft and battleships. This improvement in battleship capability is a reminder of the danger of assuming that a weapons system is necessarily static, which is a conclusion too often drawn when discussing battleships. As an armored, mobile, big-gun platform, the battleship had much to offer, both on its own and in combined operations, and battleships were readily understood in that light.

Indeed, in the Second World War, although there were spectacular losses, notably the *Prince of Wales* to Japanese torpedo bombers in December 1941, and major problems in protection methods,[7] many battleships took considerable punishment before being sunk by air attack. At Pearl Harbor, only two battleships were a total loss, while two others damaged were back in service as early as March 1942. Battleships were not supposed to operate by themselves, but in tandem with auxiliary ships that could serve to enhance antiaircraft capabilities, as in the successful American (and British) response to Japanese kamikaze air attacks in 1944–45. During the war, air attack could be less effective than some had expected, in part due to very effective anti-air coordination, which included air cover. Battleships provided the required offensive armament and defensive armor with which to fight, and thus deter and control, other battleships.

There was no experience, from the First World War or subsequently, with conflict between carriers, but there was considerable confidence in their potential. Interwar British planning called for a carrier to every two or three capital ships. The key to British attitudes was that aircraft had to be integral to the fleet, whereas, in the American and Japanese navies, although that doctrine was present, there was a greater willingness for carriers to operate separately. In America, the National Defense Act had placed air power under the army air service (rather than creating an equivalent to the RAF), but naval aviation was kept separate.[8]

PLANNING FOR THE PACIFIC

Speculation about the likely role of carriers, and of carriers as opposed to battleships, focused on the Pacific. It was there that Japan, the United States, and Britain competed. Indeed, in 1919, an Admiralty memorandum warned that the British navy was likely to be weaker than that of Japan in the Far East. It suggested that using Hong Kong as a base would expose the British fleet to overwhelming attack from Japan, a reasonable view about the vulnerability of forward bases, and notably, but not only, to surprise attack. Instead, the memorandum recommended that Singapore be developed, as it was sufficiently far from Japan to permit reinforcement without peril.[9] The Treasury proved reluctant to share the Admiralty's concern, which was a tension familiar to all powers, but the creation of a Singapore base and the development of the so-called Singapore Strategy were critically important to the Royal Navy in the 1920s.

Japan represented a different threat to the British Empire from that earlier posed by Russia. The British response to Russia had been military and diplomatic policies focused on the Asian landmass, crucially to protect the land approaches to India, with the Royal Navy playing only a supporting role.

Now there was the prospect of a naval challenge to Britain in Far Eastern or even Indian waters, one that could not be countered by British strength in home waters and that required a regional capability.[10] In his *Rulers of the Indian Ocean* (1927), George Ballard, a retired British admiral, argued that the rise in Japanese and American naval power meant that it was no longer sufficient for Britain to prevail over European rivals in order to win global naval dominance. This was a challenge that was more direct for Britain than for other European naval powers. The rise of a potentially hostile Japanese navy changed the traditional Royal Navy strategic landscape. Earlier, if all naval rivals could be locked up in Europe or chased when they evaded blockade, then Britain had global command. However, fiscal issues, combined with the Japanese navy, created a situation in which Britain had a two-ocean empire, threatened at each end, and a one-ocean navy to defend it.

A collision of American and Japanese interests in the Pacific region had been building since Japan's stunning victory in the 1904–5 Russo-Japanese War eliminated her sole naval threat in the region. That same year, America strengthened its fleet in the Philippines as a Japanese buffer in the event of war. Both countries now recognized each other as a potential threat to their respective interests and ambitions. Japanese naval commanders, fearing Japan would lose in a sustained war, hoped that quick decisive naval battles would enable it to establish a defensive perimeter against the American navy, as Japan had done against Russia in 1905. In 1921, America regarded Japan as the most probable enemy.[11] The tonnage limitations of the Washington treaty assumed that America, Britain, and Japan could each only dominate its own geographic sphere in the Pacific.

There were specific American interests in the western Pacific, including the territories of the Philippines, Guam, and Samoa; trade; and a strong commitment to the independence of China and to an "open door" allowing other powers that had not had territorial bases there, notably the United States, to share in Chinese trade. This concern led to American planning for war with Japan, which was correctly seen as menacing all these interests.

The likely character of a major future war in the Pacific led to a new geography of commitment and concern that was reflected in the development of naval bases or the consideration of alternatives. The switchover from coal to oil as the power source of major warships helped to ensure that the previous system of coaling bases was obsolete. In addition, the expansion in the size of battleships from the deployment of dreadnoughts in the mid-1900s had made the existing imperial harbors inadequate. The British chiefs of staff urged that Singapore should be not only a modern naval base but also the location of an army able to act as a strategic reserve forward of India,[12] a measure aimed at Japan and to protect India, Malaya, and Australasia. In turn, the strategic value of Pearl Harbor for controlling the eastern Pacific and advancing across the western Pacific was clear to the American Joint

Army and Navy Planning Committee in 1919. More than any other navy, the American one got the war it expected in the 1940s. Naval exercises that were a bridge from the naval thought of the pre-1914 Mahanian period to the American strategy in the Second World War were pursued. War Plan Orange of 1924 called for the "through ticket." This was a rapid advance directly from Pearl Harbor, the American base in Hawaii, to Manila, the capital of the Philippines, in order to relieve it from Japanese attack, followed by a decisive naval battle and then starving Japan by blockade.[13]

Pearl Harbor would be crucial for the planning that superseded the "through ticket," planning in which there was now greater interest in a slower, three-year process of seizing the Japanese islands in the Pacific—the Marshalls, Carolines, and Marianas—which they had gained from Germany as mandates in the Versailles peace settlement. The capture of these islands would provide the Americans with forward bases en route to the Philippines and deny them to the Japanese. Without control of this area, it was argued, a naval advance to the Philippines would be unsuccessful. The logistical challenge of projecting power into the western Pacific was formidable. It included an erosion of efficiency as warships responded to fouled hulls and reduced speeds. The more cautious voices had prevailed over the "through ticket" advocates by the mid-1930s, the "Cautionaries" prevailing over the "Thrusters." The evolution of American strategy reflected the sophistication of American planning, notably the War Plans Division within the Office of the Chief of Naval Operations. American naval leaders and planners responded to the lack of adequate bases in the western Pacific by favoring technological, operational, and force structure solutions, including underway replenishment and carriers.[14]

The Americans and Japanese made major advances with naval aviation and aircraft carriers, in part because they would be key powers in any struggle for control of the Pacific. The Japanese commissioned six carriers between 1922 and 1939, some converted, but others purpose-built as carriers. In 1927, as part of his graduation exercises at the Japanese Naval War College, Lieutenant Commander Tagaki Sokichi planned an attack by two Japanese carriers on the American Pacific base at Pearl Harbor, although, in the evaluation, he was held to have suffered heavy losses. In 1929, the American *Saratoga* launched eighty-three aircraft in a simulated raid on the Panama Canal.[15] At sea, however, whatever their apparent potential, air power was restricted in the 1910s and 1920s by the difficulty of operating aircraft in bad weather and in the dark, by their limited load capacity and range, and by mechanical unreliability.

The American navy was experienced in large-scale movements and maneuvers. The Atlantic Fleet would regularly join the Pacific Fleet in the Caribbean or the eastern Pacific for maneuvers. For example, in 1925, the Pacific Fleet engaged in maneuvers with the Atlantic Fleet off Panama; then both fleets went up the West Coast of the United States for "fleet week" events, after which they engaged in maneuvers from California to Hawaii, and then, while the Atlantic Fleet went home, the Pacific Fleet went to Australia and New Zealand. By 1940, no other fleet had as much experience in such large-scale movements.

Options were tested in fleet exercises and in war games.[16] In an American 1933 war game, Captain Ernest King chose a northern attack route on Japan, via Hawaii, Midway, Wake, and the Marianas, while the president of the Naval War College, Rear Admiral Harris Laning, preferred a southern route, beginning with Micronesia, and criticized King's plans as the worst possible. A decade later, King put his plan into action, while Douglas MacArthur put Laning's plan into action, but they each took far longer than expected. Moreover, practicalities such as fuel and ammunition were underplayed in the planning and exercises. When operating at peak performance, carriers need to refuel very often. To cope with the speed and range of Japanese battleships, the Americans relied on better fire control and on spotter aircraft. Fighters to cover the latter were to be launched from carriers, which thus served to enable the battleships to range accurately. It was assumed that the carriers would be sunk quickly, but if they allowed the battleships to win, they had done their job.

There was also a focus on increasing the range, size, and speed of submarines. The American S class of 1918–21, with a range of five thousand to eight thousand miles at a surface speed of ten knots, was replaced by the B class (twelve thousand miles at eleven knots), and then by the P-boats of 1933–36, which were the first American submarines with a totally diesel electric propulsion. These were followed by the *Gato* class introduced in 1940: double-hulled, all-welded-hull submarines with a range of 11,800 miles and a surface speed of twenty to twenty-five knots. By the time of the Japanese attack on Pearl Harbor, the American navy had 111 submarines in commission, although their cautious use in the first year of the war reflected deficiencies in interwar doctrine.[17] Poor torpedoes were also a major issue.

In turn, the Japanese had sixty-three oceangoing submarines. Their *Sentoku*–type 1-400 submarines had a range of 37,500 nautical miles, a surface speed of 18.7 knots, and a submerged speed of 6.5 knots and carried two seaplanes and supplies for sixty days. In the event of war with the United States, the Japanese planned to use their submarines to sink American warships steaming from Hawaii into the western Pacific. They therefore intended to employ the long range of their submarines as a major preliminary component in subsequent fleet action. In the event, Japanese submarines repeatedly failed to fulfill expectations, which was unsurprising, as prewar exercises had indicated significant deficiencies.

The need to plan for conflict with Japan accentuated the problems for Britain and the United States, powers with major commitments in both the

Atlantic and Pacific, for they had to think about how best to distribute naval forces and how vulnerabilities would affect policy. There was a de facto division of spheres of activity, with the United States dominant in the Pacific but having no role in the Indian Ocean, which was very much a British sphere. The British were more prominent than the Americans in the South Atlantic and in East Asian waters, although the Americans had a small Asiatic Fleet to defend the Philippines and their interests in China. As Admiral Montgomery Taylor, the Asiatic Fleet commander from 1929 to 1933, pointed out, this force was too small to thwart Japanese moves, and any intervention would probably prove counterproductive.[18]

With the exception of carriers and cruisers, the American surface navy was smaller in 1938 than it had been in 1925, while the marines were a small and inadequately equipped force.[19] Nevertheless, although the size of the navy was limited as a result of the treaty holiday in shipbuilding, the American navy was being expanded rapidly by the late 1930s. In addition, the navy's tactical doctrine had become reasonably sophisticated. It focused on all-arms coordination, tactical flexibility, and a decentralized command structure.[20] As a result of the earlier freeze on battleship construction, the Americans had devoted appropriate attention to carriers and submarines, while the lack of base fortifications in the islands of the northwest Pacific ensured that the navy had had to focus on warships of greater range, build floating dry docks, and invest in logistical capability.[21]

The British failed to agree among themselves, or with the Americans, on how best to contain the Japanese threat. In response to Treasury opposition in 1934 to sending a fleet to the Far East and, instead, concern about Germany and support for a British focus on air power, it was argued by both the Admiralty and the Dominions Office that this was an unacceptable stance due to the impact on Australia and New Zealand of leaving them without support.[22] More generally, whereas the Royal Navy sought to focus on Japan, the politicians, the Treasury, and the RAF wanted to concentrate on Germany. The British government was developing serious doubts at the highest level about its ability to project power effectively into the Pacific. The Admiralty was ready to consider a forward policy of projecting a battle fleet into Far Eastern waters (and thus protecting Hong Kong), to provide support against Japan, but that policy required an American willingness to move naval units to East Asian waters as an aspect of a coordination that did not yet exist. Fearing that this would leave Hawaii vulnerable, the American Naval Department, which anyway included anglophobes, was unwilling to support such a scheme.

A forward policy of sending much of the fleet to Singapore in the event of a crisis with Japan was developed in the early 1920s and then went through several significant shifts in timing and force structure, notably in 1937–41 as Britain grappled with the problems of risking fighting a three-front war and facing substantial risks in European waters. By April 1939, the Admiralty was no longer willing to specify how soon and what size a force would be deployed to Asian waters in the event of an Anglo-Japanese war arising. In 1941, Churchill decided to send the *Prince of Wales*, a modern battleship, and the battle cruiser *Repulse* to Singapore in order to deter the Japanese and impress the Americans. However, this decision rested on a misreading of the strategic situation in the Far East as the Japanese could not be deterred. Moreover, the availability of warships for Singapore depended on commitments against Germany and Italy in home, Atlantic, and Mediterranean waters, and on the fate of the British fleet in any conflict that might arise with these powers. After the sinking of the *Prince of Wales*, Churchill told a secret session of the House of Commons on April 23, 1942, "While we are at war with Germany and Italy we do not possess the naval resources necessary to maintain the command of the Indian Ocean against any heavy detachment from the main Japanese fleet."[23]

In 1935–36, in the Second London Naval Conference, Japan demanded equality of tonnage with Britain and the United States, which would have meant Japanese naval superiority in the Pacific and Far East. British attempts at negotiating compromise failed, and the Japanese left the talks in January 1936. Already, in December 1934, Japan had provided the necessary two years' notice under the treaty regime to end their commitments.

Japan, therefore, launched the Marusan Program of shipbuilding, which was designed to prepare for victory over American and British fleets. Japan focused on the force structure of a large navy based on battleships and on the goal of victory stemming from a decisive battle. This was the lesson the Japanese had taken from their victory at Tsushima in 1905. The buildup of their navy included the largest capital ships in the world, the "super battleships" *Yamato* and *Musashi*, ordered in 1937, each displacing seventy-two thousand tons and carrying nine 18.1 inch guns. Their size and gunnery were designed to compensate for Japan being heavily outnumbered by American battleships, but they were to be sunk by the Americans in 1944 and 1945, air power, or rather the lack of their own air power, proving the nemesis of this class.

Seeking international power through naval strength, and naval strength through international power, many Japanese naval commanders and planners opposed the naval limitation treaties because they believed that the Japanese navy should be closer in size to the American navy, an idea first expressed in 1907 when a ratio of 70 percent or more had been advanced. As a consequence, the 1922 Washington Naval Treaty ratio of 60 percent was regarded as unreasonable, a humiliation, and a threat both to national defense and to the ability of the navy to act as a deterrent force. Indeed, in November 1930, the prime minister was assassinated after he signed the London Naval Treaty. The militarist/nationalist resentment against the ratio system ignored the fact that, in an all-out arms race with the United States, Japan had no chance of achieving a 60 or 70 percent ratio. Therefore, arms control actually worked to their advantage.

Both the Japanese and the American naval leadership focused on a decisive battle centered on battleships, with air and submarine attacks being preliminary blows, while mundane items like support ships and salvage training were ignored by the Japanese. The Japanese also put an emphasis on preliminary damage from nighttime cruiser and destroyer torpedo strikes and produced an effective surface-launched torpedo, the oxygen-fueled Type 93 or "Long Lance." Training was significant. Realizing that their torpedo-launching skills were inadequate, the Japanese analyzed the situation, tested alternatives, and improved their skills. Moreover, as an instance of the relationship between tactics and equipment, the Japanese increased their capability for nighttime attack by developing impressive light-gathering optical devices, as well as high-explosive propellants that were nearly flashless. The Americans lacked a comparable torpedo (and comparable propellants), and the contrast in tactics affected conflict in the Guadalcanal campaign in the Solomon Sea in 1942. As far as warships were concerned, the Japanese added armor, upgraded engines, and increased the gun elevation of their warships in an attempt to outclass the Americans at extreme range, and thus be able to damage them prior to conflict at closer range. In response, the Americans did the same in an effort to secure an initial advantage. At the same time, Japanese naval tactics have been seen as overly dogmatic.[24]

NAVAL AIR POWER

Improvements in naval air effectiveness in the interwar years were particularly the case of the 1930s. New arrester gear was fitted, which helped slow down aircraft while landing on carriers, and, in addition, the equipment could be reset automatically, which was useful when more than one aircraft were landing. Hydraulically reset traverse arrester gear was in use by the British navy by 1933. Improvements in carriers and aircraft helped to ensure that carriers, rather than seaplanes, which were indeed significant, or airships, were seen as the way to apply air power at sea and made it easier to envisage using carriers for operational and strategic ends. Naval air doctrine and tactics also advanced. The value of attacking first was understood as what would hinder the chance of an opponent's carrier responding, notably as it was difficult for defenders to stop an air attack. Defending fighters and their control system lacked this capacity, while antiaircraft guns at the time were of only limited value, not least in protecting such a big target as a carrier.

There were some distinctly Japanese approaches to naval aviation. In particular, the Japanese navy focused not only on carriers but also on land-based bombers as an offensive force. These long-range bombers were capable of bombing and torpedoing ships, which was not the case with the American and British navies. This was partly because the Japanese navy thought it convenient to utilize the Pacific colonies it controlled, notably the Marianas, to provide forward air bases from which to intercept the advancing American fleet. Moreover, the Japanese navy enjoyed relative organizational autonomy in developing naval aviation as far as its army counterpart was concerned. While there was notoriously severe interservice rivalry between the army and the navy over budget, personnel, and resources, the Japanese navy was less restricted in terms of developing naval aviation and less threatened by proponents of an independent air force than the British and American navies. This was linked to the extent to which the Japanese Naval Air Force was larger in size and better in equipment than the Japanese Army Air Force, a contrast with the situation in the United States. In 1938, the Japanese concentrated all maritime and shore-based air power into a combined force. Moreover, in 1940 the Japanese navy took over part of the air war in China, providing long-range fighter protection for bombers with the Zero introduced that year.

However, Japanese naval aviators were mostly noncommissioned officers: officers comprised fewer than 15 percent of its aviators. The Japanese navy initially tried to have an all-officer pilot corps, but it gave this up for fear of destabilizing the existing personnel hierarchy because a lot of aviators were needed. Instead, the navy introduced the Yokaren system, recruiting civilians between fifteen and seventeen in order to train sufficient noncommissioned officers to fill the lower ranks. This practice led to less organizational and political representation of aviators within the navy, which hampered the necessary transformation from a battleship-oriented navy to an air-centered one. Although that was not the sole reason hampering this transformation, it was important.

Britain and the United States had carrier fleets that were intended to compete with that of Japan. In contrast, Germany, Italy, and the Soviet Union did not build or complete carriers in the interwar period, and France only had one, the *Béarn*, a converted battleship that was insufficiently fast to be considered an important asset. The Soviet emphasis, not on carriers but on shore-based aircraft, reflected the extent to which it was assumed by the Soviets that their naval operations would take place in the Gulf of Finland or otherwise close to Soviet-controlled coastlines and the air cover they offered. So also with Italy and the Mediterranean, much of which sea is not well suited for carrier operations. In 1920, Admiral Katō Tomsaburō, the navy minister, stated that the navy had no interest in obtaining carriers, as it could rely on coastal air bases.

British and American carrier and aircraft design diverged because of differing conceptions of future naval war. In the Second World War, the British armored deck carriers proved less susceptible to bombs and Japanese kamikaze aircraft than the American wooden-deckers, as they tended not to penetrate the former. Japanese carriers also had wooden decks. The lighter-weight wooden decks were linked to the larger fuel capacity necessary for the longer range of Pacific operations. Moreover, the wooden-deck carriers had capacity for more aircraft. In contrast, the British navy's most important task was protecting national waters and the major imperial trade route through the Mediterranean. Both tasks were well within the existing and forecast zones vulnerable to attack from land-based aircraft, notably from Italy. In the 1920s and 1930s, it was held that such aircraft would have a major advantage over the slower and longer turning circle of carriers and the problems posed by headwinds for aircraft taking off and landing. However, that was not the key reason for armored decks. Instead, the British navy sought a line of carriers sailing in parallel with, but further away from, the battleships, which would be the primary ships to engage the enemy. This need for carrier protection was enhanced by the limited range of aircraft, which meant that carriers had to approach their targets, which made them vulnerable. The original carrier specifications called for the armor to stretch over both sides of the ship as protection against naval gunfire. Cost was the reason the side armor was dropped. Armor ensured that there was less space below the deck for the repair and storage of aircraft, and British carriers carried fewer aircraft per tonnage than their American and Japanese counterparts.

Despite pressure from the Royal Navy, naval air power in Britain lacked a separate institutional framework. The RNAS merged with the RFC (Royal Flying Corps) into the RAF in 1918. The RAF was primarily concerned with land-based aircraft and had little time for their naval counterparts, and indeed for maritime operations: RAF Coastal Command was short of aircraft in the Second World War. In 1931, the RAF had pressed for major cuts in naval aviation. The decision to separate embarked (onboard) aviation and its necessary shore support, but not land-based maritime air or aircraft procurement, from the RAF and return it to the navy was announced by the Inskip Award of 1937 and came into effect in May 1939.[25]

In France, the Air Ministry, established in 1928, gained nearly all naval air assets, and this helped ensure that plans for more carriers were not pursued there until 1938. In 1936, the French navy had regained control of naval aviation. In Germany, the Luftwaffe took control over all military aviation, angering the navy, which had earlier developed an air capacity even though that was forbidden under the 1919 Versailles peace settlement. In Italy in 1923, the navy lost the control of its air branch, which had been organized in 1913, and in 1925 all its aircraft and airships passed to the newly established Regia Aeronautica. This lessened the navy's interest in carriers, as, if built, their aircraft would belong to the air force.

In the United States, there was a very different situation thanks to the Bureau of Aeronautics of the American navy created in 1921. The bureau stimulated the development of effective air-sea doctrine, operational policies, and tactics. American air-to-sea doctrine emphasized attacking capital ships. The number of aircraft in the American naval air arm rose from 1,081 in 1925 to 2,050 in 1938, a larger figure than in the Army Air Corps. The United States had a third air arm in the Marine Corps. In the Netherlands, the navy was able to resist political pressure and maintain a separate naval air service.

Aside from the construction and enhancement of carriers, there were also marked improvements in naval aircraft, notably as airframes became larger and more powerful in the 1930s, although carriers could not accommodate twin-engined bombers in this period. The Americans and British developed dive-bombing tactics in the 1920s and, subsequently, dive-bombers. However, they did not replace torpedo bombers, aircraft that launched torpedoes. Torpedo bombers were vulnerable to defensive firepower but were best able to sink armored ships.[26] Improved torpedoes were deployed. In 1931, the Japanese introduced the Type 91 Mod 1 antiship torpedo.

The emphasis on carrier attack should not crowd out other uses for naval air power. Many aircraft were employed at sea to help battleships spot the fall of their shells. They were launched from catapults on the top of the turrets. Aerial reconnaissance, notably by seaplanes, which had a much better range than the smaller carrier or cruiser aircraft, was also crucial in the location of shipping.[27] A clear future for air power at sea was suggested by the British fleet reconstruction program of 1937, which aimed, by the late 1940s, to have twenty new battleships and twenty new carriers at the core of the battle fleet. In America, the emphasis was also on carrier support for battleships. From hindsight, the battleship appears redundant, but that was not how it seemed to contemporaries.[28] Instead, it was believed that battleships could be protected against air attack, while carriers appeared vulnerable to gunnery, and thus to require protection, as well as being essentially only fair-weather and daytime warships.

EUROPEAN CHALLENGES

It was not only in the Pacific that a revisionist power threatened the existing international order. The same was true of Europe, with Italy and Germany. Benito Mussolini, the Italian Fascist dictator from 1922, greatly expanded the Italian navy in rivalry with France and in order to challenge the British position in the Mediterranean. This was the crucial axis of the British Empire as the shortest route to India, Australasia, and the Far East, via the Suez Canal. It was an axis that was dependent on naval power and related bases at

Gibraltar, Malta, and Alexandria (in Egypt), with Cyprus also a British colony.

However, like Hitler, Mussolini was less interested in naval affairs than in the situation on land, and he lacked both relevant knowledge and an understanding of the strategic situation. It was possible to talk of unlocking the gates of the Mediterranean at Gibraltar and Suez, but, as the ambitious Italian Naval Staff noted, there was really only hope of Italy controlling the central Mediterranean. A lack of carrier air cover, and a battle fleet that could not match those of Britain and France, rendered other schemes futile. Despite some new warships, including battleships, cruisers, and submarines, the Italian navy also had tactical, resource, and weaponry deficiencies, especially weaknesses in gunnery training and shell manufacture, a shortage of oil, and some of its numerous submarines being outdated.

Britain and Italy came close to conflict as a result of the Italian invasion of Ethiopia in 1935–36, a step condemned by the League of Nations. The Royal Navy, despite weaknesses, including a lack of sailors, reserves, and antiaircraft ammunition, and concerns about Italian submarines based at Leros in the Dodecanese Islands (an Italian colony in the Aegean), was confident of success. It had bases at Gibraltar, Malta, and Alexandria, although the Mediterranean Fleet was withdrawn from Malta to Alexandria due to fear of Italian air attack. The significance of naval bases was such that the priority thereafter was to improve Malta's defenses against air attack, rather than against bombardment or invasion. Matching their confidence that antiaircraft guns could protect warships, the Royal Navy was certain that such improvement could be made, whereas senior airmen were convinced that sustained and heavy air attack could prevent safe use of the island and its naval base.

As a might-have-been war, the confrontation in 1935–36 was significant in the establishment of relative capability and in the development of plans. During the confrontation, the British planned a carrier attack on the Italian fleet in harbor at Taranto. One, indeed, was to be successfully launched in November 1940. However, the government did not wish to provoke war with Italy, not least as it hoped to keep Mussolini and Hitler apart, and it did not intend to antagonize the Americans by stopping their oil tankers. The British failure to intimidate Italy was more a consequence of an absence of political will than of a lack of naval capability. A failure to secure a promise of French naval cooperation was also significant.

Mussolini pushed forward naval construction from 1936, improving Italy's battleship and submarine fleet. By the outbreak of war for Italy in 1940, the fleet included 6 battleships (two of them new), 19 cruisers, and 113 submarines, but no aircraft carriers. In Eritrea, Italy had a colony on the Red Sea, with a port at Massawa, where destroyers were based, and, in Somalia, a colony on the Indian Ocean, with a port at Mogadishu. Yet, with the British in control of Egypt, the Italians were in no shape to aid these colonies.

Germany had a greater industrial capacity but was more restricted by treaty in the 1920s and early 1930s. Under the Weimar Republic, which was the government system between the First World War and the Nazi takeover of power in 1933, the Germans enhanced their naval strength by responding to the Versailles (1919) constraints on the maximum tonnage of German battleships by designing the *Deutschland* class. The *Deutschland* was classified by Germans as a *Panzerschiff* or armored ship, and by others as a "pocket battleship." Exploiting the discrepancy between the Versailles treaty, which bound them, and the Washington treaty, which bound everyone else (eleven-inch guns against eight-inch), the firepower of this class was superior to the cruisers of other navies. The *Deutschland* had six eleven-inch guns. Moreover, their new diesel propulsion gave them a speed of twenty-eight knots, which was faster than most other battleships, offering a mobility designed to allow the *Deutschland*-class ships the prospect of engaging with a target of opportunity, but to escape if the situation proved hazardous. Laid down in 1928, the *Deutschland* was commissioned two months after Hitler came to power in 1933. Over the following years, the specifications of the class improved. The development of this class was an instance of German strategic culture. The stress was on using technology to permit a major change in the international system. Surface warships and submarines provided key instances, whereas, in Britain, technological developments, such as changes in battleships, were pursued according to a more defensive strategic culture.

Britain sought to use naval issues as a means to stabilize Nazi Germany's position in the international system. The Anglo-German Naval Treaty of June 18, 1935, was a British attempt to provide an acceptable response to German demands for rearmament. Under this, the Germans were to have a quota equivalent to that of France or Italy under the 1922 Washington treaty, with a surface fleet up to 35 percent the size of that of Britain, and a submarine fleet of 45 percent, later 100 percent. Hitler, however (characteristically), ignored these restrictions in his naval buildup.

Like Stalin, Hitler was fascinated by battleships, ordering the 42,000-ton *Bismarck* and *Tirpitz* (not the 35,000-ton figure provided to the British),[29] and he then planned another six battleships. This focus was to the detriment of smaller, frequently more effective warships. Indeed, Germany only had fifty-seven submarines, of which twenty-three were seagoing, and all of obsolete design, at the outset of the Second World War. The navy's commander, Admiral (Grand Admiral from 1939) Erich Raeder, was also committed to battleships, arguing that antisubmarine warfare by Germany's rivals, notably the development of ASDIC (sonar), would counter the German submarines. Raeder planned a balanced fleet. The buildup of the navy was designed for conflict with France and the Soviet Union, and, after relations deteriorated, Britain from 1938; but, in accordance with an assurance to Raeder from

Hitler, it did not assume war until the mid-1940s. By then a far larger German navy was planned, one able to compete with the Royal Navy in battleships and also to contain carriers. Plan Z, approved by Hitler in January 1939, proposed to have 13 battleships, 3 battle cruisers, 2 carriers, and 194 submarines by 1944, and 13, 12, 8, and 249 eventually.[30]

Karl Dönitz, a First World War submarine commander who was appointed chief of the submarine force in 1935, sought to create a capability, aimed at the British, that was more effective than that seen in the First World War. He developed wolf-pack tactics in which a group of submarines, coordinated by radio, was to attack convoys on the surface at night, overwhelming the escorts. Dönitz planned an autonomous role for submarines focused on attacks on trade and wanted as many submarines as possible, whereas Raeder saw submarines both in this role and as performing those of fleet support and screening, for which he sought a small number of large, fast, and long-range submarines. However, the Germans did not carry out adequate cost-benefit analyses of naval power, whether surface or submarine, and did not properly think through their strategic weaknesses in this respect. Dönitz, a fanatical Nazi, appointed those of similar views rather than more proficient alternatives.

BRITAIN

Although equality of size had been conceded to the Americans at the Washington Conference, the Royal Navy remained the world leader in prestige and reputation, while also having an unrivaled chain of fleet bases, which, in effect, were battleship bases. Nevertheless, as a consequence, in part of the economic difficulties, social policy, and disarmament priorities of the Labour government of 1929–31, British naval expenditure had been cut seriously in 1929–34. Cuts in fuel and ammunition hit training. By 1936, there was a degree of obsolescence in parts of the navy.

However, the British then responded to the buildup of German strength.[31] British naval planning correctly anticipated that war with Germany would result in a determined air-sea offensive against the British maritime system, with a naval dimension proving central to a lengthy struggle of industrial attrition. From 1936, the Admiralty was free to pursue ambitious policies. Many carriers, battleships, cruisers, and destroyers were laid down. The first two of the *King George V*–class battleships, which had ten fourteen-inch guns, the *King George V* and *Prince of Wales*, were laid down on January 1, 1937, the first date permitted under the naval limitation regime. In 1937, the first *Dido*-class cruiser, a dedicated antiaircraft cruiser, was laid down, offering a new cruiser design, although it suffered from inadequate armor and firepower. The fleet air arm was greatly expanded. Radar sets were installed in British (and German) warships from 1938.

There were, nevertheless, weaknesses in 1939, notably a lack of mines and torpedoes, as well as a failure to appreciate that convoy protection was best ensured by escorts and not by hunting groups at sea.[32] There was only limited equipment for, and experience in, amphibious operations.[33] British naval bases, for example, Alexandria, Malta, and Hong Kong, lacked adequate defenses against air attack. The Royal Navy was in a much better state than it had been in 1931, but it faced major commitments around the world. For example, Admiral Sir Geoffrey Layton noted in his war diary that, in early 1942, in the face of Japanese advance, "the problem of retaining control of the coastal waters of Burma was quite beyond our powers in the absence of either air superiority or fast patrol craft with good AA [antiaircraft] armament so numerous that we could afford substantial losses."[34]

FRANCE

France and the Soviet Union could be classified as having medium-sized navies relative to the world's leading fleets. Each played supportive roles to the army and operated within defined waters. France's focus was on its army and fortifications. Nevertheless, there was also concern with naval strength and over protecting links with the colonies. Having competed with Italy in the 1920s and responded in particular to the Italian-Spanish alignment, including with preparations for coastal defense, the French were challenged by the laying down of the *Deutschland* in 1928. This led the French to lay down new battleships in the early 1930s, the *Dunkerque* and the *Strasbourg*. The name of the latter, an affirmation of France's commitment to the territory regained from Germany in 1918–19, was, as so often, an indication of the symbolism of naval power. In turn, these ships were followed by the 35,000-ton *Richelieu*-class battleships, such that in 1939 France had the fourth-largest navy in the world. In response to the German naval buildup, the French navy refocused its attention from the Italians and the Mediterranean and established a battleship-based Force de Raid at Brest, France's major Atlantic base. This force was designed to protect French trade routes. From 1938, in part as a result of Italian naval expansion, an ambitious three-year shipbuilding program was pursued. As a result, the French fleet had effective ships that were to be important to the power politics of 1940–42, notably in the Mediterranean. France also had the *Béarn*, a dreadnought converted into a carrier, and laid down a second carrier, the *Joffre*, in 1938. However, more effective land-based aircraft in the 1930s threatened carrier operations in European waters, especially from the Italians in the Mediterranean, and this lessened French interest in carriers. France's strategic situation posed major problems. It was dependent on transporting troops from North Africa and also drew most of its oil supplies from the Caribbean, thus being dependent on Britain for control of the North Atlantic sea-lanes.

THE SOVIET UNION

The development of the Soviet navy underlined a point that is more generally true, the role of political considerations in strategy and doctrine, rather than the centrality of weapons capabilities. There was significant continuity from the Tsarist period into the Soviet era that began in 1917, not least continuity in terms of doctrine and leadership. The emphasis, under what was later called the "Old School," was for a defensive posture in both the Gulf of Finland (to the west of St. Petersburg/Petrograd/Leningrad) and the Black Sea. Submarines and torpedo boats were to weaken attacking fleets—most probably the Royal Navy, which had played a major role against the communists in the Russian Civil War—prior to a battle in which the Soviet navy would use its full power in a decisive engagement. This strategy accorded with the state and size of the Soviet navy, which did not benefit from new construction in this period and was very much overshadowed by the army.[35] Unlike in the 1890s and 1900s, there was no strong naval concern with the Far East.

The drive for something more than a defensive strategy, combined with ideological, political, and generational contrasts, led the "Young School" (based on the French Jeune École of the 1880s) to challenge these ideas from the late 1920s. The Young School were communists and also sought a strategy that conformed more to the attacking plans of the Red Army. Arguing for the role of submarines and aircraft, the Young School questioned the idea of command of the sea as well as belief in a superior navy, with the attendant stress on powerful surface ships which the Soviet Union did not have. In contrast to the Old School, and the more general international adherence to Mahanian ideas, the Young School claimed that a decisive battle was a mistaken goal and, instead, that the submarines, torpedo boats, and aircraft of the Soviet navy could nullify the impact of the opposing fleet, so as to enable the Soviet navy to assist the army.

This approach pleased Josef Stalin, the Soviet dictator, who, in 1930, purged the navy and promoted the Young School. As a result, in the early and mid-1930s, their ideas shaped doctrine, training, and procurement. The Second Five-Year Plan (1933–37) pressed for submarine production, while the annual maneuvers of the Baltic Fleet, the main Soviet fleet, focused on amphibious attacks in support of the army. Such attacks could be launched against the Baltic republics, Poland, and Germany. Stalin considered a new naval response following Hitler's rise to power in 1933.

In 1937–38, there was another transformation in leadership and a related reversal in doctrine. Imposing total control, Stalin purged the navy in 1937 at the same time as he brutally purged the army and air force.[36] The Young School was destroyed, while political commissars were given the task of jointly signing orders with commanding officers. This purge reinforced and reflected Stalin's commitment to big ships. Stalin had come to focus on them, in part in response to the commitment to such ships by Germany, Japan, and Britain. In particular the development of the German fleet challenged the Soviet position in the Baltic and was interpreted in that light by Stalin. Stalin saw the battleship as the foundation of naval power. He was thwarted in his plans to order the world's largest battleship from an American yard, but, by 1939, there were three 59,000-ton battleships under construction in the Soviet Union, as well as two 35,000-ton battle cruisers, which were designed to be faster.[37]

None, however, was ever completed. In part, there was no time to create a fleet of big ships before the Soviet Union was plunged into war with Germany in 1941, but the purges were also a factor. They affected the shipyards and greatly exacerbated the problems created by Stalin's unrealistic assumptions. This situation led to a serious decline in quality. Much of the armor of Soviet warships was inadequate, and complex gun mountings posed a particular problem. Due to such problems, much of the investment of resources was wasted.

In addition, Stalin's purges, which were continued into the 1940s by fresh killings, helped to ensure a serious shortage of experienced officers and noncommissioned officers, as the latter were promoted to fill gaps. Training regimes were seriously affected, the frequency of accidents rose, and there was less emphasis on annual maneuvers. As a result, the effectiveness of the navy at combined-arms operations, notably coordination with aircraft, declined.

The range of naval capabilities that had to be established and maintained at an effective pitch was indicated by the significant deficiencies in the Soviet naval forces at the close of the 1930s. These included the absence of dive-bombers, advanced torpedoes or sonar equipment, and the fact that only one ship was equipped with radar. Although there was a large submarine force, it was poorly trained, and, in the event, its wartime effectiveness proved limited. In part, this was because submarine aiming and firing techniques were poor, while Soviet doctrine emphasized remaining in fixed positions and waiting for enemy vessels to appear. The situation underlined the more general difficulty of developing capability and the requirement for more than resources.

The Soviet Union could have been exposed to naval warfare, but the clashes with Japan in 1938 and 1939 were both limited and restricted to land combat in border regions. Thereafter, after an agreement in 1941, the two powers did not fight until 1945. Moreover, alliance with Germany in 1939–41 ensured that the Soviet Union was not exposed to attack by the larger German navy until such time as the latter was largely engaged by Britain, which had not gone to war with the Soviet Union when it was allied with Germany.

NAVAL CONFLICT IN THE 1930s

Warships played a role in many of the conflicts of the 1930s, in both civil conflicts and those between states. The Japanese employed only a portion of their navy in the attack on China from 1937, and notably few of their aircraft carriers, but had fleets on the Yangzi and off China. Naval gunfire played a major role in stemming the initial Chinese attack on the Japanese positions in Shanghai. Subsequently, the Japanese made much use of amphibious attacks. An amphibious landing that threatened to cut off the Chinese forces there was crucial to the capture of Shanghai in 1937, the ports of Xiamen (Amoy) and Guangzhou (Canton) fell in 1938, and the island of Hainan in 1939, while Japanese warships sailed up the Yangzi and bombarded Chinese positions.

Largely as a result of initiatives by the army, Japan made the most progress among the powers, both in developing types of landing craft and in building a reasonable number of ships. Their *Dai-Hatsu* had a ramp in its bows and was to become the key type of landing craft. The navy built up its amphibious capability by developing units that specialized as *rikusentai* (landing parties). They were given infantry training and, by the late 1930s, the navy had permanent landing units that were based ashore and armed with heavy weaponry including artillery. This represented a type of jointness in that amphibious capability was enhanced, but also the extent to which the army and navy fought separate wars.

With far more expertise than other powers, the Japanese developed an amphibious doctrine and practice. They put the emphasis on attacking at night or at dawn and on landing at several points simultaneously and then concentrating on land. Their experience was to stand them in good stead in 1941–42, especially in their rapid conquest of Malaya, the Philippines, and the Dutch East Indies. This was a key bridge between the interwar period and the Second World War.

CONCLUSION

Doctrine, planning, and procurement all reflected tasking. For example, the need for deep-sea British air capability in any war with Germany appeared lessened by the vulnerability of German naval power to land-based air attacks. The lesson of the First World War appeared to be that the Germans could be bottled up in the North Sea. In 1940, however, they were to transform the situation by seizing Norway and France. More generally, the British, American, Japanese, and German navies failed to realize fully the contribution that air power could make to the conduct of war at sea.

The navies built up in the 1930s were to be those that fought the Second World War. At the same time, the war involved the destruction of all or most of these navies. In doing so, the war increased the need to construct new warships. This proved a test for strategic prioritization, resource allocation, and industrial capacity. In particular, America was to build a bigger and better fleet (as well as merchant fleet), and one that incorporated both prewar lessons and those of the early section of the war.[38]

Chapter Seven

The Interwar Years in the Air

The potential for air warfare also appeared immense. The Allied generalissimo on the Western Front in 1918, Marshal Ferdinand Foch, wrote two years later,

> Today, the ability for aviation to carry increasing weight furnishes a new method for abundantly spreading poison gases with the aid of stronger and stronger bombs, and to reach armies, the centres of population in the rear, or to render regions uninhabitable.

That his remarks appeared in a book, *The Riddle of the Rhine: Chemical Strategy in Peace and War* by Victor Lefebure, a wartime gas officer, indicated the extent to which military issues were presented to the public.[1]

In the aftermath of the First World War, air power was considered, at least in part, as a way to learn lessons from the conflict, particularly in waging another major war of this type more successfully. At the same time, national variations played a key role, as each state interpreted air power in a different fashion, notably in light of its specific wartime track record, its institutional organization of air power, and its particular requirements of the moment.[2] Looking to the future, and fearing another major conflict, commentators sought to make sense of the experience of the First World War and to present that experience as a war-winning formula. They were influenced by a belief in the fragile nature of morale, both military and civilian, and the problems and opportunities this would provide for future conflict.

Chapter 7
PLANNING THE FUTURE

This belief provided the basis for the theory of the knockout blow that could be delivered only by air and that would lead to rapid victory. As a result, it was argued, for example by Giulio Douhet of Italy, that air power would be able to overcome the stasis and high casualties of intractable conflict at the front, which was how the First World War was recalled. The major impact on public morale caused by German raids on London in the "Gotha Summer" of 1917 appeared a menacing augury of what could happen as a result of the deployment of more powerful aircraft. There was an idea, prevalent in Britain in particular, but not only there, that aerial bombardment in any future war was going to be more devastating in practice and decisive in consequence, more strategic in impact, than, in fact, it proved to be until supplemented by atomic bombs in 1945. The Air Ministry in Britain was more moderate in its claims about the potential of air power than independent air enthusiasts,[3] but the latter made the running in public and had an impact. Concerns were ventilated in the press, in novels, and in supposedly analytical works, such as Basil Liddel Hart's *Paris, or the Future of War* (1925). There were particular air scares in Britain in 1922 and 1935. In John Galsworthy's novel *A Modern Comedy* (1929), Sir Lawrence Mont wondered how the English nation could exist with "all its ships and docks in danger of destruction by aeroplanes." The prospect of civilian losses in millions arising from attacks with gas and high explosives on major cities was frequently held out.[4] Widespread international concerns about air attacks indeed encouraged the idea of "qualitative disarmament": banning aggressive weapons such as aircraft, submarines, and gas. Much speculation and some diplomatic and legal activity were devoted to the subject in the 1920s and early 1930s.

In practice, there was no genuine danger in the 1920s, as Britain's principal opponent then, the Soviet Union, a threat to the Middle East, Persia (Iran), Afghanistan, and India, was in no position to mount an attack on Britain. In the mid-1920s, British bombers with a full load of fuel were designed to take off from Kent, bomb Paris, and return home. However, despite serious concerns, France, as was widely appreciated, was not the principal threat to Britain.[5] Moreover, the French were using virtually the same aircraft as in the First World War into the early 1930s, while the Soviet Union did not develop a modern long-range bomber capability until the 1930s. Even then, aimed against Japan, this capability was not suited for any attack on more distant Britain. However, concern about the Soviet Union was a reason for the British deployment of air power in Iraq, formerly part of the Ottoman (Turkish) Empire, where Britain had become the imperial power. There was therefore a strategic purpose alongside the counter-insurrectionary use of aircraft based in Iraq that tends to attract attention.

There was a large-scale use of air power by imperial states against insurrections in the 1920s, for example with Britain in Somaliland and Iraq, with France in Syria, and with the United States in Nicaragua, which was a state where American power was dominant. This use of air power, in an asymmetrical fashion and in small-scale conflicts, looked ahead to more modern patterns, notably with the role of air power in COIN (counterinsurgency) operations. Anticipating arguments made by American advocates of air power in the 1990s and 2000s, air attack was seen as a rapid response combining firepower and mobility; it did not entail the deployment of large forces and was therefore presented both as cost efficient and as appropriate for the much-reduced military establishments arising from postwar demobilization and expenditure slashing. Western public opinion readily accepted the use of air power for imperial and quasi-imperial control. Indeed, air power appeared to marry what was presented as inherently desirable Western control to modernization, which was very much a theme of imperial ideology and governance in this period. The logic of air power was empire, while empire's logic was enhanced by air power. The interwar use of air power, however, had already suggested that it might be less effective in conflict and deterrence in the future than its protagonists claimed. The use of air power for imperial or quasi-imperial control and power projection did not look toward its employment during the Second World War. Nevertheless, this use was highly significant, both in terms of the 1920s and with reference to the situation since 1945.

Moreover, the capacity for mobility and tactical advantage offered by air power ensured that it was increasingly seen as a major strategic asset and one that offered a new approach to geopolitics.[6] Indeed, geopolitical considerations encouraged the development of air services to link imperial possessions, notably by the British to Hong Kong, Australia, and South Africa, a process encouraged by Trenchard. These services enjoyed government support and were regarded as an important counterpart to the development of an imperial military air presence. This prefigured the American case after the Second World War. Imperial Airways, a company founded with government support in 1924, pioneered new routes and services. The Britain-to-Australia airmail service began in 1932. Weekly flights began to Cape Town (1932), Brisbane (1934), and Hong Kong (1936). Air travel was very important to the development of individual British colonies and offered a way to administer a global empire.[7] French airlines crossed the Sahara en route to French West Africa. The Soviet Union also saw the possibilities of air travel for political integration in the 1920s.

DEBATING AIR POWER

In his *Il Dominio dell'Aria* (*The Command of the Air*) of 1921, which was soon translated into English, Giulio Douhet claimed that aircraft would become the most successful offensive weapon and that there was no viable defense against them. Stressing the value of wrecking enemy morale and thus creating a demand for peace, a theme he had advanced from 1915, Douhet advocated the use of gas and incendiary bombs against leading population centers. Thus, bombing would accelerate the potential earlier seen to rest in blockade. He came to argue that air defense was impossible.[8] In *The Reformation of War* (1923), J. F. C. Fuller argued that the bombing of cities would be important in future war.

More generally, the political struggle entailed in creating separate air forces caused air-power advocates to make grandiose claims for the ability of strategic bombing alone to win wars. This political-institutional context encouraged an emphasis on long-range strategic bombing at the expense of tactical air power, and in procurement accordingly. Brigadier General Billy Mitchell, the top American combat air commander and assistant chief of the American air service in 1919–25, told the presidential inquiry on air power in 1925 that the United States could use Alaska to launch effective air attacks on Japan, which was already seen as a major and growing threat to American interests in the Pacific and the Far East.[9]

However, critics claimed that these commentators exaggerated the capability of air power. Thus, in Italy, Amedeo Mecozzi, a former pilot, criticized Douhet, not least by emphasizing the capacity of antiaircraft guns. Indeed, the transition from First World War biplanes, used mostly for reconnaissance, with very light bombing, to more modern aircraft had to take place before major strategic bombing could develop.[10] This transition only really happened in the 1930s, although, from the First World War, water-cooled aircraft engines were replaced by the lighter and more reliable air-cooled engine. Similarly, it was important that aircraft came to be made of Dural or Duraluminium (and a number of other variations, all of them trade names), an alloy of aluminum which was stronger and more durable than aluminum alone. Dural was first used in the Junkers J1 monoplane of the First World War. In the 1920s, foreign offices and war ministries anticipated the development of strategic bombing, but it had only just begun to happen in reality.

In part, this was a matter of capability in the shape of the implementation of technological possibilities, but tasking was also a key issue. In the late 1920s, Russia seemed contained, Japan was not pursuing expansionism, and Germany was engaging actively and positively with the Western international community, notably in the Locarno treaty negotiations. The United States, the world's leading industrial economy, and Britain, with its most far-flung empire, each followed policies of maintaining the status quo and cutting expenditure. The interacting paranoia and justified fear of the 1930s that began with the Japanese invasion of Manchuria in 1931 was to drive forward investment in symmetrical warfare capability and cutting-edge technology. Despite anxieties, this was not the case in the 1920s.

Alliance building and political display were not the sole issues in air power. This decade saw a shift toward a clearer focus on the potential of air power in symmetrical conflict: war between similarly armed states. In particular, there was an emphasis on the apparent war-winning capacity of the bomber in such conflict, conflict that increasingly appeared a prospect. Centering on bombing, there was a growing social and governmental concern about what air power would bring in a new large-scale war, and the apparent possibility of social breakdown as a result, notably in cities, underlined military concern about the need to be able to respond adequately. Deterrence through inflicting serious damage by means of bombing appeared the best response.[11]

More generally, there was a greater sophistication of aircraft in the 1930s, notably the development both of improved fighters and of more effective bombers. These were seen as bringing the potential of air power to fruition, rather as the development and diffusion of new aircraft and munitions toward, and after, the close of the Cold War were, in turn, to be presented. In each case, there was the press of the modern. In the 1920s and 1930s, major advances in aircraft technology, including improved engines and fuels, and variable-pitch propellers, provided opportunities to enhance military aircraft. They came to the fore with metal aircraft in the 1930s. The massive adoption then of German aerodynamic developments was important to a general process of change. Major advances included all-metal monocoque construction, which gave aircraft strength and lightness: loads were borne by the skin as well as by the framework. Retractable (as opposed to fixed) landing gear were significant. The significance of wind resistance led to an emphasis on these undercarriages. The range of advances in the 1930s was impressive and included flaps, variable-pitch propellers, stressed skin construction, night-flying instrumentation, radio-equipped cockpits, and high-octane fuels.[12] Wooden-based biplanes were replaced by all-metal cantilever-wing monoplanes with high-performance engines capable of far greater speeds.

As ever, the placing of priorities in discussing both developments and usage is problematic, not least because these priorities can suggest a clarity to patterns of causation that, in fact, was absent. In the 1930s, there was no abrupt demonstration of a new capability, comparable to the use of atomic bombs in 1945, and therefore no obvious new start. Instead, it was the combination of a more menacing international environment, the extent of change in aircraft technology, and the greater apparent capability of air power that provided the key element in encouraging a renewed and more urgent move from ideas about air warfare to detailed planning and procurement for it. In this, and notably in the contextualization of these ideas, an ideology of modernity, movement, and power, focused on what aircraft could apparently do, played a highly significant role. The ideology was so potent that Colonel Emilio Canevari, the most prominent Italian commentator, covering the successful Italian invasion of Albania in 1939, reported the attack of nonexistent motorized formations in cooperation with the air force.[13] The Italians, however, did transport part of the invasion force by air.

Alongside the implication so far of a clear developmental pattern in air power, it is important to note the impact of particular economic and political contingencies. The economic and fiscal crisis known as the Slump and the Depression led, across the world, to a marked fall in government expenditure in the early 1930s, and this fall greatly affected aircraft procurement. So did the pressure to order aircraft from national companies, a pressure that influenced the response to technological possibilities.[14] Similarly, domestic political demands pressed on military spending, as did the perception of the international situation.

INNOVATION IN THE 1930s

Airships still appeared to have potential, and there was interest in their cooperation with aircraft. In 1926, two Gloster Grebes, British fighters, were launched from an airship as an experiment. However, accidents, notably the crash of the British R 101 on October 5, 1930, and of the *Hindenburg* on May 6, 1937, ended British and, later, German interest in airships. More centrally, they were too vulnerable to airplanes, lacked the maneuverability of the latter, and required the availability of helium.

The British Ministerial Committee on Disarmament Dealing with Air Defence noted in July 1934 that "development in aircraft design and construction is rapid in these days," with consequent risks of obsolescence.[15] The range and armament of fighters, and the range, payload, and armament of bombers all increased.[16] The Handley Page Heyford, which served from 1933 to 1937, was the last of the RAF heavy-bomber biplanes. In contrast, introduced from 1937, the American B-17 Flying Fortress was the first effective, all-metal, four-engined monoplane bomber. It was seen as a key expression of American power. Thirty-five were deployed by 1941 at Clark Field, America's leading air base in the Philippines. This bomber was not simply a weapon, but it also embodied the dreams of glory of American air-power enthusiasts.[17] Both Boeing, with the XB-15, and Douglas, with the XBLR-2, renumbered as the Douglas B-19, had developed gigantic long-range bombers, the latter named the "Hemisphere Defender," as part of the air force's XBLR (experimental bomber, long range) program; but success came with the B-17. It was conceived of as extending America's coastal perimeter by attacking an incoming fleet well out to sea, in short as a form of mobile coastal fortress, and not as a strategic bomber; but it was pressed into that role in the Second World War.

Both Britain and the United States procured bombers that were designed or redesigned as strategic bombers at a considerable rate in the 1920s and 1930s, whereas Germany and the Soviet Union preferred tactical attack aircraft. Britain and the United States were also more concerned than Germany and the Soviet Union with defensive fighters or pursuit aircraft and procured many more aircraft designs. Quite a few of the British and American designs did not work out, but excellent fighter-bombers (the Typhoon and P-47) resulted, able to fight their way home in hostile airspace in a way that attack aircraft such as the German Stuka and the Soviet Il-2 could not: against fighter opposition, the last two were very vulnerable.

As an example of the pace of change, the Blenheim I, a fast monoplane bomber, first entered British service in 1937, in which year the Miles Magister entered the RAF as its first monoplane trainer. The British Air Ministry issued specifications for a four-engined bomber in July 1936, followed in September by specifications for a twin-engined all-metal medium/heavy bomber. A series of new aircraft entered British service in the late 1930s. These included the Wellington, the first model of which flew in December 1937. Until the arrival of the four-engined bombers, the Wellington played a key role for Britain's Bomber Command. Its airframe offered more resistance to opposing fire than earlier models, as it was made with a geodetic metal "basket weave" or lattice construction. The Hampden I, which entered service in September 1938, was a twin-engined monoplane, although it was an example of an aircraft being designed without an understanding of how the bomber would fare against fast single-seat fighters. It proved ineffectual and poorly protected and also carried a small payload. The Hampden was last used on bombing operations in September 1942, with almost half of those built having been lost. Another example of an ill-conceived multirole aircraft, the Fairey Battle, proved ineffective in France in May 1940 and was withdrawn that year after heavy losses. Also in 1938, the Short Sunderland I was the first RAF monoplane flying boat, replacing earlier biplanes. It was to be important to Coastal Command in the Second World War.

Innovations spread. Although they largely turned out 1932-design aircraft until 1938, the French development of power-operated turrets for bombers strengthened hopes that they would be able to beat off fighter attacks. The Boulton Paul Overstrand, a biplane that began service in 1935, was the first RAF bomber with a power-operated turret.

Improvements ensured the obsolescence of existing planes, such as the He-51 and He-60 biplanes flown by the Germans in 1935, and the need for fresh investment. In Britain, the Hawker Fury I, a biplane fighter with a maximum speed of over two hundred miles per hour that entered service in

1931, was made obsolete by the introduction of the Hawker Hurricane I in 1937. Alexander de Seversky, a veteran of the Russian naval air arm who had become a protégé of Mitchell, inventing an air refueling system and a gyroscopically stabilized bombsight, developed, in the early 1930s, an all-metal aircraft with enclosed cockpit, the BT-8, which was a forerunner of a sort of the P-36, a fast, long-range, all-metal monoplane fighter, which was to be the basis of the P-40 Warhawk. Whereas, prior to the mid-1930s, despite the bold claims made by the protagonists of air power, its effectiveness was very limited, in contrast, from then to the early 1950s, aero-technology was relatively inexpensive, but potent enough to produce an age of mass industrial air power, provided investment was forthcoming.

The Soviet TB-3 was the first mass-produced, four-engined, all-metal bomber. Andrei Tupolev also produced the SB light bomber, which, with Nikolai Polikarpov's I-16 fighter, entered service in large numbers in 1934, being among the most advanced aircraft in the world. However, as a pointed instance of the rapid development of new types and capabilities, these aircraft quickly became obsolete. Seventy-six I-16s were among the 409 Soviet aircraft sent to Spain by June 1937, but they were no match for the early variants of the German Me-109 (B and C) they encountered there. In response, the Soviets pushed forward the production of new aircraft, notably the I-22, I-26, and MIG-1 fighters, and the TB-7, DB-3, and Pe-2 bombers, but the fighters were not a match for their German counterparts. In the Soviet Union, as in the West, there was a big aviation cult, lauding pilots such as Chkalov who flew over the North Pole in 1937.

The increasing size of aircraft also led to interest in the use of airborne troops. A number of powers, especially the Soviet Union and Germany, trained parachute and glider-borne units. From the late 1920s, the Italians made a major effort to develop such a capacity, and they had several parachute battalions, but they never did a parachute drop in action and were used as elite infantry in the Second World War. The Soviets dropped an entire corps by parachute in 1935, but probably largely for impressing foreign observers rather than as a practical military operation. The Germans began training parachutists in 1936. There were also developments in air transport: in 1935, the Soviets moved a fourteen-thousand-strong rifle division by air from near Moscow to the Far East, a demonstration of the ability to respond to Japan, while, in 1937–38, they practiced dropping artillery and tanks by parachute.

GERMANY

Under the 1919 Versailles peace settlement, German air power had been banned, although, following the Treaty of Rapallo of 1922, the Germans and

Soviets had secretly combined on aircraft design and manufacture, and on pilot training. After Hitler came to power in 1933, the Germans prioritized a new air force, the Luftwaffe, which was officially created in 1935, and they spent accordingly: about 40 percent of the defense budget in 1933–36. Air power appeared to offer both a counter to German fears of vulnerability and a way to embrace a modern technology that promised victory. There was a fascination with air power that, in part, reflected its apparent potency, but also the desire to take revenge on Versailles and intimidate other powers. Air power was important to Nazi propaganda, as with Hitler's use of flight in his tours around Germany and Goebbels's film treatment of these tours.[18] Air power also shaped German industrial and economic planning. Already in March 1935, Hitler had told British ministers that his air force was the same size as that of Britain, which was a false claim, but one that indicated his drive. That October, the ambitious existing Luftwaffe program for expansion was stepped up.

However, the German air industry did not develop sufficiently to support an air force for a major conflict, while investment in infrastructure was inadequate. The Spanish Civil War also suggested to the Germans that large long-range bombers were not crucial: they used dive-bombers there instead and developed dive-bombing tactics. Seeking a strategic bombing force that could act as a deterrent, Germany had initially made progress in the development of the long-range bomber—the "Ural bomber"—but had only made prototypes. The capability to produce the engines necessary for the planned heavy bombers was lacking, while there were also shortages of key materials necessary for their production and use. Nevertheless, the Germans expected to have the four-engined He-177 (the first prototype flew in 1939) in production by 1940–41.[19] In the event, nicknamed the Flaming Coffin, the He-177 never came into full-scale production, did not become operational until late 1942, and was weakened by overcomplicated engineering. The failure of the He-177 led to the attempt to develop the four-engined bomber He-277, for which a few prototypes were built. However, it was not ready for testing until July 1944. There was also the Me-264 four-engined bomber, which also only saw prototypes being developed. The Ju-390 had six engines, but only two prototypes were built in 1943. This had been developed from the four-engined Ju-290, which saw service as a maritime bomber (sixty-five built), like the FW-200 Condor, developed from a passenger airliner, of which 276 were built. Both had multiple roles, including transport and reconnaissance, as well as being used as bombers and for maritime patrol. The lack of a large long-range bomber force adversely affected German capability during the Second World War.

More generally, there were problems with the availability of aviation fuel for the Luftwaffe and with its training program. There was also a preference for numbers of aircraft as opposed to a balanced expenditure that would include investment in infrastructure, for example logistical provision, especially spares. This preference owed much to the poor quality of leadership. Hermann Göring, a veteran of the air struggle during the First World War, became Germany's minister of aviation in 1933 and commander in chief of the Luftwaffe in March 1935. He was not interested in the less glamorous side of air power, and this helped to weaken the Luftwaffe in the subsequent war. Göring also was less than careful in his appointments. Ernst Udet, whom he made technical director, was overly interested in dive-bombing. Göring's concern for aircraft numbers helped to lead, in 1937, to the postponement of the four-engined bomber program, as it was easier to produce large numbers of twin-engined bombers.

Furthermore, German military doctrine and planning resulted in a lack of support for strategic bombing. Hitler's preference for quick wars, as well as the structure of the German economy, led to the search for a force structure that would make a success of combined operations focusing on a rapid attack, a system later described as blitzkrieg. Strategic bombing was seen, instead, as a long-term solution in warfare. Blitzkrieg entailed no obvious requirement for a strategic bombing force.[20] Big "terror" bombing raids, as were practiced by the Germans, first in the Spanish Civil War and then, with greater force, in the Second World War, did not amount to sustained strategic bombing of the type of the Allied air offensives on Germany and Japan.

Instead, the Germans became increasingly committed to air-land integration, with the Luftwaffe designed to provide both close air support and interdiction in support of the land forces in order to enhance the possibility of obtaining a decisive victory, and thus a successful strategic outcome. The Luftwaffe was to be employed as mobile artillery in order to provide tactical support at the front of the army's advance. Wolfram von Richthofen, chief of staff and then commander of the Condor Legion dispatched by Hitler to help the Nationalists in the Spanish Civil War, pressed for close coordination in both space and time and used the war to test and improve relevant techniques. The practice and philosophy of jointness was very important to blitzkrieg.[21] Alongside later criticism of the German failure to develop strategic bombing can come the contrary argument that the proper role of aircraft in ground support was grasped.[22] As in this case, differing modern perceptions affect the reading of the past.

Aircraft suitable for ground support were developed. First flown in 1935, the Ju-87, or Stuka, was more accurate than most aircraft, remaining stable in near-vertical dives. This capability increased the Stuka's accuracy against moving tanks, although, in practice, fighting the Poles, the Luftwaffe in 1939 proved far more effective against static units. Organizationally, the Luftwaffe benefited from avoiding the RAF's division into functional commands, namely the separation into a Bomber Command and Fighter Command in 1936, and instead created *Luftflotten* (air fleets). Each of these contained

SPANISH CIVIL WAR, 1936–39

It is not clear that the conflicts that did occur were adequately analyzed. For example, the bombing of cities, such as Madrid (1936), Guernica (1937), Barcelona (1938), and Cartagena (1936 and 1939), by German and Italian aircraft sent to help Franco's Nationalists in the Spanish Civil War did not actually play a central role in the result of that conflict. These cities were civilian targets, as were Pamplona, Burgos, Valladolid, and Palma, which were among the cities bombed by the Republicans, but more was generally at stake. Thus, Cartagena and Barcelona were major ports, and the attacks on them were aspects of the attempt to prevent the Republicans from importing arms. The German bombing of Guernica possibly affected the resistance mounted when the Nationalists moved on to take the more important city of Bilbao in June.

Bombing captured the imagination of many, sowing fears that the bombing of civilian targets would be decisive in a future war. This affected British thinking at the time of the Munich Crisis in 1938 when confrontation with Germany led to the possibility of war. Indeed, British intelligence exaggerated German air capability. The resulting concentration on air defense was crucial for Britain in 1940, but some of the preparations for air attack led to a misapplication of scarce resources. Yet, the impact of the bombing on the war in Spain, although deadly, was exaggerated. Moreover, as the Second World War was to show, Douhet and others had exaggerated the potential of bombing (as well as underestimating the size of the bomber forces required) and underplayed the value of tactical air support.

The Italians sent 759 aircraft to Spain, the Germans about 700. In turn, the French sent the Republicans aircraft in the early stages of the war, while the Soviets provided them with 623 aircraft. The Nationalists had a clear superiority. Aside from bombing cities, there were also attacks on Republican ground positions. At the Battle of the Ebro (July–November 1938), the last major Republican offensive of the war, the Republicans suffered from being seriously outnumbered in the air and lacked sufficient antiaircraft guns. As a result, their forces proved vulnerable to Italian and German aircraft, not least to their air attacks on the pontoon bridges built across the river. The Germans found that their use of aircraft required effective ground-air liaison and developed it—tactics that were to be important in the early stages of the Second World War.

The war also saw developments in other fields such as air reconnaissance[24] and air transport. In August 1936, German Ju-52s and Italian Savoia-

Marchettis, escorted by He-51s and Italian CR 32s, transported Spanish Nationalist troops from Morocco to southern Spain, providing mobility and speed and overcoming the Republican naval blockade. Separately, in 1935–36, Italy successfully and regularly air-supplied its columns advancing into Ethiopia from Eritrea, dropping all the needed supplies of food, water, and ammunition by parachute.

THE ISSUES OF BOMBING

In many countries, the ability to learn lessons from the Spanish Civil War about the value of air support for ground forces was limited by interservice rivalry and the nature of air force culture, notably the emphasis on strategic bombing, and a degree of reluctance in some quarters to adopt an analytical approach. This was especially so in Britain where there was a pronounced fear of air attack [25] and a major commitment to strategic bombing as a way to break the will of an opposing population. [26] In November 1932, Stanley Baldwin, the previous (and next) prime minister, had told the House of Commons that "the only defence is in offence, which means that you will have to kill more women and children more quickly than the enemy."[27] Bombing was seen as a way to avoid a military commitment to Continental Europe and the political entanglements to which this would give rise.

There was resistance to the possibilities of ground-support operations on the part of those committed to strategic bombing. Indeed, RAF bomber crews were not trained to operate over the battlefield. Moreover, the need to provide fighter escorts for bombers was not appreciated by the British or the Americans until they suffered heavy casualties in the Second World War.[28] The B-17 Flying Fortress was heavily armed in the belief that they could defend themselves, but the reality proved otherwise.

The focus on bombers offers a parallel to attitudes toward the inappropriate reliance on tanks alone in mobile warfare, rather than on mixed-armed forces and combined operations. A key point is the value of jointness. The history of air power suggests that much of its capability rested on being part of an integrated fighting system with an operational doctrine that relied on cooperation between arms and sought to implement realizable military political goals. The same was true of the impact of mechanization on land warfare. However, cooperation between ground-attack aircraft and tanks was limited because of ethos and practicality. Such cooperation required effective radio communications, as well as training and commitment. Moreover, both ground-attack aircraft and tanks tend to work independently if they aim to play to their strengths.

In France, there were significant disagreements on the strategic question, disagreements that adversely affected procurement, leading, in particular, to a failed attempt at multirole aircraft. There was an attempt to develop a strategic role for aviation, notably, in 1937, a drive to create an ambitious bomber force; but the powerful army staff was not prepared to support this pressure from the Air Ministry. Instead, tactical requirements prevailed. Rather than stressing strategic bombing, the French put the emphasis on reconnaissance aircraft and tactical roles. Despite some good aircraft, France lacked an air force to match that of Germany.[29]

The Soviet Union lacked an independent air force, but, despite weaknesses in relevant industrial capability, had, thanks to the buildup of its aircraft industry from the late 1920s, the largest number of aircraft in the 1930s, as well as a strong aviation culture.[30] Furthermore, although the air force was largely an extension of the army, the Soviets had an interest in strategic bombing. The long-range TB-3 was intended as a deterrent against Japan. By the end of 1935, the Soviets had a 170-strong bomber force able to reach Japan and to threaten Japanese communications with Manchuria. However, the murderous purges of the military launched by Stalin in 1937 hit the air force hard. Yakov Alksnis, the longtime head of the air force, was arrested in 1937 and executed in 1938. An extremely competent and effective manager, his loss had a severe impact on operational effectiveness. The purges were linked to a move of the Soviet air force from strategic capability to army support, although the Soviet Union had the largest number of multi-engined bombers until 1941.

Separate from this, it is unclear how effective Soviet air power might have been. A successful buildup required more than developing capability and the allocation of resources. As the Soviets did not have to fight, except for the limited case of Spain, until after the purges, there are two difficult counterfactuals: how would the Soviets have fought in 1936, or how would they have fought in 1941 if they had not suffered the purges? They were producing aircraft in quantities that were extraordinarily impressive, and when not overwhelmed by surprise, as happened at the hands of the Germans in 1941, quantity has a quality all its own. Their designs, however, were not world beaters, and Soviet aircraft manufacturing did not have a reputation for innovation or creativity. Moreover, as with their tanks, although the Soviets had an enormous force, only a fraction were of the most modern types: in 1941, 1,300 of the 8,300 in the five Soviet western military districts plus long-range aviation. Yet many of the German aircraft in 1941 were also older types, although that does not necessarily mean bad: the Me-109 held up very well, but not the He-111.

Both the British and the French devoted attention to fighter defense in the late 1930s, seeing this defense as a necessary response to German power, although the British Air Staff possessed scant evidence to support its belief that the Germans had plans for an air assault on Britain.[31] Concern about the Luftwaffe encouraged threat-based expenditure, as well as research and development, which ensured that the French air force won a bigger share than the navy or, still more, army in the increased defense expenditure in 1934–35. The weakness of the French air force was a contributory factor to vulnerability at the time of the Munich Crisis in 1938, but, by 1939, France had 1,735 frontline aircraft. These included the Farman 222, which could carry an unprecedented load of bombs (over four tons), as well as the Dewoitine D520, a well-armed fighter with an exceptional range. However, French fighters were not as fast as the Me-109. Although, after Japan, the most active user of aircraft in combat in 1935–38, Italy suffered from the mismatch between Mussolini's bold plans for a large and modern air force and the limitations of Italian industry, notably in engine manufacturing. Political favoritism in procurement was a major problem. Italy had the third-largest force of multiengined bombers in the world, but the emphasis in the war plan drawn up in late 1939 was on acting in conformity with the operations of the land army, not on strategic air warfare and concentrated bombing.[32]

In March 1934, Baldwin told the House of Commons that Britain would not accept inferiority in air power, and, that July, a large majority voted in the Commons for a substantial increase in the size of the air force by 1939. While the War Office may have started rearmament efforts relatively late, the Air Ministry's rearmament program was already in play before 1936.[33] This was underscored by large British investments in the aircraft industry.[34] The British developed two effective monoplane fighters, the Hawker Hurricane and the Supermarine Spitfire. In November 1934, the government issued specifications for a fighter with improved speed, rate of climb, and ceiling, and with eight, not four, machine guns. The prototype Hawker Hurricane was ordered in February 1935 and made its first flight that November. In December 1937, the Hawker Hurricane I entered service, beginning a new period of eight-machine-gun monoplane fighters that could fly faster than three hundred miles per hour. In March 1936, the prototype Supermarine Spitfire made its first maiden flight, and the aircraft entered service in June 1938.

In 1937, in a speech titled "Fighter Command in Home Defence," Sir Hugh Dowding told the RAF Staff College that the major threat to British security would be an attempt to gain air superiority in which the destruction of airfields would play a key role. This would leave the way clear for attacks on industry, London, and the ports. A system of defense was therefore the key necessity.[35] Alongside early-warning radar, Spitfires and Hurricanes were to help rescue Britain in 1940 from the consequences of devoting too much attention to bombing. At that stage, Britain had a numerical superiority over Germany in single-engined fighters. In 1938, the Anschluss (German annexation of Austria) and the Munich Crisis further encouraged an emphasis on air power in British rearmament and, by September 1939, the RAF had replaced most of its biplanes. In response to the German threat, new RAF air bases were built in East Anglia, Lincolnshire, and Yorkshire, and squadrons were moved there from elsewhere in Britain.

Ethics were not to the fore when strategy was discussed by the military. There was some uneasiness about the ethical nature and practical consequences of strategic bombing against civilian targets. However, this uneasiness tended not to be expressed by air-power advocates who focused on the idea of a "magic bullet" promising victory without casualties at the front. In an undated memorandum that contains a reference to a document of March 1930, Field Marshal Sir George Milne, the chief of the British Imperial General Staff, brought ethical issues about air power into organizational questions. He wrote of

> the highly organised and unscrupulous propaganda of the Air Staff . . . the separation of the Air Staff from the General Staff which prevents problems of defence being considered as a whole, and with a proper sense of proportion as to their cost . . . the Air Staff have found it necessary, in order to find support for their separate and independent existence . . . to devise a special form of so-called air strategy. . . . There appears to be two principles or catch words upon which it is based . . . attack against the nerve centers of an enemy nation . . . and the moral effect of the air arm. In dealing with problems of war on a large scale against civilized countries the former term is usually employed. The objectives of such strategy are the centres of production—nominally of munitions, which, be it marked, is a term of very wide significance. In effect this new form of strategy takes the form of attack against civilian workers, including their women and children. The hitherto accepted objectives of land and sea warfare have been the armed forces of the enemy, and whether or no we as a nation are justified morally in adopting a military policy which is so totally at variance with the accepted dictates of humanity, there is no doubt that we should be the first to suffer if the next war were to be waged on such principles.[36]

Public responses to the threat of bombing varied. H. G. Wells's rewrite of *The War in the Air*, *The Shape of Things to Come*, was made into a film in which a world war begins in 1940 with terrifying air attacks on Everytown. Alongside alarm, there were calls for more bombers in order to provide deterrence through the threat of reprisals. There were also internationalist responses aimed at limiting the threat, not least, from the 1920s, the idea of an international air force under the control of the League of Nations. The Geneva Disarmament Conference in 1932–34, held under the auspices of the League, discussed such a force as well as the abolition of bombing and accepted a Czech proposal to prohibit the bombing of civilians. However, although these ideas continued to circulate, they lacked diplomatic traction.[37]

Instead, in the late 1930s, improvements in fighters began to undermine the doctrine of the paramountcy of the bomber. Thanks to the Rolls-Royce Merlin engines developed from 1932 and part of the major British advance in aero-engines,[38] British fighters by 1939 could intercept the fastest German bombers. The introduction of radar on the eve of the war was another blow to the bombers.

LOOKING TOWARD THE FUTURE

Far-reaching innovation was seen in many fields. In 1930, Frank Whittle, a British air force officer, patented the principles that led to the first gas turbine jet engine, which he first ran under control in 1937. However, Whittle's engine did not generate much interest in the Air Ministry or the RAF: they saw it as something of an expensive novelty but with no practical use. He and two other former RAF officers formed Power Jets to develop the engine without government funding. His patent had lapsed in 1935 because he was unable to afford the renewal fee, thereby allowing the patent to come into the public domain. The technology rapidly spread, with the Germans producing the first operational jet engine. The Germans, in 1939, and the Italians, in 1940, beat the British jet into the air. In 1938, Germany began the development of radio-guided gliding bombs, a precision weapon, which became operational in 1943.[39]

With its capacity for long-distance detection of movement, radar developed rapidly. In 1904, Christian Hülsmeyer had first used radio waves to detect the presence of distant metallic objects. Thirty years later, the French CSF company took out a patent for detecting obstacles by ultrashort wavelengths, while, in 1935, Robert Watson-Watt published *The Detection of Aircraft by Radio Methods*, and the Air Ministry decided to develop radar. The following year, the American Naval Research Laboratory demonstrated pulse radar successfully. In the Battle of Britain in 1940, the British benefited greatly from an integrated air-defense system founded on a chain of radar early-warning stations built from 1936 to 1939, but still incomplete at the time of the Munich Crisis. These stations, which could spot aircraft one hundred miles off the south coast of England, were linked to centralized control rooms where data were analyzed and then fed through into instructions for fighters. No other state had that capability at that stage.[40]

PLANNING AIR WARFARE

More immediately, there was the development in the 1930s of a potential for air warfare that brought to fruition in planning, procurement, and training some of the ideas of the 1920s. At the same time, contemporaries found it difficult to make a realistic assessment of the potential. The conflicts of the 1920s and 1930s offered only limited guidance because they did not happen between equally balanced air forces, while rapid technological developments soon outdated experience. International crises increasingly involved much thought about the aerial aspect.

Thus, there was an air dimension in the Anglo-Italian crisis of 1935–36 over Ethiopia, although, in the event, there were no hostilities between the two powers. Nevertheless, the crisis showed the greater extent to which air power played a role in planning for war. Reflecting the dependence of strategic bombing on nearby airfields, the RAF proposed to bomb the industrial centers of northern Italy, notably Turin and Milan, from bases in southern France, assuming that France joined Britain. The British indeed were to do so in June 1940. There was also a need to protect British colonies from neighboring Italian colonies, and, in turn, to permit attacks on the latter. As a result, the RAF moved aircraft to Egypt (against Libya), British Somaliland (against Italian Somaliland and Eritrea), and Malta (against both Libya and Italy). Fear of the vulnerability of Malta to Italian air attack led to the decision to withdraw the British Mediterranean Fleet to Alexandria in Egypt. The significance of air attack was such that the priority thereafter was to improve Malta's defenses against that rather than against bombardment or invasion. Matching their confidence that antiaircraft guns could protect warships, the British navy was certain that such improvement could be made, whereas senior airmen were convinced that sustained and heavy air attack could prevent safe use of the island and its naval base. This argument has been linked to the RAF's struggle for funds for Bomber Command.[41]

At the time of the Munich Crisis in 1938, British intelligence and the Air Staff exaggerated German military capabilities. In practice, despite bold claims by Göring about its potential, the Luftwaffe lacked the training and range to launch a bomber offensive against Britain.[42] Similarly, the RAF had only a few modern fighters, while its bombers were weak and its radar network incomplete, and France was seriously short of new aircraft. Alongside widespread anxiety, indeed fear, there was a measure of skepticism about air power, with a degree of confidence in Britain's ability to withstand bombing; but, notably on the part of the "Bomber Barons" of the RAF, there was no lack of belief in the potential of bombing as such.[43] Technological capability was misread, and strategic consequences were misleadingly assumed on the basis of doctrine and of growing tactical effectiveness.

THE FAR EAST

In 1933, the British Chiefs of Staff Subcommittee referred to the Japanese air force as having "air equipment and a standard of training fast approaching that of the major European powers" and presented it as "the predominant factor in the air situation of the Far East."[44] Indeed, in 1937, Japan deployed about 1,500 planes at a time when only 87 of China's 300 aircraft were able to fly. Air power was used from the outset of the Sino-Japanese War, with the University of Tianjin, a prominent source of opposition to Japan, bombed in July 1937. As was to happen during the Cold War, there was intervention in this regional struggle from other powers. The Soviet Union delivered 297 aircraft to China in the winter of 1937–38. Flown by Soviet pilots, they began operating in defense of the capital, Nanjing. However, Japanese air power was greater, and this advantage proved important to Japanese advances in China. Nanjing fell in December 1937. Moreover, there was heavy Japanese bombing of positions at a distance from the battlefield. In 1939, once winter clouds and fog had ended, Chongqing, Chiang's next capital, proved the prime target. With no effective antiaircraft support or air cover, the city was badly damaged by a series of long-distance heavy raids by twin-engined bombers, raids which continued into 1940. This attempt to break Chinese morale, however, had no strategic or political effect. Lessons were not drawn from the war. Japanese air superiority could not dictate developments on the ground. Not only did bombing fail to end Chinese resistance, but, also, the tactical impact of air power was limited. For example, the Battle of Shanghai in 1937 showed that Chinese losses made during the day could be regained at night when Japanese air power was less effective, a frequent experience.

CONCLUSION

The hope of air power in the 1930s was not matched by the capability and technology necessary to deliver it. Some of the hopes, expectations, and fears were fantastical when it came to aircraft and what they might be capable of achieving. Aircraft, both individually and collectively, were more potent than when the First World War had ended in 1918. At the same time, demonstrating the improved capability that both wars were to bring, the air forces available in 1939 lacked the strength that was to be deployed by 1945. Moreover, there were serious deficiencies in the range of aircraft available when war broke out in Europe in September 1939. None of the air forces had an effective purpose-built transport aircraft and, with the exception of Japan, they did not have fast enough reconnaissance aircraft. In addition, there were significant problems in the design of some aircraft that had originally appeared promising.[45] It was far from clear what the next war would bring.

Part III

The Second World War

Chapter Eight

Causes

Debate over the causes of the Second World War links contemporaries with those born after 1945. For contemporaries, such debate was largely political, an attempt to mobilize support, both domestic and international, behind the war effort. For subsequent generations, in contrast, debate links the issue of war guilt, on the part of wartime opponents and others, to more general questions of justification and vindication and to related political dynamics. Thus, some blamed the Second World War on the Versailles peace settlement of 1919, which, in practice, was far less harsh than that of 1945.

Consideration of the war certainly demonstrates that the combatants, and their alignments, were far from inevitable and were definitely not seen in that light by contemporaries, whatever the views of contemporaries. Therefore, the discussion of how these alignments arose is a key issue in the politics involved in the war and its recollection.

Debate is particularly difficult because of the number of different conflicts involved. This number is reflected in the widely contrasting titles, dates, and periodization offered for the war, as well as the dangers of assuming clear causal links between these conflicts and of arguing that there was a common struggle. Whereas the British, French, Germans, and Poles date the war from 1939, the Chinese turn to 1937, when they were attacked by Japan, and there are Spanish commentators who see the Spanish Civil War (1936–39) as the first stage of the Second World War. Italy entered the war in 1940, but the Soviet Union and, later, the United States did not enter the war until 1941, while the Soviets did not declare war on Japan until the closing days of the war in August 1945.

JAPAN ATTACKS CHINA

The interactions of ideological inheritance, strategic culture, institutional drives, and political and economic circumstances were certainly shown in Japanese bellicosity in the 1930s. Hit in the global economic Depression by a collapse in vital exports and mass unemployment, Japan became more bellicose, breathing, as the British diplomat Sir Victor Wellesley put it in 1932, "an atmosphere of gun-grease."[1] In part, this bellicosity arose because sections of the military followed autonomous policies ignoring civilian restraint, and in part because the military as a whole supported a militarism that challenged civil society and affected government policies, leading to what was called "government by assassination."

In 1930–31, Japanese soldiers, angered by what they felt was the failure of the government to defend national interests, planned a coup and the creation of a military government. Instead, they found it easier to seize control of the Chinese province of Manchuria, where they were concerned that Japan's existing leased rights were under threat and where China had been put under pressure by the Soviet Union in 1929 in a brief conflict won by the latter.[2] On September 18, 1931, Japanese soldiers of the Kwantung Army blew up part of the South Manchurian railway near the city of Shenyang (Mukden). This incident, one of what were to be a number of staged episodes during the 1930s, served as the basis for taking over the city and for an advance north and west from the Kwantung Leased Area, the established Japanese sphere of influence in southern Manchuria. The Japanese separately increased pressure on China by attacking the Chinese section of Shanghai in 1932.

A lack of support by the government in Tokyo led to the murder of the prime minister, and civilian views became less important in the government. Party politics continued but became less significant, and in 1936 the killing of senior officers in an attempted coup by younger officers served to quiet voices of reason and caution among both civilians and military. Moreover, the impact of the Depression, and the popular relief at what was seen as decisive action in Manchuria, hit Japanese internationalism. The League of Nations criticized Japanese policy, which led to Japan leaving the League in 1933 in its most public abandonment of internationalism but suffering no effective consequences.[3]

Success in Manchuria did not suffice to guarantee Japan's security and satisfy its ambition. In 1933, the neighboring province of Jehol (modern Hebei) was invaded. A conviction that large-scale war between Japan and the United States or the Soviet Union was inevitable had developed in Japanese military circles. This conviction led to pressure for the strengthening of the military, the state, and Japanese society, with the latter two seen in an authoritarian and militaristic perspective. China was regarded as a base for the vital resources necessary for preparing for this conflict. Manchuria was developed by the Japanese army as a military and industrial base that was outside civilian control, and was used as a basis for expansionism in China and for greater strength in the event of possible war with the Soviet Union, which was greatly feared in Japanese army circles. A military-industrial complex in Manchuria, drawing on its coal and iron, served as the basis for a system of planning that sought to include the enhancement of industrial capacity.[4]

There was also concern in Japan about military developments in China, notably the expansion of Guomindang power and pretensions, especially the buildup of the German-trained divisions of the Central Army. In practice, Jiang Jieshi, the Chinese dictator, proved willing to accommodate Japanese demands in the early 1930s, in large part because he wished to strengthen and unify China, not least by destroying the rival communists. Jiang saw this as a necessary step before confronting Japan, but it turned out to be an intractable goal.

Some in the Japanese army were inclined to despise their opponents and to exaggerate both the significance of their "honor" and the ability of their will and military machine to overcome the problems posed by operating in China, an attitude that prefigured that of the Germans toward the Soviet Union in 1941. These problems were not simply a matter of the ratio between Chinese space and Japanese resources, important as that was, but also of the determination and fighting quality of the Chinese. These Japanese were misleadingly confident that China would fall rapidly, although others in the army knew better.

In the event, conquest turned out to be an impossible goal: the limited warfare and amphibious-based expeditions of Britain and France in the nineteenth century were a more realistic response to the nature of the military balance between China and the outside powers, and to the problems of campaigning in China. A similar point could be made about the Anglo-French Crimean War attacks in 1854–56, as opposed to attempts to conquer Russia itself in 1812, 1919–20, and 1941–42.

Overlapping with and helping to mold discussion in Japan of policy in "rational terms," there was both a social basis for militarism in what remained mainly an agrarian society[5] and a sense of imperial mission, a sense that for some, but far from all, was linked to a radical Shintō ultranationalism, in particular, a belief in a divine providential purpose of Japanese superiority and expansion and a god-given purpose and right to rule.[6] The attitudes and impact of Zen Buddhism have been a source of controversy, but one school of scholarship emphasizes their bellicosity.[7]

After the violence of 1930–36, it is difficult to speak of moderates in the Japanese government. In particular, compromise was regarded as failure. However, the Sino-Japanese War that broke out in 1937 was unintended. An unplanned incident between Chinese and Japanese troops near the Marco Polo Bridge outside Beijing on July 7–8 during Japanese night exercises occurred at a time when many Japanese leaders favored preparing for war with the Soviet Union and communism. Ideally, it was felt that, as part of this preparation, China should be persuaded to accept its fate as a junior partner of Japan. Jiang's uncooperativeness prompted Tokyo to try to give him a short, sharp lesson.

Jiang's attitudes reflected a recent strengthening of Chinese nationalism, as well as the marked improvement in the German-trained Chinese army. He moved divisions north across the Yellow River into the part of China that in 1933 had been left demilitarized by the Chinese Central Army, and thus toward the Japanese. While not wanting large-scale conflict, the Japanese government felt the nation's honor had been challenged by the Marco Polo Bridge incident and sent fresh forces to the region. Refusing to yield to Japanese pressures to withdraw, Jiang proved willing to fight and eager to assert Chinese sovereignty, and large-scale conflict broke out in late July as the Japanese moved large numbers of troops into the area. This conflict, which was not declared as a war, and is still referred to in Japan as the "China Incident," continued until 1945 and proved the vital context for Japan's later wars.

THE SPANISH CIVIL WAR

Like international conflicts, civil wars could also show the role of the unexpected, and certainly not turn out as had been anticipated. In Spain, a group of right-wing senior army officers, who called themselves the Nationalists, sought to seize power in 1936 from the elected government in a rebellion that began in Spanish Morocco on July 17 and on the Spanish mainland on July 18–19. They were opposed to the modernizing policies of the left-leaning Republican government. They were also concerned about the possibility of a communist seizure of power via the Frente Popular (Popular Front) after the narrow left-wing electoral victory by the Popular Front in the hard-fought elections of February 16, 1936. The army's attitude toward politics explains the rebellion by much of it. Claiming that the government had lost control (which in practice was due to right-wing as well as left-wing violence), they were really against the Republic itself, and, with it, democracy and freedoms.

The Nationalists, however, achieved only partial success in 1936. They conspicuously did not take control of Madrid, let alone Barcelona. Moreover, the failure of any attempt by the rebels to negotiate a settlement or to defeat their opponents led to a bitter civil war which only ended on March 28, 1939, when the Nationalists seized Madrid.

The Spanish Civil War is commonly seen as a harbinger of the Second World War, and the ideological division between the two sides is stressed. Indeed, the Nationalists, who very much emphasized religious themes, depicted the Republicans as the servants of the Antichrist. Caution, however, is required in seeing the civil war as a harbinger of the world war, while the ideological dimension was scarcely new. Moreover, the practice of military violence was well established as a political tool in nineteenth-century Spain, as in Portugal and Latin America. In part, this was a baleful consequence of the destabilization wrought by the Napoleonic conquest in 1808. Against this background, the twentieth century offered a new iteration of old themes and methods, a situation also seen in the Balkans. Extreme violence was employed, as by the Nationalists in Seville in 1936, irrespective of the degree of violence required to achieve specific goals. Repression employing disproportionate force continued after particular places had been captured and, indeed, after the war. It was part of the war.

The Spanish Civil War also throws light on another aspect of the causes of war, namely the conflicts that did not break out. The combatants received extensive international support, but no formal war broke out as a consequence. This reflected a willingness and ability to fight by indirect means, a situation that raises questions about the definition of war. Italy and Germany sent substantial assistance to the aid of the Nationalists. Their forces that were involved were at war, but not formally waging it. So also, albeit to a lesser extent, with Soviet aid to the Republicans.

APPEASEMENT

The most controversial aspect of the causes of the Second World War relates to the argument that the British and French were partly responsible because of a failure to adopt a robust stance toward Germany, Japan, and Italy, the Axis powers, prewar. Voiced at the time, this argument was much employed by the Left during the Cold War that followed the war in order to hold the West partly responsible for Axis policies and, indeed, the Second World War. This approach shifted the blame to Britain and France, a rather curious response to the goals and actions of the Axis, and one, to a degree, matched by the argument that much of the responsibility lay with the global economic situation, with the sustained global economic Depression of the 1930s encouraging international competition and political support for extremists.

In practice, while systemic factors, such as the Depression, were highly significant in destabilizing the international system, Hitler's responsibility for the war was the key element.[8] You do not blame a lake when a murderer drowns someone in that lake. Like other politicians, Hitler operated in response to a background that he did not create, as well as to international circumstances and developments. Nevertheless, Hitler also played a major role in shaping them and in encouraging a mistrust that made compromise appear a danger. He built on German anger with the territorial losses and reparations of the 1919 peace settlement (each of which Germany had imposed on France in 1871), but gave it a new inflection. The racial ideology and policy of the destruction of Jewry and the subjugation of the Slavs presented an agenda in which racial conflict was linked to an exultation of violence. Ironically, as it sought to direct popular anger, the Nazi Press Office was subsequently to attribute the outbreak of the war to the Jews, which was a classic instance of blaming the innocent, and one that mixed cynicism with paranoia. Subsequently, the Jews were again to be (inaccurately) blamed in Germany for Allied bombing, while (on a different basis but again blame shifting) the Allies were to be criticized for not bombing the extermination camps.

The focus on appeasement continues to play a significant role in current controversies. Aside from this specific argument about the origins of the Second World War, there was also the use of appeasement outside this context, but as part of a call for action. A lack of deterrent firmness is presented as responsible either for war or for weakening the recourse for war. Thus, in 2003 and 2013, opponents of international intervention in Iraq and Syria, respectively, were described with reference to the appeasers, as part of a long process of castigating caution.[9]

The scholarly dimension is very different, for appeasement emerges as in large part a matter of circumstances, notably, in the case of Britain, the interaction between far-flung imperial commitments and strategy. There is a corresponding emphasis on the extent to which British policy options were constrained by the need to protect threatened interests across the world, which prefigures the current American situation. The uncertainties affecting British policy related in part to this situation, but also to the extent to which it was by no means clear, prior to 1938, whether Nazi Germany or the Soviet Union was more of a threat. Furthermore, wherever the emphasis was placed, it was unclear how best to confront these threats. The eventual outcome was far from predictable. In the case of the Soviet Union and Britain, there was hostility short of war in 1939 to 1941, then alliance against Germany until 1945, and then sustained opposition between the Soviet Union and Britain in the Cold War.

Some British and French commentators saw Germany as a potential ally against the Soviet Union. Moreover, Hitler initially hoped that Britain would join Germany in a war against communism. However, in Britain, Hitler's determination to overturn the (much criticized and misrepresented[10]) 1919 Versailles peace settlement and to make Germany a great power anew was correctly regarded as a growing challenge to Britain's interests, which included the international order. In the winter of 1933–34, Nazi Germany was identified as Britain's ultimate potential enemy by the Defence Requirements Subcommittee.

Germany was seen as a graver security threat than Japanese expansionism, even though the latter was already apparent in Manchuria. Britain's unwillingness to accept Japanese expansionism in China helped lead the Japanese navy in 1934 to begin preparing for war with Britain. This was a major step, as the Japanese navy had developed on the pattern of the British navy, and with its assistance. Moreover, Britain and Japan had been allies from 1902, notably in the First World War.

Focusing on Germany, Neville Chamberlain, Britain's prime minister from 1937 to 1940, made a major effort to maintain peace, and thus both domestic and international stability and the chance for economic recovery. However, Chamberlain was weakened by his inability to accept other points of view or to learn from experience, as well as by his self-righteous and continuing optimism about his own assumptions. Indeed, these flaws helped vitiate the conduct of British policy, ensuring that, however sensible in practice and/or as a short-term expedient, appeasement was developed in a fashion that did not secure its purposes. Moreover, the implementation of appeasement helped to ensure that it was open to subsequent criticism, as did its presentation.

Chamberlain knew that Britain and France were not well prepared for conflict and feared that war would lead to the collapse of the British Empire and would also wreck the domestic policies of the Conservative-dominated National Government. He was indeed correct on both counts, although he was at error in seeing these outcomes as worse than the victory of Nazism. It was assumed that, if conflict broke out with Germany, Japan might be encouraged to attack Britain's Asian empire, which was rightly seen as militarily and politically vulnerable. This vulnerability encouraged the British government to search for compromise with the rising nationalism in India, not least with the Government of India Act of 1935, and with Ireland over naval bases in 1938. A sense of vulnerability also led to the attempt to create a viable policy of naval support, based on the new base at Singapore, for the British Empire in the Far East: Hong Kong, Malaya, Singapore, north Borneo, British interests in China, and links to the Dominions of Australia and New Zealand. However, the deployment of modern aircraft was focused on the challenge from Germany.

An American alliance did not seem a welcome solution, as the Americans were regarded as posing a challenge to British imperial interests and, correctly, as unlikely to provide consistent support. This is a viewpoint that can be difficult to recover from the perspective of subsequent wartime and postwar cooperation with America, both of which were crucial to Britain. Nevertheless, it is a viewpoint that helps to explain the importance of this later cooperation. British responses to Japanese, Italian, and German expansionism were affected by the nature of Anglo-American relations, and, in turn, the legacy of these years helped underline later calls for a strong alliance. Isolationist

America, which, under President Franklin Delano Roosevelt, president from 1933 to 1945, had had cooler relations with Britain than those in 1929–31, and which passed Neutrality Acts from 1935, was regarded in the 1930s as self-interested. This, indeed, was a key element in American isolationism. Moreover, the two powers had failed in 1932 to cooperate against Japan during the crisis caused by its invasion of Manchuria.

Isolationist sentiment was strong in the United States, notably so from the reaction against President Woodrow Wilson and his role in the establishment of the League of Nations at the close of the First World War. In 1937, this sentiment led Congress to consider the Ludlow Resolution, which would have required a national referendum before Congress could declare war, unless in response to a direct attack. That October, Roosevelt's "Quarantine" speech, proposing that aggressor states be placed in quarantine, enjoyed only limited support in the United States in the face of strongly expressed isolationist views.

Such views were linked to a conviction that the United States should focus only on the defense of the New World—hemispheric defense—and, despite signs of a broader engagement, such as the 1938 trade agreement with Britain, this approach helped make the United States a problematic potential ally. The situation was exacerbated by limited expenditure on the American military in the 1930s. This was not as bad as was later suggested. The oft-repeated comment that the army was smaller than that of Portugal is unhelpful, as Portugal had extensive colonies in Africa to protect (and from which to raise troops), notably Angola and Mozambique, while, conversely, the United States spent much more on the navy and air force. Portugal, for example, had no equivalent to the B-17 Flying Fortresses.

Nevertheless, the United States had a smaller military than it could afford as the world's leading economy and a major center of population. Crucially, the United States in the 1930s did not press forward with rearmament as its wartime opponents did, as well as the Soviet Union, France, and, indeed, Britain. In 1938, the American army could only put six divisions in the field, although it had one of the world's leading navies, an improving air force, and valuable developments in military planning. The United States could do far more than solely defend its own immediate geographical region. Moreover, during the subsequent world war, the United States benefited from not having earlier devoted massive expenditure to weapons that were out of date by 1940, notably with aircraft.

As far as Britain was concerned, appeasement was designed to avoid both war and unwelcome alliances, and it responded to the domestic mood. Britain in the 1930s certainly lacked a powerful alliance system comparable to that in the First World War. Although hopes for the French defense of Western Europe in the event of German attack were high, France had been greatly weakened by that war. It increased its military from 1935 in response to the

German remilitarization of the Rhineland. However, despite increasing expenditure in response to the German remilitarization of the Rhineland, France did not spend as much as a Germany solely focused on a military buildup; had a much smaller population than Germany as a pool from which to recruit, as well as a smaller industrial base; had major colonial commitments; and also put strenuous and successful efforts into developing its navy, a navy in large part designed to act against Italy's new navy.[11]

Confidence in the ability of an Anglo-French alliance to prevent German expansionism in Eastern Europe was limited. Indeed, prior to the outbreak of a new war, Germany did well in the bitter competition for influence and markets in Eastern Europe that was a key aspect of the rivalry between the great powers. In seeking cooperation there, the Germans benefited from the "democratic deficit" across much of the region as well as from bitter opposition there to the Soviet Union. This opposition reflected the significance of ideological factors.

Moreover, unlike in 1914, neither Russia nor Japan was an ally of Britain. This absence was a key contrast, even more so because both powers allied with Germany: the Soviet Union in 1939–41 and Japan throughout. However, despite significant economic assistance to Germany, the Soviet Union did not fight Britain directly, while Japan only did so from December 1941.

In the 1930s, the British government was unhappy about Britain's allies and potential allies. It was also unwilling to explore the path of confronting Hitler by making him uncertain about the prospects of collective action against Germany. Instead, as another instance of choice, the British government preferred to negotiate directly with the expansionist powers, especially Germany. This political response was matched by Chamberlain's focus on deterrence through a stronger navy and air force, each of which was to be based on Britain, rather than through an army that was to be sent to the Continent and therefore have to cooperate with France. This buildup was an aspect of what was an unprecedented international arms race, unprecedented as it involved air power over both land and sea, as well as more conventional weaponry.[12]

The policy of negotiating with the Axis focused on Germany, because it was felt that Japan would be cautious if peace was maintained with Hitler. This was a reasonable view, at least insofar as Britain and its determination to preserve its colonies was concerned. It was certainly not so for China, which was the repeated victim of Japanese aggression. Italy, from 1922 under the bombastic and opportunistic Fascist dictator Benito Mussolini, was not treated as a serious threat and instead was regarded by Britain as a possible ally. Mussolini indeed long saw Hitler as a rival in Austria and the Balkans, although he shared both Hitler's contempt for the democracies and his opposition to Britain and France. These views became more important for him in the late 1930s with Hitler's growing power.

On the part of Britain, a sense that compromise with Germany was possible, combined with a lack of interest in the areas threatened by German expansionism, encouraged a conciliatory search for a settlement, as did the extent to which few were in other than denial about what Nazism was really like, both in domestic and international policy. In some respects, there was an attempt to reintegrate Germany into the international order that was comparable to the treatment of France after the Napoleonic Wars ended in 1815. Thus, Hitler was treated as another Napoleon III, the expansionist and bellicose ruler of France (first as president and then as emperor) from 1848 to 1870. Yet such an approach was mistaken. The search for compromise with Hitler was not only unsuccessful, other than as a series of concessions, but it also arguably discouraged potential allies against Germany.

The attempt to contain the Axis powers short of war failed in the 1930s. Nevertheless, however mishandled, the realpolitik involved in appeasement was not inherently dishonorable. In the 1930s, a wish to seek a negotiated alternative to war was widespread across the political spectrum. Far from being a characteristic of reprehensible Conservatives, not to say fellow-traveling neo-Fascists, the desire to avoid war and opposition to rearmament were also notably strong among liberal opinion and on the Left, and particularly so prior to the Czech Crisis of 1938. This point needs to be underlined because of the subsequent politicized placing of appeasement, notably in Britain, as a means to criticize the Right.

As "Britain" as a term stands for the British Empire, it is also necessary to discuss the response of the Dominions: Australia, New Zealand, Canada, and South Africa. Their attitude and effort had been crucial to the British effort in the First World War, not only in the fighting but also in the economic sphere. Yet, from the Chanak Crisis in Turkey in 1922 on, it had been clear that the Dominions were not only pursuing independent tracks but also ones that could be at variance with those of Britain. In the Chanak Crisis, there was an unwillingness, apart from on the part of New Zealand and Newfoundland, to support Britain when Turkish nationalist forces under Kemal Atatürk approached the Dardanelles and Bosporus, which were garrisoned by British forces in accordance with the postwar settlement imposed on Turkey in 1920. In the event, with most of the cabinet unwilling to risk war, Britain backed down, and the settlement was revised in 1923. There was no comparable difficulty in political relations with the Dominions until the late 1930s. However, at the time of appeasement, and notably the Czech Crisis of 1938, the unwillingness of the Dominions, especially Canada, to risk war was a critical element.

WAR IN EUROPE

Appeasement was a key issue in 1931–38 in the response to Japanese, German, and Italian expansionism. The situation changed on March 15, 1939, when Germany seized Bohemia and Moravia: the modern Czech Republic, bar the Sudetenland, which had been gained already by Germany as a result of the Munich Agreement. This loss had gravely weakened the Czechs' capacity to defend themselves. By this seizure, Hitler destroyed the Munich Agreement, the most public product of appeasement, exposing its total failure.

Despite his ambition to ally with the British Empire, Hitler broke the Munich Agreement, as he would have broken other understandings that restricted him. Indeed, this helped to give the Second World War a moral legitimacy as a "good" war, with Hitler bearing the responsibility for the failure of appeasement, which, indeed, conformed to the Augustinian ideal of seeking to avoid conflict. Hitler was interested, not in a revision of the Versailles settlement in pursuit of a German nationalist agenda, but in a fundamental recasting of Europe. This goal meant war, for only in defeat could an agreement that left the Continent at Hitler's disposal be seriously contemplated by Britain and France.

Moreover, Hitler was not a ruler with whom lasting compromise was possible, as Joseph Stalin discovered in 1941 when Hitler attacked his Soviet ally, which had provided Germany with crucial geopolitical and economic assistance in 1939–41. Hitler's quest for a very extensive, eventually continent-sized empire reflected his belief in the inherent competitiveness of international relations, his system of aggressive racist geopolitics, and his conviction that widely flung territorial power was necessary for effective competition with the other empires or imperial-strength powers: Britain, the Soviet Union, and the United States. This was a conviction shared with Japan. Hitler wanted both to overthrow Versailles and, with increased urgency from late 1937, to redraw Eastern Europe. Ideally, this was to be on the lines, at least, of the victorious Treaty of Brest-Litovsk negotiated with the Soviet Union in 1918 at a stage when Germany had done very well on the Eastern Front. In contrast, Hitler had less interest in Western Europe until 1940 and never showed the same commitment to territorial or ethnic changes there.

Violence was at the heart of Nazism. Violence was allegedly for the "good" of the "Race" and was seen as the ultimate purpose of life. This was a creed born of a violence that required the destruction of alleged enemies. All were linked: domestic dissidence, the Nazis claimed, had to be prevented in order to strengthen Germany for war. There were simple elements in the causes and nature of governmental support for Fascist or Fascist-style bellicosity and expansionism in Italy and Japan. Alternative measures of power were to yield, as with Hitler overriding budgeting considerations and the limits they might play on rearmament.

In March 1939, it became clear that Hitler's ambitions were not restricted to bringing all Germans under one state, which was the case argued when his acquisition of Austria (1938) and the Sudetenland (1938) were discussed, and, indeed, also the German excuse when, on March 23, 1939, an ultimatum demanding the immediate return of the Memel (Klaipeda) region was successfully issued to Lithuania.

In response to the destruction of the Munich Agreement, an attempt was made to create a collective-security alliance system that would contain Hitler through deterrence. This system, however, was weakened by the failure to include the Soviet Union. Again, as with appeasement, and in some respects linked to it, there has been considerable debate over responsibility for this failure. Critics have argued that Anglo-French anticommunism bore much of the responsibility. While that attitude was indeed significant, far more was involved. Again, this issue throws light on the more general problems of deterrence, particularly clashes of interest and views in conception and implementation.

First, Stalin was hostile to the West, indeed as hostile as he was to Germany, whereas Hitler was hostile to both the Soviet Union and the West, but more so to the former. Stalin's hostility to the West owed much to an opposition to democracy and bourgeois liberalism, as well as a legacy of hostility from the Russian Civil War when Britain and France had intervened against the communists. The Soviet Union was far more hostile to liberal democracies than Romanov Russia, Britain's ally in the First World War, had been. There was also an incompatibility in long-term goals between Britain and the Soviet Union, one that provided a key context for diplomatic relations, as had been the case with the failure of Anglo-Soviet naval armaments diplomacy in 1935–39.[13] As the world's leading imperial power, Britain opposed Soviet views and moves in a number of areas, notably China and Afghanistan.

A shared interest in revisionism and opposition to democracy, together with a shared mentality of the "leader," provided a basis for agreement between Hitler and Stalin. Moreover, with their ideologies and practices of terror and violence, each appeared equals between whom an agreement could be made, indeed as a natural partner of the other. Indeed, in the summer of 1938, Stalin had planned to approach Hitler for an alliance; in August 1939 they were to ally, notably against Poland; and, in early 1940, there was to be pressure in Britain and France to send military assistance to Finland, a neutral power that had been attacked by the Soviet Union.

Secondly, serious differences between Poland and the Soviet Union played a key role in 1939. Negotiations for a triple alliance of Britain, France, and the Soviet Union, an alliance that might have deterred Hitler from acting, collapsed, largely because Britain and France could not satisfy the Soviets on the issue of Polish and Romanian consent to the passage of Soviet forces in the event of war with Germany. Romania was suspicious of Soviet intentions about Bessarabia, which Romania had gained from Russia after the First World War. Events were to vindicate this suspicion. Romania was also fearful of the German reaction if it agreed to the British approach.

Earlier, the idea of a four-power declaration by Britain, France, Poland, and the Soviet Union had fallen foul of Polish opposition. In light of the Soviet invasion of Poland in 1920 and treatment of Poles in the Soviet Union during the 1930s purges, as well as what was to happen in 1939–41 and 1944–45, with the Soviets brutally occupying much and all of Poland, respectively, Polish concerns are understandable. However, the Poles were also naive in imagining that Germany could be restrained without active Soviet assistance. Stalin was totally untrustworthy, but the Poles had no viable alternative bar becoming a German client-ally.

The German-Soviet Pact of August 23, 1939, named after their manipulative foreign ministers Ribbentrop and Molotov, who negotiated the agreement, was crucial in encouraging Hitler to invade Poland, given the unexpected (and implausible in the light of their policy in 1936–38) determination of Britain and France to fulfill their guarantee of Polish independence and the failure of his major ally, Italy, to act in Hitler's support. Hitler persisted against Poland despite the guarantee. He believed that Britain and France would not fight, especially as a result of his pact with Stalin. This freed Germany from a two-front war,[14] the disastrous situation that had faced Germany for most of the First World War. However, the pact greatly alienated Germany's ally Japan, notably because Japanese and Soviet forces were involved in a major clash that August. Thereafter, Japanese policy makers did not feel that they could trust Hitler, a situation that looked toward very different policies toward the Soviet Union in 1941.

In 1939, the British chiefs of staff advised that it would not be possible to offer Poland any direct assistance. This was to be borne out by the course of the war in both 1939 and 1944, and was also true of Britain's military posture toward Czechoslovakia in 1938 and 1948. Britain itself was left reliant in 1939 for military action in Europe on the French, who were to be revealed, when Germany attacked in 1940, as a flawed ally, both militarily and politically. Already in 1939, France, despite its large army, was unable and unwilling to attack Germany's western frontier, in part because the army lacked the resources to sustain an offensive. Such an attack could only have been an indirect help to Poland (important as that would have been), whereas, with a long common frontier, the Soviet Union could readily have sent forces to Poland's assistance.

In the event, cooperation between Germany and the Soviet Union was initially directed against Poland and was also linked to an anti-Western turn in German policy. Indeed, Germany's war in the West was an ideological struggle like that for lebensraum (living space) in the East.[15]

The outbreak of war on September 1, 1939, was not the only conflict in Europe that has to be explained as part of the Second World War. Far from seeing a process of inevitable expansion of the conflict, it is important to underline the extent to which the expansion of the war was hesitant. Moreover, this hesitancy provided opportunities for the Axis powers. Crucially, Hitler's successive attacks from 1939 to the spring of 1941 found the Soviet Union neutral and complicit (or an active participant against Poland from September 17) and, very differently, the United States unwilling to come to the aid of fellow neutrals. Thus, as in the Wars of German Unification (1864–71), Hitler was able to fight single-front conflicts. Film provided historical endorsement for Hitler's diplomatic policy, with *Bismarck* (1940) showing the firm and iconic chancellor, the maker of German unification and a model of leadership on the Right, favoring a Russian alliance to protect Prussia's rear.

Moreover, when Hitler invaded in 1939, Romania did not aid Poland, while Norway and Sweden provided only limited assistance to Finland when it was attacked by the Soviet Union in the "Winter War" of 1939–40.

Similarly, Japan was able to attack China from 1931 without the intervention of the other powers (including the neighboring Soviet Union), despite the fact that they were not otherwise engaged in warfare. Japan was also able to fight limited border wars with the Soviet Union (1938 and, more seriously, 1939) that did not escalate, and to attack Britain and the United States in 1941 without fear of Soviet entry into the war. When Roosevelt, Churchill, and Jiang Jieshi met in Cairo in November 1943, Stalin was not present, as he did not wish to attend a conference of the powers at war with Japan. As a result, he was not a party to the Cairo Declaration of December 1, by which Roosevelt and Churchill agreed to support the return to China of Taiwan (lost to Japan in 1895) and Manchuria (lost in 1931–32). In contrast, Stalin was willing to meet Roosevelt and Churchill at Teheran in December 1943: Jiang was not present.

Yet, despite the reluctance of most of the powers to fight, Hitler's inability to consider limits on his ambition, or to understand the flaws in German economic and military capability, acted as an inexorable factor encouraging the expansion of the war. A correct sense that Hitler could not be trusted also meant that the rapid defeat of Poland did not lead to negotiations for peace. In the Reichstag (Parliament), on October 6, 1939, Hitler called for peace with Britain and France, but no real attempt was made to compromise with them, let alone with conquered Poland. Moreover, Britain and France were determined to fight on to prevent German hegemony in Europe, and they planned for success through a long war involving naval and economic blockade and the active pursuit of alliances. There was also the hope that Hitler would be overthrown. The strength of the British war machine and the global range of the British economy were significant to this planning.[16] It provided a measure of confidence in victory that encouraged persistence in a struggle for which, in practice, there was no clear way out.

NEW COMBATANTS IN 1940

The German invasion of Norway on April 9, 1940, in turn, required that of Denmark the same day. The Japanese were to adopt a similar logic of attack by successive dominoes in their drive south in late 1941. A determination to break the British naval blockade and to give the German navy operational flexibility and strategic possibilities played a major role in German policy against Norway.[17] There was also concern to protect the Swedish iron ore the Germans received through the Norwegian port of Narvik, which the Germans feared the British would seek to block.

In the event, the conquest of Norway brought relatively little benefit to German war making, in part because serious weaknesses in the German surface navy made Norwegian bases less valuable than might otherwise have been the case, while the German conquest of France swiftly provided submarine bases closer to Atlantic trade routes. Brittany indeed was so positioned as if designed to threaten British maritime links. Furthermore, concern about the possibility of British attack ensured that the Germans tied up a large force in garrisoning Norway, a force that, in the event, had no strategic value, as there was no comparable risk of it being used to invade Britain. This force was not needed to coerce neighboring Sweden, which was very willing to trade with Germany.

Similarly, the German conquest of Yugoslavia in 1941 led to an even larger garrison obligation because of the serious problems posed by guerrilla opposition there. This opposition encouraged British intervention in favor of the guerrillas. Planning the invasion of Yugoslavia, the Germans did not consider the possibility of large-scale postconquest resistance and the need subsequently to deploy large numbers of troops there accordingly.

The neutrality of the Netherlands and, more particularly, Belgium, and their failure to create a joint defense,[18] gravely weakened the Anglo-French response to German attack on May 10, 1940. This attack was an aspect of the conquest of France launched the same day. The failure to allow the prior deployment of British and French forces in these countries, a deployment that, however, would have provoked German invasion, meant that these forces had to advance and to expose themselves to the German attack without the benefit of holding defensive positions. The rapid and total success of this attack was a striking contrast to the situation in the First World War, and the 1940 campaign, culminating in the fall of France in June, was important to the politics of the war, both those at the time and those subsequently. The outcome of the campaign also permitted a vindication of Germany's decision for war the previous autumn. The failure of Allied deterrence appeared to rest on a sensible German assessment of the situation, an approach that underplayed the major risks taken.

WAR WITH VICHY

With France's surrender in June 1940, there was no longer the prospect of a main-force conflict with the Germans on the Western Front, as in the First World War. Instead, there was now the need to limit the consequences of France's surrender and of Italy's entry into the war. A key characteristic of Churchill's strategy was a determination to attack. He responded to the threat that the French navy, now in the hands of the Vichy regime that was aligned with Germany, would be taken over by the Germans, or would cooperate, by ordering action against it. This turn to war remains a controversial step.

Moreover, driving the Vichy French from their possessions was regarded as a crucial way to win the global struggle for power. On September 18, 1940, Churchill wrote to Sir Samuel Hoare, the ambassador to Spain, explaining his support for the Free French attempt to capture Dakar, the capital of Senegal, the leading French colony in West Africa. Churchill presented a classic account of the indirect approach, observing that, if Charles de Gaulle was to establish himself in Dakar and become "master of Western and Central Africa, Morocco is next on the list."[19] The struggle was to broaden out to encompass Vichy possessions elsewhere, notably Syria (1941), Lebanon (1941), and Madagascar (1942), each of which was conquered by British-led Allied forces.

ITALY ENTERS THE WAR

In June 1940, the Italian dictator, Benito Mussolini, an ally of Hitler in the Pact of Steel, joined in the war. He did so once the French had been clearly defeated by the Germans, yet while the conflict with France and Britain was still continuing, because he feared that he would otherwise lose the opportunity to gain glory and territories from France and Britain. Longer-term ambitions also played a major role. German victory in 1940 brought to a head Mussolini's ideological affinity with Hitler, his contempt for the democracies, and the inherent violence and aggressive expansionism of his regime, and overcame his awareness of the poor financial and military situation of Italy and his realization of little popular support for war. At the same time, Mussolini's awareness could be overcome by his delusions.

Italian expansionism in the late 1930s and 1940 represented a continuation of Mussolini's breach with both Britain and France and, instead, alignment with Germany as a result of the Ethiopian Crisis of 1935–36. In November 1938, the Italian Chamber of Deputies had echoed to calls for acquiring "Tunisia, Corsica, Nice, Savoy,"[20] all from France. Mussolini judged Corsica, purchased by France from Genoa in 1768, as traditionally Italian,[21] but did not have the same view of Savoy.[22] In his forceful report on February 4, 1939, to the Fascist Grand Council, he showed a clear opposition to France. Even though relations were close with Hitler, notably with the Pact of Steel signed on May 22, 1939, this depended on a verbal understanding given by the German foreign minister on October 28, 1938, that neither Germany nor Italy would provoke war before 1943.[23]

Mussolini's son-in-law and foreign minister, Count Galeazzo Ciano, opposed this alignment. He claimed that Mussolini was furious with Hitler for not consulting him about the invasion of Poland. Mussolini appreciated that Hitler, rather than being Mussolini's equal, was becoming more prominent. The invasion of the Low Countries and France made the worried Mussolini conclude that he could not remain neutral. He was convinced that war would be short and that Germany was powerful enough to win, and he was fearful of Germany's reaction to Italy at the end of the war. This appeared a reasonable conclusion.

War with Britain and France was conflict in a very different league for Italy than Mussolini's earlier wars, and it matched the process of escalation also seen with Germany and Japan. Feeling that his vision of Italian greatness required domination of the Mediterranean and, therefore, British defeat, Mussolini, who had built up a large and expensive modern fleet to that end, sought gains from France and the British Empire. This policy, which entailed overcoming the pronounced pessimism of his service chiefs, destroyed the conviction in the British Foreign Office that Italy would remain neutral and the linked illusion that Mussolini could be a moderating "back channel" to Hitler. This had been hoped by those on the Right in Britain keen to see a negotiated end to the war.

Assisted by the alpine terrain, by prepared defenses, and by the earlier Italian emphasis on the defensive and on a deployment (accordingly) in depth, the French mounted an effective resistance to Italian attacks in June 1940. The Italians were outgunned. In the subsequent peace, signed on June 24, Italy's territorial gains were very modest. These terms reflected the success of the French resistance to Italian attack and Hitler's concern to bolster Vichy France.

Whatever the arrangements that would have been offered by Germany had Britain accepted peace (i.e., surrendered) in 1940, Britain fought on. Aside from the subsequent air war over Britain (the Battle of Britain and then the Blitz) and the U-boat (submarine) assault on its trade, most of the initial fighting on the part of the Axis involved Italy because the projected German invasion of Britain, Operation Sealion, was not launched. Although vulnerable British Somaliland fell rapidly, Italian campaigning in East and North Africa was a humiliating failure. Mussolini's planned advance on the Suez Canal, the vital axis of British imperial power, failed totally. In turn, in 1940–41, Somalia, Eritrea, Ethiopia, and much of Libya were captured by British troops (many from the British Empire). This failure led to a major shift in the politics of the Axis, with Germany ever more dominant.

The same shift in Italian policy, from ambition to action, occurred in the Balkans. Mussolini's ambition for Balkan gains, concern about Greece's alignment with Britain, and anxieties about Greece's wish to attack the Dodecanese led Italy to attack Greece in October 1940.[24] The two powers had had poor relations from the 1910s over rival territorial interests in the Balkans and the Aegean. Thanks to the Italian colony of Albania, they also had a common frontier.

In turn, Italian failure in this conflict, failure that resulted in a successful Greek invasion of southern Albania, ensured that Hitler decided to intervene in Greece, partly in response to Greece's alignment with Britain. This operation, however, when launched on April 6, 1941, was an attack on both Greece and Yugoslavia, because an unexpected nationalist coup by the military in Yugoslavia on March 27, a coup encouraged by Britain, challenged German influence there, and Hitler was not prepared to accept such a challenge.

SOVIET EXPANSION

A focus on German, Italian, and Japanese expansionism in 1939–41 can lead to an underplaying of that of the Soviet Union, which instead sought to keep pace with that of Germany, not least to give effect to the division of Eastern Europe agreed in the Nazi-Soviet Pact in August 1939. There is a tendency to underplay this expansion, but for Poland, Finland, the Baltic republics (Estonia, Latvia, and Lithuania), and Romania, it was a brutal process. The Soviets only annexed part of Finland and part of Romania, but in eastern Poland (overrun in 1939) and the Baltic republics (1940), their complete control was accompanied by the large-scale deportation to the gulags, the often-deadly Soviet concentration camps, of large numbers of those judged potentially hostile.

To the Soviet Union, this expansion was in part a matter of recreating the pre-1914 Russian Empire, which had included all these areas. For those affected by Soviet expansion, the situation was very different: sovereign states whose independence was internationally recognized were forced to surrender independence (the Baltic republics and, in concert with Germany, Poland) or territory (Finland and Romania).

GERMANY ATTACKS THE SOVIET UNION

The causes of the war between Germany and the Soviet Union in 1941, launched by Germany on June 22, the largest-scale land conflict of the Second World War, can be firmly found on the German side. There have been repeated claims that the Germans preempted plans for a Soviet attack, a claim initially made by Josef Goebbels, Hitler's minister of propaganda, in June 1941. Whatever the nature of long-term Soviet intentions and military expansion, and Stalin might well have attacked after 1943 if Germany had been weakened by its conflict with Britain (and maybe the United States), this claim was not an accurate account of the situation in 1941.[25] Instead, Hitler's overconfidence and contempt for other political systems reinforced his belief that Germany had to conquer the Soviet Union in order to fulfill what he alleged was her destiny and to obtain lebensraum.[26] The earlier reversal, from 1933 to 1940, of the Treaty of Versailles, was secondary to the reestablishment of Germany's victory in the East in 1918, a victory rapidly overthrown as a consequence of Germany's defeat later that year on the Western Front.

Such a war would also permit Hitler to pursue the extermination of the European Jews that he had promised the Reichstag on January 30, 1939. To Hitler and his supporters, "International Jewry" was an active worldwide force, responsible for Germany's plight, and therefore had to be destroyed in order to advance the German cause.[27] Hitler's metahistorical goal of racial superiority, especially over Slavs, and the slaughter of all Jews was not an outcome possible without total victory. At the same time, success encouraged Hitler to make his ambitions more central, not least to move from an emphasis on revising Versailles, so as to ensure a Greater Germany, to creating, instead, a new European order, one in which there would be no Jews.

Hitler was convinced that a clash with communism was inevitable, as well as necessary. Soviet pressure over the future of the Balkans, notably during the Molotov-Ribbentrop discussions in Berlin in November 1940, encouraged this view. Although Britain in 1941 was still undefeated, and Germany deployed considerable forces in France and Norway, Hitler correctly felt that Britain was no longer able to make any effective opposition to German domination of mainland Europe, and therefore believed that her continued resistance should not deter Germany from attacking the Soviet Union. Indeed, Soviet defeat was seen as likely to weaken Britain by ending hopes of a war between Germany and the Soviet Union, and thus to encourage Britain to negotiate.

Furthermore, indicating the different timelines of anticipation that play a role in the causes of war, Hitler was convinced that the United States would enter the war on Britain's side. Indeed, on August 25, 1941, he told Mussolini that Roosevelt was controlled by a Jewish group, a totally inaccurate view similar to his flawed assessment of Churchill. The influence of Jews in the Soviet Union was also greatly exaggerated. Hitler believed that an attack on the Soviet Union was necessary in order to win rapid victory before such an American intervention.

Hitler's adventurism and conceit were a reflection of his warped personality and also the product of a political-ideological system in which conflict and hatred appeared natural. Moreover, Hitler was confident that the Soviet system would collapse rapidly and was happy to accept misleading intelligence assessments of the size and mobilization potential of the Red Army. German optimism was enhanced by the successful conquest of Yugoslavia and Greece in April 1941.

Equally distrustful of Britain and suspicious of plans for an Anglo-German peace, Stalin totally ignored numerous warnings from German opponents of Hitler via Soviet intelligence. Warnings that were ignored also came from Roosevelt, and from Churchill (derived from Enigma decrypts), about German invasion plans.[28] As also with Hitler in 1941, this was a key instance of a war leader's willfulness—that linking a misunderstanding of the context of policy to its flawed implementation. Aside from Hitler, the German way of war, with its emphasis on short wars characterized by offensive operations designed to lead to total victory, encouraged the resort to war and, indeed, helped cause German failure.[29]

GERMANY'S ALLIES

Allies of Germany were expected to support the attack on the Soviet Union, and indeed did so, although for their own reasons. The Finns were determined to regain the territories they had lost to the Soviet Union in 1940 and saw what they termed the "Continuation War," of 1941–44, as a second stage of, and response to, the Soviet attack in the Winter War of 1939–40. The same goal of recovering territory was sought by Romania, which aimed to regain Bessarabia and northern Bukovina from the Soviet Union. Thus, Romania wished to reverse the consequences of the Nazi-Soviet Pact. In order to help overcome communism, and under pressure from Germany, Hungary declared war on the Soviet Union. Hungary's government had an explicitly Christian nationalist ideology[30] and was, by the early 1940s, moving the country toward becoming a racial state.[31] Moreover, in 1938–41, Hungary had benefited greatly territorially from alliance with Hitler at the expense of

Czechoslovakia, Romania, and Yugoslavia, recovering losses under the Treaty of Trianon of 1920.

Yet, as is inevitably the case, these explanations are far too brief. To take Romania, there was a complex interplay between King Carol II, the Fascist Iron Guard, liberal politicians, and General Ion Antonescu, the minister of war, an authoritarian nationalist seen as above politics, with the Germans also playing a major role. Carol called in Antonescu as prime minister in 1940 as a way to contain the Iron Guard, and Antonescu, a nationalist who did not want to be a client of Germany, nevertheless turned to Hitler, as he was convinced that Germany was going to win the war, which indeed seemed a reasonable conclusion in September 1940. In turn, although the SS backed the Iron Guard, the German government, influenced by its army and the Foreign Ministry, supported Antonescu because they saw him as a reliable ally and a source of stability, neither of which was true of the Iron Guard. In light of the forthcoming war with the Soviet Union, reliability was more desirable than the ideological affinity offered by the Iron Guard. At the same time, Antonescu and his government were to be murderously anti-Semitic.

Underlining the interaction of domestic politics with foreign policy, Antonescu bullied the unreliable Carol into abdicating in favor of his son, Michael, on September 6, 1940. The following January, Antonescu saw Hitler, telling him that he was ready to support Germany in defense of Eastern Europe against a possible Soviet attack, and, eight days later, Antonescu was able to crush the Iron Guard without German intervention on behalf of the latter. In June 1941, Romania joined in the attack on the Soviet Union, declaring a "holy war" to free Bessarabia. Antonescu saw Germany and the Soviet Union as the only alternatives.[32] This was an analysis that France's defeat and British weakness encouraged many to share.

WAR IN THE PACIFIC

The outbreak of the Pacific War in December 1941 is harder to study because, in part due to the nature of the surviving sources, Japanese policy making has proved more opaque than that of Germany. Nevertheless, the general situation is clear. Japan was already at war with China. The wider conflict begun in 1941 amounted for Japan to more enemies to beat and was not the much bigger step of going from being a peaceful to a wartime society.

Alongside an expansionism based on the self-confident assumptions of the Japanese ruling elite, resource issues, particularly access to oil, were important precipitants to the decision for war.[33] These issues played a key role in clashing geopolitical priorities focused on Southeast Asia. The collapse of France and the Netherlands to German attack in 1940, and the weakening position of Britain, already vulnerable in the Far East (of which the Japanese were well informed), created an apparent power vacuum in East and Southeast Asia. This vacuum encouraged Japanese ambitions southward into French Indochina (Cambodia, Laos, and Vietnam), British Southeast Asia (Malaya, Singapore, North Borneo, and Burma), and the Dutch East Indies, while leading the Americans to feel that only they were in a position to resist Japan. The last was accurate.

Jiang Jieshi, the Chinese leader, had argued in his diary on September 2, 1939, that it was crucial to link the Sino-Japanese War with the Allied cause in Europe.[34] Although this did not happen in the way he predicted, Jiang was correct in feeling that, to move beyond checking Japan, it was necessary for China to win allies and therefore benefit from developments in the international system. Furthermore, the unresolved character of the war between Japan and China, which entered a state of attritional stalemate in 1939,[35] not only embittered Japanese relations with America, which provided some support for China, but also exacerbated resource issues in Japanese military planning, as well as placing a major burden on Japanese finances. Thirty-four divisions were bogged down by 1939; by that September, Japan had lost half a million troops killed or badly wounded in China. Japan had had to settle on a policy of consolidating the territory it controlled in China and launching punitive expeditions into the remainder of China.

Moreover, Japanese economic weakness was such that her trade deficit was condemning her to the prospect of national bankruptcy in the spring of 1942. This was a repetition of the serious fiscal and economic strain that had confronted Japan during the militarily successful and far shorter Russo-Japanese War of 1904–5, but, as for Germany with the Franco-Prussian War in 1870–71, it had proved possible to end that conflict more speedily.[36] There was no reason to believe that the war with China could be ended so readily. The failure of Japanese policy makers was clear but unacknowledged.

Germany's victory over France in 1940 encouraged Japan to revive relations with Germany that had been dimmed when Hitler, without warning, concluded his nonaggression pact with Stalin the previous year: Japan was opposed to the Soviet Union for ideological and geopolitical reasons and had sent a large force into the Soviet Far East during the Russian Civil War, as well as briefly fighting the Soviet Union in Mongolia and Manchuria in 1938–39. On September 27, 1940, in response to pressure from the military, Japan joined Germany and Italy in the Tripartite Pact. The Japanese government and military, although divided, were determined to expand at the expense of others, particularly, from 1940, into Southeast Asia, which was, to Japan, the "Southern Resources Area," a region rich in raw materials, notably oil, tin, and rubber, all of which Japan lacked. From June 1940, the Japanese navy had begun full mobilization, although the German failure to invade Britain in the autumn of 1940, as planned, discouraged ideas of a Japanese attack on Britain's colonies that year.

Continued Japanese aggression against China and, more particularly, expansion into southern French Indochina in July 1941 helped to trigger American commercial sanctions, specifically an embargo on oil exports to Japan. This was tantamount to an ultimatum because, without oil, the operations of the Japanese armed forces, notably the navy, would grind to a halt. Unlike the United States, a major exporter as well as producer, Japan did not produce oil. The embargo helped provoke the Japanese to act against the United States in order to protect their position and potential, because they were unwilling to accept limitations to their expansion in the Far East. The latter was more an "idealist" than a "realist" position: there was no inevitable need for Japan to confront the United States in this fashion.

In 1941, the Japanese increasingly focused on the raw materials to be gained from Southeast Asia and the East Indies. They also planned to seize British-ruled Burma in order to block Western supplies to China, a goal that had already led them to occupy the northern part of French Indochina in September 1940. It was misleadingly believed that blocking these supply routes would lead to the serious weakening, if not collapse, of Chinese resistance. The Dutch East Indies (modern Indonesia) posed a problem for Japan as, despite the German conquest of the Netherlands in May 1940, the Dutch colonial officials rejected Japanese efforts to acquire oil and instead sought to align policy with Britain and the United States.

Supplies for Japan and China had become far more of an issue with the development of American policy. The Americans considered themselves entitled to react forcefully to events on the other side of the Pacific, and they also felt threatened by the fall of France in 1940 and by the possibility that Britain would follow, thus completely exposing the Atlantic to German action and the United States to attack by a worldwide coalition.[37] These anxieties encouraged Congress to support rearmament, particularly naval preparations, and also led Roosevelt, in part in order to demonstrate bipartisanship, to appoint Henry Stimson, a prominent Republican who argued that American security required the maintenance of British power, as secretary of war on June 19, 1940. The Neutrality Act was repealed, military equipment was sold to the British, and steps were also taken to confront Japan.

At the same time, there were strong divisions in public opinion and public politics. The isolationist America First Committee was formed in September 1940 to oppose intervention against Germany. The Committee to Defend America by Aiding the Allies and, later, the Fight for Freedom Committee took a very different stance.[38] The Two-Ocean Naval Expansion Act was passed on July 19, 1940, when Britain appeared defeated by Germany and certainly could no longer rely on the French navy. This act, increasing the authorized tonnage of American warships by 70 percent and providing for a cost of $4 billion, served notice on the Japanese that the Americans were going to be in a position to dominate the Pacific in the near future. This fleet would enable the Americans to wage naval war with modern ships against both Germany and Japan, a necessity that seemed increasingly apparent.

This buildup had an impact on Japan comparable to pre-1914 German fears of Russian military developments: the vista appeared threatening, but, in the short term, a window of opportunity seemed to be present. In turn, although it did not seek war with Japan, the American government was resolved to prevent Japanese expansion yet was unable to make an accurate assessment of Japanese military capability. The latter issue was linked to an American exaggeration of the effectiveness of American air power.[39] There was no experience of long-range Japanese naval and amphibious capabilities, especially the ability to mount multiple landings at the same time over a large distance, and there was a degree of racial discrimination in the assessment of the Japanese.

French Indochina, especially Vietnam, came to play a crucial part in the crisis. America registered responses to what she saw as aggressive Japanese steps there. After the fall of France, Japan ordered the closure of the border between China and Indochina in order to prevent the movement of supplies into China. Indochina was also of strategic importance as an axis of Japanese advance to the "Southern Resources Area." From air bases in Vietnam, it was possible to threaten Thailand and the British colony of Malaya, a point that anticipated later American concerns about Vietnam in communist hands. The declaration, on July 24, 1941, of a joint Franco-Japanese protectorate over all French Indochina led to an American trade embargo and the freezing of Japanese assets in America. Under the Hull Note of November 26, a memorial presented by Cordell Hull, the secretary of state, the Americans demanded that the Japanese withdraw from China and Indochina. Long-standing Japanese fears of encirclement now focused on anxiety about the so-called ABCD group: America, Britain, China, and the Dutch.

Within Japan, there were attempts to explore the idea of better relations with Britain and the United States, but these required an ability to restrain the military that did not correspond to the dynamics of Japanese politics. These explorations, already seen in 1939–40, were pursued in late 1941 in order to ascertain if the United States could be persuaded to lessen its support for China. Britain and China were anxious about this point, but, in November 1941, Roosevelt agreed that the United States could not sacrifice China in order to maintain relations with Japan. Thus, a Japanese recognition of Chinese independence became a key American objective, continuing a pattern of international restraint on Japanese expansion there seen episodically from the mid-1890s. To Japan, this was American intervention in its sphere.

After staging war games in August 1941, the Japanese decided to launch a war if diplomacy failed to lead to a lifting of the trade embargo. On October 17, 1941, a hard-line ministry under General Hideki Tōjō gained power. At the same time, as a reminder that it is necessary to appreciate the divisions and strains within states and their governments, Tōjō rose to power against the background of long-standing tension within the army, as well as within the government. There were disagreements over policy, especially over whether there should be compromise with the Chinese Nationalists, an option opposed by Tōjō, and also over the Neutrality Pact signed with the Soviet Union on April 13, 1941, so as to enable Japan to focus on war with Britain and the United States. This pact, which matched the Molotov-Ribbentrop Pact of 1939 in allowing an Axis power to fight the Allies with a one-front war, reflected Hitler's assurances to Japan that he would attack Britain in 1941. The alignment of Germany–the Soviet Union–Japan apparently provided the necessary opportunity. This helped explain Japanese anger when Hitler attacked the Soviet Union in June 1941. Equally, by late 1941, Japan was not interested in German requests for an attack on the Soviet Union.

In late 1941, pressure from Admiral Yamamoto Isoroku, the commander of the Japanese Combined Fleet, for an attack on the American naval base at Pearl Harbor in Hawaii (using the same military technique of the "knockout" blow as had been seen with Germany) as a prelude for covering Japanese invasions of Malaya, the Philippines, and the Dutch East Indies was successful. This plan won the day on November 3, 1941.[40] The devastating (but also unfinished) surprise attack on Pearl Harbor on December 7, "a date which will live in infamy" according to Roosevelt the next day, was to play a key role in American public memory,[41] as well as indicating that war did not begin with a declaration of hostilities, but, rather, with an event. As against the Russians in 1904, Japan started fighting before the declaration of war. Most of the damaged warships returned to service, and the battleships that were sunk were replaced with either more modern battleships or large aircraft carriers.

The Japanese suffered from the lack of a realistic war plan, a lack, already apparent in the case of the attack on China, that was based on their assumption of their superiority over the Chinese and others. As with Hitler in the case of both Britain and the Soviet Union, a misleading conviction of the internal weakness of the opposing systems led the Japanese to a failure to judge resolve accurately, a failure that was important to the reading of the international system. In particular, there was a certainty that Britain and the United States lacked the willpower of Japan and Germany. The British and Americans were believed to be weakened by democracy and consumerism, an extrapolation of authoritarian views within Japanese politics and about Japanese society onto other states. In the event, the initial Japanese ability to mount successful attacks, to gain great swathes of territory, and to establish an apparent stranglehold on the Far East and the western Pacific behind a defensive perimeter did not deter the Americans from the long-term effort of driving back, and destroying, Japanese power.

GERMANY AND THE UNITED STATES

Hitler followed the unexpected blow at Pearl Harbor by declaring war on the United States on December 11, 1941, as (necessarily as an ally) did Mussolini. Hitler claimed that this declaration was in accordance with German obligations under the Tripartite Treaty with Italy and Japan signed on September 27, 1940. However, strictly, the terms of the treaty did not require such cooperation, and Japan did not declare war on the Soviet Union in June 1941. Already angered by American cooperation with the British against German submarine (U-boat) operations in the Atlantic, operations that were part of a growing pattern of Anglo-American cooperation[42] and that had brought the war to the seas off North America, Hitler claimed that his decision to declare war was in response to American "provocations" in the Atlantic. Like Goebbels, Hitler saw the United States as part of a global Jewish conspiracy directed against Germany, and Roosevelt as the key instrument of this conspiracy. Already on December 21, 1940, Germany had claimed that American assistance to Britain constituted "moral aggression."

In practice, there was no real appreciation in Germany of the impact of American entry and no sign of any informed analysis of the likely trajectory of war between Japan and the United States, nor of the consequences for Germany of war with America. This was an aspect of the more general failure of German intelligence, and notably of Hitler's unwillingness to consider the views and capabilities of his opponents other than in terms of his own ideological suppositions, but also of a more general German politico-military naïveté.

As in 1917, there was a mistaken confidence in Germany that the U-boats would weaken the United States, providing Germany with a strategic weapon that could operate to strategic effect and that would negate the American effort in Europe. This was a belief necessary to Hitler's attempt to regain the initiative by a bold step and to limit the West while trying to conquer the East. In reality, the U-boats only provided an operational capability, a situation exacerbated by serious mismanagement of the submarine fleet, notably a lack of large, long-distance boats.

In addition, this capability was gradually to be eroded by improved Allied antisubmarine warfare tactics and by the vast capacity provided by American shipbuilding and, in particular, the development of the latter thanks to large-scale investment, the availability of raw materials, and labor flexibility. By the end of the third quarter of 1943, the Allies had built more ships than had been sunk since the start of the war. The Americans could build them faster than the Germans could sink them.

Hitler, moreover, regarded the United States as weakened by deracination resulting from interbreeding, by consumerism, and by democracy, and as lacking in martial spirit, all views also shared by Japanese commentators. He felt that Japan and the U-boats would keep the United States busy until after Germany had successfully settled the war with the Soviet Union, which he hoped to do with his 1942 offensive. In January 1942, Hitler told Lieutenant General Hiroshi Oshima, the Japanese ambassador, that he did not know how he would defeat the United States, but such lucid moments were overtaken by an emphasis on will and by rambling fantasies.[43]

As a result of Hitler's declaration of war, the struggle was now truly global. The United States, in response, declared war on Germany on December 11, and its influence in Latin America was such that most of the world's remaining neutrals followed suit. Cuba, the Dominican Republic, Guatemala, Nicaragua, and Haiti also declared war that day. Honduras and El Salvador followed the next day, and Panama, Mexico, and Brazil in 1942. The declaration by Brazil, on August 22, was influenced by American pressure and the Brazilian determination to exploit America's need for support. German attacks on Brazilian shipping were cited as the major cause, but American influence and pressure were more significant.[44]

These entries marked a major blow to German and Italian diplomatic and espionage attempts to build up support in Latin America. In part, these attempts reflected the desire to exploit opportunities, not least those presented by local German and Italian populations and by authoritarian governments, such as the Perón dictatorship in Argentina. In part, the attempts were a product of the global aspirations of key elements in the German government. As in the case of Mexico in the First World War, there was also a desire to weaken the United States by causing problems in its backyard. Thus, there was a strategic intention underlying Germany's Latin American policy. This policy had many flaws, not least encouraging American hostility and a central problem with implementation: the inability of Germany to give teeth to its hopes. This inability reflected British naval strength as well as the German focus on operations in Europe. Yet, despite the flaws of Germany's Latin American policy, there was a potential for causing trouble.

This potential was one of the victims of Hitler's decision to declare war on the United States. Instead, the Rio Conference in January 1942 saw the creation of the Inter-American Defense Board, which was designed to coordinate military matters throughout the Western Hemisphere. In effect, the United States assumed responsibility for the protection of the region. It, not Germany, benefited from Britain's declining role.

America's success in Latin America nevertheless had limitations, which in part reflected the appeal of the German authoritarian model. Indeed, many Latin American states delayed entry into the war: Bolivia and Colombia until 1943, and Ecuador, Paraguay, Peru, Venezuela, Chile, and Argentina (in which there was much sympathy for Germany) until 1945. Although, once they joined the war, none of the Latin American states played a major, let alone crucial, role in the conflict, their experience, as combatants and neutrals, reflected the global impact and nature of the struggle, at once military, political, ideological, and economic. The state that played the leading military role was Brazil, which sent twenty-five thousand troops to fight in the Italy campaign. Northeast Brazil also played a staging role in the 1942 Operation Torch, an American amphibious attack on French-held North Africa. Mexico sent units to the Philippines in 1944.[45] Other late entrants into the war, all on the Allied side, were Liberia in 1944 and Saudi Arabia, Egypt, and Turkey in 1945.

Moreover, the alliance between Britain, the United States, and the Soviet Union led these three powers to declare war on those who were already at war with their allies. Thus, Britain and the United States went to war with Hitler's allies that had attacked the Soviet Union, while, keen to gain the spoils of victory, the latter went to war with Japan on August 8, 1945, after the end of the war with Europe. This was two days after the first atom bomb was dropped on Hiroshima, an event that encouraged Stalin to act rapidly in order to seize opportunities.

CONCLUSION

The Second World War, therefore, was a number of conflicts, differently closely connected and partly separate. Their interactions were crucial to the diplomacy and strategy of the war. As with the First World War, the causes of the conflicts varied greatly, while the number of these conflicts poses major problems for the statistical analysis of the causes of war. Again, as with the previous war, the context was crucial, notably the fear and opportunism created by the conflict; the extent to which it was not shut down but, instead, escalated dramatically; and the pressures from the two sides for new allies. The ideological drives of the war leaders and the regimes they controlled were central. They explained why alignments were both created and transformed. Ideological factors played a central role in the content and means of policies pursued, in short, in both formulation and implementation.

Chapter Nine

The Second World War, Land Warfare

The image of land warfare over the last 160 years is very much dominated by the two world wars. The First World War is particularly important for the Europeans, but it is less dominant an issue, image, and memory for the United States, still more for Japan, and even more for China. As the latter three became the world's leading powers, so this situation ensured that images changed. The views, indeed images, held in the United States were particularly prominent further afield, notably as a consequence of the influence of Hollywood. However, the Second World War also supplanted the First because it was more recent, defined personal and collective experiences that were more strongly present, and left more, and more varied, photographic images. The First ceased to be *the* World War or, as it was known in Britain, the Great War.

The Second World War was a global one from 1939 because it was then that Britain and France went to war with Germany, mobilizing their global empires, the largest in the world, in doing so. Moreover, war between these powers and Germany added a far-flung naval dimension that was missing in the case of that already started between Japan and China, which had broken out in 1937. Rapidly conquering France in 1940, and defeating British forces in France (and Norway) at the same time, the Germans brought to a final end the interwar period, both militarily and politically. German victory was also, to a degree, the final end of the revived First World War that had broken out in 1939: Germany and Russia had produced a de facto alignment in 1918 that prefigured their alliance in 1939. By late 1939, as in 1918, Germany was at war with Britain and France, although not with Italy or the United States, both of which (eventually) had been members of the coalition that had defeated Germany in 1918: from 1915 and 1917 respectively.

The defeat in 1940 of the imperial systems of France and, to a far lesser extent, Britain in their European heartland ensured that Germany would only be overthrown as a superpower if the Soviet Union and America came into the war. This factor also meant that a major American role would be necessary to defeat Japan once it entered the war in December 1941. Britain and China would be able to deny Japan victory, which the British did by holding on to India, and the Chinese by continuing the war begun in 1937. However, these two powers were not able to defeat Japan.

The fall of France in June 1940 also marked the end of limited war with Germany because the new British government under Winston Churchill was not interested in a compromise peace dictated by a victorious Germany, which was all that was on offer. Churchill's decision, and the inability of Germany later that year, as rapidly planned, to invade Britain, or to bomb it into submission, meant that the conflict would continue until the actions of the Soviet Union and the United States could play a decisive role.

POLAND AND SCANDINAVIA, 1939–40

The Germans conquered Poland in 1939 in a rapid campaign of maneuver launched from several directions against an opponent that had a long and vulnerable frontier to protect and that dispersed its army to defend this perimeter. The Germans lost fewer than fifteen thousand in defeating an opponent whose armed forces totaled over one million men. The Germans greatly outnumbered the Poles in aircraft, tanks, and other mechanized vehicles and enjoyed the initiative. The Luftwaffe having gained air superiority, the German armored forces broke through and isolated and enveloped Polish positions, making it difficult for them to maintain supplies or launch counterattacks. Much of Poland was good tank country, and it was good tank weather, in marked contrast to the situation in the Soviet Union by late 1941.

Nevertheless, the campaign was not a walkover for the Germans, and the Poles showed how a determined foe, although outclassed technologically, could make a superior conquering force pay for its conquests. The major individual battle, that of the Bzura, saw an initially successful Polish attack on exposed German forces, but ended with a German victory that benefited from air and artillery superiority. Largely reliant on railways and draft animals, the Germans also benefited greatly from Soviet intervention against the Poles. This denied the Poles defense in greater depth and contributed to the sense of a collapsing military and political situation. As agreed before the war, the two victors partitioned Poland, which ceased to exist as an independent state.

By the end of 1939, Germany was allied with Japan, Italy, and the Soviet Union and had cooperated with the last in conquering Poland and determining spheres of influence in Eastern Europe, which left the independent states there with few options other than looking to Germany, as Hungary and Romania, and then Bulgaria, did. The United States was neutral. Britain and France, while supported by their mighty empires, were reduced to somewhat dubious hopes of long-term success, in particular through a naval-based economic blockade. That, in practice, was not going to work due to the Russo-German alignment. Hitler's certainty about his strategic ability and Germany's confidence in its army had been increased greatly by victory over Poland.

In turn, in 1940, the Germans switched between opponents in a fashion they had not been able to do in 1914. First, they expanded their Western Front, hitherto only on a largely inactive French frontier, by attacking neutrals. In Denmark and Norway, the Germans proved highly successful, in part due to their use of air power. This was of great significance for land warfare. General Auchinleck, who commanded the Anglo-French expeditionary force to Narvik, attributed the German victory primarily to air power:

> The predominant factor in the recent operations has been the effect of air power. . . . The actual casualties caused to troops on the ground by low-flying attacks were few, but the moral effect of continuous machine-gunning from the air was considerable. Further, the enemy made repeated use of low-flying attacks with machine guns in replacement of artillery to cover the movement of his troops. Troops in forward positions subjected to this form of attack are forced to ground, and until they have learned by experience its comparative innocuousness, are apt not to keep constant watch on the enemy. Thus, the enemy was enabled on many occasions to carry out forward and outflanking movements with impunity . . . the first general lesson to be drawn is that to commit troops to a campaign in which they cannot be provided with adequate air support is to court disaster.[1]

Far more was in fact involved in Allied failure in Norway, not least the inability to implement strategic decisions at an effective operational level and to appreciate the need to make these decisions in the light of tactical and operational circumstances. These included the problems of tri-service fighting, the lack of Allied coordination, and the dynamic of German operations, which was seriously underestimated by the Allies.[2] Yet they were not alone in this underestimation of opponents. Indeed, the problems of inadequate training, organization, preparation, and intelligence of particular environments were revealed throughout the war, for example in the fighting between Japan and the Americans on the Pacific island of Guadalcanal in 1942, which became the first Japanese defeat on land at American hands.[3]

Alongside German expansionism, there was its Soviet counterpart, as Stalin sought to gain control over neighboring territories in order to provide defensive buffers for the Soviet Union, as well as to advance the cause of communism.[4] This policy led to the invasion of eastern Poland in 1939 in agreement with the Germans, as well as to an attack on Finland in 1939–40, and, in 1940, to the enforced occupation of Estonia, Latvia, and Lithuania and the extortion of territory from Romania.

These operations, notably the most violent, the Winter War with Finland, revealed serious limitations with the Soviet army, particularly its unfamiliarity with operating in the snow in extensive forests. However, ultimately, applying far larger forces, the Soviets prevailed. The key campaign, that in the Karelian Isthmus, saw Soviet artillery provide the means to break through the Finnish Mannerheim Line of fortifications, which was far weaker than the French Maginot Line. The war ended with Finland agreeing to cede territory.

THE COLLAPSE OF THE WESTERN FRONT, 1940

Before Norway had finally fallen, the Germans, on May 10, also attacked Belgium and the Netherlands, both hitherto neutral, as well as invading France. The rapid defeat of the Dutch, who surrendered on May 14, indicated the success of German methods against a far weaker opponent that lacked defenses-in-depth. Swiftly gaining and employing air superiority, the Germans advanced rapidly, using paratroopers, glider-borne forces, and tanks to weaken the cohesion of the defenders. Heavy civilian casualties caused by the bombing of the undefended city of Rotterdam speeded the surrender.

The crucial victory occurred further south: poor Allied strategy had led the Allies to move their strategic reserve on their far left into Belgium, in order to protect northern Belgium and the southern Netherlands, before they were aware of the main direction of the German attack. As a result, these forces were not available in a reserve capacity. Thus, taking the initiative did not do the French much good.

The German attack came further south, through the supposedly impenetrable hilly woodland of the Ardennes, bisecting the Allied line, outflanking the fortifications of the French Maginot Line and their defensive forces, and exposing the Allies' failure to prepare for a fluid defense-in-depth. The Maginot Line, which contained about four hundred thousand troops, guided the direction of the German attack to the north of the line through southern Belgium. However, advancing to break through the French positions on the middle Meuse, like the advance through the Ardennes, in theory a reckless plan, the Germans gained and retained the initiative in the area in which they advanced. The failure of the Maginot Line continues to be a much-cited instance of the failure of fortification and defensive strategies as a whole, as well, more particularly, of the French in 1940. This failure is often held up as the product of the drawbacks of resting on the defensive. The line was penetrated in places on June 16, but, more seriously, the forces in it were cut off by German advances to their rear, while, earlier, they had not been able to intervene against the German offensive.

Moreover, the French attention to a continuous front greatly limited their ability to respond to the German breakthrough, as did the speed of the German advance, which was far faster than in 1914. The French did not maneuver well for, or in, defense. The French also lacked an effective doctrine for their armor and tended to see it in terms of infantry support. Helped by air superiority, the German panzer (tank) divisions proved operationally effective as formations, maximizing the combat characteristics of tanks. German signaling capacity was also superior. When tank conflict occurred with the British or French, the Germans tended to control its pace, although they were not invariably successful. French failures, which included a lack of peacetime training for reserve units, magnified German efforts at innovation. In contrast, these efforts were subsequently in the war to be revealed as inadequate against defense-in-depth, notably in the Soviet Union in late 1941.

The effectiveness of the German blitzkrieg attacking methods in 1939–41 was exaggerated by contemporary, and later, commentators, both German and others, under the spell cast by the sheer shock and drama of the German offensives.[5] Writing on the "essentials of total war," three senior British military figures, the army one being Major General (retired) J. F. C. Fuller, claimed,

> Thus were the greater powers divided into two antagonistic ideological camps, and, so far as war was concerned, into two military groups. One group still believed in the comparatively leisurely mass warfare of the nineteenth century, whereas the other put its trust in the strenuous machine warfare of the twentieth. When war came in 1939, and these ideological differences rendered it inevitable, one factor alone saved the democratic powers from annihilation, and that factor was the English Channel.[6]

As far as outcomes were concerned, and notably on the Western Front in 1940, the situation certainly contrasted greatly with the First World War. As a result, commentators then, and subsequently, have overrated the impact in 1939–41 of military ideas and methods that, in practice, represented more of an improvisation than the fruition of a coherent doctrine, or, at most, an evolution rather than a revolution. Rather than focusing on blitzkrieg, particularly on the use of tanks and ground-attack aircraft, the Germans benefited in their early campaigns from the army's doctrine, training, and leadership, notably from the stress on flexibility, personal initiative, and action. Germany's opponents could not match these elements, either individually or in combination. It was the combined characteristic of German advantages that gave particular advantages, which had also been the case for the attacking British against the Germans in 1918.

However, in 1940, aside from issues of preparedness, the margin between success and failure was closer than was generally appreciated, which was different from the situation with Allied success in late 1918. Furthermore, the potential of weaponry and logistics based on the internal combustion engine, the tank, and the lorry (truck) was less dramatic than talk of blitzkrieg might suggest. Artillery, for example, remained a key factor, as was to be seen on all the military fronts during the war. It was the major killer among weapon systems.

German success against Poland, Norway, the Netherlands, Belgium, France, Yugoslavia, and Greece in 1939–41 also owed much to poor strategic decisions by Germany's opponents, notably in terms of defensive planning and the allocation of reserves, particularly as a consequence of having to defend an overlong perimeter. Moreover, German generalship and organization displayed serious shortcomings in 1940. Indeed, there was a parallel between French and German military conservatism.

German successes in 1939–41 were also a product of the existing geopolitical situation, because Germany was able to fight a one-front war and thus maximize its strength. In short, Stalin was the root cause of the German triumph in the West in 1940. In 1939, by allying with Hitler, Stalin had followed Lenin in 1918 by joining the cause of international communism to that of Russian state advancement in concert with Germany.

Having broken through, via the middle Meuse, to reach the English Channel on May 21, 1940, the Germans had cut off the Allied forces to the north. Many of these troops were evacuated from Dunkirk, but the Germans meanwhile rapidly regrouped before pressing south. Numerous French troops fought bravely, notably at the Meuse, Somme, and Aisne, and also at Lille, a key position in protecting what became the Dunkirk defensive perimeter. However, there was to be no repetition of the blocking of the German advances in 1914 and 1918, advances that had lacked the benefit of mechanization. The German superiority in generalship and tanks prevailed in 1940, and, having broken through French defenses on the Somme and the Aisne, the Germans rapidly advanced into central and southern France, seizing cities as far south as Bordeaux.

Moreover, the necessary political will to fight on, while displayed by the new Free French movement under Charles de Gaulle, was largely absent in France. With the commander in chief, General Maxime Weygand, critical of the political system and pressing for an armistice, and Marshal Henri Pétain, the deputy prime minister, also pessimistic about the future and opposed to fighting on, the cabinet, on June 15, agreed to find out what armistice terms the Germans would offer. This sold the pass. There would be no union with Britain as suggested by Churchill, no attempt to mount continued resistance from a Breton redoubt, no guerrilla warfare, and no retreat of the government to the North African colonies.

The army could not have withdrawn to North Africa before being cut off, encircled, and destroyed by the advancing Germans, because there was a considerable distance to the Mediterranean ports and, once arrived, a lack of sufficient merchantmen for a rapid withdrawal. The navy could not act without air protection, and there was a lack of spare parts and ammunition in the air bases in North Africa. The French also feared that a continuation of the war would lead to German intervention in North Africa, either an invasion or provoking local uprisings.[7]

This collapse was of global significance. The Germans imposed an armistice far harsher than that imposed by them in 1871 or envisaged in 1914. Part of France was occupied, while a government cooperative with Germany was established in Vichy in order to rule the remainder. In an echo of the terms imposed on Germany in 1919, Vichy France was only permitted a small and weak military (other than for its fleet). French control of Syria, Lebanon, Madagascar, French North and West Africa, and French Indochina (Vietnam, Cambodia, and Laos) created the possibility of German and Japanese penetration into the Middle East, Africa, and Southeast Asia. The Japanese aircraft that sank British warships off Malaya in December 1941 operated from bases in southern Vietnam.

This collapse also made the British decision to fight on of greater significance, and also far riskier. German naval and air forces could now be moved far closer to Britain than had been the case in the First World War. German hope for a negotiated settlement with Britain reflected the difficulties of invasion, but also Hitler's interest in war with the Soviet Union. The ideological thrust of his policy would be served by a peace by which Britain retained her empire in return for accepting German dominance of the Continent. Moreover, such a peace would match the German commitment to a quick war, one in which a single campaign solved the issues of policy and strategy. Indeed, the German army began to demobilize in the summer of 1940.

There was interest in Britain in a compromise peace, but it was pushed aside by Churchill. In part, the weakness of the Far Left was an element. Left-wing trade unionists looked to the example of Stalin, who was then allied to Hitler, but communism was relatively weak in Britain, while both the Conservatives and Labour were characterized by a robust patriotism.

WAR IN THE WIDER MEDITERRANEAN

Meanwhile the war had spread in a new direction, as Italy, under Mussolini, came in on the German side on June 10, 1940. However, the Italian attack on France in June was thwarted by a firm resistance resting on good prewar defensive positions in the Alps. The umbrella nature of the war was indicated by the number of struggles it now included, which increased with the Italian attack on Greece from Albania on October 28, 1940. This attack was mounted at Mussolini's insistence, despite the Italian forces used being outnumbered and also lacking supplies, as the General Staff had been warned. There was a lack of good ports in Albania through which the Italian navy could land supplies, and a shortage of trucks to move sufficient supplies from the ports. Within two weeks, the Italian advance was stopped by a lack of supplies, which was repeatedly a key element in the war.

The Greeks counterattacked in a campaign that tends to be neglected, which underlines the selective nature of the coverage of the war. The Italians had nine divisions, the Greeks thirteen plus additional forces, while the individual Greek divisions had more soldiers than Italian ones. Finally, when the Greek government realized that it did not have to fear Bulgarian or Turkish intervention, it concentrated the entire army against the Italians. This was an instance of the subordination of strategy to international politics that was particularly apparent in the first half of the war when the combatants were less fixed than from 1942.

As later with Allied operations in Italy in 1943–45, the terrain added further difficulties. Albania and Northern Greece have mountain chains running north to south, and the front ran west to east, perpendicularly cut by mountains. Due to its lack of numbers, the Italian army concentrated its army in the valleys to stop Greek attacks along the roads, only for the Greeks to attack along the ridgelines and overwhelm any Italian troops that might be there.

By December 1940, the Italian army had been driven from Greece and a third of Albania. In bitter cold, the Italians lacked food, artillery, and organization. In late January 1941, the situation stabilized, although an Italian counteroffensive in early March failed. The Italians were not able to prevail until, attacking on April 15, they took advantage of the successful German invasion of Greece earlier that month. Italian total casualties were 155,172, the majority wounded or ill.

Furthermore, in December 1940, the Italian forces that had invaded Egypt from Libya were driven back by the British, a term that should be taken to include Dominion and empire forces, particularly, in this case, Australians. The British went on to conquer eastern Libya and, in early 1941, to reconquer British Somaliland and overrun Eritrea and Italian Somaliland, finishing the conquest of Italian East Africa in northern Ethiopia that November, after overcoming formidable logistical difficulties as well as those posed by the environment. The British benefited from the Italians having built roads linking Ethiopia, Eritrea, and Italian Somaliland and used these to advance from the last into Ethiopia.[8] As a reminder of the significance of linkage between different fronts, the skills developed in the conquest proved of value for the British when later operating in Burma.[9]

More generally, the Italian military lacked good equipment, in part due to the limitations of its industrial base.[10] There was also an absence of realistic political direction by Mussolini, a shortage of able commanders, and serious problems with supplies. The last encouraged large-scale surrenders when the fighting went badly, as in 1940–41 in Libya and Italian East Africa. A lack of trucks greatly affected food and water distribution to the front line, notably in the Tobruk defensive ring in 1940. This situation was exacerbated by a shortage of drivers and car repairers: in 1939, Italy had only about three hundred thousand vehicles.[11]

Hitler responded to Italian defeats by sending help to the Italians in Libya, in the shape of the Afrika Korps, which led to the British being driven back. Moreover, on April 6, 1941, the Germans attacked Greece, as well as Yugoslavia, which had defied German wishes. Virtually surrounded by its opponents, the strung-out Yugoslav defense proved vulnerable, and the country fell rapidly, as Poland had done. The Germans also benefited from both the international and the domestic political situation. Bulgarian, Hungarian, and Italian forces joined in the invasion, each receiving part of Yugoslavia as their reward. Within Serb-dominated Yugoslavia, there was considerable division, and many Croats were unwilling to fight against the invaders, who were enthusiastically greeted when they reached the Croat capital of Zagreb.

The British sent an expeditionary force to help the Greeks, but, with inadequate air support, it was pushed back with fifteen thousand casualties. The tempo of the German advance, especially its rapid use of airborne troops and armor, brought a decisive advantage, as did the effective use of ground-support aircraft. This enabled the Germans to overcome successive defensive lines in Greece. At the same time, analysis is complex. For example, it was also the case that, due to poor weather and roads, among other factors, German aircraft and armor only had a limited impact. In practice, the weakness of the Greek army, notably in command, equipment, and logistics; the lack of coordinated Anglo-Greek command; and the readiness of the hesitant commanders of the British forces to withdraw in the face of fear of being outflanked were all significant.[12] The last was also to be important when the British lost Malaya to boldly operating Japanese invaders in 1941–42.

The campaign culminated with the capture of the Greek island of Crete by German parachute and air-transported troops. This was a risky attack, launched on May 20, 1941, as such forces were unable to bring heavy arms with them, while the formidable British naval presence thwarted the planned maritime support for the invasion. German air attacks, however, inflicted serious damage on the British navy, while the German airborne assault force, although it took heavy casualties, was able to gain the initiative from a poorly directed resistance, to seize airstrips, and to secure resupply by air. The Crete operation was a close-run thing as the parachutists were nearly beaten, but a failure of communications led the British to believe that the situation was never as close to failure for the Germans as it was. The British evacuated their forces, those remaining surrendering on June 3. Because of the very high casualties suffered by the paratroops, Hitler never engaged in a major parachute-landing operation again. The paratroops became, in effect, conventional infantry thereafter, albeit of a more elite nature than those in the regular army.[13]

The conquest of Crete took the Germans forward into the eastern Mediterranean. However, the possibility of exploiting the advance into the eastern Mediterranean was lessened by continued British naval strength and by successful British action to secure Iraq (April–May 1941), and Lebanon and Syria (June–July 1941), the first from a pro-German government and the latter two from Vichy France.

The Iraqis were defeated in a rapid campaign that was a mix of the flying columns, river steamers, and use of native allies employed in the wars of imperial conquest of the nineteenth century, and the application of modern weaponry, especially aircraft and armored cars. This enabled the British both to overrun a large country and to overcome far larger forces. Moreover, the German focus on war with the Soviet Union, which broke out on June 22, 1941, directed German priorities. The Mediterranean was no more than a sideshow for Hitler, one where he acted in order to prevent Britain from exploiting Italian weaknesses.

More generally, the Germans benefited in their early campaigns, in 1939–41, from the army's doctrine, training, and leadership, and, notably, the stress on flexibility, personal initiative, and action. Germany's opponents could not match these elements, either individually or in combination. It was the combined characteristic of German advantages that gave them particular significance.

INVADING THE SOVIET UNION

On June 22, 1941, nearly 3.6 million German and allied troops, supported by 3,350 tanks and 1,950 aircraft, were launched in a surprise attack that had been postponed from May due to unusually wet weather that made the roads impassable. The badly prepared Red Army, which had about 2.7 million troops and 10,400 tanks deployed in the western Soviet Union, suffered heavy defeats at the outset and in initial counterattacks, losing large quantities of men, tanks, and aircraft.

However, lulled by overconfidence in the value of a swift offensive, and completely failing to appreciate Soviet strength, both numerically and in fighting quality,[14] the Germans had neither planned nor prepared adequately for the conflict. Most German generals were confident that they had developed a military system able to defeat the Soviet Union. They did not understand Soviet geography, including the impact of the weather on the roads. German assessments drew on the flaws revealed in the Soviet invasion of eastern Poland in 1939 and, even more, in the initial stages of the Soviet attack on Finland in 1939–40, the Winter War, as well as on assumptions based on the effect of Stalin's extensive purges of the military leadership from 1937 to 1941, purges themselves fed by the German provision of forged information. These assessments failed adequately to note the success of the Red Army in the last (successful) stage of the Winter War as well as postwar improvements, while, anyway, there was a major contrast between weaknesses on the offensive and capabilities in defense.[15] Furthermore, Russian military defeat and total political collapse in 1917 encouraged the Germans to feel that victory could again be had. Letters indicate that many German troops were confident that the war would be speedily over. Nevertheless, despite their misjudgment of the Red Army, appreciable casualties were anticipated by the Germans, who deployed as many troops as they could. The Germans did not understand the Soviet ability to compensate for casualties and lost equipment, and notably the potential of the Soviet economy, especially in tank production. They also planned to overrun production facilities fast, thus making them unimportant.

Much of the German infantry was not fully combat ready, in part due to a lack of sufficient training, while the armor was short of drivers and radio operators and was outclassed by the Soviet T-34 tank. Because it was assumed that the war would be over before winter, there was a complete lack of the winter equipment and uniforms that were to be required.

From the outset, Soviet forces, notably in northern Ukraine, fought better than the Germans had anticipated, and the large amount of Soviet territory conquered, and the millions of troops killed or captured, were at the cost of heavier-than-expected German losses. Soviet doctrine, with its emphasis on defense and its stress on artillery, proved effective once the initial shock and surprise of the German attack had been absorbed. Although there was very serious failure at the operational level, including leaving large numbers to be surrounded, the Soviets fought hard, and the Germans were unable to sustain success and, more seriously, to achieve it in a manner that would enable them to overcome the space and resolve of the Soviet Union.[16] Instead, their victories left them exhausted.

German strategy and fighting methods proved deeply flawed, and there were related doctrinal problems. German doctrine was based on the notion of a rapidly obtained and decisive land battle. This goal was realizable if the opposing power was readily accessible, focused its strength on the army, lacked adequate space in which to retreat or maneuver, and accepted the same doctrinal suppositions. These factors, however, were absent in the case of Britain, the Soviet Union, and the United States; and German war making was the story of failure to suppress the will of others: the inability to make opposing states accept German assumptions. In the case of Germany, will could not be a substitute for an inability to set sensible goals or to implement implausible ones.[17]

There was a serious disjuncture in the case of Germany, notably, but not only, in 1941, between tactical and operational effectiveness, and, on the other hand, strategic folly and economic preparedness. The problems posed in 1941, and again in 1942, by the vastness of the territory to be conquered by the Germans, were compounded by the failure to secure the support of Germany's ally Japan, which instead had signed a nonaggression pact with the Soviet Union, and by a lack of consistency and appropriate prioritization in German strategy. As a result of the former, the (far larger) Soviet Union did not face attack from west and east, as Poland had done in 1939. The German invasion plan represented an attempt to seize all objectives in the Soviet Union simultaneously, but this reflected a serious source of confusion that arose from the failure to settle the core target of the operation and the mistaken assumption that the Soviet Union would rapidly fall. The Germans also pursued murderous, brutal, and expropriatory antisocietal policies that ensured that they were not long seen as liberators by the civilian population who had earlier been brutalized by the Soviet regime.[18]

The inconsistently conceived and executed offensive stemmed from a failure to set sensible military and political goals. Even if the Soviet Union was defeated, there was no viable peace policy on offer for its leadership or people other than total submission. Strategy shifted over the emphasis between seizing territory and defeating Soviet forces, and also over the question of which axes of advance to concentrate on. This led to a delay in the central thrust on Moscow in September, while forces were sent south to overrun Ukraine and destroy Soviet armies there: the gain of the resources of Ukraine (notably grain) and the crushing of Soviet forces there then appeared more important than a focus on Moscow. Hindered by Stalin's refusal to consider advice to withdraw, the Soviet army lost three-quarters of a million men, killed or captured in Ukraine, but victory was won at the cost of serious losses in the German armored forces.[19]

The delay in the advance on Moscow hindered the Germans when they resumed it in late 1941 in Operation Typhoon,[20] not least because the Soviets, helped by the transfer of troops from Siberia where they had faced the Japanese, proved better than the Germans at operating in the difficult winter conditions, and that winter proved very difficult. The Germans, moreover, had very poor logistical support. More seriously, it was unclear what their attack could achieve. Although the Soviet government was evacuated to Kuibyshev on the River Volga, the Red Army was able to hold the assault on Moscow, their communications and command center, and to mount a counterattack launched on December 5–6, 1941. At the end of the 1941 campaign, the Germans had captured neither Leningrad nor Moscow. Further south, having captured the city of Rostov on the River Don on November 21, 1941, the Germans evacuated it a week later as Field Marshal Gerd von Rundstedt, the Army Group commander, feared they had become overextended. Rundstedt was sacked by Hitler.

Moreover, the Soviet counteroffensive revealed the continued vitality of the Red Army, with its effective artillery and increasingly potent tanks.[21] This vitality encouraged resistance activity in the occupied territories. Once their advances had been held, the Germans lacked strong operational reserves to cope with counterattacks, and they found it difficult to stabilize the front in the face of these attacks. The counteroffensive was eventually held, but the Germans never again came so close to Moscow as they had done prior to its launch.

To the north, Leningrad (St. Petersburg) held off German attacks but was besieged, and its inhabitants suffered grievously as the Germans sought to starve out the city, the birthplace of Soviet communism. About one million people died there. The German operations against Leningrad, however, used up troops to scant strategic purpose.[22]

A broader German failure was that arising from the Soviet ability to move large quantities of industrial plant and many millions of workers to the east, far beyond the range of likely German advance or air attack. About 16.5 million people were evacuated between the summer of 1941 and the autumn of 1942. Once relocated, these industries turned out vast quantities of military matériel, outproducing the Germans, for example, in numbers of tanks.

THE JAPANESE ATTACK

In December 1941, the war broadened out when Japan attacked Britain, the United States, and the Dutch, while Hitler then declared war on the United States. Much of the Japanese triumph reflected the ability to direct operations permitted by gaining and using superiority at sea and in the air. Yet this ability still required success on land. Despite having much of its army committed in China, Japan was able to win repeated successes on land. Its opponents, weak and poorly prepared, were outfought. The combat quality and determination of Japanese units were matched by the operational flexibility of their plans. This was particularly seen in Malaya, where the attacking Japanese were outnumbered by British forces. Much of the fighting there involved infantry assaults on British positions, but with the forest cover giving the British scant warning. The Japanese also proved able to outmaneuver the British positions by outflanking them as a result of advances through the forest.

Chapter 9
AXIS ATTACKS HELD, 1942

In Russia, the Germans were able to recover from the Soviet counterattacks of the winter of 1941–42 and mount a major new offensive, whereas the Japanese failed to recover comparably from the first defeats they encountered. The new German attack, however, was to be disastrous. From the outset, the 1942 offensive—Operation Blue—was jeopardized by a poorly conceived and executed plan. In this, the Germans planned the seizure of the Caucasian oil fields, notably around Baku on the Caspian Sea, in order better to prepare for the lengthy struggle that American entry into the war appeared to make inevitable: most of the world's oil supplies were under Allied control or closed to the Axis by Allied maritime strength. The Allies dominated oil production in the Western Hemisphere (the United States and Venezuela) and also in the Middle East (Iran, Iraq, and Saudi Arabia), which helped to make the seizure of oil fields in Borneo and Sumatra important for Japan.

Hitler, however, underestimated Soviet strength and also failed to make sufficient logistical preparations, both consistent problems with his military leadership. Furthermore, there were serious flaws in the development of the operation, specifically in the decision to attack simultaneously eastward toward the River Volga as well as southward into the Caucasus. As the British and Americans showed in advancing against Germany through and beyond France in 1944, the Germans were scarcely alone in their difficulty in fixing on an axis of advance. Nevertheless, the German failure to do so on the Eastern Front was of particular seriousness due to the size of the opposing forces and the extent of the area of operations. Moreover, in 1941, the German advance had already suffered greatly from this factor. As with the determination to devote so many resources to destroying Leningrad, Hitler's conviction, in 1942, that the city of Stalingrad, on the Volga, had to be captured foolishly substituted a pointless symbolic goal for the necessary operational flexibility: German strategy was both misguided and poorly implemented. Despite a massive commitment of resources, the Germans were fought to a standstill at Stalingrad, which had been turned by their air and artillery attacks into an intractable urban wasteland that, in practice, offered major advantages to the Soviet defenders. The fighting there became attritional, and the German force was "fixed." This was an appropriate image of strategic failure. Both strategic and operational elements were swallowed by the tactical dimension.

Soviet losses in combat at Stalingrad were heavy, but they helped stop the Germans. Moreover, the Soviets had mass, some good commanders, and effective artillery. At Stalingrad, as elsewhere, the Soviets benefited from their ability to take heavy casualties, an ability that owed something to the willingness to shoot commanders and ordinary soldiers for failure: about fifteen thousand in the battle for Stalingrad and at least two hundred thousand during the war as a whole. In October 1941, Georgy Zhukov, the commander of the Leningrad front, announced that all the families of those who surrendered would be shot. In 1945, many tens of thousands of surviving prisoners freed from German captivity at the end of the war were shot or sent to the gulags (Soviet concentration camps).

In the Second World War, the attritional character of the conflict was particularly pronounced on the Eastern Front after the initial German successes in late 1941 and mid-1942. This was not least because that was the European land sector in which conflict lasted longest, as well as the largest in Europe, although, in the world as a whole, the Chinese-Japanese conflict lasted the longest. In Europe, the human mass and cost involved was throughout greater on the Eastern Front[23] than in the Mediterranean or Western Europe. The Germans had not planned for such an outcome, for neither their military and its doctrine nor the military-industrial complex was prepared for the lengthy conflict that resulted. Instead, the Germans sought the *Kesselschlacht* (battle of encirclement and annihilation) that they had pursued in earlier conflicts, and, as in 1914, there was no plan B and a failure to give adequate weight to other possibilities.[24] Not envisaged in 1941, the 1942 offensive did not prove an adequate stage two.

In November 1942, a Soviet counterattack drove in the flanks of the German Sixth Army bogged down in Stalingrad. Shortages of troops had led the Germans to cover their flanks with allied troops, mostly Romanians, but their allies also were short of men and lacked tanks. The Sixth Army was rapidly encircled, and the Soviets then expanded their new position in both directions. Attempts, in difficult winter weather, to break through to its relief failed. Despite Hitler's insistence that the army fight on, its remains surrendered in February 1943.

In a separate conflict, the German-Italian invasion of Egypt was blocked and subsequently defeated by British and British Empire forces at El Alamein. The systematic British use of artillery proved important in the successful offensive at El Alamein that drove in the German-Italian defenses with their extensive minefields and well-sited antitank guns. The British artillery first overcame the German artillery and then weakened their defenses. The British, who had earlier tended not to match German skill in combined-arms tactics, now proved more adroit in doing so. Indeed, in some respects, the battle was not only attritional but also a replay of their successful fighting methods in 1918.[25] The British followed up their victory by advancing into and across Libya, albeit without destroying the retreating Germans.

Moreover, Operation Torch, an American-British (largely America) invasion of Morocco and Algeria in November 1942, achieved rapid success in transferring Vichy-run northwest Africa to the Allied camp and thus greatly lessened Axis dominance of the Mediterranean. By causing an angry Germany to occupy Vichy-run France, the invasion also caused a breakdown of the German alliance system.[26]

In response to Torch, the Germans moved troops into Tunisia to help stiffen the Italians retreating from Libya and in order to retain a presence in North Africa. However, the German forces there were to be attacked not only by American troops advancing from Algeria but also by British forces advancing from Libya. The Allies were beginning to mount, not a series of counterattacks, but rather a planned and increasingly coherent attempt, first, to undo Axis conquests and, second, to take the war to the Axis states themselves.

THE EASTERN FRONT, 1943

The Americans and British dominated the struggle at sea and in the air, for example engaging far more German aircraft in 1943 and 1944 than saw service on the Eastern Front. They also made a very important contribution on land by their successes in the Mediterranean and, from 1944, in Western Europe. Nevertheless, the Red Army absorbed the bulk of the German army: over two-thirds was always engaged on the Eastern Front after Germany attacked the Soviet Union. After Stalingrad, this front was largely a prolonged struggle of attrition, although there was usually much more obvious movement than on that front in the First World War.

Formidable foes on the defensive, certainly at the tactical level, the Germans succeeded in stabilizing the front in early 1943 after the loss of the Sixth Army. In part, this was thanks to Field Marshal Erich von Manstein's skilled employment of counterattacks,[27] although they pressed on limited fuel supplies. The stabilization was also due to the difficulties the Red Army encountered in sustaining the offensive, difficulties already seen in early 1942. The relationship between these factors was complex, and this complexity enhances the difficulties in analyzing their respective weights. It was not easy to move from the defense to the offense, nor for the Soviets to provide the logistical support to help maintain an offensive. Thereafter, however, the Germans were outfought.

The German generals agreed with Hitler that, while Germany could not attack along the entire Eastern Front, it nevertheless could not afford to relinquish the initiative in Russia. The panzer divisions were in part rebuilt, including, to a degree, with new tanks, the Tiger and Panther. However, their logistical support was inadequate, not least with a lack of spare parts and fuel. The Battle of Kursk was launched on July 5, 1943, to win a victory, although it also represented the last chance to stabilize an economical front line. In Operation Zitadelle, the Germans launched formidable tank assaults on the northern and southern sides of a large Soviet bulge or salient on the front line around the city of Kursk, intending not only to shorten the front line but also to strengthen their prestige and strike a major psychological blow. Manstein was the principal architect of the plan.

However, the Soviets were well prepared. They had constructed concentric lines of defenses, and these weakened and finally stopped the German assaults. The Germans suffered especially badly at the hands of Soviet artillery, yet again demonstrating that artillery is the most underrated arm in the war; antitank guns indeed were the most underrated weapons. The availability of large Soviet armor reserves was also important to the flow of the battle. The Germans did not fight well. There were many command mistakes. For example, in accepting battle at Prokhorovka on July 12, Lieutenant General Hermann Hoth, the commander of the Fourth Panzer Army, knowingly gambled on the tactical skills and technical superiority of the outnumbered and unsupported divisions of II SS Panzer Corps because he remained committed to his view that the decisive engagement would be fought there. In the event, although their losses were less than often claimed, the Germans failed to break through.[28]

Once the German offensive had been blocked, in a way that had not happened in 1941 or 1942, in each of which the Germans had long advanced, the Soviets rapidly switched over to the attack, making far more gains than the Germans had done in the battle. The Soviets were far better able to replace their losses, notably of tanks. The Soviets drove the Germans out of eastern Ukraine and crossed the Dnieper River. For the remainder of the war, the Germans stood on the strategic defensive on the Eastern Front. Meanwhile, the Red Army proved increasingly successful in attack, adept at developing cooperation between armor, artillery, and infantry; at making the latter two mobile; and at building logistical support so as to maintain the impetus of attack, the last a key element.

Defeat for Germany at Kursk was followed on the Eastern Front by longer fronts defended by weaker forces, and notably so when the Soviets pushed into the Balkans in 1944. Overall German losses rose and, as a percentage of army strength, were, at 15 percent in 1943, heavier than in 1941 (less than 7 percent) or 1942 (10 percent). This was largely due to the conflict on the Eastern Front. The new soldiers, moreover, were less experienced than those who became casualties.

The Germans were unable to translate their central position into lasting political or military success because, due to Hitler's attitudes, peace was not an option. Despite soundings, notably by the Soviets in 1943, there was to be no second Nazi-Soviet pact.

Chapter 9

NORTH AFRICA AND ITALY, 1943–45

Meanwhile the Germans and Italians in North Africa had been forced to surrender by American and British forces in May 1943. The Germans had initially made good use of their interior lines in Tunisia in order to fight the advancing American and British forces separately. Their attack on the Americans in the Battle of the Kasserine Pass in February 1943 had inflicted much damage on outnumbered and poorly commanded units that were not adequately prepared for high-tempo conflict. In part, this was a matter of the blooding or experience that the Germans had gained through earlier conflict, just as Japanese effectiveness in 1941–42 owed something to earlier experience in China, not least in amphibious operations.

American combat effectiveness rapidly improved, however, while the Axis forces in Tunisia suffered from the impact of Allied air superiority, especially on their supply links from Italy. Once the Allies had gained the initiative, the British outflanking the defenses of the Mareth Line, they were able to win a speedy victory and to take more prisoners than the Soviets had captured at Stalingrad. The Allied success in Tunisia hit Japanese confidence in its Axis allies hard.[29]

The Allies pressed on to invade Sicily that July and mainland Italy that September. Amphibious power and air support allowed the Allies to seize the initiative.[30] However, while the overthrow of Mussolini in July by his own ministers, followed in September by an armistice with the Allies, temporarily wrecked Axis cohesion, a rapid German response gave them control of central and northern Italy. This response left the Allies in a far more difficult position. The mountainous terrain and the east–west river lines made Italy excellent defensive terrain. Prefiguring the situation in Korea in 1950–53, much of the fighting proved to be conventional infantry combat, with artillery playing a major role: the terrain was not well suited to armor.

The Allied attempt to bypass German defenses with the Anzio landing in January 1944 was totally mishandled, as in the initial stages there were no German forces to block an advance on Rome. However, the opportunity was lost, the Germans moved up troops, and the exploitation of the landing to create and secure a strong defensive perimeter then proved difficult. Rome did not fall until June.

In the end, a series of hard-fought offensives were required to surmount successive German defensive lines, and Milan, the major city in northern Italy, only fell in April 1945. The Germans not only resisted Allied advances but also suppressed resistance by Italian partisans (guerrillas). In turn, the latter also fought the puppet, pro-German republic of Salò to which Mussolini, once he had been rescued by the Germans, had been reduced. Thus, the war in Italy was both a civil war and a struggle between regular forces.

Although the war in Italy did not fulfill Allied hopes until the very close, the German units sent to Italy were not available to fight the Soviets, nor to resist the Allies in France. Indeed, Mussolini (like Japan) wanted a separate peace between the Soviet Union and Germany so that the latter could concentrate on Britain and the Americans.

Moreover, the Italy campaign was not a strategic irrelevance as far as the goal of the defeat of the Germans in France was concerned. Allied amphibious operations in the Mediterranean in 1943–44 provided valuable experience in planning and execution, notably in air support, airborne attacks, and the use of landing craft. The landings of 1943–44, especially that at Salerno in 1943, also provided warnings about the difficulty of invading France, not least in terms of the German response. The interdependence of land and air warfare was shown by Hitler's concern to retain control of as much of Italy as possible in order to keep Allied bombers as far from German targets as possible. This interdependence had been seen at a tactical level during the First World War, but now it was operational and strategic.

NORMANDY LANDINGS, 1944

The German position in Europe was reasonably strong in the spring of 1944 as, despite the Anglo-American invasion of Italy in 1943, the German army was still largely fighting a one-front war, that with the Soviet Union. Despite the marked decline in the strike power of the German navy and air force, the army was still effective, and there was no serious threat from the hostile population of occupied areas. However, Allied effectiveness had greatly improved. Success in part reflected preparation, as with the Anglo-American invasion of Normandy, which benefited greatly from extensive preliminaries, notably in developing amphibious capability and in intelligence gathering.

On June 6, 1944, in Operation Overlord, American, British, and Canadian forces landed in Normandy. The invasion benefited from the experience gained by the British and Americans in North African and Italian landings in 1942–44, although the scale of the operation and the severity of the resistance, both anticipated and actual, were each more acute in Normandy.

Overlord was a triumph for combined operations, but also a product of the success of the Allied military over the previous two years. In part, this success was a matter of victory in conflict. The British, Canadian, and American navies had won the Battle of the Atlantic, without which it would not have been possible to sustain the major preparations required in Britain prior to the launch of any invasion. In order to confront the German forces in France, it would be necessary to land and support far more troops than had been the case with Operation Torch in North Africa in November 1942, although at a much closer distance to base, which greatly affected the shipping possibilities. The ability to arm and support these numbers was an aspect of the Allied success in mobilizing the productive resources of much of the world's economy, but especially that of the United States. The Allied ability to mount amphibious operations, and in both the European and Pacific theaters at the same time, rested ultimately on American shipbuilding capacity. Moreover, by the summer of 1944, absolute air superiority over northern France had been obtained. The effectiveness of Allied ground-support air power there owed much to the long-term strategy of gaining air superiority over the Luftwaffe.

As important as success in conflict was the process of training and other preparations that contributed to an increase in confidence in the overall fighting quality of land forces and, crucially, in the consequences of the major expansion in the size of the armies.[31] Uneasiness over this factor remained, however. This was unsurprisingly so because, as in the First World War, the use of large numbers of men with little or no combat experience posed major problems for prediction. Training is the factor most underrated in discussing Allied competence, and for each world war.

Prediction was at issue for both sides. Anticipating an attack, which Hitler was confident could be repelled, the Germans, nevertheless, could not prioritize it because of the serious Soviet pressure in Eastern Europe. Soviet successes forced a reallocation of German units intended for the West.

In France, although they had developed the wide-ranging Atlantic Wall system of fortifications, many of which were built of ferroconcrete, the Germans lacked adequate naval and air strength to contest an invasion. Indeed, the Germans were in a far worse state for both naval and air support than the British had been when threatened with invasion in 1940. Furthermore, in large part due to the needs of the Eastern Front, much (although by no means all) of the German army in France was of indifferent quality, as well as short of transport, training, and, in many cases, equipment. The German forces in Normandy were reliant on huge numbers of captured weapons, and for their mobility on horses and bicycles. Many of the officers and men were recovering from wounds suffered on the Eastern Front.

These problems made the quality of German command decisions particularly important, but alongside an extraordinary command chain, these proved inadequate. For long, such failings during the war, for example during Operation Barbarossa in 1941, were generally blamed, notably by captured German generals being questioned, on Hitler's untutored and maladroit interventions. More recently, alongside this factor, there has come a stress also on drawbacks in German planning as a frequent aspect of more widespread deficiencies in German war making.

In the particular case of Overlord, the serious German failure related both to their assessment of where the attack was likely to fall and about how best to respond to it. The Germans were surprised by the Normandy landing. In part due to Allied attempts, including the apparent buildup of units in Southeast England, they had concentrated more of their defenses and forces in the Calais region, which offered a shorter sea crossing from Britain and a shorter route to Germany. Normandy, though, was easier to reach from the invasion ports on the south coast of England, particularly Plymouth, Portland, and Portsmouth. Even after D-day, Hitler remained anxious about a subsequent additional landing near Calais. As another instance of German intelligence failures, the Germans anticipated a Soviet assault in Ukraine in 1944, instead of in Belarus further north where it actually came, and to devastating effect in Operation Bagration. In contrast, the Allies benefited in the invasion of Normandy from a mastery of aerial reconnaissance.

The German commanders in the West were also divided about how best to respond to any landing, particularly over whether to move their ten panzer (tank) divisions in France close to the coast so that the Allies could be attacked before they could consolidate their position, or whether to mass the divisions as a strategic reserve. The eventual decision was that the panzer divisions, whose impact greatly worried Allied planners, should remain inland, but their ability to act as a strategic reserve was lessened both by the decision not to mass them and by Allied air power. This decision reflected the tensions and uncertainties of the German command structure, the tensions around Hitler, and those around the army leadership at many levels.

The German response was also affected by Allied operations, which again underlined the significance of combined operations. Air power helped ensure that the Allies were able to secure the flanks of their landing by the use of parachutists and glider-borne troops. These landings were particularly important to the landing on the right flank of the Normandy operation, at Utah Beach on the eastern base of the Cotentin Peninsula, as the Germans were unable to bring up reserves to support their coastal defenses there. The disorganized nature of the American airdrop, which matched that in the invasion of Sicily the previous year, further handicapped the defense as it disorientated it, not least because there were no coordinated targets to counterattack. The Americans took very few casualties on Utah, in large part because the crucial fighting had already taken place inland.

On the next beach, Omaha, the situation was less happy. The Americans were badly prepared in the face of a good defense, not least because of poor, overly complex planning and confusion in the landing, including the launching of assault craft and duplex drive (amphibious) Sherman tanks too far offshore, as well as a refusal to employ the specialized tanks developed by the British to attack coastal defenses, for example, crabflail tanks for use against minefields. A strong wind and a current did not help, and most troops did not land where or when they were supposed to. There was also a lack of working radios. Under intense machine-gun and mortar fire, the Americans sustained about three thousand casualties, both in landing and on the beach, from German positions on the cliffs that had not been suppressed by air attack or naval bombardment. The experience of Mediterranean and Pacific landings had not been taken on board. Air power could not deliver the promised quantities of ordnance on target on time, and ferroconcrete was highly resistant to bombardment. Eventually, the Americans on Omaha were able to move inland by gaining the bluffs and overcoming the outnumbered defenders there.[32]

However, at the end of D-day, the beachhead was shallow, and the troops in the sector were fortunate that the Germans had no armor to mount a response. This lack of support owed much to a failure in German command that reflected rigidities, in part stemming from Hitler's interventions. More broadly, the pressure from the Soviet army on German resources was significant.

The British and Canadian forces that landed on Gold, Juno, and Sword Beaches further east (the Canadians on Juno) faced active opposition and equipment issues but benefited from careful planning and preparation; from the seizure of crucial covering positions by airborne troops, who landed within their planned drop zones; from the effective use of specialized tanks; and from German hesitation about how best to respond, although there was particularly hard fighting on Gold, where D-day objectives were not attained.[33] The Twenty-First Panzer Division, the sole German armored division in the area, did not counterattack until the early afternoon. German tanks approached the Channel between Juno and Sword beaches but were blocked. At the cost of 2,500 troops killed that day across the entire invasion zone, the Allies were back in France: 132,000 troops had been landed, while the airborne force was 23,000 strong.

The over eleven thousand sorties flown by Allied air forces that day had a major impact: the Luftwaffe was kept away, while, although air support could not always suppress defensive fire, it made a valuable contribution. Had invasion been attempted in 1943, it would have faced a more serious situation in France than it was to do in 1944 as, although the Germans had not proceeded so far with their defensive preparations as they were to have done by D-day, the Allies did not yet have sufficient air dominance to seek to isolate the area of operations, nor had they the capacity to construct an oil pipeline under the English Channel. The naval armada, largely British, both provided heavy supporting fire—heavier fire than from air attack—and also prevented disruption by German warships.

This brief summary of what occurred also helps to indicate what was distinctive about Overlord. In Operation Dragoon, the large-scale Allied landing in Provence in the south of France on August 15, for example, the weakness of the defending force ensured that there was no major battle comparable to that in Normandy: resistance, both on the beaches and inland, where an Anglo-American parachute force landed, was light, and casualties were few. An assault on a fortified coastline on the scale of Overlord was unique.

If Overlord was unique in scale, it also indicated the unpredictable nature of force requirements. There had been interwar interest in enhancing amphibious capability, but it had been a low priority. For both the British and the Americans, it was highly unlikely at that stage that there would be a future need to invade a hostile French coastline. Were Germany to attack in the West again, the more likely scenario was, as in the First World War, of France resisting and receiving assistance from Britain, and maybe the Americans, through the Atlantic and Channel ports. Instead, France had fallen.

The unexpected nature of the challenge facing the Allies in 1944 was a problem, as, very obviously, it had earlier been for the Germans when they had planned an invasion of Britain in 1940, and, as the latter showed, improvisation was not an option. It could not be a substitute for the necessary capability and preparations, a lesson the British had learned at Gallipoli in 1915. In contrast, in a context of greater technological possibilities than were available in 1915, the Allies benefited in 1944 from a purposed process of planning that applied resources to tasks clearly defined in the light of experience. This achievement, however, sounds far easier than was the case, not least because each invasion posed unique issues and problems. Furthermore, by 1944, the combined experience of such invasions, which included American amphibious operations in the Pacific, ensured that very different lessons could be drawn, for example, concerning the desirability of surrendering surprise by mounting a lengthy prior bombardment, which was, in particular, to be an issue in discussions over how best to prepare for the landing on Omaha Beach. The targets in Pacific landings were small compared to those in Italy and Normandy in 1943–44, and there was no strong prospect of resupply for the Japanese defenders.

BATTLE FOR NORMANDY, 1944

Even with the success of Overlord, it proved very difficult for the Allies to break out of Normandy, and they both faced a hard battle and fell behind the anticipated phase lines for their advance. With surprise now lost, Allied casualty rates were far higher than in the initial landings. Training and command issues posed problems. Despite air attacks, especially on bridges, the Germans were able to reinforce their units in Normandy, although the delays forced on them both ensured that the Allies gained time to deepen their beachheads and obliged the Germans to respond in an ad hoc fashion to Allied advances, using their tanks as a defense force rather than driving in the beachheads.

In the subsequent struggle, the Germans learned how to adapt in the face of concentrated firepower and air attack and fought well in defending the *bocage* landscape of Normandy with its many hedges, which provided good cover for antitank guns. In what was a highly constricted battle sphere, the Allies, notably the British and the Canadians, found it difficult to break through and restore maneuver. In contrast, the American capacity to innovate tactics stood them in good stead in defeating the Germans. The Americans broke through at the base of the Cotentin Peninsula and defeated a German counterattack. The German defenders in Normandy were then threatened with envelopment in the Falaise Pocket, although an Allied failure to close it ensured that many were able to retreat.[34]

SOVIET OFFENSIVES, 1943–45

Alongside improvements in organization and equipment,[35] the Soviet learning curve in implementation was apparent in 1943 as they developed the theories of "deep operations" which had been advanced in the 1930s, neglected in 1941, but now implemented and refined in the cauldron of war. Rather than seek encirclements, as the Germans had done in 1941–42, the Soviets deployed their forces along broad fronts, launching a number of frontal assaults designed to smash opposing forces and maintain continued pressure.[36] This was similar to the Allied offensive on the Western Front in 1918.

Taking and using the initiative, the Soviets denied the Germans the ability to recover from attacks, lessened their ability to move units to badly threatened positions, and searched out the weakest points in their positions. As in 1918, at the tactical level, this undermined the value of German defensive "hedgehogs." While they had an operational importance on narrow-front campaigns, narrowing the advance and challenging its flanks and rear, these hedgehogs were less significant in resisting broad-front attacks, particularly when the German defenders could not rely on air support or armored counteroffensives. The loss of air support also ensured that it would not be possible to reinforce encircled positions by air.[37] The Soviet focus on deep operations, and the encirclement and annihilation they permitted, helped ensure the destruction of otherwise tactically proficient, endlessly resourceful, and determined German formations.[38] There was also an ability to use their armor more effectively than the Germans.[39]

The degree of success increasingly enjoyed by Soviet offensives instilled uncertainty in their opponents. This helped to ensure that the defensive effort required by the Germans on the Eastern Front meant that the mobile reserve necessary to oppose successfully a Second Front in France was being destroyed.

Although not always successful and also facing major problems with logistics,[40] the Red Army indeed achieved what has been seen as its own blitzkrieg. This was especially so in the breakthrough attacks in June–September 1944 (Operation Bagration), which overran Belarus and took the Soviets close to Warsaw. In the process, the Red Army destroyed much of the German Army Group Center and caused over half a million casualties.

Although fighting determinedly,[41] the Germans were badly outgeneraled and totally outfought. In less than two and a half years of fighting, the Red Army drove the Germans from the Volga to the Elbe, a distance greater than that achieved by any European force for over a century, and one that showed that a war of fronts did not preclude one of a frequent movement of those fronts. This was not simply an advance on one axis but one from the Black Sea to the Baltic across much of Eastern Europe, and an advance that destroyed much of the German army. The achievement was greater than that of the German advance east in 1941–42, not least because the opponent was unable to recover and, instead, was totally defeated. The Soviets both captured territory and destroyed their opponents.

Germany's allies were also defeated and knocked out of the war. The Soviet advance into the Balkans led in 1944 to the overthrow of pro-German governments in Romania and Bulgaria, and to the German evacuation of Greece, Albania, and Yugoslavia. Thus, the campaign of that year was important to the fate of a number of states. It does not receive the matching attention. Once they had changed sides, the Romanians provided considerable numbers of troops to fight the Germans. The Soviets pressed on to invade Hungary and Slovakia.

Moreover, under pressure, Finland responded to the shift of fortune by abandoning Germany in 1944. The Finns subsequently joined the Soviets in attacking German forces based in Arctic Norway.

Soviet operational methods toward the end of the war stressed firepower but also employed mobile tank warfare: attrition and maneuver were combined in a coordinated sequence of attacks in which heavy losses were accepted. Once they had broken through, mobility and the sustained pace of the offensive allowed the Soviets to prevent their opponents from falling back in order, while strong German defensive hedgehogs were enveloped and then bypassed. In 1945, when the Soviets declared war on Japan, operational effectiveness led to the very rapid conquest of Manchuria despite its large garrison.

THE CLOSE OF THE WAR, 1944–45

Improvements, tactical and operational, on the part of the Americans, British, and Soviets were such that it proved repeatedly possible to defeat German forces in 1944 and to inflict heavy casualties on them. However, despite the July 20, 1944, bomb plot, an unsuccessful effort by some senior officers to kill Hitler and overthrow his regime, the war did not end that year as was overoptimistically hoped by some Allied commentators. Making the difficult transition from the breakout from Normandy to a wide-front advance toward Germany, a lack of command coordination and skill hit the Allies, as did serious supply problems. The British and Americans failed to handle the operational level of war adequately, and, as a consequence, there was scant focus on theater-level action or the synchronizing or sequencing of major operations. The emphasis, instead, on a broad-front advance ensured that the gaining of land, rather than the destruction of German forces by far more risky maneuverist deep operations, was the option followed.

This, however, ensured that the Germans were not destroyed and helped them to play to their tactical strengths.[42] Moreover, in what was a poorly conceived operation,[43] the failure of the British parachute and glider attack on Arnhem showed the operational and tactical weaknesses of airborne troops in the face of supply problems and the heavier weaponry of opponents' units, as well as the difficulties of staging a breakthrough. More generally, the Allies were faced by a shortage of manpower and motor transport. In addition, the German defense hardened as the campaign of maneuver in the West was forced to a close in late 1944 and the weather deteriorated. The German army did not collapse. Its units, both large and small, retained cohesion.[44] The German army did not have the degree of class division seen in 1918.

Continued determination in the face of heavy odds was also the American experience when attacking Japanese garrisons on Pacific islands, as on the Gilbert Islands in 1943, the Marshall and the Mariana Islands in 1944, and Iwo Jima and Okinawa in 1945. Few Japanese surrendered, and their willingness to fight to the death created an alien fighting environment for the Americans, compounding the difficulties of operating in hostile terrain, thick cover, and a harsh climate. This fighting to the death provided a dimension of total war, as did the high casualties suffered over what were relatively small islands. Before the island assaults, American air and sea power offered a massive technological advantage, but, once landed, the Americans found that the capability gap was far narrower and, instead, that fighting was a matter of closing with the enemy in circumstances that favored the defense.

The Americans could choose where to land, but the fighting and logistical problems of operations on shore both remained formidable. Having successfully invaded the Philippines in late 1944, the Americans found that operations on land involved them in heavy casualties. The invasion served as a reminder that Japanese forces could tie down large numbers of Americans and thus underlined the need to select targets carefully. Indeed, the invasion seemed to some critics to be a cul-de-sac on the route to Japan. In the background were service rivalries and the views of individual commanders, especially Douglas MacArthur, who pressed for the operation. This was not a unique episode, nor a characteristic only of American war making. Instead, for all militaries, abstractions, such as national policy or strategic culture, have to be understood in terms of support from particular interests, as well as pressure for specific views. Rivalries between generals were exploited by political leaders, notably Stalin, while Hitler manipulated German generals, especially by providing secret extra payments, including land in conquered territory. Yet, as a reminder of the need to be cautious in explanation, MacArthur's pressure can only be used to a degree. At the same time, faced by a formidable logistical prospect, the American navy knew that it needed Subic Bay and other ports for an invasion of Japan, and American politicians saw the Philippines as American: they therefore had to be retaken by force of American arms as soon as possible.

Early in 1945, the Americans seized the islands of Iwo Jima and Okinawa in order to provide air bases for an attack on Japan. The overcoming of the well-positioned and determined Japanese forces, fighting in defense of their homeland, was slow and involved heavy casualties. The Japanese fought to the end, a sacrificial policy perhaps emerging out of the earlier stress on "spirit" that matched the use of kamikaze (suicide) aircraft against American warships. These policies affected American tactics and armaments. This resistance was of strategic as well as tactical and operational significance because of the likely costs of American attacks.

That was not the only strategic dimension. Although very successful in their offensive in southern China in 1944 and gaining much territory there, the Japanese had failed then, as in earlier offensives, to knock China out of the war. However, controlling, for the first time, a continuous ground route from Manchuria to Vietnam gave Japan a land axis that was independent of American maritime intervention. This provided Japan with valuable strategic depth. Furthermore, Japanese forces overran Chinese airfields from which American aircraft could otherwise have bombed Japan. This obliged the Americans to focus on seizing islands that could provide air bases, such as Saipan. This Japanese campaign also gravely weakened the idea of a China-based American invasion of Japan.

In Burma, in contrast to China, the Japanese were outfought on the ground. The simplicity of their determined offensive tactics were no longer adequate against British troops (very much British imperial forces) who, thanks to improved training focused on the task in hand, were better able to operate in the jungle, not least to patrol and fight there. The well-motivated

British also benefited from superior logistics, medical support, air power, and artillery. In March to July 1944, they heavily defeated a poorly planned and executed Japanese invasion of northeastern India, designed to provoke a rising by Indian nationalists, followed by a Japanese advance on Delhi. Instead, in hard fighting, British forces held on to their positions at Imphal and Kohima in Assam. Lacking heavy weapons and sufficient mortar shells, the Japanese launched unsuccessful frontal attacks. They suffered from poor logistics and a misguided confidence that they would be able to seize British supply dumps. The Japanese were totally defeated.

In turn, in an impressive feat of generalship that also reflected the improvement of British military capability, the British invaded Burma that December, defeating the Japanese at Meiktila in March 1945 and reconquering the country. This campaign was a major defeat of large Japanese forces. It is one that tends to be ignored by the American public and, now, increasingly by its British counterpart, which has forgotten Britain's role as an imperial military power. To assess Japanese war making as well as the war with Japan, it is necessary to understand the very different requirements, course, and consequences, for both sides, of operations in Burma, China, and the Pacific, and also to appreciate the important contrasts between the parts of the Japanese military.

Although they knew they had lost, the German and Japanese commanders fought on, at great cost, because they wished to avoid a shameful defeat and, in the case of the Germans, because many were committed Nazis. Following a pattern clearly shown from Operation Barbarossa on, senior German officers (like their Japanese counterparts) tended increasingly to disregard military reality when they took decisions. So, even more so, did Hitler, who responded to the July 1944 bomb plot by taking more control and determining to take the initiative.

This lack of realism was very apparent with the Ardennes offensive in late 1944, the Battle of the Bulge launched on December 16. This surprise attempt to break through to Antwerp, the key Allied supply port, isolating the British forces, and to inflict defeat on the Western Allies, was designed to strategic effect, notably to persuade Britain and the United States to abandon the war with Germany so that Germany could focus on the Soviet Union in a one-front war. In practice, although feared by Japan, which did not want Britain and the United States to concentrate on her, this was a total misreading of the political situation. In addition, in the face of Allied military power and resilience, there was not the room for the maneuver warfare the Germans had earlier used so well. Moreover, the Germans lacked the strength to exploit early gains. Confused German command structures did not help. Allied, essentially American, combat quality and responsiveness, such as the superb American defenses of the towns of Bastogne and St. Vith,[45] were both underrated. The Germans advanced to within sight of the River Meuse near Dinant but could neither sustain their advance nor overcome fierce American resistance in flank positions.[46] German propaganda, however, still managed to suggest to the people that the fate of the war remained undecided.

Despite flaws, the Allied achievement in 1944 was formidable, not least in comparison with the extent of Allied advances in 1918, although in 1918 the Allies had the disadvantage that Germany was essentially fighting a one-front war and that the Germans took the initiative for part of the year. In 1944, the German army lost 1.8 million troops, a third of its strength. These losses also hit both accumulated experience and training, as a result affecting the quality of both officers and men. The Wehrmacht also found itself on the defensive, trapped in an attritional warfare it could not win, and attempts to regain mobility, notably by means of the Battle of the Bulge, failed.

Alongside for the Allies (and the Axis) the significance of resources and the role of improvements in fighting technique, it is also important to note other factors. These included the extent to which the quality of officers rose under the serious pressures of their tasks. There were certainly improvements in the steps taken to monitor and maintain troop morale.[47]

Having checked the German Bulge offensive, the Western Allies resumed the advance, and across a broad front, unlike that German counterattack. The Allies fought their way to, and across, the River Rhine, while Germany was incessantly bombed. There was then a rapid advance, although a fanatical German willingness to fight to the end ensured that the fighting remained costly and brutal until the close. In April 1945, nearly as many American soldiers were killed in action in Europe as had been killed in June 1944.[48] The Germans and Japanese continued to fight hard until the end, which helps explain the decision to continue bombing them so much. German resistance in Berlin and that of Japanese forces in Manila had to be overcome by block-to-block fighting, but this was done, by Soviet and American forces respectively. These were not Stalingrad-type offensives. Hitler's suicide in Berlin was followed by Germany's surrender.

MILITARY STYLES AND STRENGTHS

The difficulty of making general statements about military style, and notably about national characteristics, is underlined by the different conclusions of detailed studies. For example, American fighting quality in the winter of 1944–45 against the Germans has been underlined in discussion of the Vosges campaign, but questioned for the Huertgen Forest operation. Command skills in the latter have been criticized. In part, such differences can reflect scholarly emphasis. However, there is also the frequently underrated issue of variations between units, as well as the extent to which particular command decisions could accentuate the nature of such variations.

The relatively small size of the American army ensured a lack of reserve divisions, and the resulting duration of combat without a break for individual units in 1944–45 created serious difficulties as well, again, with variations between units. At the same time, the Americans did not suffer the heavy losses the Germans were cumulatively hit by on their various fronts, losses that affected their fighting quality and that lessened the earlier capability gap in Germany's advantage. Allied strength, including in air power, meant that the Germans, forced into attritional warfare on the defensive, were no longer able to demonstrate their earlier superiority in maneuver warfare and were unable to match Allied tactical and operational skills.

The war repeatedly demonstrated the value of doctrine and, very differently, of training. As far as the former was concerned, Major General Eric Dorman-Smith, deputy chief of staff for the British Eighth Army in North Africa in 1942, and a critical commentator, then and subsequently, of British fighting methods, saw doctrine as a crucial factor in conflict there in 1941:

> In the Middle East Command, during the autumn of 1941, there arose the tactical heresy which propounded that armour alone counted in the Desert battle, therefore the British . . . should discover and destroy the enemy's equivalent armour, after which decision the unarmoured infantry divisions would enter the arena to clear up what remained and hold the ground gained.

Dorman-Smith contrasted this situation with Rommel's Afrika Korps and its tactical preference for a "mixed formation of all arms," and attributed British deficiencies to the sway of generals with a cavalry background: "the romantic cavalry mystique of horsed warfare" led to "basic tactical fallacies . . . the dichotomy between the unarmoured infantry divisions and the relatively 'uninfanterised' armoured divisions."[49] Dorman-Smith correctly picked out the impact of earlier cavalry practices in British armored warfare. However, just as cavalry had been hit by infantry firepower, so tanks were stopped by antitank guns.

In practice, armored divisions that were balanced between the arms were more effective, rather as the Napoleonic division and corps had been. The British eventually adapted their doctrine and closed this capability gap, dismissing some commanders in the process, although the initial doctrine for infantry-armor operations imposed by General, later Field Marshal, Bernard Montgomery, commander of Eighth Army in 1942–43 and of the Allied Ground Forces (Normandy) in 1944, was flawed and required change after the serious problems encountered in Normandy. Armor there too often advanced without adequate support, despite commanders urging their officers to wait for it, which was a sensible response to the German skill in defensive warfare, especially the careful siting of guns to destroy advancing tanks. That July, Lieutenant General Sir Richard O'Connor, the commander of Eighth

Corps in Normandy, instructed the commander of a British armored division to "go cautiously with your armour, making sure that any areas from which you could be shot up by Panthers [tanks] and 88s [antitank guns] are engaged. Remember what you are doing is not a rush to Paris—it is the capture of a wood by combined armour and infantry."[50]

The German army, like that of other states, was expanded very rapidly, and this caused problems for its training. From 1.1 million strong at the start of 1939, it reached 5.76 million in June 1940, an expansion that worried German commanders. Combat effectiveness, however, was helped both by the training that took place during the "Phony War" of inactivity between the conquest of Poland and the attack on Scandinavia in the spring of 1940 and by the limited number of casualties, which meant that the experienced manpower was not chewed up, as had happened in 1914. Between the start of September 1939 and the end of August 1940, the German army lost seventy-six thousand dead and very few prisoners, low figures compared to what had been expected as a result of the experience of combat in 1918. In contrast, French combat effectiveness did not improve during the Phony War. A capability gap in favor of the Germans was readily apparent into late 1941 and for the Japanese until mid-1942.

The learning curves subsequently and successfully followed by Allied forces,[51] however, helped not only to close the capability gaps with their Axis opponents but also to provide gaps in favor of the Allies. This element tends to be ignored because of the widespread presentation of the war in terms of superior German and Japanese fighting quality that was only overborne by greater Allied resources. The latter interpretation, however, faces many problems, including the failure to make any sense of the ultimately flawed Italian contribution to the Axis. Aside from the failure to address variations within armies, there is a more general lack of appreciation of wartime changes in overall effectiveness, a situation also seen with the assessment of the First World War. In the case of Japan, American, Australian, and British-Indian fighting effectiveness on land all greatly increased between early 1942 and 1944. So also with the Allies fighting Germany.

Training was very important, and success in it had tactical and thus operational consequences. Training conditioned men to machines (and to the machine, at once complex and simple, that is the army); enabled troops to assimilate new tactical thinking and to convey an instructive response; provided experience of the unit in, and with, which troops would fight; and gave a psychological form of empowerment, providing an understanding of what was to happen as troops became "combat-wise." Night training and the use of live firing in training were both significant. It was necessary to overcome the civilizing effects of peacetime and to prepare troops for killing. Bayonet drill was a classic instance, even though bayonets were rarely used for that end, other than by the Japanese, the others preferring to use light automatic weapons effectively.[52]

Training was far more complex than in the late nineteenth century. In large part, this was because the nature, range, and challenge of combined-arms operations were more difficult, on a battlefield that included not only indirect fire but also tanks and aircraft. The nature of formations, and the responsiveness of troops to officers and noncommissioned officers, also changed as close-order formations, whether lines, squares, or columns, were replaced, in the "empty battlefield," by more dispersed formations. As a result, officers could not readily give orders, and individual soldiers as well as noncommissioned officers now had to make their own choices. That troops were more educated, better read, and less familiar than in the past with the rural experiences of coping with weather, understanding terrain, and seeing death in the case of animals was also significant in affecting training and the experience of combat.

WEAPONRY

The roles of cultural and doctrinal differences were seen in weapons procurement, although other factors were also involved, including the nature of links between the military and industry. Unlike the Germans, the Americans and Soviets concentrated on weapons that made best use of their industrial capacity because they were simple to build, operate, and repair, for example, the American M-1 Garand infantry rifle and Sherman M-4 tank, and the Soviet 120 mm Type 38 mortar. In contrast, German tanks were complex pieces of equipment and often broke down, compromising their value. For example, whatever its impressive specifications, the unreliability and high maintenance requirements of the Tiger tank weakened it. The Americans emphasized tanks that were fast and maneuverable, rather than heavily armored, and produced the Sherman, which exemplified these characteristics, in large quantities. Although under-armored and under-gunned for much of the war, the Sherman was the first truly universal fighting vehicle, able to fight in such different environments as Europe, the southwest Pacific, and the North African desert. The Americans also benefited in late 1944 from the introduction of high-velocity armor-piercing shells for their tank armament. There were long-term problems with the conception, planning, production, deployment, and use of British tanks, although by 1943 these had improved as production was concentrated on fewer designs.[53] The unwillingness of Italian industrialists to abandon their quasi-monopolies helped to ensure that Italy lacked effective heavy and light tanks. Thus, the M 13/40 was slow, its gun inadequate, and its armor thin.

Tanks were not alone. Motorizing antitank weaponry was important. The resulting self-propelled tank destroyers had a major impact. The Italian self-propelled howitzer was a surprise to British tanks, while effective German tank destroyers were matched by American versions armed with 76 mm and 90 mm guns.

More generally, the absence of adequate mechanization, and at nearly all levels, affected the effectiveness and range of German advances. However, even had there been more German vehicles, there were the issues both of their maintenance and, more seriously, of the availability of petrol (gas). Italy was in an even worse position.

A very different example of German overprovision from that of tanks was provided by uniforms. That of German soldiers looked good but required far more wool than its British counterpart. The Germans also lacked the winter clothes that the Soviet troops had. This hit them especially hard in the very difficult winter of 1941–42.

The Allies had important advantages in artillery and in motorized infantry. Artillery was more effective than in the earlier world war because of better shells and fuses, for example, proximity fuses, which were used by the Allies in land warfare from the Battle of the Bulge. Benefiting from impressive guns, such as the American 105 mm howitzer, Allied artillery was more intensive and overwhelming in firepower, although the British lacked an adequate modern heavy artillery. The Soviets had particularly plentiful artillery and, in 1945, used short and savage artillery bombardments to prepare the way for tank assaults. The Americans, British, and Soviets were very keen on using big artillery bombardments to accompany their offensives, as with the successful and rapid Soviet advance across the River Oder on Berlin in 1945. The Germans, who used artillery when they could, had no real answer. Although, unlike the Germans, the Italians favored a doctrine of massive artillery fire, Italian artillery was old and had too little ammunition. In the Pacific, the Japanese relied on the terrain, frequently digging in underground. In contrast, Allied firepower there was largely provided by warships and air attacks, although the plunging fire of mortars was important to conflict on the islands.

Artillery fire, especially that of the Americans, benefited from improved aiming and range that reflected not only better guns, but also radio communication with observers, as well as meteorological and survey information. The Americans, with their high-frequency radio, were especially adept at this combination. The use of self-propelled and mechanized guns increased the mobility of artillery. Artillery dominance remained a decisive factor into the closing campaigns of the war.[54] It tends to be underrated in film portrayals of the war in favor of tanks.

The Germans were not without good weapons. In the MG-42, introduced in 1942, they had a flexible, easy-to-use machine gun, which gave considerable strength to their defensive positions and made it important to suppress their fire before they were stormed. However, the value of weapons depended on fighting conditions. For example, on the Eastern Front, the impact of the effective German long-range antitank guns was lessened by the close distances of actual engagements.

Whereas the Americans, who first used the Bazooka antitank rocket in 1942, failed to upgrade it as tanks got heavier, the Germans developed the design into the more powerful *Panzerschreck* rocket grenade. They also developed the handheld *Panzerfaust* rocket launcher. The British lacked a satisfactory antitank weapon.

The ranges at which rifles were used were often no more than four hundred yards, and often much less. This led to the development of the assault rifle, firing a round of intermediate power with a range of about four hundred yards. American infantry companies were armed with automatic and semiautomatic rifles and reliable light machine guns, bazookas, mortars, and grenades.

The expansion of the range of weaponry and capabilities included decrypting encoded radio messages. This capability was important to the Allies, against both Germany and Japan.

MOVEMENT

Building on their prewar peacetime society as well as on military developments, American forces were motorized to an extent greater than those of any other state, and this was not only a question of the armor, while the British had made impressive advances with mechanization. No other power matched either. American weapons production was closely linked to the objective of movement. German success on the Western Front in 1940 had led American tank commanders to foster a doctrine in which their armor alone brought success. However, American force structure and training was organized by Lieutenant General Lesley McNair, the head of Army Ground Forces from 1942 to 1944 (who was killed by "friendly fire" in Normandy), to emphasize combined-arms attacks. McNair was not in favor of heavier tanks with bigger guns. Instead, he favored antitank guns and tank destroyers. He also created airborne units and light divisions.[55]

American infantry and artillery were fully motorized, which helped maintain the pace and cohesion of the advance. The Germans, Japanese, and Soviets, and even the British, could not match this integration, although that did not prevent major Japanese advances in southern China in 1944–45. The image of German mechanized movement, an image carefully disseminated in propaganda films that are still regularly shown as part of modern documentaries, was deceptive, as *Panzergrenadiers* were only a minority of the German infantry. Most of the German infantry were slow-moving infantry, dependent on horse-drawn transport. In contrast, the Soviets, notably in 1944–45, were able to make much of their infantry and artillery mobile, in part thanks to the American provision of trucks.

American mobility was intended to allow for "triangular" tactics and operations, in which the opposing force was frontally engaged by one unit while another turned its flank, and a third, in reserve, was poised to intervene where most helpful. British observers were impressed by the value of motorized infantry, and, in late 1944, some individual commanders, such as O'Connor, sought to find ways to follow suit.[56] So also for lesser forces. In its planning in 1940–42, the Vichy army had responded to German victory by envisaging a more motorized force so that the infantry and artillery could move at the same speed as the armor.[57]

American force structure and tactics were a direct product of the economy's ability to produce weaponry and vehicles in large numbers and were closely related to American logistical capacity. The force structure and logistics also helped to ensure the strength of the economy, as the relatively small number of combat divisions, eighty-nine, made it easier to meet demands for skilled labor in manufacturing. President Franklin Delano Roosevelt's call, in his radio broadcast on December 29, 1940, for America to be "the great arsenal of democracy" was fully met.

Given the size of the United States, it was necessary for the economy there to be effective at transportation and logistics. This experience helped the Americans greatly in the war. The flexibility of both economy and society had direct consequences in terms of American production and fighting quality.[58] Institutional and cultural factors were very significant, notably the widespread existence of management abilities stemming from the needs of the economy, as well as a high degree of appointment and promotion on merit, albeit not as far as African Americans were concerned. In addition, in the United States, there were widely disseminated social characteristics that had military value, including a can-do spirit, an acceptance of change, a willingness to respond to the opportunities provided by new equipment, a relative ease with mobility, and a self-reliance that stemmed from an undeferential society.

At both tactical and operational levels, mobility and firepower were seen by the Americans as multipliers that compensated for relatively few troops. These facets had resource and logistical implications, not least in the need for oil (gas), ammunition, and shipping. Thus, the *relatively* small size of the American combat arm increased its mobility, although there was need, on the part of Americans, for a substantial backup and for a higher level of resources than enjoyed by other armies.

That account of American fighting style, however, does not allow for the variety of methods employed by the Americans in response to the many military environments they confronted, methods that benefited from the quality of their combat leadership.[59] For example, although it was not only against the Japanese that the Americans employed close-in infantry techniques, these techniques became more significant in the Pacific in 1944–45 as the Japanese on the islands increasingly focused on resting on the defensive in well-fortified positions rather than attacking landing forces. Underground fortifications provided the Japanese with a myriad of interconnected firing positions. From 1944, the Americans employed "corkscrew and blowtorch" tactics, involving satchel charges and flamethrowers, in order to kill Japanese in situ or to force them into the open to be killed by overwhelming fire.[60] In Okinawa in 1945, the coral limestone hills had been fortified by the determined defenders with tunnel positions, pillboxes, mortar emplacements, and machine-gun nests. American casualties were heavy. The Americans deployed all the facilities of available weaponry to aid their slow progress: they dropped napalm and explosive charges into the entrances of Japanese positions and made extensive use of tank-mounted flamethrowers, the successful use of which depended on the crucial protection provided by the infantry. Demolition teams of combat engineers also proved an important part of this well-integrated force which reflected the value of accumulated experience.

RESOURCES

Allied resource superiority and economic sophistication[61] affected the conduct of the war at the strategic, operational, and tactical levels. For example, as the Americans advanced across France in 1944, they generally did not storm villages and towns where they encountered resistance. Instead, they stopped, brought in aerial, armor, and artillery support, and heavily bombarded the site before moving in, with limited loss of American life, although this did not lessen the contribution made by their effective infantry.

To some American commentators, the British were overly keen on waiting to bring up artillery, a course that could lead the Germans to strengthen their defenses or to disengage successfully and retreat. However, the British had learned, by hard experience at German hands in North Africa in 1941–42, the wisdom of methodical preparation and superior firepower when closing with the Germans. Moreover, their doctrine for offensives emphasized consolidation to repel counterattacks rather than follow-ups to exploit enemy weaknesses.[62]

Montgomery used artillery and air support to preface his attacks in 1944–45. His employment of the former reflected First World War doctrine and practice as well as the significant defensive strength of the Germans.[63]

At the same time, Montgomery adapted to new ideas from subordinate officers and created doctrine accordingly, notably with combined-arms tactics.[64]

Resource superiority made it easier for the Americans to support combined-arms tactics, although it was also necessary to have the relevant doctrine and training. In part, this entailed knowing how best to respond to the combined-arms tactics of opponents. The Germans, in contrast, proved unable to do so. In particular, their moving armor was vulnerable to Allied close air support, which helped to close the capability gap from which they had initially benefited. This was an instance of the manner in which resource factors were very important in providing the basis for successful combined-arms tactics, although, again, they could not in themselves provide the necessary doctrine. Doctrine had to adapt to weaponry, but it also involved other factors. Tactical capability, in turn, made it easier to implement operational planning.

RESOURCE TARGETING

The importance of resources helped provide direction to the land war. Hitler was aware of the role of resources, and this affected his military planning. In 1940, Hitler invaded Norway in part to control Swedish iron ore exports through the Norwegian port of Narvik. Subsequently, he kept large numbers of men in northern Finland in order to hold Petsamo and its nickel reserves, sought to secure the manganese at Kivri Rog in Ukraine, wished to seize the Caucasus oil fields, and tried to hold on to Crimea in order to prevent Soviet aircraft that might be based there from being able to bomb the Ploesti oil fields in Romania.

Yet these goals led to major problems. Planning for the German offensive in 1942, Hitler included an advance on the Soviet oil fields at Baku, although it was not clear how this oil would be transported. This advance ensured that there were fewer tanks available for operations near Stalingrad and also increased the vulnerability of the German offensive to flank attack. In the event, the Germans did not reach Baku. They conquered territory in the northern Caucasus, but to no strategic effect.

Attacking industrial resources, by land and air, was also important to Allied strategy. In his "General Situation" memorandum of January 21, 1945, Montgomery, now commander of the Twenty-First Army Group, wrote of the leading German industrial region, "The main objective of the Allies on the western front is the Ruhr: if we can cut it off from the rest of Germany the enemy capacity to continue the struggle must gradually peter out."[65]

CONCLUSION

The role of subsequent assessment of the war remains significant to the perception of land warfare because, for all leading powers bar China, which was to wage a large-scale civil war in 1946–49, it was the last existential conflict they waged. At the level of the personal experience of individual soldiers, the memory, or rather memories, have been disseminated in part by publications[66] but also, more commonly, by extensive treatment in the media. Unfortunately, this process can not only be misleading for the war itself but can also lead to a neglect or underplaying of the significance of what happened. There are also the persistent issues arising from different national and other treatments of the same episodes or developments.[67]

As a result of the interest in mechanized warfare shown by societies for whom such mechanization was, with the motor car, part of the experience and facts of life, the impression of combat changed. Images created at the time also proved highly seductive. These images were of movement *and* force, and the war was very much seen in these terms, and thus as different from the First World War. With the tank, firepower became an aspect of mobility, and the combination dominated the image of fighting and, more particularly, of success. Plucky infantry could be shown as defeating armor, as in the climax of the American film *The Battle of the Bulge* (1965). However, the general theme in television documentaries on the History Channel, were those of armor advances.

This theme led to an underplaying of the role of artillery, which, in both world wars, was the principal killer of combatants, although, due to its range, not generally a significant killer of civilians. The role of artillery was classically underplayed in accounts of battles and continues to be in film treatments. However, this role proved of great importance not only in suppressing defenses, as used by the British against the Germans and Italians at El Alamein in Egypt in 1942, the key battle in the North African theater of the war, but also in thwarting counterattacks. This role was one of the principal aspects of the continuity between prewar circumstances and the world wars, as well as between the two of them, of which it is all too easy to lose sight. A sense of continuity can be seen in an extract from the draft report of 30 Corps, part of the British Eighth Army. Dated November 21, 1942, this report was drawn up after its victory at El Alamein:

> The operations proved the general soundness of our principles of training for war, some of which had been neglected during previous fighting in the desert. In all forms of warfare, new methods should never disregard basic principles. The operations involved a reversion, with the difference due to the developments in weapons, to the static warfare of the war of 1914–18. This reversion should not be regarded as an isolated exception unlikely to recur . . . our

organisations and weapons must remain suitable both for mobile and periodical static operations.[68]

Moreover, the use of armor could in part be countered by the development of antitank defenses, notably in the form of antitank guns and minefields. The quality and quantity of each increased greatly during the war. Artillery, however, whether static or mechanized, was employed to suppress antitank defenses.

There were major changes in land operations during the Second World War, as there had also been during the previous world war. In each world war, these changes reflected the inability of Germany (and of Japan in the Second World War) to translate their initial victories into lasting political or military success. In each case, this failure helped to give an attritional character to the war, both at the strategic level as well as in the nature of fighting.[69] Even then, differences in war aims, operational culture, force structure, resource availability, and the terrain and weather features of the area of combat, combined to ensure great diversity in conflict, as well as undermining the idea that the two wars were a unit. German and Japanese attempts to improve their war economy faced the structural weaknesses of their ideologies and wartime conditions. Will was no substitute, and violence was part of a process of hasty improvisation that could not act as a replacement for the rational crisis management required. Moreover, reflecting in large part their prewar character and training, both the German and the Japanese militaries were more tactically and operationally adept than strategically oriented.

Alongside the systemic flaws in German war making that were readily apparent from late 1941 (and in practice there earlier), and those of the Japanese from the winter of 1942–43, Allied improvements in fighting effectiveness by 1944 reflected the general Allied success in directing resources, in appreciating the interdependence of weapons and operations, and in improving training. The last was particularly necessary for the Americans and British, and 1943 in particular was a year focused on training and preparation. Alongside the marked improvements in American and British capabilities, the Soviets, having recovered from the purges of the late 1930s, showed that they had mastered the capabilities of their weaponry and fighting systems, had learned how to outfight their opponents, and had developed not only a "deep battle" doctrine that drew on prewar ideas but also the ability to maintain the pace of a rapid fighting advance.

Allied attacks simultaneously from a number of directions proved more successful than they had done in 1915, 1916, and 1917, making it harder for the Germans, once committed, to shift forces between theaters. In late 1942, Operation Torch coincided with the Soviet counterattack at Stalingrad; in 1943, Operation Husky, the Allied invasion of Sicily, helped lead Hitler to call off the Kursk offensive; and in 1944, Operation Bagration, the Soviet advance through Belarus, was launched soon after D-day. The cumulative pressure was intense. Moreover, cooperation between the Allies, notably between Britain and the United States, greatly multiplied their contribution.[70] The Axis could not match this.

Chapter Ten

The Second World War at Sea

The Second World War saw the largest-scale naval warfare in history, and notably so from December 1941 when the Japanese attack on the American naval base of Pearl Harbor, and the subsequent German declaration of war on the United States, increased the number of participants and greatly widened the geographical range of conflict. The "world ocean" became a unified theater of naval warfare. Already, however, the naval warfare had involved the European powers, notably Britain, Germany, and France, all from 1939; Italy from 1940; and the Soviet Union from June 1941, and, while focused on European waters, the Mediterranean, and the North Atlantic, had, thanks to German commerce raiders, ranged across much of the world. In that warfare, as well as in that from December 1941, there was a full variety of types of naval conflict, including battles between surface warships, amphibious operations, submarine warfare, carrier-based missions, and blockades.

Any narrative of the naval dimension of the war poses issues of explicit or, far more commonly, implicit emphasis. Much derives from differing national perspectives. There are contrasts and sometimes somewhat clashing comments, occasionally childish, in American and British views. In part, issues of emphasis relate to one aspect of naval warfare as opposed to another. However, there is also the question of the significance of cooperation of naval forces with others, both in combined operations and otherwise. Separately, there is the issue of the relative importance of naval power as opposed to other forms of power. These factors should be considered as implicit within the narrative.

In many respects, the war represented *the* crisis for the prime naval power, Britain and, as a linked but separate matter, its empire. Yet France, the Soviet Union, Italy, Germany, and Japan suffered far more serious blows to their navies, and these require due attention while also shedding light on the resilience of the Royal Navy, which was responsible for most of the damage to the German and Italian navies. The war also saw the triumph of American naval power and a significant rise in that of Canada. The Americans crushed the Japanese navy. In each case, fighting quality, leadership, strategic roles, and organizational sophistication were linked to impressive feats of shipbuilding.

It is also important to note the importance of the war at sea for states not generally seen as naval powers, such as Thailand and Sweden. For example, Vichy French warships defeated the Thais in January 1941 at the Battle of Koh-Chang when Thailand attacked French Indochina. The Vichy navy launched an incursion in response to the Thai attack on land. Five Vichy ships, including a light cruiser, used their overwhelming firepower against three Thai warships (two of them torpedo boats), causing heavy casualties. The Thais suffered from not using their four newly acquired Japanese-built submarines to patrol their waters, as these submarines could have destroyed the Vichy warships. As a reminder of the need to contextualize naval achievement, the success of Thai forces on land and, even more, the geopolitical situation—with Japan supportive of Thailand and Vichy France, in contrast, isolated—were such that peace was obtained at the price of French territorial cessions to Thailand in Indochina.

Sweden remained neutral during the war, but its navy, 47 vessels strong in 1939 and 126 in 1945, escorted convoys bound across the Baltic for Germany so as to protect them against Soviet submarines, being helped by the limitations of the latter. This naval strength, which included six destroyers commissioned during the war, was very important to the continued movement of iron to supply Germany's steel industry and thus its munitions production. For such states, the war repeatedly indicated the importance of the maritime dimension and of naval power.[1]

Neutrals faced differing vulnerabilities and threats in part due to power politics, but also to the extent to which they had a coastline and could therefore be more readily invaded. The significance of their territories for maritime routes, for example of the Azores, a Portuguese possession, for air cover over a large part of the mid-Atlantic, was also notable.

THE WAR BEGINS

In 1939, Britain, despite its strengths, lacked a navy capable of fighting Germany, Italy, and Japan simultaneously. That was the product of the stop on capital ship construction under the Washington Naval Treaty, as well as the lack of sufficient British industrial capability and fiscal strength. At the same time, the buildup of the strength of these three powers and the political context were key elements. To expect the arithmetic of naval power to provide for conflict at once with all three states was to anticipate a margin of superiority that was unreasonable given the state of Britain and the fact that its potential enemies were well apart, but also one that diplomacy sought to avoid the need for. British naval strategists planned that, if necessary, operations against threats arising simultaneously would be conducted sequentially in separate theaters. This strategy assumed that operational flexibility could help lessen the constraints posed by tough fiscal limits.

In addition, war was likely to bring Britain the support of allies. France was seen as a key help against Italy if the latter entered the war, which it did not do until June 1940.[2] The loss of French naval support in the aftermath of German conquest in May–June 1940 was unexpected. However, Japanese entry into the war in 1941 led to a crucial alliance with the United States. The naval history of the war thus demonstrated the importance and unpredictability of the political dimension of warfare.

Naval warfare played a key role from the outbreak of the Second World War. It was crucial to the Allied plans to weaken Germany by means of containment, blockade, and cutting it off from the non-European world, and thus lessening its appeal to potential allies and leading Hitler to negotiate or be overthrown. This approach, the so-called long-war policy, represented a reading from the role of naval blockade in Germany's defeat in 1918, a desire to avoid the casualties of a large-scale land conflict, as well as a reflection of where Britain had its greatest power.[3] However, the German-Soviet alliance enabled Germany to obtain supplies from the Soviet Union, including food and oil. Germany was given a strategic depth that thwarted the oceanic strength of its opponents.

Thanks to naval dominance, Britain and France were able to move their forces, with the British Expeditionary Force transported to France in 1939, as were French forces from North Africa. Britain and France, however, were unable to provide naval assistance to Poland, whose small fleet was rapidly overwhelmed by the Germans, although the best Polish warships (two recently built large destroyers) and some others escaped to Britain. In order to cut off Swedish iron ore supplies to Germany, supplies necessary for steel production, Churchill advocated the dispatch of a fleet to the Baltic especially prepared to resist air attack. This rash idea, a new version of that considered prior to the First World War, would have exposed the fleet to German air attack in confined waters and without local bases, but it was thwarted by his naval advisers.

NORWAY, 1940

Naval power was important to amphibious capability, and there were plans for such Allied attacks on a number of places. Amphibious capability came to the fore with the Norway campaign in April–May 1940. Anxious to preempt the danger of British moves against German imports of Swedish iron ore by sea through Norwegian waters, and keen to establish submarine (U-boat) bases from which to attack British shipping,[4] the Germans invaded Norway, conquering Denmark in addition in order to ease this invasion. In Norway, the Germans largely relied on amphibious landings, although the capital, Oslo, was captured by airborne troops after the loss to coastal-based torpedo fire of the *Blücher*, a heavy cruiser escorting an attempted German amphibious landing that was thereby blocked.

The German ability to mount landings represented a success as well as a failure for naval power, notably a failure of the poorly directed Royal Navy to prevent the initial landings or, subsequently on April 9, to disrupt them. It was part of a more general failure of intelligence and naval management, with the British initially wrongly convinced that the Germans were planning to sail into the Atlantic.[5] A Luftwaffe attack ended moves by the British surface fleet on invasion day, although British submarines had a valuable impact on German warships. Moreover, the possibility of naval action was shown on April 10 and 13 when British warships sailed into Ofotfjord to wreck the German squadron that had attacked and occupied the town of Narvik in northern Norway, destroying ten German destroyers. These destroyer losses effectively scuppered naval support for any cross-Channel invasion of southern England: thereafter, the Germans did not have enough to ward off a British destroyer attack. More generally, German losses of warships in the campaign had a long-term strategic consequence by weakening the German surface fleet.[6] As such, there was a parallel to German losses of warships in 1914–16.

Thanks, however, to German air power, the British forces in Norway were totally defeated. The Royal Navy had also been shown to be unable to cope effectively with German air power, and a doctrine of reliance on antiaircraft fire had been revealed as inadequate: there was a lack of enough rapid-firing antiaircraft guns. Admiral Sir Dudley Pound, the First Sea Lord, remarked to one of the senior admirals, "The one lesson we have learnt here is that it is essential to have fighter protection over the Fleet whenever they are within reach of the enemy bombers."[7]

The Royal Navy also took hard knocks from German surface warships, especially when covering the forces withdrawing from Narvik. The vulnerability of carriers to surface ships was shown, on June 7, when the *Glorious* was sunk by the battle cruiser *Scharnhorst*, although this was to be the sole British carrier sunk by surface ships during the entire war. The British failure in Norway was to be serious for the subsequent course of the naval war, as it increased the possibilities for German access to the Atlantic and, from 1941, also provided bases for German submarines, surface ships, and aircraft that threatened the maritime route from Britain to northern Russia.

FRANCE, 1940

Naval conflict played essentially no role in the rapid German conquest of France, the Netherlands, and Belgium in 1940, thus repeating the situation with the Franco-Prussian War in 1870–71 and the German invasion of Belgium and France in 1914. However, naval power was significant in permitting the evacuation of much of the British army from France. This was a pivotal military event of the Second World War, allowing Churchill to push the case for Britain fighting on. From May 27 to June 4, 338,000 troops, including 123,000 French troops, were evacuated from Dunkirk. Although private boats and French warships took off an important number, the Royal Navy evacuated most of the troops, an evacuation that was crucial to the subsequent strength of Britain in the event of invasion. The navy took serious punishment from German aircraft in the process.

THE THREAT TO BRITAIN

France surrendered on June 22, 1940. Much was occupied by Germany, including all of the Channel and Atlantic coastlines. Britain's security was now greatly at risk. German air power and submarines threatened Britain's vital sea lines of communication and supply with the outside world. Moreover, Operation Seelöwe (Sealion), an invasion of southern England, was planned, and preparations were made. The Luftwaffe was instructed to prepare the way, especially by driving British warships from the English Channel. Despite the failure to prevent their success in the earlier Norway campaign, it had indicated the potential vulnerability of German amphibious operations to British naval power as well as causing the German navy heavy losses. Moreover, although Italy's entry into the war in June 1940, in alliance with Germany, had increased pressure on the Royal Navy in the Mediterranean, sufficient warships remained in British home waters to challenge any German naval attack. Although successful against Norway, the Germans lacked adequate experience or understanding of amphibious operations, as well as specialized landing craft. The towed Rhine barges they proposed to rely on could only manage a speed of three knots and would have failed to land a significant number of troops had any of them managed to reach England's southern coast. Even had the Germans landed troops, they would not have been able to sustain and reinforce them. In practice, the invaders would probably have been killed at sea given the willingness of the Royal Navy to lose ships as required to defeat an existential threat.[8] Moreover, British bombers destroyed nearly 40 percent of the barges and obliged the Germans to disperse the others.

The failure of the Luftwaffe in the Battle of Britain in August–September 1940 to overcome the Royal Air Force in a struggle for air superiority over southern England helped ensure the failure of Operation Sealion, which was never launched. However, the Royal Navy was probably strong enough to thwart invasion even had the Luftwaffe been more powerful, not least because of the limited nighttime effectiveness of air power. The navy's vulnerability to German dive-bombers was an important factor, but these bombers were themselves vulnerable to British fighters and to antiaircraft guns. Moreover, the Germans lacked the torpedo bomber capability that the British and Japanese were effectively to display in 1940 and 1941, respectively. The Royal Navy and the RAF contributed greatly to the abandonment of Sealion by raids on the invasion ports and the barges they contained.

WAR IN THE MEDITERRANEAN

In the Mediterranean, June 1940 introduced a period of grave danger for Britain, both with Italy's entry into the war and with the fall of France. The sympathy of Spain's Fascist regime for Germany was also an issue. Anxiety about the position of the new French government based in Vichy, and the possibility that the Germans would be able to take over the French fleet, led to the contentious, but necessary, British attack on the Vichy fleet at Mers el Kébir near Oran in Algeria on July 3, 1940, in which one battleship was sunk and two were damaged.[9] They also led to a subsequent, poorly coordinated, mishandled, and unsuccessful British attack on September 23–25 on Dakar, the main Vichy base in West Africa, an attack in which surprise had been lost. This was very much a case of the war spreading.

Whereas Germany was a Continental power with added naval interests and strength, Italy was a far-flung empire, with colonies in North Africa (Libya) and East Africa (Eritrea, Ethiopia, and most of modern Somalia). As such, Italy was dependent on maritime links and thus exposed to British naval power while, in turn, challenging the Mediterranean axis of the British Empire from Gibraltar via Malta to the Suez Canal, and then on via the Red Sea to India and Australasia. Admiral Domenico Cavagnari, the cautious chief of the Italian Naval Staff, had planned a fleet able to seize control of both ends of the Mediterranean so that it could operate on the oceans, but, aware of the true capability of the Italian air force and navy, he adopted a far more cautious stance once war broke out. Despite the success of individual units, especially their "human torpedoes" that fixed mines crippling two British battleships in Alexandria in Egypt in December 1941, the Italians, notably their large submarine force, were unable to make a major impact on British naval strength. The Italians were short of oil and confidence, and it was difficult, with their limited industrial base and shortage of raw materials, to replace losses. The Italians also lacked an effective naval air arm, and their radar was far weaker than that of Britain.

Instead, the British repeatedly took the initiative. This was true at the strategic level. Britain was able to move the forces that recaptured British Somaliland and that carried out the conquest of Italian East Africa. Part of the advance was overland, but distance, communications, and the coastal location of key Italian positions (Massawa and Mogadishu) made naval capability and amphibious operations especially significant. Moreover, in the invasion of the Italian colony of Libya in December 1940, a British naval inshore squadron played a role. The Italian colonies were unable to provide mutual support.[10]

The British seizure of the initiative was also true of the operational and tactical levels. The successful night attack by twenty-one torpedo bombers on Italian battleships moored, without radar cover, in Taranto in southern Italy on November 11, 1940, badly damaged four of them and encouraged the Japanese attack on Pearl Harbor just over a year later. This was also so at the tactical level with the technique of shallow-running the torpedo. Unlike with the Americans at Pearl Harbor, the Italians did not have carriers at sea elsewhere and, in addition, lacked the shipbuilding capacity to create a replacement navy. Indeed, in terms of the damage inflicted and the number of attacking aircraft, this raid was more effective than the Japanese raid on Pearl Harbor. The long-term effect on the Italian navy was different from that on the US Navy.

In response to the raid, the Italians withdrew units from Taranto northward and thus lessened the vulnerability of British maritime routes and naval forces in the Mediterranean, notably by increasing the problems of concentrating Italian naval forces and maintaining secrecy. In addition to the senior commanders understanding the limitations of their ships and industrial base, Italian admirals were also averse to taking risks because they believed the war would be won or lost by Germany and that in a postwar world, the navy would be Italy's most important military asset. For Britain, Taranto served as a crucial boost to public and governmental morale at a time of isolation and being under assault.

Each of these elements was more generally significant to the multiple contexts of strategy. The likely postwar consequences of these steps appeared more significant due to a lack of knowledge of when and how the war would end, and notably with what alignments. Similarly, the significance of morale and the need to ensure or prevent success accordingly was important to all combatants.

On March 27–28, 1941, off Cape Matapan, thanks to torpedo bombers from the carrier *Formidable*, battleship firepower, and ships' radar, the British, who had broken the German codes, sank three of the best Italian cruisers, *Fiume*, *Pola*, and *Zara*, and damaged the modern battleship *Vittorio Vento*.

The British benefited from the interaction between aerial reconnaissance, the use of radar, and the squadron at sea. The Italian cruisers were wrecked by the fifteen-inch guns of British battleships. This defeat ended meaningful Italian fleet operations. The Royal Navy benefited from knowing that Sealion had been canceled, which enabled them to focus their forces in the Atlantic and Mediterranean, where they had superiority in battleships and carriers.

In response to Italian defeats, and to the need to put pressure on Britain, which he wanted to drive to negotiate, Hitler sent German aircraft to Sicily from January 1941. The Tenth Fliegerkorps, specialists in maritime strike attacks, challenged the British position in the central Mediterranean. This was a form of indirect assault on Britain, but the emphasis was on air power and not, as in British doctrine, on sea power. In January 1941, German dive-bombers sank the cruiser *Southampton* and crippled the carrier *Illustrious*, underlining the vulnerability of carriers.[11] The damage to *Illustrious* was significant in that it was intended to accompany the warships sent to Singapore, and the inability to send the ship deprived them of air cover. German submarines also made a major difference in the Mediterranean, attacking warships and merchantmen.

The German presence increased that April–May 1941 with the conquest of Yugoslavia and Greece. Much of the Yugoslav navy was captured by the invading Axis forces, while many Greek warships were destroyed by German bombers. British intervention in Greece was unsuccessful. Maintaining their momentum, the Germans invaded the Greek island of Crete by parachute and glider troops, an invasion accompanied by successful resupply by air. Two German convoys en route for Crete in order to support the invasion were successfully intercepted, but the British attempt to reinforce, supply, and eventually evacuate Crete by sea led to heavy British losses, including three cruisers and six destroyers sunk.

Naval operations within the range of land were now clearly vulnerable to attack unless air superiority could be gained. The British navy off Crete lacked air cover and adequate air defense in its ships. Such vulnerability affected the rationale of naval operations, because the risk of a rapid and serious loss of ships was now far greater. Moreover, such a loss would mean a failure of relative naval capability, because there would be no accompanying loss of opposing naval forces. Air power thereby threatened to limit the attritional possibilities of naval operations.

Admiral Andrew Cunningham, the able British naval commander in the Mediterranean, feared that the Germans might press on to invade the island of Cyprus, a British colony, and to deploy forces in Vichy-run Syria, threatening the British position in the Middle East.[12] In the event, there was no such exploitation, and instead the Crete invasion was a distraction for the Germans from the more important target of Malta, a British island colony that threatened maritime and air links between Italy and North Africa. The

Royal Navy helped in the British conquest of Syria in 1941, defeating a Vichy flotilla.

The value of air cover was such that operations on land were regarded as crucial to naval operations, as they offered the possibility of moving airfields forward. In August 1941, General Thomas Blamey, the commander of the Australian forces in the Middle East, reported about eastern Libya, "Cyrenaica is regarded as most urgent problem of Middle East as control to Benghazi [the major city] would give fleet freedom of movement as far as Malta and advance air bases to allow cover of sea operations."[13] German and Italian air attacks on Malta's harbor and airfields, and highly damaging air and submarine attacks on British convoys supplying Malta in 1941–42, especially on the convoy code-named Pedestal in 1942, were central to a sustained, but unsuccessful, attempt to starve the island into surrender. Spitfires that were delivered by carrier from March and, more successfully, May 1942 ensured that the air war over the island was won by the British that year. However, the Italians were able to keep the rate of loss on the Libyan convoy route low, which was their key naval goal, not battle.[14]

Hypotheticals or counterfactuals, the "what-ifs" of history, come into play, as the fate of Malta leads to the question of whether air and sea operations against an island were inadequate unless supported by an invasion. As far as the Second World War itself was concerned, this is a question that also arises with the German threat to Britain itself, with American "island-hopping" in the Pacific, and with the "endgame" for Japan. Similar questions can be raised about areas that were not islands but were nevertheless vulnerable to amphibious attack, notably Italy in 1943–45. In short, had a combination of naval pressure and air attack made the actual presence of invading troops less necessary or even redundant?

These hypotheticals are of value because many of them played a role in strategic debate at the time. In the specific case of Britain in 1940 and of Malta in 1941–42, the German and Italian naval pressure was far less direct than that of the Americans against Japan in the case of the war in the Pacific. The Germans and Italians enjoyed a surface presence in the Atlantic and Mediterranean but in each case were outnumbered by the British. Air power and submarine attacks could try to counter this but did not succeed in doing so to the extent of closing the sea to British shipping. Submarines provided the capacity for a blockade, but not one that was complete, and certainly not one to match the American blockade of Japan in 1945. As a consequence, the alternatives were invasion or enforced surrender. The latter was to be the case with Japan as a result of the use of atom bombs. However, in the absence of such a strategic means, and the aerial resources of Germany did not provide one, it was necessary to invade.

Chapter 10
THE STRUGGLE FOR THE ATLANTIC

The Royal Navy was under wide-ranging pressure by the summer of 1941. The German conquest of Norway and France ensured that the naval situation was totally different from that in the First World War, with a German presence now in Atlantic ports in France, especially Brest, while it was now far harder for the British to enforce a blockade on German-occupied Europe.

Instead of using their surface fleet as a unit and providing the British with a concentrated target, the Germans relied on raids by small squadrons or individual ships. These were designed to attack Allied shipping, but the ships were hunted down. Thus, in December 1939, the "pocket battleship" *Graf Spee*, which had attacked shipping in the Atlantic, was damaged off South America by less-heavily gunned British warships in the Battle of the River Plate. Taking refuge in Uruguay rather than fighting its way into the open Atlantic, the ship was scuttled before the arrival of British reinforcements. Thus, there was no equivalent to the Battle of the Falkland Islands in 1914.

The most spectacular of these raids was that by the 42,000-ton battleship *Bismarck*, the leading warship in the German navy, in May 1941. The threat posed by this well-armored ship, with eight fifteen-inch guns and capable of going at more than twenty-nine knots, helped drive American preparations, encouraging a determination to expand the American navy, and also defensive steps around Norfolk, Virginia, the main American naval base on the Atlantic. These included the deployment of land-based sixteen-inch guns with a maximum range of 45,100 yards, capable of outfiring the *Bismarck* with its gun range of 39,900 yards.

The *Bismarck* was sent on a three-month cruise to devastate British shipping, a raid designed to show that surface warships could make a major impact on the North Atlantic lifeline to Britain. The *Bismarck* was strong enough to defeat convoy escorts. Well aware of the threat, the British mounted a considerable effort to keep tabs on German warships and to respond to any moves they made. British bombers failed to find the *Bismarck* in Norwegian waters but, on May 23, she was spotted by patrolling British warships in the Denmark Strait between Iceland and Greenland, a large choke point into the Atlantic. The following day, the *Bismarck* and the cruiser *Prinz Eugen* encountered a British squadron sent to intercept them southwest of Iceland, with the British helped by radar to shadow the Germans. In the subsequent gunnery exchange, which lasted for only twenty minutes, the *Bismarck* sank the elderly battle cruiser *Hood*, with all bar three of the crew killed, and seriously damaged the battleship *Prince of Wales*. Three shells from the latter, however, had hit the *Bismarck*, causing a dangerous oil leak that led the commander to set course for France for repairs.[15]

As a testimony to British naval strength and the capability for a "deep response," the *Bismarck* swiftly faced a massive deployment, including the battleships *King George V* and *Rodney*, two carriers, two battle cruisers, and thirteen other cruisers. The *Bismarck* was eventually crippled by a hit on the rudder by an aircraft-launched torpedo (May 26), a further demonstration of the vulnerability of surface ships to air power. Heavily damaged by fire from the battleships, the *Bismarck* fell victim next day to a cruiser-launched torpedo.

THE SUBMARINE ATTACK

Submarines were less vulnerable than surface ships to blockade, detection, and destruction. Moreover, they could be manufactured more rapidly and in large quantities. However, the Germans did not focus their entire naval construction effort on them until the spring of 1943. In addition, too many of their U-boats (submarines) had only a restricted range and could not therefore operate in the Atlantic. Nevertheless, submarines were more sophisticated than in the First World War; the Germans had the effective Type 7c, operational from 1940; and they now had bases from which it was far easier to threaten British shipping. As a result, the amount of shipping sunk by U-boats rose from the summer of 1940, at a time when British warships were focused on home waters to cover the evacuation of forces from France and to retain control of the Channel. There were also severe losses in the winter of 1940–41, as the U-boats attacked Atlantic convoys and developed wolf-pack tactics against their slowly moving targets. The German U-boats were supported by thirty-two Italian submarines that operated out of Bordeaux, from July 1940, sinking a little less than six hundred thousand tons of shipping. It is necessary to underline the difficulties both sides faced in operations, notably the small size of the ships and submarines and the roughness of the weather and seas in the vast Atlantic.

The situation improved for the Allies in the summer of 1941 as a result of an increased number of escort ships and aircraft, in part thanks to the lend-lease agreement with the United States. The British also cut the number of ships sailing independently. They had experimented with letting more fast ships sail outside convoys, an idea Churchill championed but gave up when Admiralty statistics made it clear that this was a bad idea. The American willingness to play a major role in the defense of shipping in the western Atlantic from September 1941 was important. In effect, there was a state of war between America and Germany in the Atlantic prior to Pearl Harbor, which makes Hitler's declaration of war on the United States less surprising. The British also benefited from a hard-won ability to decipher German naval codes.

As in the First World War, the Germans had insufficient submarines to achieve their objectives, and those they had lacked air support. In 1940, the

Germans lost U-boats more speedily than new ones were being brought into service. Changing goals were also significant. For example, U-boat pressure in the Atlantic was reduced in late 1941 as submarines were moved to Norwegian and Mediterranean waters in order to attack Allied convoys to the Soviet Union and to deny the Mediterranean to Allied shipping. These movements reflected the range of strategic options the Germans had, but also the inability to focus that was to be seen during the invasion of the Soviet Union in 1941. German strategic direction was repeatedly inconsistent and flawed.

Submarines were responsible for about 70 percent of the Allied shipping destroyed by the Germans during the war. Aircraft, especially the long-range, four-engined FW200 Kondor, were also significant, benefiting from bases in France and Norway. However, the Luftwaffe was not committed to the war against trade. Navy and army complaints about the Luftwaffe reflected the unreliability of its megalomaniac leader, Göring. In this, as in much else, the Germans suffered from a lack of a unified command structure and joint staff. German mines and surface raiders were also significant in the destruction of shipping.

Alongside the use of intelligence, air power played a key role in resisting the German submarine assault. Most U-boat "kills" of shipping were made by attack on the surface, which rendered Allied ASDIC (sonar) less effective. In contrast, aircraft forced U-boats to submerge, where their speed was much slower and it was harder to maintain visual contact with targets. On the surface, submarines operated using diesel engines that could drive the vessel three to four times faster than underwater cruising, which was powered, by necessity, from battery-powered electric motors. This factor affected cruising range and the number of days that could be spent at sea. Long-range air power was the vital element that reduced the killing power of the German submarine fleet to the point that its effectiveness, measured by Allied tonnage lost, decreased steadily.

Nevertheless, as a reminder of the significance of tasking or goals, neither the RAF, which was interested in strategic bombing and theater fighters, nor the Royal Navy, which was primarily concerned with hostile surface warships and was content to rely on convoys, hunter groups, and ASDIC, of which there were very few sets, to limit submarine attempts, had devoted sufficient preparation to air cover against submarines. There were strategic, operational, and tactical flaws.

In addition, land-based aircraft operating against U-boats faced an "Air Gap" across much of the mid-Atlantic, although Iceland's availability as an Allied base from April 1941 increased the range of such air cover. Again, as a reminder of choices, the British had used carrier-based aircraft against U-boats at the start of the war, but the sinking of the carrier *Courageous* by a U-boat ended the practice, and the remaining fleet carriers were deployed against Axis surface warships. Moreover, the demands of the bomber offensive against Germany on available long-range aircraft restricted the numbers available for convoy escort, while it took time to build escort aircraft carriers: the first entered service in late 1941. It was destroyed not long afterward, although it fully demonstrated the value of this class of ship during its short operational life. The next escort carriers (all American built) did not begin to enter service until late 1942, but so great was the need for naval aviation in a variety of roles that they were not initially used for trade protection and were not used to cover the Air Gap until April 1943.[16]

NAVAL POWER POLITICS

The German naval leadership had wide-ranging interests, with the Naval Staff committed to Germany becoming a power with a global reach provided by a strong surface navy, a policy seen as the way to secure resources and to gain Hitler's favor. There was interest in acquiring bases in the Atlantic, notably the Azores from Portugal and the Canaries from Spain. From these, it would be possible to threaten British convoy routes further from Europe, increase German influence in South America, and challenge American power. There was also naval pressure for an increased German effort in the Mediterranean. Hitler focused instead on creating a new Europe by attacking the Soviet Union in June 1941, launching Operation Barbarossa. However, concern about German naval intentions affected American planners and played a role in the public debate within the United States over policy.

Concern about German capabilities, as well as plans and anxiety about the strength of the British response, encouraged America to expand its Atlantic presence. On September 3, 1940, the United States agreed to provide fifty surplus and elderly destroyers (seven of them to the Canadian navy, the remainder to Britain) in return for ninety-nine-year leases on British bases in Antigua, the Bahamas, Bermuda, British Guiana, Jamaica, Newfoundland, St. Lucia, and Trinidad, bases that enabled President Roosevelt to claim to be supporting the defense of the Western Hemisphere. In practice, the deal was of limited military value as the largely obsolete ships took time to prepare. However, aside from the considerable psychological value at a time when Britain was vulnerable, no other power was in a position to provide such help.[17] More generally, the critical importance of American supplies was exaggerated by the British for political reasons so as to make Britain appear stronger. In 1941, the United States went on to establish bases in Greenland and Iceland, which strengthened their commitment in the Atlantic and lessened the burden on Britain.

THE EASTERN FRONT

Launched on June 22, 1941, the German assault on the Soviet Union had a naval dimension even though the planning largely left the navy aside. Rapidly gaining superiority in the air, the Luftwaffe was able to destroy ships of the Soviet Baltic fleet. German and allied conquests also lessened the ports and areas where Soviet warships could operate in the Baltic and Black Seas. In the Baltic, where, although the Soviets had a larger fleet, the Germans had the naval forces and air dominance they lacked in the Black Sea, the Soviets were bottled up in St. Petersburg by late 1941, in part as a result of German mine laying.

The Germans were less successful in the Black Sea than in the Baltic. In mid-October 1941, the Soviets evacuated their besieged and outnumbered garrison from the port of Odessa, an evacuation that reflected the strength of the Black Sea Fleet and the neutrality of Turkey, which, unlike in the First World War, did not support Germany. The Soviets were also able to make major landings on the Kerch Peninsula in December 1941, which were important instances of short-range amphibious warfare. In early 1942, in turn, the Axis naval flotilla—essentially of torpedo boats and submarines, mostly German and Italian, moved via the Danube—that had been built up in the Black Sea played a role in harassing Soviet naval links with besieged Sevastopol in Crimea, which contributed to its lack of supplies and fall to the Germans. However, in practice, Axis naval units, which included four Italian-built Romanian destroyers, could do little beyond protecting supply lines from the Danube mouth to the front.[18] Both sides lost warships to air attack, and this led Stalin in late 1943 to ban the employment of the larger Soviet warships in the area. They therefore served essentially only as a deterrent.

JAPAN ATTACKS

The passage of the Two-Ocean Naval Expansion Act on July 19, 1940, was designed to produce a fleet that would enable the United States to wage naval war against both Germany and Japan. It provided for the building, at a cost of $4 billion, of a truly massive additional complement that was designed to increase the authorized total tonnage of American warships by 70 percent, including 18 fleet carriers, 11 battleships, 6 battle cruisers, 27 cruisers, 115 destroyers, and 43 submarines. Most of these ships, however, were not due for completion until 1946–48, a similar timetable for the planned German navy. Keels were laid down for four 45,000-ton *Iowa*-class battleships in 1941, and seven were projected at over 60,000 tons each. The act served notice on the Japanese that the Americans were going to be in a position to back up their hostility to Japanese expansionism, more particularly in Southeast Asia. The *Iowa*-class battleships were well armored and also, at thirty-three knots, very fast. American planning increasingly presumed a focus first on defeating Germany because it was feared that, otherwise, Germany might be able to knock Britain out, putting America in a much more difficult position.

PEARL HARBOR

On December 7, 1941 (December 8 on the other side of the International Date Line), Japan attacked the naval base of Pearl Harbor on the Hawaiian island of Oahu without any prior declaration of war. Thanks in part to total radar silence, it achieved a degree of surprise that indicated considerable deficiency in American intelligence gathering and assessment and has led to a morass of conspiracy theories. The Americans had considered the prospect of a Japanese preemptive strike, but thought the more vulnerable Philippines the most probable target, while the Pacific Command in Hawaii focused on the threat from the nearest Japanese territory, the Marshall Islands, and not from the north, the direction from which the Japanese came. The defenses on Oahu were manned for sabotage, not air attack, which helped the Japanese greatly.

In Japan, in place of separating vulnerable carriers, there was a conviction of the value of massed air power at sea, and thus of a carrier group. The Japanese used Type 91 Mod 2 torpedoes, which, with their heavier charge, thinner air vessel, and antiroll stabilizers, were first delivered in April 1941. The attack on Pearl Harbor was a dramatic assault that was tactically successful but that also indicated the problems with achieving strategic results. It was a classic case of an operational-tactical success but a strategic failure. Three hundred fifty-three aircraft from six Japanese carriers totally destroyed two American battleships and damaged five more, while, in an attack on the naval air station at Kaneohe Bay, nearly four hundred American aircraft were destroyed or damaged on the ground.

The attack, however, revealed grave deficiencies in Japanese (and American) planning, as well as in the Japanese war machine. Only 45 percent of naval air requirements had been met by the start of the war, and the last torpedoes employed in the attack were delivered only two days before the fleet sailed. Modifications of aircraft to carry both torpedoes and heavy bombs were last minute, and there was a lack of practice. Furthermore, the Japanese target-prioritization scheme was poor, attack routes were conflicted, and the torpedo attack lacked simultaneity. These problems more generally indicated the difficulties of effective implementation, even in planned surprise attacks, and these difficulties should encourage caution in judgment.

Because of the focus on destroying warships rather than strategic assets, there was no third-wave attack on the fuel and other harbor installations. Had the oil farms (stores) been destroyed, the Pacific Fleet would probably have had to fall back to its Californian base at San Diego, gravely hindering American operations in the Pacific. Had the Japanese invaded Oahu, the Americans would have had to do so, but the logistical task facing the Japanese in supporting such an invasion would have been formidable.

The Japanese had embarked on an attack that was not essential. Their fleet was larger than the American Pacific and Asiatic Fleets, especially in carriers, battleships, and cruisers, and the American fleets, as a result, were not in a position to have prevented the Japanese from overrunning British and Dutch colonies, which was their major expansionist goal. From the point of view of the Pacific naval balance, the Americans had too many warships in the Atlantic. The devastating nature of the surprise attack encouraged a rallying around the American government. Moreover, the damage to America's battleships (some of which were to be salvaged and used anew) forced an important shift in American naval planning toward an emphasis on their carriers, the *Lexington*, the *Yorktown*, and the *Enterprise*, which, despite Japanese expectations, were not in Pearl Harbor when it was attacked.[19] All of these underlined the problems with addressing strategy largely in action-oriented military terms.

THE JAPANESE ADVANCE, 1941–42

Naval strength was crucial to the Japanese conquest of Southeast Asia, although it was the army that had the key experience, equipment, doctrine, and responsibility for amphibious operations. Fear of Japanese air power and concern about the relative ratio of naval power led the American navy, mindful of the wider strategic position, to fail to provide the support for the Philippines requested by the commander of the US Forces in the Far East, General Douglas MacArthur, who had not taken the necessary precautions. A convoy of reinforcements turned back, the navy refused to fly in aircraft, and the submarines were evacuated. This left the defenders in a hopeless position. Superiority in the air (over the poorly prepared American local air force component) and at sea enabled the Japanese to land where they pleased. The main force landed in Lingayen Gulf in northwest Luzon, with supporting units landing in south Luzon at Legaspi and Lamon Bay, threatening Manila with a pincer attack.

Further east, American islands in the western Pacific were captured, Guam falling on December 10, 1941, to an expedition from the Mariana Islands. Wake Island was attacked on December 12, but the marine garrison drove off the attack, sinking two destroyers. An American failure to relieve the island ensured, however, that, on December 23, a second attack, supported by carriers from the Pearl Harbor operation, was successful, although only after heavy casualties.

The successful Japanese attack on Hong Kong benefited from air support in order to block interference from British torpedo boats there. The Japanese invasion of Malaya was an amphibious assault. A powerful (by prewar standards) British squadron was sent to threaten Japanese landings on the coast of Malaya, but, on December 10, 1941, eighty-five land-based naval bombers sank the battleship *Prince of Wales* and the battle cruiser *Repulse*. Based at Saigon in French Indochina, these bombers showed that, in a sense, when France fell, Malaya fell. When sunk, the *Prince of Wales* had the best radar suite of any operational warship in the world, including close-in radar for her antiaircraft guns as well as radar for her main guns. A modern ship, she had good compartmentalization.[20] The sinking reflected the extent to which, although the success of high-level bombers was mixed, torpedo bombers could be deadly. Japanese tactics were impressive. On the British side, there was inadequate antiaircraft armament and gunnery, but a lack of land-based air cover to compensate for the absence of a carrier was crucial. This arose primarily from the mistakes of the force commander, Admiral Sir Tom Phillips. His poorly conceived and executed plan reflected a serious personal misreading of the situation but also wider problems: a lack of strategic foresight about what the ships could achieve, and operational weaknesses, including the problems of air-sea coordination.

As part of a more general Allied self-deception about Japan, Churchill had mistakenly thought that Japan could be deterred, and there was no proper contingency plan for the British force. In addition, the hope that the British would benefit from the strength of the American fleet in the western Pacific proved seriously mistaken.[21] Subsequently, the Japanese advance south in Malaya, and their consequent successful invasion of Singapore, were supported by naval action. The British hope that Singapore could hold out until it was relieved by the navy was wrong on both counts.

The Japanese pressed on to attack the Dutch East Indies, now Indonesia, beginning on January 11, 1942, with a landing at Tarakan, and that month saw amphibious forces leapfrog forward through the Straits of Makassar and the Molucca Passage, to the west and east of Sulawesi, capturing ports there and in Borneo. Other forces captured Ambon in the Moluccas and advanced from Sarawak to leapfrog down the western coast of Borneo. These gains provided bases, notably air bases, from which Japanese attacks on Java (the most important island), Bali, and Timor could be prepared.

Allied naval forces tried to protect Java, unsuccessfully attacking a Japanese invasion fleet in the Battle of the Java Sea on February 27, which was the first fleet action of the Pacific War. The two fleets were relatively balanced, with five cruisers and ten destroyers in the Allied fleet, and four and thirteen in that of the Japanese. However, the latter was well coordinated, enjoyed superior air support, and benefited from good air reconnaissance and better torpedoes. In contrast, the American, Australian, British, and Dutch warships lacked an able commander or unified command structure, experience of fighting together, air reconnaissance, and air cover. Heavy Allied losses, then and subsequently, including all of the cruisers, left the Japanese in a dominant position, and, on the night of February 28–March 1, they landed in Java, which surrendered soon after.

Naval support was valuable for the Japanese conquest of Burma from January to May, although far less so than that of the Dutch East Indies as island seizing was not involved. Japanese strength in the region was displayed in April 1942 when a force of five carriers sailed into the Indian Ocean and mounted destructive air raids on ports in eastern India and Sri Lanka, as well as sinking two British heavy cruisers and a carrier that were inadequately protected from dive-bombers. After the sinking of these warships, the British withdrew their Indian Ocean Fleet to East Africa or Mumbai. Admiral Somerville, the commander, was now having to think about the need to protect the Arabian Sea (the waters west of India), and thus tanker sailings from the Persian Gulf, as well as the route from both the Gulf and the Red Sea down the coast of East Africa to the Cape of Good Hope.

The crisis ended in April with most of the Japanese warships being withdrawn to be deployed for an attack on Port Moresby in New Guinea. The crisis led, however, to acute concern about the security of the Indian Ocean, which, indeed, greatly worried the British with their commitment to an imperial network and strategy [22] and also interested Axis naval commanders. This led the British to invade the island of Madagascar, which was held by Vichy forces. The British fleet successfully covered this invasion in May, deploying aircraft from two carriers to support the attack on Diego Suarez, the main port. In response, Japanese midget submarines torpedoed a British battleship there, which encouraged the British, urged by South Africa to capture the other ports, to press on to conquer the rest of the island. [23]

Japanese pressure in the Indian Ocean is one of the great naval counterfactuals (what-ifs) of the war, one linked to contrasting strategic requirements and to the difficulty of subsequent analysis. The British Empire was more vulnerable to Japanese attack than the United States was in the far larger Pacific. However, the Japanese transfer of their carriers back into the Pacific theater reflected the navy's correct certainty that the United States was the major challenge. The Japanese rejected Axis attempts at coordination at sea, as well as on land. Aside from their strategic priorities in the Pacific, the Japanese did not trust their allies.

WAR IN THE PACIFIC, 1942

Having brought French Indochina into their orbit and conquered the Philippines and the Dutch East Indies, the Japanese planned to press on to fix and strengthen the defensive shield with which they wished to hold the western Pacific against American attacks. However, initial successes led to interest in a more extensive perimeter, which proved a serious mistake in terms of the eventual loss of units. The Naval General Staff considered an attack on Australia or operations against India and Sri Lanka, but the army was unprepared to commit the troops required and instead favored a more modest attempt to isolate Australia.

Having captured Rabaul on the island of New Britain on January 23, the Japanese decided to seize Port Moresby, as well as New Caledonia, Fiji, and Samoa, in order to isolate Australia. Their plan, however, was thwarted as a result of the Battle of the Coral Sea on May 7–8. This, the first battle entirely between carrier groups in which the ships did not make visual contact, indicated the failure of the Pearl Harbor attack to wreck American naval power. The Americans had intercepted and decoded Japanese messages and, in a major forward deployment of American naval power that demonstrated the threat it posed to Japan, were waiting in the Coral Sea for the Japanese. In the battle, the Americans suffered serious losses, especially the carrier *Lexington*. However, the Japanese, who had failed to achieve the necessary concentration of strength and had an overly rigid plan,[24] also suffered, not least with the loss of aircraft and pilots. Crucially, the Japanese, whose naval commanders were divided over strategy, failed to persist with the operation, while American pilots acquired experience in attacking Japanese carriers. It was necessary to develop carrier warfare techniques, a formidable task, including cooperation with other surface warships. This had not been a task in the previous world war.

Rather than focusing on Australia, where Darwin and parts of the north were being repeatedly attacked from the air,[25] and the southwest Pacific, Yamamoto preferred a decisive naval battle aimed at destroying American carriers. The decision was made in February, but the Doolittle raid, a symbolic American air attack on Tokyo on April 18 launched from the carrier *Hornet*, both raised American morale and, by demonstrating Japanese vulnerability, further encouraged the Japanese to act. Yamamoto proposed to seize Midway and other islands that could serve as support bases for an invasion of Hawaii, which, he thought, would lead to such a battle. Yamamoto hoped to lure the American carriers to destruction under the guns of his battleships, in what would therefore be a decisive battle.

The continued capacity of the American navy, however, was shown clearly, on June 4, with the American victory in the Battle of Midway, a naval-air battle of unprecedented scale. This battle also reflected the superiority of

American repair efforts and intelligence. The combinations of fighter support with carriers (in defense) and of fighters with bombers (in attack) were crucial. The Americans encountered serious problems in the battle, and contingency and chance played a major role, but at Midway and, increasingly, more generally, the Americans handled the uncertainty of war far better than the Japanese. The Japanese navy, which had doctored its war games for Midway, was affected by the tension between two goals: those of a decisive naval battle and of the capture of Midway. This ensured that the Japanese had to decide whether to prepare their aircraft for land or ship targets, an issue that caused crucial delay during the battle.

While the American ability to learn hard-won lessons from Coral Sea was highly significant, the dependence of operations on tactical adroitness and chance played a major role in a battle in which the ability to locate the target was crucial. The American strike from the *Hornet* failed, with the fighters and dive-bombers unable to locate the Japanese carriers. Lacking any, or adequate, fighter support, the torpedo-bomber attacks suffered very heavy losses: forty-four out of fifty-one aircraft. However, the result of these attacks was that the Japanese fighters were unable to respond to the arrival of the American dive-bombers, not least because they were both out of position to intercept them and at a low altitude, a fortuitous instance of coordination on the American part. In only a few minutes, in a triumph of dive-bombing, three carriers were wrecked, a fourth following later; once wrecked, they sank.

These minutes shifted the arithmetic of carrier power in the Pacific. Although their aircrews mostly survived, the loss of 110 pilots was especially serious as the Japanese had stressed the value of training and had produced an elite force of aviators. The Japanese looked upon a carrier and its combat aircraft as an inseparable unit, with the aircraft as the ship's armaments, much like guns on fighting surface craft. Once lost, the pilots proved difficult to replace, not least because of a shortage of fuel for training. More seriously, the loss of four carriers' maintenance crews could not be made up.[26]

The Americans won decisively in the carrier battle, the Japanese losing all four of their heavy carriers present, as well as many aircraft. There was no opportunity for the Japanese to use their battleships, as the American carriers prudently retired before their approach, while the American battleships had already been sent to the West Coast. This was one of the respects in which Midway was no Tsushima, the decisive Japanese naval victory in the 1904–5 Russo-Japanese War. Yamamoto's inflexible conviction of the value of battleships in any battle with the Americans had served him ill. This poor judgment ensured that the Japanese had lost their large-scale offensive capacity at sea, at least as far as carriers were concerned. Conversely, the American admirals may have acted differently had they had battleships at their disposal. Learning as they went along, American carrier strategy was in part a shortage-of-battleships strategy.[27] The battle ensured that the congressional elections on November 3, 1942, took place against a more benign background than if they had been held earlier in the year.

The introduction in the late 1930s and early 1940s of carrier-capable aircraft that had substantial range had significantly improved carrier capability. Before that, it was not unusual for carrier aircraft to be limited to an operational range of only about one hundred miles, which made the carriers very vulnerable to surface attack. Indeed, during the American "fleet problems" or planning exercises, carriers were quite often "sunk" or at least threatened by battleships. The Battle of Midway demonstrated the new power of carriers, but also their serious vulnerability, not least if, like the Japanese, they had poor damage-control practices. Carriers were essentially a first-strike weapon, and their vulnerability to gunfire and air attack led to a continued stress on battleships and cruisers, both of which were also very important for shore bombardment in support of amphibious operations. Air power in the Pacific was seen as a preliminary to these operations rather than as a war-winning tool in its own right.

In addition, battleships were still necessary while other powers maintained the type. Furthermore, until reliable all-weather day and night reconnaissance and strike aircraft were available (which was really in the 1950s), surface ships provided the means of fighting at night. Surface ships, moreover, provided a powerful antiaircraft screen for the carriers, while the Americans also had dedicated antiaircraft cruisers in the Pacific.

GUADALCANAL, 1942-43

Midway did not mark the end of Japanese advances as they sought to strengthen their perimeter. The advance on Port Moresby in New Guinea was now mounted overland from the northern shore of New Guinea, but, on July 7, 1942, the Japanese landed at Guadalcanal in the Solomon Islands in the southwest Pacific. The island, then a British colony, had strategic importance, being seen as a key forward base to cut off the American reinforcement and supply route to Australia and New Zealand, but the American attempt to regain it launched a month later took on a significance to contemporaries that exceeded both this and the size of the Japanese garrison. It was important to the Americans to demonstrate that the Japanese could be beaten not only in carrier actions but also in the difficult fighting environment of the Pacific islands. It was also necessary to show that air and sea support could be provided to amphibious forces, both when landing and subsequently. In addition, Coral Sea and Midway had been defensive successes, but, at Guadalcanal, the attack, or rather counterattack, was clearly taken to the Japanese in what was the first American offensive operation in the southwest Pacific.

Eventual American naval success in the naval battles off Guadalcanal compromised the ability of the Japanese to support their force on the island. The naval campaign indicated the key role of warships other than carriers. Aside from their heavy losses at Midway, carriers could play little role in nighttime surface actions. Destroyer torpedo attacks could be highly effective, as when used by the Japanese, with their effective "Long Lance" torpedoes, off Guadalcanal on November 13 and 30, the last, the Battle of Tassafaronga, leading to one American cruiser sunk and three more badly damaged. The Japanese maintained a capability in naval night fighting. Moreover, their submarines were responsible for important American losses, whereas the poorly managed American submarine role was inadequate.[28] In mid-November 1942, however, in what was to be a turning point in the conflict off Guadalcanal, success was won by the Americans in a three-day sea action focused on surface warships fighting by night. For example, on November 14, the radar-controlled fire of the battleships *Washington* and *South Dakota* hit hard the battleship *Kirishima*, which capsized on November 15. Japanese battleships lacked radar-controlled fire and were badly trained in night-fighting. The Americans inflicted important losses on the Japanese in the Guadalcanal campaign in what was attritional fighting. There was an equal loss of warships, but the buildup of American naval resources ensured that they were better able to take such losses. Moreover, the Japanese suffered from the repetition of their tactical methods, a repetition to which the Americans quickly responded.

Victory offshore was crucial to the American success on Guadalcanal in January 1943. In the campaign, the Americans developed a degree of cooperation between land, sea, and air forces that was to serve them well in subsequent operations. The naval battles around Guadalcanal involved more uncertainties than during the Battle of Midway. The latter was a classic battle, within a limited timetable and with a clear order of battle. Guadalcanal involved a much longer period. Moreover, as later with the Leyte Gulf theater in 1944, there were many small islands and other underwater obstacles, and these made the struggle for Guadalcanal much more challenging than the open ocean of the Battle of Midway.

WAR IN THE PACIFIC, 1943

In July 1942, the Australian War Cabinet cabled Churchill: "Superior seapower and airpower are vital to wrest the initiative from Japan and are essential to assure the defensive position in the southwest Pacific Area."[29] Due to their superior industrial capability, the Americans were able to build up their naval strength far more successfully than Japan in late 1942, and this success proved crucial both in 1943 and to the key 1944 campaign. This buildup included not only the carriers and submarines that tend to dominate attention, but also other classes of vessel, including destroyers, which played a key role in escort, patrolling, and amphibious support tasks.[30] Ten cruisers were completed or commissioned in June 1942, the production of *Fletcher*-class destroyers began in June 1942, and of the first escort carriers that summer.

Moreover, the Americans developed important organizational advantages. These spanned from shipbuilding to the use of resources. The American advance across the Pacific would have been impossible without the ability to ship large quantities of supplies and to develop the associated infrastructure, such as harbors and oil-storage facilities, and the ships of the support train. In many respects, this was a war of engineers, and the American aptitude for creating effective infrastructure was applied to great effect in the Pacific.

Naval and air superiority were crucial to the American advance. They permitted the identification of key targets and the bypassing of many of the islands the Japanese continued to hold, a sensible strategic and operational decision given the time, effort, and casualties taken to capture Guadalcanal. Thanks to a growingly apparent American superiority at sea and in the air, the Japanese would be less able to mount ripostes, and any bypassed bases would be isolated. Thus, the Pacific War was to become one that was far from linear. Bypassing at the strategic level was not matched at the tactical level where the navy and marines attacked island defenses frontally, frequently taking heavy casualties.

The process of island-hopping in the Solomon Islands began in June 1943 with an attack on New Georgia. Carriers played a major role in the American campaign in the Solomons, but so also did other surface warships. Covering the landing on the island of Bougainville in the Solomons on November 1, 1943, a force of American cruisers and destroyers beat off an attack that night by a smaller Japanese squadron, with losses to the latter, in the first battle fought entirely by radar. The Solomons' advance culminated with the capture of Admiralty Island at the end of February 1944.[31]

In the central Pacific, the Americans opened up a new axis of advance, capturing key atolls in the Gilbert Islands in November 1943 in hard-fought amphibious attacks in which well-prepared and highly motivated defenders fought to the death inflicting heavy casualties, notably on Tarawa. Clearing the Gilberts prepared the way for operations against the Marshall Islands in early 1944. This route revived the prewar American Plan Orange and represented the shortest route for an advance on the Philippines. The army wanted a southern drive, the navy a central Pacific drive, but the real story was that the Americans had enough resources to do both. The choice of strategy was important alongside the availability of resources because, however out-resourced, there were a large number of Japanese bases, and it was important not to lose too much time or manpower.

Resources were far from the only element. For example, the Americans gained cumulative experience in amphibious operations, in their coordination with naval and air support, and in naval logistical support. Superior American interwar leadership development, based at the war colleges and focused on solving complex higher operational and strategic problems, contributed to wartime successes.

SUBMARINES IN THE PACIFIC

The tendency is to put the submarine war in the Atlantic first. It was, indeed, crucial to the war against Germany and to the war as far as Britain was concerned, but this emphasis can lead to a stress on the failure of submarines, as in the German case in the Atlantic and that of the Italians and Germans in the Mediterranean. The American story in the Pacific eventually reveals a very different outcome. The submarine war in the Pacific had major strategic implications. Although they had large, long-range submarines that, indeed, were used to maintain links with Germany, the Japanese did not launch a submarine war against America's lines of communication in the eastern Pacific. Nor did Japan mass submarines for use in offensives elsewhere. The prestige of their submarines had suffered from their failure to make a major impact in the Pearl Harbor operation. This affected subsequent Japanese consideration of submarines as a strategic and operational tool. Instead, with a cleaving to prewar doctrine, Japanese submarines were more commonly employed as part of the battle fleet, stalking American warships, sometimes successfully but without decisive results.[32]

This Japanese failure to attack their communication links made it easier for the Americans to deploy resources against Japan and to plan for attack. As a result, there was a clear contrast with the war with Germany. An Allied invasion of France, which was not mounted until June 1944, was not feasible until after the Allies had won the Battle of the Atlantic. This victory permitted the safe buildup and supplying of Allied forces in Britain. In contrast, there were no such constraints affecting the forward movement of forces in the Pacific by the Americans.

The Americans used submarines to greater strategic effect, notably to lessen the economic value Japan derived from its conquests.[33] Japanese industry was heavily dependent on the import of raw materials, especially oil, rubber, and tin, from the new Japanese Empire, while rice imports were also significant. The United States increasingly employed submarines to attack Japanese trade, and this stymied Japanese plans to raise munitions production. Whereas the wartime German Empire, in both world wars, was a land one with few maritime routes, the Japanese one was heavily dependent on such routes.

The Americans faced serious problems with their Mark XIV torpedo and Mark VI exploder torpedoes until mid-1943. Early German torpedoes also faced problems. However, effective long-range American submarines made major inroads on Japanese trade, especially from late 1943, establishing one of the most successful blockades in naval history. Unrestricted submarine warfare, for which the Americans had no experience, had been ordered without hesitation immediately after Pearl Harbor, with the naval leadership playing the key role in this decision.[34] The Americans benefited from the quality of their submarines, including good surface speed and range, from the ability to decipher Japanese signals, and from a clear determination to attack. The Japanese did not inflict enough casualties to cause a deterioration in American submarine leadership or in the quality and motivation of the crew. Indeed, the United States became the most successful practitioner of submarine warfare in history. This provided a core basis of skill and confidence from which to use hunter/killer submarines to confront Soviet submarines in the Cold War.

The Japanese in the Pacific proved less effective than the Allies in the Atlantic at convoy protection and antisubmarine warfare and devoted far fewer resources to them, notably by not providing adequate air support for convoys. In 1942–44, successful American submarine attacks forced the Japanese to abandon many of their convoy routes. Lacking a large enough merchant fleet at the start of the war, notably of tankers, the Japanese failed to build sufficient ships to match their losses, their trade was dramatically cut, and the Japanese imperial economy was shattered. By the end of the war, American submarines had sunk 5.32 million tons of Japanese merchant shipping (and Japan had a lower tonnage than the British Empire), and there was no area of Japanese overseas and coastal trade that was free from attack. As with the air attack on Germany, this greatly increased the uncertainty that sapped the predictability on which industrial integration depended.

Japanese losses made it difficult to move raw materials or, indeed, troops rapidly. Thus, the flexibility seen in the initial Japanese conquests had been lost. Expedients, such as postponing the maintenance of shipping and leaving garrisons to fend for themselves (an equivalent in its impact to Allied island-hopping), proved deleterious for overall effectiveness.

The American submarine assault was supplemented by the dropping of mines by naval aircraft, as well as by air attacks on Japanese shipping, both of which proved deadly. These means became more significant in 1945 as American air bases were established closer to Japan, and as carriers also operated closer in and therefore more intensively.

THE SURFACE NAVAL WAR WITH GERMANY

Surface warships played a far greater role in the naval war with Japan than with Germany. In part, this was a result of the German focus on commerce raiding, not battle; of the sinking of the *Bismarck* in 1941; and of the withdrawal, on February 12, 1942, of major warships from Brest, the leading Atlantic base in German hands. This withdrawal, which owed much to the vulnerability of the warships there to British bombers, as well as to concern about a possible British invasion of Norway, was a success as the British attempt to intercept them in the Channel totally failed due largely to the jamming of British radar and to effective and well-coordinated German air defenses. At the same time, the withdrawal was a strategic mistake as it lessened the threat posed by these warships to the Allied position in the Atlantic and thus their danger as a fleet in being.

The following month, the British launched an attack that wrecked the dry dock at St. Nazaire, the only dry dock on the French Atlantic coast big enough to accommodate the 42,000-ton battleship *Tirpitz*. Thus, the very requirements of the warship lessened its usefulness, although Hitler's insistence that she only go to sea when free from real risk was also a key restriction. This insistence was a telling mark of Hitler's ignorance in naval warfare. He saw warships as jewels to be hoarded away for their propaganda and potential value, rather than as military units with strategic purposes involving risk. The attack on St. Nazaire illustrated the importance of geomilitary considerations in both strategy and operational planning. Naval bases had more complex requirements than in the First World War.

Norway was an important base for operations against British convoys sent from August 21, 1941, to take supplies to the Soviet Union. These convoys were a key source of supply that provided 4.43 million tons of matériel. One-sixth of the heavy tanks the Soviets used in the Battle of Moscow in late 1941 had come from Britain. Initially, confident of victory over the Soviet Union, the Germans largely ignored the convoys, but, from December 1941, they increased the warships and aircraft available in northern Norway to attack them. From March 1942, convoy losses mounted, notably for convoys PQ16 and PQ17 in May and July 1942, respectively. As such, the focus of German naval strength could be regarded as in synergy with the German strategic concentration on the Soviet Union, rather than on being extraneous to it. Overall, 7 percent of the matériel sent was lost to German attack. The supply route from Alaska to Siberia lacked this danger but did not provide supplies so close to the zone of Soviet operations. The Arctic ice forced ships closer to Norway than they would have preferred. The convoys were escorted by warships (mostly British but also American), including, from late 1942, escort carriers, and were protected, where possible, by Allied air and submarine patrols, although the range of air cover was insufficient.

The serious inroads of German aircraft and, in particular, submarines on these convoys, however, were not matched by surface ships. On December 31, 1942, in the Battle of the Barents Sea, German surface ships failed to destroy a British convoy which was ably defended by its destroyer escorts, much to the fury of Hitler. In the Battle of North Cape on December 26, 1943, the battle cruiser *Scharnhost* was slowed by a destroyer torpedo attack and then sunk by fire from a British fleet escorting a convoy. The *Tirpitz*, which had sailed to Trondheim in Norway in January 1942 and had sortied out in early March 1942 in an unsuccessful attempt to intercept a convoy, was first damaged by British midget submarines and then sunk by British aircraft on November 12, 1944, after two twelve-thousand-pound (5,430 kg) Tallboy bombs developed for the purpose hit the ship. These heavier bombs also ensured that the RAF was able to inflict damage on the concrete submarine "pens" in Bergen in Norway.

BATTLE OF THE ATLANTIC

In 1942, the German U-boats inflicted heavy losses on Allied shipping, creating a serious situation, while U-boat losses were less than new launchings. For the first time, there were enough U-boats to organize comprehensive patrol lines across North Atlantic convoy routes. For the Germans, the naval opportunities presented by American entry into the war came not from cooperation with Japan but from the poorly defended nature of American waters, although nothing better encapsulated Hitler's lack of grasp of maritime strategy and its relationship to international policies than the declaration of war on the United States. Due, in part, to an American reluctance to learn from earlier experience, one that the British could also display, and to a focus on hunting U-boats, it took time for convoys to be introduced in American waters, and there were very heavy losses to U-boat attacks in early 1942, their so-called "happy time." However, in the Caribbean, in Operation Neuland, the Germans failed to focus on the particular strategic vulnerability offered by these targets (or to shell oil refineries), or to make the submarines suitable for tropical operations by fitting air conditioning.[35]

In May, when U-boat attacks also led Mexico into the war, the situation improved as effective convoying, introduced from Halifax to Boston in March, spread. As a result, the U-boats, from July, focused anew on the mid-Atlantic. After the summer of 1942, the effectiveness of individual submarine patrols, in terms of the tonnage sunk, fell. This fall reflected the increase of convoying and the greater strength of convoy escorts. The majority of merchantmen sunk that year were sailing independently.

New emphasis was given to the submarine war from January 1943 because, as a result of Hitler's anger with the failure in the Battle of the Barents Sea, Karl Dönitz, the head of the U-boat service, replaced Raeder as the naval commander in chief. Thus, there was a parallel to the German response to the Battle of Jutland in 1916, again with stronger emphasis on submarines.

In 1943, however, the Allies successfully responded to the U-boats with improved resources, tactics, and strategy. They introduced more powerful depth charges, better sonar detection equipment, and an increased use of shipborne radar. Enhanced antisubmarine weaponry, especially effective ahead-throwing guns, was important to the Allied success. So was signals intelligence, the ability to intercept and decipher German naval codes and to use the resulting material to operational and tactical effect. After serious problems for most of 1942, the Allies' intelligence on the U-boats improved from December.[36] Effective antisubmarine tactics by both convoy escorts and aircraft was also important. Accumulated experience increased Allied operational effectiveness. In addition, as in the First World War, minefields were responsible for many U-boat losses.

In 1943, antisubmarine air resources became more plentiful, equipment more impressive, and tactics more effective. There was an increasing number of VLR (very long range) aircraft for the Air Gap and the first use of escort carriers in the mid-Atlantic. With convoy escorts, there were incremental steps not only in numbers, detection equipment, and weaponry, for example improved fuses for depth charges and better searchlights, but also in the experience of operating together and thanks to the development of effective formations and tactics. From late 1940, ASV Mk II radar, combined with the Leigh light, proved highly effective at detecting and targeting surfaced submarines. However, the radar lost its potency when the Germans were able to introduce listening receivers on U-boats. In turn, in March 1943, the Mk III radar, which could not be detected by these receivers, proved a crucial addition to British capability. Radar sets small enough to be carried by aircraft, and yet able to pick up submarine periscopes at five miles, were a key tool. Increased resources in the struggle with submarines owed much to the growing Canadian commitment.[37]

The building of far more merchant shipping from 1942, especially by the Americans, was also very important to Allied victory, as was the availability of more escort vessels and their improved armaments. In early 1943, U-boat losses rose. In May, forty-three U-boats were sunk, and, on May 24, Dönitz ordered a halt to attacks on convoys in the North Atlantic and the withdrawal of submarines to areas where there was less Allied air power. To believe that tonnage sunk, no matter where, was the critical factor was a strategic error, for the percentage of Allied ships sunk fell considerably in 1943, while the ratio of ships sunk to U-boats destroyed was 2:1, a rate of success well down from the 14:1 of 1940–42.

Germany throughout was at a clear disadvantage in the Battle of the Atlantic, both in warship numbers and as a result of Allied shipbuilding. Moreover, the needs of the Eastern Front, and of countering Allied bombing attacks on Germany, exacerbated the failure to provide adequate air support for the antishipping campaign. Yet, aside from these highly important elements, a range of factors helped the Allies win, including effective antisubmarine tactics, by both convoy escorts and aircraft, and intelligence. As a consequence, the number of submarines sunk per year was much greater than in the First World War, while the percentage of Allied shipping lost was lower. The strategic issue posed for the Germans by Allied shipbuilding interacted with the tactical and operational challenges imposed by improved Allied proficiency in antisubmarine warfare, and German submarine construction methods were not significantly accelerated until 1944.[38]

May 1943 was not the end of the Battle of the Atlantic and should only be seen as a turning point for the Allies if the need to continue to overcome the submarine challenge is also stressed. Indeed, in the battle of technological innovation, the Germans made important moves. When they introduced the T-5 acoustic homing torpedo in the late summer, they were, at once, able to sink three escorts and to launch a renewed attack on Allied shipping. This, however, was successfully counteracted by Allied air power, the application of which benefited from intercepted signals information. The determined German attempt to regain the initiative failed, and they suffered heavy losses, including thirty-seven submarines in July. The German failure confirmed and underlined their defeat that May. The success of stronger convoy defenses had been apparent from late 1941 and was now combined in a more effective overall antisubmarine strategy. Moreover, the Germans proved less adept in adapting to changing tactics and technology than the Allies.

In the event, air power in the shape of long-range aircraft was important. Already based in Britain, Iceland, and Canada, land-based American four-engined Liberators flying from the islands of Terceira and Santa Maria in the Azores were the key to closing the mid-Atlantic Air Gap in October 1943 and thus to denying submarines their safest hunting ground, which was to the west of the Azores.

Mass was a key element and demonstrated anew the ability of American industry to produce large quantities of all sorts of weapons. The production of escort destroyers began in June 1943, and the United States built over three hundred of these warships. The number of aircraft deployed against submarines in the Atlantic rose from 595 in late 1942 to 1,300 a year later, and the number of escort carriers increased.[39] The availability of more aircraft meant that submarines could not safely sail from their French bases across the Bay of Biscay on the surface and thus used up some of their supply of electricity, as the recharging of batteries had to be done on the surface, which made submarines increasingly vulnerable to air attack. There was also an important shift in the relative quality of personnel. German U-boat losses cost the Germans the crew and therefore the experience they offered, while the Allies built up a bank of experience.

In early 1944, the Germans fitted snorkel devices to their U-boats. These allowed them to charge their batteries while submerged, as well as enabling the underwater starting and running of diesel engines, thus reducing their vulnerability to Allied air power. The U-boats were becoming true submarines, as opposed to just submersibles. However, the snorkel did not permit running the diesels at sufficient depth to avoid detection. A submarine just below the surface was visible from the air, so that submarines operating in waters within the range of aerial antisubmarine patrols had to be either on the surface and maintaining aircraft watches continuously or far enough below the surface to prevent detection from the air. The gun on the Type 7c submarine was replaced by antiaircraft guns.

The change in the specifications of U-boats did not increase significantly their attack capability vis-à-vis escorts. The improvement in Allied escort capability outweighed U-boat advances, and, demonstrating that the war in the Atlantic had been largely won, the Germans sank relatively few Allied ships in 1944–45. Furthermore, the production of a new type of submarine, the high-speed Type 21 "Electro," was badly affected by Allied bombing. The strategic failure of the U-boat offensive was clarified by Allied, especially American, shipbuilding.

Allied success in the Battle of the Atlantic was crucial to the provision of imports to feed and fuel Britain, as well as to the buildup of military resources there. Only three Allied merchantmen convoyed across the Atlantic in the first three months of 1944 were sunk. This was the background to the Second Front sought by the Allies, and it underlined the strategic quandary faced by the Germans, with an intractable conflict on the Eastern Front likely to be joined by fresh commitments in France. Despite the hopes placed by their advocates, the U-boats were proven to have had only an operational capability.

PACIFIC WAR, 1944

The vast extent of the Pacific created unprecedented problems of war making and infrastructure. Substantial fleets had to operate over great distances and required mobile support and maintenance. The scale of planning was large in resources, space, and time. The American problem-solving, can-do approach to logistics permitted a rapid advance. The fleet train that provided logistical support was greatly expanded, while processes for transferring fuel and ammunition and other supplies from ship to ship at sea were developed.[40] In addition, the use, from 1944, of shipping as floating depots for artillery, ammunition, and other matériel increased the speed of army resupply, as it was no longer necessary to use distant Australia as a staging area for American operations.

The vast extent also created important opportunities. It was easier to isolate island targets in the Pacific than in the Mediterranean, and there was less naval exposure to Axis air attack. As a result, the American navy could concentrate force more effectively.

The Japanese continued building warships, but their numbers were insufficient and their navy lacked the capacity to resist the effective American assault. It also suffered from poor doctrine, including a lack of understanding of the naval air war[41] and an inadequate grasp of respective strategic options. Indeed, the deficiencies in Japanese planning indicated serious systemic failings, including an inability to understand American policy and to respond to earlier deficiencies in Japanese strategy and operational planning. The Japanese military tended to lack the mental flexibility to choose an option that would be against their moral compass. Defensive strategies were unwelcome.

The Japanese aimed to destroy the spearhead of the advancing American fleet by concentrating their air power against it. There was the hope, even conviction, that the decisive success of the Japanese fleet over the Russians at Tsushima in 1905 could be repeated. This reflected a more general conviction, also seen in the Midway operation in 1942, that a decisive victory could be obtained on one front, which could overcome the more general role and impact of Allied resources. Similar goals were pursued in 1944 at the expense of Britain (on the India-Myanmar border) and of China (in southern China). As seen from the outset of the attack on the United States in 1941 (as indeed also that on China in 1937), Japanese assumptions arose from the sway of historical examples that supposedly represented national greatness and, even more, from the role of factors of will in Axis thinking. There was a conviction that victory would sap the inherently weaker will of opponents and thus give the Axis the success to which they were entitled.

Aside from the lack of political understanding underlying this policy, it was anachronistic militarily. Defeat in 1944 on one front would have delayed the Americans, but nothing more; and, by concentrating a target for the Americans, Japanese strategy made it more likely that the American attack would succeed in causing heavy casualties. The Americans had a better and more mobile fleet, a far greater ability to replace losses, and far more capable leadership than the Japanese. There were now sufficient American aircraft both for a carrier battle and for protecting an amphibious assault, and the fast-carrier task forces, combined with surface escorts, constituted a major operational-level weapon with the necessary tactical cohesion. Air power could be applied from the sea as never before, and as part of an effective and well-supported modern combined-arms force.[42]

The campaigning in 1944 saw the collapse of the Japanese Empire in the Pacific, although not in East and Southeast Asia, a contrast that both emphasized the significance of the maritime dimension and the difficulties of the task facing the United States. Without air superiority, Japanese units and logistics were highly vulnerable, which repeatedly ensured a lack of tactical, operational, and strategic capability. In addition, the Japanese were fooled by American strategy and deception. Having two simultaneous American drives created serious problems for the Japanese navy, which itself had less influence than in 1941–42 as the army became more powerful. The two services fought over resources, command, and priorities, a rivalry that affected Japanese war making more than that of the other major powers.

In January–February 1944, the Americans successfully attacked the Marshall Islands. American success reflected the lessons learned at Tarawa, notably the need for closer and sustained inshore bombardment from appropriate ships and the use of underwater demolition teams to clear man-made and natural obstacles, particularly routes through coral reefs. Success there made it easier to strike at the Mariana Islands—Saipan, Tinian, and Guam—in June.

This offensive led to the Battle of the Philippine Sea on June 19–20, the major battle the Japanese had indeed sought. American Task Force 58, with fifteen carriers and over nine hundred aircraft, was attacked by the nine carriers and four hundred aircraft of the Japanese First Mobile Fleet. However, located by American radar, Japanese air attacks, launched on June 19, were shot down by American fighters and by antiaircraft fire from supporting warships, with no damage to the American carriers. The Americans also benefited from radio interception. The following day, a long-range American air attack in the failing light sank the carrier *Hiyo* and damaged three others. The Japanese carriers were protected by a screen of Zero fighters, but, as a clear sign of growing Japanese weakness in the air, this was too weak to resist the fighters escorting the American bombers. Although the Japanese still had a sizeable carrier fleet, once again the loss of pilots and carrier-based maintenance crew was a crippling blow. As part of the combined capability of the American navy, its submarines sank two large carriers, *Shokaku* and *Taiho*.

This victory enabled the Americans to overrun the Marianas, a decisive advance into the western Pacific. The determination of the Japanese resistance was shown on Saipan where nearly the entire garrison died in a strong defense in the jungle-covered mountainous terrain or in costly frontal counterattacks. The Marianas provided not only sites for American airfields, but also an important forward logistical base for the navy and for subsequent amphibious operations. The cumulative nature of warfare was readily apparent.

The Americans used their naval and air superiority, already strong and rapidly growing, to mount a reconquest of the Philippines from October. That operation helped ensure a naval battle, that of Leyte Gulf of October 23–26, 1944, the largest naval battle of the war and one (or rather a series of engagements) that secured American maritime superiority in the western Pacific. The availability of oil helped determine Japanese naval dispositions and, with carrier formations based in home waters and the battle force located just south of Singapore, any American movement against the intervening Philippines presented a very serious problem for Japan. There was growing pessimism in Japan, and losing honorably became a goal for at least some Japanese naval leaders. The head of the Naval Operations Section asked on October 18 that the fleet be afforded "a fitting place to die" and "the chance to bloom as flowers of death."

In Operation Sho-Go (Victory), the Japanese sought to intervene by luring the American carrier fleet away, employing their own carriers as bait, and then using two naval striking forces, under Vice Admirals Takeo Kurita and Shoji Nishimura, respectively, to attack the vulnerable American landing fleet. This overly complex scheme posed serious problems for the ability of American admirals to read the battle and control its tempo, and, as at Midway, for their Japanese counterparts in following the plan. In a crisis for the American operation, one of the strike forces was able to approach the landing area and was superior to the American warships there. However, instead of persisting, the strike force retired, its exhausted commander, Kurita, lacking knowledge of the local situation, not least due to the difficulties of identifying enemy surface ships. The net effect of the battle, which, overall, was dominated by American naval air power, was the loss of four Japanese carriers, three battleships including the *Musashi*, ten cruisers, other warships, and many aircraft.[43]

AMPHIBIOUS OPERATIONS IN EUROPE, 1943–44

Naval strength proved a key element in a series of Allied invasions, with the American and British navies playing the crucial role. Operation Torch, the invasion of Morocco and Algeria in November 1942, was followed by the invasion of Sicily in July 1943 (which involved 3,600 ships) and of mainland Italy in September. The direction of Allied success in North Africa and Italy reflected the transformation of the situation in the Mediterranean and developed it. Naval superiority made any sortie by Vichy or Italian capital ships unlikely to succeed and prevented a Dunkirk-style Axis retreat from Tunisia. As a result, a large number of Axis troops surrendered there, troops who would otherwise have proved a major asset in subsequent fighting. This was a major achievement for the Allied naval war.

Most of the Vichy navy, 250,000 tons of warships, was scuttled by the French on November 27, 1942, when, having occupied Vichy France, German forces attacked the great naval dockyard at Toulon. Similarly, the Danish fleet was to scuttle to avoid German takeover. Moreover, the Italian armistice in September 1943 was followed by the surrender of practically the whole of the Italian navy to the Allies, with the fleet sailing to Malta, although it lost its most modern battleship to German glider bombs. This transformation of the naval situation enabled the British to withdraw warships from the Mediterranean, both to support the invasion of Normandy and for operations against Japan.

At the same time, substantial Allied naval forces remained in the Mediterranean where they supported operations in Italy and the invasion of southern France. The Torch landings had revealed a lack of appropriate Allied equipment, doctrine, and experience. Many of the faults, however, had been rectified by the time of Sicily, not least through proper reconnaissance for, and organization of, the process of landing. Moreover, Anglo-American naval bombardment was important to the landings at Salerno in September 1943, Anzio in February 1944, and southern France in August 1944, the last of which was particularly impressive, with 887 warships, including 9 carriers, 5 battleships, and 21 cruisers, supporting the 1,370 landing craft.[44] Carriers played an important role: five were present for the Salerno landings.

Naval dominance provided the background for consideration of an invasion of southeast Europe. However, this idea, although supported by Churchill, who saw it as a way to preempt Soviet expansionism, was largely blocked by American opposition. The exception was a British amphibious campaign in the Aegean in late 1943, a campaign defeated by German land-based air power. As a result, British warships tended to keep to the dark. Despite this, six destroyers were lost. This failure indicated that command of the sea involved far more than warship numbers.

Control of much of the Mediterranean made a major contribution to the flexibility of Allied supply links, greatly shortening the route from the North Atlantic to the Middle East. It was no longer necessary to face the choice of risking Axis interception in the Mediterranean or of sailing around South Africa, the latter a far longer route.[45]

Allied naval power was employed on a greater scale and more decisively in British home waters in 1944. In the invasion of Normandy, launched with Operation Neptune on "D-day," June 6, the Allies benefited from well-organized and effective naval support, as well as from absolute air superiority. Maritime considerations were important at the strategic, operational, and tactical levels. The Germans concentrated more of their defenses and army units in France in the Calais region, which offered a shorter sea crossing and a shorter route to Germany. Normandy, in contrast, was easier to reach from the invasion ports on the south coast of England, especially Plymouth, Portland, and Portsmouth. While the largely British naval armada provided heavy supporting fire, which in general was more effective than the bombers, the steel-reinforced concrete of the German casements and bunkers proved very resistant to high explosives.

The naval armada also prevented disruption by German warships. There was no equivalent to the challenge posed by the Japanese fleet to the American landings in the Philippines later that year. Nevertheless, attacks by destroyers, torpedo boats, and submarines based in French Atlantic ports were a threat to the landing fleet and to subsequent supply shipping, a threat that was successfully guarded against.

Naval power included bringing across the Channel two prefabricated harbors composed of floating piers, the Mulberry harbors. The laying of oil pipelines under the Channel was also an impressive engineering achievement that contributed to the infrastructure of the invasion.[46] In late 1944, against far weaker German opposition, Soviet amphibious operations cleared the islands in the Gulf of Riga.

THE LAST STAGES OF THE WAR AT SEA WITH GERMANY

The buildup and supply in, and from, Britain of the massive American and Canadian forces that landed in Normandy, and subsequently, were a reflection of the failure of German submarines to achieve strategic results. After the Allied breakout from Normandy, the Germans evacuated their submarines from their bases in west France and concentrated their force in Norway. From there, however, the U-boats were able to inflict scant damage on the Arctic convoys and focused instead on British waters where their inshore campaign proved deadly, although they were no longer able to sink large numbers of merchantmen. Instead, the U-boats suffered serious losses, in part as a result of air attacks, notably on their bases, as well as at sea, although the sinkings at sea were due more to convoy escorts and their use of forward-firing weaponry.

Nevertheless, the submarine threat remained potent, as construction maintained the overall numbers of U-boats. This obliged the Allies, as in 1918, to continue to devote considerable naval resources to escort duty and antisubmarine warfare, including coastal convoy routes in British waters. Given Allied, especially American, shipbuilding capability, and the resulting size of the Allied navies, this task did not, however, limit or prevent other uses of Allied naval power, particularly the movement of British warships to the Indian Ocean and the Pacific.

At the close of the war in Europe, as earlier in 1918, there were still large numbers of U-boats, but they were unable to inflict serious losses on Allied shipping. Had new types become operational, they would have posed a more difficult challenge, but, thanks to bombing, the construction of a new, faster class of submarine—the Type 21, which had a much greater battery capacity and mechanically reloaded torpedo tubes—was delayed so that it did not become operational until April 1945. This was too late to challenge Allied command of the sea, although, even had it become operational earlier, it would not have been in sufficient numbers to determine the struggles. Indeed, the trajectory of German air power, first with rockets (V-1s and V-2s) and then with jet aircraft, neither of which brought significant improvements, suggests that the possibilities from improved submarines should not be pushed too hard.

However, in a continued determination to fight on and divide and defeat the Allies, Hitler's regime placed much reliance not only on a stronger will, but also on what it saw as wonder weapons, including the development of new submarine types.[47] There was Allied concern that the top underwater speed of the Type 21, 17.2 knots, would improve its capacity for evasion tactics and make it harder to destroy, but the Allies were also developing new tactics and technology, including electromechanically controlled, ahead-thrown ordnance.[48]

The German surface navy, far weaker in 1945 than had been the case in 1918, was concentrated in the Baltic in order to cover the retreat of German units and civilians in the face of Soviet advances, and also to supply German beachheads, notably in Courland (western Latvia). In the face of a weak and poorly managed Soviet navy, both of these goals were successfully executed, and about 2.5 million people were evacuated, albeit for the loss of fifteen thousand, mostly as a result of Soviet submarine attack.

THE COLLAPSE OF JAPAN, 1945

In the closing months of the war, as American operations neared the Japanese Home Islands, the Japanese increasingly turned to kamikaze (suicide) attacks in order to counter overwhelming American naval superiority: aircraft were flown into ships, making them manned missiles, although they had little or no penetrative power against large warships. Such attacks were a product not only of a fanatical self-sacrifice but also of the limitations, by then, of the Japanese naval air arm. First mounted on October 25, 1944, these attacks led in 1944–45 to the sinking of forty-nine ships, with another three hundred damaged, and were designed to sap American will. Initially, the percentage of hits and near misses was over a quarter, but the success rate fell the following spring as the Japanese increasingly relied on inexperienced pilots, while American air defenses improved, with more antiaircraft guns and also fighter patrols, notably Hellcats, which were dispatched miles from the fleet in order to shoot down outclassed Zeros. The Americans benefited from the large number of fighters carried by their numerous carriers and from the radar-based system of fighter control. Bomber attacks on Japanese air bases also helped. The Japanese lost about five thousand men in the kamikaze attacks.

From April 1945, the Japanese also used Ohka (cherry blossom) flying bombs powered by three solid-fuel rocket motors and launched from aircraft twenty-three miles from their intended targets. They had pilots but no propeller or landing gear, thus serving even more as manned missiles. About 750 were used, mostly in response to the American conquest of the island of Okinawa in April–June 1945, but only three American ships were sunk or damaged beyond repair as a result.

The Americans invaded the island of Okinawa on April 1, 1945. The Japanese sent their last major naval force, led by the battleship *Yamato*, on a kamikaze mission, with only enough oil to steam to Okinawa. However, it was intercepted by 380 American carrier-based aircraft, and the *Yamato*, a cruiser, and four of the eight accompanying destroyers were sunk on April 7. The vulnerability of surface warships without air cover was amply demonstrated. The battleships on which the Japanese had spent so much had become an operational and strategic irrelevance.

The fighting on the islands of Iwo Jima and Okinawa was fierce, a bland remark that gives no guidance to the difficulty of the conquests and the heavy casualties involved in defeating the well-positioned Japanese forces. They fought to the death with fanatical intensity for islands seen as part of Japan, although under heavy pressure from the attacking marines with their massive air and sea support. The skillful Japanese exploitation of the terrain, not least by tunneling into Iwo Jima, ensured that the bombing and shelling that preceded the landing of the marines there on February 19 inflicted only nominal damage. As a consequence, the conquest was slow and bloody. So also with Okinawa.

Japan's position in 1945 indicated the great value of Allied naval power, most of which, in these operations, was American. Although the Japanese still occupied large areas in East and Southeast Asia, for example much of China, Malaya, Sumatra, and Java, these forces were isolated. American submarines operated with few difficulties in the Yellow and East China Seas and the Sea of Japan. Carrier-borne aircraft attacked Japan, dominated its airspace, and mined its waters, while warships bombarded coastal positions as they had earlier done at Iwo Jima and Okinawa.

American naval and amphibious operations and planning benefited from their mastery of logistics, not least in ensuring the availability of sufficient oil. The Americans could plan where they wanted to mount an invasion. Cumulative experience proved important, not least in the development and testing of capabilities. The transfer of ammunition between ships at sea was tested during the Iwo Jima operation, following success earlier with fuel. The development of service squadrons by the navy, and the supporting structure of floating dry docks, was important to American forward movement, not least as existing harbors tended to be distant, exposed to the sea, and limited in their facilities.

Just as the Battle of the Atlantic had ended in Allied triumph (as also in the First World War), so the naval war in the Pacific had been decisively won. Despite logistical limitations, the British Pacific Fleet played a successful role. Nevertheless, the attack on Japan and the planning for the invasion[49] were very much an American triumph, and this looked toward postwar American naval dominance.

Allied fleets elsewhere hit the Japanese Empire. In their reconquest of Myanmar in early 1945, the British benefited from well-executed amphibious operations, notably in the capture of the city of Rangoon on May 3. The Royal Navy also launched attacks, especially with aircraft and submarines, on Japanese positions and shipping, for example, oil refineries in Sumatra. Naval support was also significant to Australasian amphibious attacks on the island of Borneo.

The Soviet Union entered the war on August 8, 1945. Most of its attack was a land invasion of Manchuria. However, the invasion of northern Korea was supported by amphibious operations from the Sea of Japan, as was that of southern Sakhalin. The Kurile Islands were also successfully invaded. Whereas earlier in the war the Soviets had suffered from a lack of preparation in their amphibious operations, the 1945 operations were ably conducted and supported by much naval infantry.

CONCLUSION

> The war we have to wage against Japan is of an entirely new type. It is no mere clash of opposing fleets. Allied naval forces must be so strong in themselves, and so fully equipped to carry with them land and air forces, that they can overcome not only Japanese naval forces but also Japanese garrisons supported by shore-based air forces. . . . The bigger the Allied fleet free to seek out the enemy, the better the chances of destroying the Japanese fleet.[50]

General Hastings Ismay, in effect Churchill's chief of staff, thus emphasized scale in his stress on the naval dimension in 1944. Scale was, indeed, readily apparent. Between Pearl Harbor and the end of the war, the Americans commissioned more warships into their navy than any other combatant. More generally, most of the forty-two million tons of shipping built by the Allies during the war was constructed by the Americans. Despite losing oil tankers with a total tonnage of 1,421,000, mostly to German submarines, the tonnage of the American oil-tanker fleet rose from 4,268,000 tons in 1942 to 12,875,000 tons in 1945. The British shipbuilding industry was affected by

German bombing, as well as by serious problems of resource supply and allocation, and the capacity for expansion was limited. The Soviet industry was badly affected by German occupation. Canadian production greatly increased, but it was the Americans who were responsible not only for much of the new Allied shipping, but also for the rapid response to needs and for the expansion in types.

Many of the new American vessels were Liberty ships, built often in as little as ten days, using prefabricated components on production lines. This was an aspect of the rapid design and production methods that characterized American procurement. All-welded ships replaced riveting, speeding up production. The flexibility of American society helped directly and conspicuously: by late 1944, over 15 percent of the workers in shipbuilding were women. In some yards, notably on the West Coast, the percentage was far higher.[51]

In contrast, Japanese shipbuilding faced major resource and organization problems, including a lack of steel, poor plants, scant use of welding, and an absence of standardization. This situation was crucial to the long haul after Midway, as the capacity of the Japanese navy to survive repeated defeats in battle by the Americans was limited. In part, this was also due to repeated American attacks on an already flawed war economy.

Differences in resources and shipbuilding were linked to the major buildup in the Allied navies. For example, Canada on the eve of war had six destroyers and fewer than 2,000 personnel, but by 1945, resting on a massive expansion in shipbuilding, there were also two light fleet carriers, two light cruisers, a very large antisubmarine force, and 110,000 serving personnel. There were administrative problems in this expansion, but the buildup was both achieved and effective.[52]

The war at sea also led to an emphasis, and far more than in the First World War, on the ability to articulate and integrate different arms. A long-established aspect of effectiveness, such integration became more important with the greater range of available technology. The integration of air and sea forces, both for attack and also in defense, was important for tactical, operational, and strategic success and proved particularly significant to the Allied achievement of strategic objectives against both Germany and Japan. This integration focused attention not only on resources but also on command skills, training, and the ability to learn and adapt.[53] In February 1943, Admiral Sir Dudley Pound, the First British Sea Lord, noted,

> At the moment we are doing all we can to produce super long-range aircraft, so that we can cover the whole of the Atlantic from one side to the other, as there is no question but that if you can put aircraft over the U-boats during the day, it prevents them getting into position for their night attacks. I am hoping very

much that we shall be able to blast them out of their operational bases in the Bay of Biscay [by air attack].[54]

The naval dimension, alongside that of the air and often, through carriers, closely linked with it, played a key role in securing Allied victory. As in the First World War, the naval dimension was crucial to the strategic axes of Allied power. In the Second, both naval and air capabilities and operations were central to the delivery of power. The Axis transport systems were repeatedly hit hard by Allied attack while also suffering from the deficiencies of the naval forces and strategy of the Axis powers. Allied attacks both lessened the mobility of Axis forces and crippled their war economy. Alongside greater Allied production, America and Britain had effective maintenance and training programs.[55]

At the same time, alongside the ease with which a clear narrative and analysis can be advanced, there are problems with both. In particular, there is the extent to which the nature of naval tasks during the Cold War affected the subsequent reading of the Second World War. In particular, the postwar significance of carriers in the American and British navies encouraged a reading back, with a downplaying of the role of battleships. In contrast, it is instructive that the war games at the American Naval War College in 1945–46 assumed the combination of fast carriers and fast battleships.[56] So also with the discussion of submarines. Because the Cold War at sea with the Soviet Union was to be dominated by the Soviet submarine threat, so the emphasis for the Second World War was on the U-boat challenge, which indeed was very real, rather than that from German surface shipping, which was also highly significant at the time.

It is necessary to remember the wider political context. For example, some of the forced labor used to make armaments and batteries for the over one thousand U-boats built was taken from concentration camps. Many workers died, in part as a result of exposure to toxic metals. Unsuccessful efforts were made to stop a German television documentary on these matters, *The Silence of the Quandts*, being broadcast in 2007. The Quandt family business made these products.

Moreover, the continuing tendency to treat the German submarine service, which, in fact, had a high rate of Nazi members, as heroes, able to keep fighting (and killing Allied merchant sailors) despite heavy cumulative losses, which was the presentation in German war propaganda, needs to be countered by a reminder of their fanaticism and of the deadly nature of their long-term goals.[57] This is particularly the case as German revisionism gathered pace in the late 2010s with the rise there of the Far Right and its increasing assertiveness in cultural as well as political matters.

It is also important to be reminded of the suffering of those sunk. In 1942, a British naval officer on another warship commented on the sinking of the carrier *Eagle* in the Mediterranean: "It was a terrible sight to see such a big ship go down so quickly. The great patch of oil and debris was full of heads, there were hundreds swimming and choking in the water."[58]

Chapter Eleven

The Second World War in the Air

> If they [the Japanese leaders] do not now accept our terms they may expect a rain of ruin from the air. . . . We are now prepared to obliterate more rapidly and completely every productive enterprise the Japanese have above ground in any city. We shall destroy their docks, their factories, and their communications. . . . We shall completely destroy Japan's power to make war.
> —Statement issued on behalf of President Harry S. Truman of the United States after the first atomic bomb was dropped on Hiroshima[1]

The hitherto unprecedented scale, scope, and sophistication of air power during this global conflict reflected the manifold use of this power: in strategic, operational, and tactical terms, and affecting both land and sea campaigning. Moreover, this use of air power demonstrated a responsiveness, indeed "quality," in terms of the rapid operation of, and improvement in, the action-reaction cycles of air power during the war. Already seen throughout the First World War, this process operated at a greater scale and range in the Second. The familiar coverage of air power focuses on bombing, fighter escort and interception, and support for airborne forces, but there is also need to devote due attention to ground support and to the role of air power in naval warfare, logistics, and communications. In particular, the integration of air power with land and sea campaigning proved instrumental in improving the effectiveness of both. In turn, the significance of antiaircraft practice increased, both that of aircraft seeking to block such activities and integration, and that of ground- and sea-based units.

Furthermore, the experience of being bombed and strafed was significant for the military and for civilians. The latter experience became an important part of the collective memory of the war and for subsequent controversies. Bombing campaigns were indeed intended to produce an overwhelming impact on political and public opinion, most notably with the dropping of atomic bombs on Hiroshima and Nagasaki in August 1945 in order to knock Japan out of the war. This use of air power had a lasting cultural impact in the shape of a debate over how far it was necessary and appropriate.

The extensive use of air power reflected the length and range of the conflict and the degree to which it involved a mobilization of the resources of societies. It was also possible to manufacture, supply, and man large numbers of aircraft, and in a variety of types, but without the high initial and ongoing costs that advanced electronics and other technological factors were to lead to by the 1980s. Technological changes did not relate solely to one model of aircraft. The standardization of screw sizes, for example, was crucial to both speedy manufacture and easy repair, helping Britain greatly in 1940 in response to German air attack. Thus, the characteristics of aircraft were particularly opportune during the Second World War. The major improvements made in aircraft and associated technology during the 1930s ensured that they were far more robust, potent, and useful than during the First World War; but, as yet, they were not overspecialized, and their specifications had not improved to a degree that was to limit and inhibit their use. The same situation was true of naval air power, of airfields, and of antiaircraft weaponry.

1939–40: GERMAN BLITZKRIEG

The first campaign in Europe, the rapid German conquest of Poland in 1939, demonstrated the use of air power in a campaign well suited to its impact. Tactical air power had three main missions: gaining or maintaining air superiority against enemy fighters, providing close air support for ground combat units, and interdiction: attacking the immediate supply and communications networks of enemy ground forces. The Germans were particularly good at the last. Greatly outnumbering the Poles in aircraft, the Germans, who began the war with a surprise assault, enjoyed the initiative, while the Polish fighters were outclassed by the Me-109. The Polish air force was rapidly destroyed, a crucial step in the German offensive. The Germans benefited from launching surprise attacks that destroyed some of the Polish aircraft on the ground, although the extent of these losses has been exaggerated, and many Polish aircraft were lost in aerial combat.

Subsequently, the rapid opening by the Germans of improvised airfields behind their advancing forces countered the short range of their aircraft and helped the Luftwaffe provide close air support, and to a degree that was hitherto unique. In contrast to very poor relations between the Luftwaffe and the navy, those with the army were less bad and could be good. Aside from providing firepower, the Luftwaffe was strong in reconnaissance. The Luftwaffe was able to associate itself with the army's success and to present itself as largely responsible. German newsreels made much of the role of the Luftwaffe. Warsaw, the Polish capital, was heavily bombed, with about seven thousand people killed. Hitler liked to watch films of the bombing.

Unlike the German attack on Poland, Soviet control of the air did not help bring rapid victory in the Winter War with Finland in 1939–40, although the winter circumstances were far more difficult. The Finns and the Soviets were both equipped with obsolescent aircraft, but the Soviet air force vastly outnumbered the Finnish one and eventually employed at least fifteen air regiments. The Finnish capital, Helsinki, was bombed. The Soviets, however, relied on artillery, not air power, to blast their way through the Mannerheim Line, the main Finnish defense position. Artillery could deliver more destruction and was less dependent on the weather. This success led Finland to terms. Poor Soviet performance, including disproportionately heavy losses, was related to the rapid expansion of the air force at the expense of training. In the late 1930s, it was plagued with an inordinate number of training accidents trying to push so many men through pilot training in a short amount of time. Also, many men were assigned to pilot training without having requested it. Finnish airmanship was definitely superior.

The Germans proved more successful than the Soviets against Finland when they launched surprise attacks on Denmark and Norway on April 9, 1940. In the case of Denmark, the Germans made effective use of their air power against a weak resistance. Airborne troops of the Luftwaffe, including the first parachute assault, complemented the troops landed by ship and those advancing overland from Germany. An amphibious landing was blocked in the Oslo fjord, but the Germans compensated by airlifting troops to the Oslo airfield, which had been captured by airborne troops.

Invading the Netherlands, Belgium, and France on May 10, 1940, the Germans again benefited greatly from air operations. Both the Dutch and the Belgians were weak in the air, and the Germans swiftly gained and, crucially, used air superiority. One of the first glider-borne air assaults, and an exceptional piece of airmanship, was against the Belgian fort at Eben Emael. The capture of bridges by German airborne forces weakened the use of river and canal defenses, hit morale, and denied defense-in-depth. The crucial step in the conquest of the Netherlands was the capture by German paratroops of the Moerdijk bridge over the combined waters of the Meuse and the Waal some sixteen miles south of Rotterdam. Air attacks supported the German advance.

However, the German use of airborne troops was only a partial success in the Netherlands. There, the German airborne troops generally failed in their attempts to take vital objects and airfields and were unable to capture either the cabinet ministers or members of the royal family. About 350 transport aircraft were lost, and of about 7,250 airborne troops, nearly 2,000 became casualties or prisoners of war. Their dire situation may well have hastened the decision by Hitler and Göring to bomb the city of Rotterdam and force a quick Dutch surrender, although the Dutch army was poorly trained and its defenses had crumbled to land assault east of Utrecht. The destruction of much of the city center caused by the bombing of Rotterdam on May 14 was a brutal demonstration of what air attack could achieve. Some eighty thousand people lost their homes and about six hundred to eight hundred were killed. The Dutch stopped fighting that day, and the surrender followed on May 15.

In part by concentrating their aircraft at critical places, the Germans also rapidly achieved air superiority over the French, inflicting heavy casualties on the French air force and then using their success to attack the French army, although there was, as yet, no direct radio communication between aircraft and ground forces. The Vichy Court of Supreme Justice was to hold the French Armée de l'Air responsible for defeat in 1940, a political judgment, but one that reflected the French failure to match the Luftwaffe in aircraft and doctrine.

Most significantly, the French failed to prevent the Luftwaffe from assisting the German crossing of the River Meuse at Sedan on May 13. Even then, however, although assisted by the impact of Stuka attacks on French morale, Guderian's breakthrough was a standard infantry-artillery fight. What was new was the German tanks' ability to exploit the gains made by the traditional arms. Air power largely played the tangential role of neutralizing French artillery in the rear areas. In the face of German aircraft and rapidly deployed German antiaircraft guns, French air attacks failed to destroy the bridges across the Meuse the following day.[2] This failure highlighted both the inflated expectation of what air power could achieve and the difficulty of destroying bridges using aircraft. British aircraft also failed dismally in their attacks on French bridges.

Maintaining the tempo of the attack, the Germans did not allow the French air force to regain the initiative, while the air force leaders anyway lacked the necessary urgent response to a rapidly deteriorating situation. In particular, the leaders were unable to compensate for their initial deployment of aerial resources across the entire frontier.[3]

The fall of France also involved the Germans fighting the British forces deployed in France as part of the alliance. The poor control of fighters against the Luftwaffe played a major role in the RAF's inability to inflict major damage, although the British fighters could hold their own against the Me-109. The German pilots had the great advantage of experience. Outnumbered, the RAF, with its focus on air conflict with the Germans, suffered from very poor coordination with the British army. As a result of this and of poor bombers, notably the Fairey Battle, the army lacked adequate close air support. Moreover, German air superiority prevented effective Allied air attacks on their advancing forces or supply lines. However, in large part thanks to the RAF, the Luftwaffe failed to prevent the evacuation of substantial Anglo-French forces from northern France, notably the beaches of Dunkirk, and this evacuation was crucial in providing Britain with the means to fight on.

BRITAIN UNDER ATTACK

The fall of France left Britain vulnerable, as well as ensuring that British air attacks on Germany would not be able to benefit from French airfields and friendly airspace. Instead, German aircraft were rapidly moved forward into France, Belgium, the Netherlands, and Norway. German airfields, notably in the Pas de Calais and Normandy, were now close to Britain, greatly cutting the journey time of bombers and allowing fighters to escort them. The situation was very different from previous occasions on which Britain had been threatened with invasion, most seriously by France under Napoleon in 1803–5. Then, British naval strength had provided strong security against invasion. In contrast, in 1940, the Luftwaffe was instructed to help prepare the way for an invasion, Operation Sealion, especially by driving British warships from the English Channel.

Instead, Luftwaffe commanders were increasingly concerned to attack the RAF and its supporting infrastructure in order to destroy the RAF and prepare the way for reducing Britain to submission by a bombing war on civilian targets. This was a strategy that would put the Luftwaffe center stage, which was very much the intention of its commanders. In practice, however, a lack of clarity in the relationship between air attack and invasion affected German strategy. There was also a serious failure to prepare for a strategic air offensive because the Germans, with their emphasis on tactical and operational imperatives, had not sufficiently anticipated its necessity. The Luftwaffe was primarily intended to act in concert with German ground forces, something that was not possible in the self-contained aerial battle with Britain.

In addition, the Germans suffered from a lack of well-trained pilots, and from limitations with their aircraft and tactics. Not only did the Luftwaffe fail to win the air superiority contest in the Battle of Britain, but its medium and dive-bombers proved highly vulnerable to fighter attack and incapable of an effective strategic bombing campaign. Their bombers' load capacity and range were too small, and their fighters were too sluggish (Me-110) or had inadequate range, affecting the time they could spend over England (Me-109). Moreover, operating near the edge of their escort range, the fighters were handicapped by having to escort the bombers. Furthermore, although the British had also lost heavily, the Luftwaffe had already lost many aircraft and pilots during the Battle of France. In a serious intelligence failure, the Germans underrated the size, sophistication, and strength of the defense and, in particular, failed to understand the role of British radar and its place in the integrated air defense system. They devoted insufficient attention to attacking the radar stations and suffered from poor target intelligence. The British control system, with its plotters of opposing moves and its telephone lines, was an early instance of the network-enabled capability seen in the 2000s with its plasma screens and secure data links. In each case, the targeting, sensors, and shooters were linked through a network that included the decision maker.[4] In 1940, Germany had radar, but it was not yet available to help the Luftwaffe.

Initial German attacks on the RAF and its airfields inflicted serious blows, especially on pilot numbers. However, fighting over Britain, it was possible to recover RAF pilots who survived being shot down, while, contesting the battle it had planned for and not needing to improvise as much as might have been the case, the RAF benefited from the support provided by radar and the ground-control organization, as well as from able command decisions, good intelligence, and a high level of fighting quality. Luftwaffe losses also reflected the vulnerability of bombers.[5] Moreover, despite issues with fuel supply,[6] the British outproduced the Germans in aircraft, so that losses in fighters were quickly made good because of more efficient manufacture that drew on superior British engineering and management. The Germans did not devote enough attention to building aircraft, in part because their intelligence underestimated RAF strength. Fighter Command was helped by the repeated spoiling raids against German airfields mounted by Bomber Command, raids made more difficult for the Germans because the airfields were not protected by radar. Aside from the availability of radar for the British, it was difficult for German bombers to put British airfields out of action, not least as the wide, grassy strips that were a key element in the latter could not be wrecked, although hangers could be destroyed.

As a reminder of the multiplicity of factors involved and the need to put explanations focused on air power into a broader context, the viability of Sealion before the onset of winter weather was dubious even had the Germans achieved air superiority over southern England, while the lack of support from advancing land forces, on the pattern of the German offensives so far, made such superiority harder to achieve. There were other British fighters further north and west in England, as well as the serious threat posed by the Royal Navy.[7] Moreover, Sealion lacked adequate planning, preparation, and resources. The hasty and improvised nature of the German plans contrasted heavily with the detailed Allied preparations for the invasion of France in 1944.

Nevertheless, however flawed the air assault was, victory in the Battle of Britain produced a significant boost to British civilian morale.[8] Moreover, the Battle of Britain served as a lasting account of valorous air combat and of the crucial role of air power. It did so not only for the RAF, but also for other air forces.

THE BLITZ

Fear about the consequences for the population of German air attack led to the mass evacuation of children (including my parents from the East End of London) when war broke out in 1939, as well as to the issue of gas masks, the preparation of a large number of cardboard coffins, and the implementation of blackout regulations. In the event, the German attacks did not come until the following autumn (by which time some of the 690,000 evacuated in September 1939 had returned) and did not include gas attacks.

From September 7, 1940, the Luftwaffe bombed London heavily and repeatedly. The German word *blitzkrieg* (lightning war) was shortened by the British to give a name to this terrifying new form of conflict: the Blitz. That day, 348 German bombers attacked. The inadequately prepared defenses were taken by surprise and failed to respond adequately. There were only ninety-two antiaircraft guns ready for action, and their fire-control systems failed. The British fighter squadrons proved unable to stop the powerful air assault. Some 430 people were killed in the East End, where the docks on the River Thames were hit hard. This was what became a German strategy to starve Britain into surrender, in part by destroying the docks through which food was imported. Liverpool, Plymouth, and Southampton were to be heavily attacked for that reason, as well as to deny the navy bases.

From September 7 until mid-November 1940, the Germans bombed London every night bar one. There were also large-scale daylight attacks as well as hit-and-run attacks. The attack on the moonlit night of October 15–16 proved particularly serious, with four hundred bombers active, of which only one was shot down by the RAF's forty-one fighters. By mid-November, when the attacks became less focused on London, over thirteen thousand tons of high-explosive bombs had been dropped on the city, as well as nearly one million incendiaries.

The German focus on attacking British cities in the Blitz from the autumn of 1940 was intended to destroy civilian morale by means of terror bombing. However, although there were occasional episodes of panic, for example, by the civic authorities in Southampton, as well as an increase in criminality, morale on the whole remained good. This campaign continued the Battle of Britain, but without an operational focus or the capability to match its destructive purpose. Moreover, the attacks on British airfields stopped.

London bore the brunt of the attack. There were also destructive raids on other cities, including Coventry, an industrial center, with 449 bombers on November 14 and Manchester the following month. Nighttime air-defense techniques were poor, and, not least because of the absence of precise aerial radar, it was hard to hit German aircraft once they largely switched to night attacks in September 1940 in part in order to cut losses. The German bombers almost always got through. Indeed, relatively few German aircraft were shot down that winter, although accidents and the winter weather led to many losses. By the late spring of 1941, however, the British defense was becoming more effective thanks to the use of radar-directed Beaufighter planes and ground defenses. From mid-November 1940 to the end of February 1941, eight major raids were mounted on London. Thereafter, the focus was on the ports, until May 1941 when the bomber forces were moved to prepare for the invasion of the Soviet Union launched the following month. The British bombing of Germany, notably the cities of Berlin and Mannheim, in late 1940 was on a smaller scale and inflicted much less damage.

In bombing London, the German High Command had set out to destroy civilian morale. In practice, there was an emphasis, in London and elsewhere, on "taking it," forbearance, and making do, notably at the docks, which continued operating. The German hope that the British people would realize their plight, overthrow Churchill, and make peace proved a serious misreading of British politics and public opinion. Instead, British intelligence reports suggested that the bombing led to signs of "increasing hatred of Germany," as well as to demands for "numerous reprisals."[9] The idea that Hitler had to be defeated and removed was strengthened. There was also a phlegmatic and fatalistic response to the bombing, one captured by the Listener Research Report organized by the BBC in 1941. For social as well as political reasons, the air assault made the home front far more significant. It became the focus of government effort, in the shape of civil defense, and of activity by the public. The bravery of the civilians was a key theme, a bravery in which women played the central role. The emphasis on a stoical response to suffering was designed to preserve morale.[10]

Attempts to shelter from the remorseless bombing led many Londoners to seek refuge in the Underground system (the "Tube" or subway), where about 177,000 people were sleeping on the station platforms by late September 1940. There was a degree of social tension in the response to the bombing. Thus, Londoners from the much-bombed working-class dockside district of Silvertown, where there was a lack of shelters, forced their way into the Savoy Hotel's impressive bomb shelter. Nevertheless, the government's theme of equality in suffering was made a reality by the Luftwaffe. Fortitude in the face of the Blitz became a key aspect of national identity, and the real and symbolic aspect of the assault on British civil society accentuated the sense of the entire country, including the royal family in Buckingham Palace, being under attack. This became a key theme in modern British public culture, indeed a central aspect of the democratization of the national heritage.

Film ensured that the Blitz was the first major episode of London's history that was captured dramatically for a wide audience. Photographs of St. Paul's Cathedral surrounded by flames and devastation acquired totemic force, and overseas as well as in Britain, including in the United States where the British were making a major attempt to win support. Documentaries, including *London Can Take It* (1940) and *Christmas under Fire* (1941), spread film of the bombing.

GERMAN OFFENSIVES, 1941

On April 6, 1941, Germany attacked Yugoslavia and Greece. The attack on Yugoslavia included the terror bombing of the undefended city of Belgrade in order to cause heavy civilian casualties: over seventeen thousand people were killed. The British sent an expeditionary force to help the Greeks, but, poorly commanded, with inadequate air support, and with its Greek allies short of equipment, it was swiftly pushed back. The tempo of the German advance, especially its rapid use of airborne troops and armor, brought a decisive advantage. German aircraft did not inflict much damage but had a severe impact on the morale of Allied troops.

The campaign culminated with the capture of the Greek island of Crete by German parachute and air-transported troops. This was a risky attack, as such forces were unable to bring heavy arms with them, a problem that was to affect the British airborne assault on Arnhem in the Netherlands in late 1944. However, on Crete, although it took heavy casualties in men and transport aircraft, the German assault force was able to gain the initiative from a poorly directed resistance, seize airstrips, and secure resupply by air. Glider troops tipped the balance during the assault on Maleme airfield, when they landed close to antiaircraft batteries which they captured. The conquest of Crete was the first time a major objective had been taken by massed airborne assault, and the operation raised important questions regarding the utility of air power.

On June 22, 1941, Hitler launched Operation Barbarossa against the Soviet Union. Despite having the biggest air force in the world, the Soviets, greatly outnumbering but outclassed by the Luftwaffe, were less impressive. In part, this was because the Soviets suffered from a lack of good pilots, as well as the extent to which effective new aircraft had not replaced obsolescent models. The Soviets had no radar, and most of the aircraft lacked radio telephones. Their pilots were poorly trained, and their morale was low. The air force had been badly affected by Stalin's purges. Benefiting from surprise (unlike against the RAF in 1940) and destroying over 1,200 Soviet aircraft on the first day, the Germans rapidly gained superiority in the air and used it both to assist ground operations and to destroy ships of the Soviet Baltic and Black Sea Fleets.

However, despite the priority placed on production for the Luftwaffe, one that hit the army hard, the Germans were short of the necessary aircraft, in part because the heavy losses suffered during the Battles of France and Britain had only just been replaced.[11] The Luftwaffe, moreover, now needed to maintain an air-defense (and attack) force to face Britain, to support German and Italian forces in the Mediterranean, to protect Germany from air attack, and to defend Norway and France, as well as to operate in the Soviet Union, none of them tasks that had to be fulfilled in 1940. In addition, the German bombers lacked the necessary range and bomb capacity to be an effective strategic force on the Eastern Front. There were more serious problems arising from the space-force ratio, with the Germans not having the number of aircraft necessary in order to have a major impact across the very extensive range of the battle zone. Furthermore, as the Germans advanced, the Luftwaffe was forced to rely on improvised airfields and was affected by the general logistical crisis of Operation Barbarossa, notably the difficulties in bringing forward and maintaining supplies. The Luftwaffe found itself overstretched and then fighting a war of attrition for air superiority, a war that it could not win. The serviceability of its aircraft and airfields deteriorated.

The rapid Soviet revival of their air force, devastated in the initial German attack, was also significant. Much Soviet industry had remained beyond the range of German power, and this proved important to this revival. Moreover, there was an introduction of better aircraft, such as the YAK-1 (1940), YAK-7 (1941), MIG-3 (1941), LAGG-3 (1941), YAK-9 (1942), LA-5 (1942), YAK-3 (1943),[12] and LA-7 (1944). The Soviets also operated aircraft supplied by Britain and the United States, notably Hurricanes, P-39s, P-40s, and P-63s. In order to provide protection for their forces on the ground, the Germans therefore had to devote large numbers of aircraft to destroying Soviet aircraft. This again reduced the option of a German bombing campaign.[13]

AIR WAR IN EUROPE IN 1942

Although aircraft were heavily involved in the war on the Eastern Front, they did not play such a major operational role as in the war in the Pacific. Air superiority, nevertheless, could still be highly significant locally. Thus, in the German capture of the Kerch Peninsula in eastern Crimea in May 1942, the Soviet lack of adequate air-land cooperation was exploited by the Germans, who benefited from effective air support. There were also heavy German air attacks on the besieged Crimean city of Sevastopol that June. However, later in the year, the German bombing of the city of Stalingrad, which became the focus of the German offensive, helped make it a wrecked terrain that made it very difficult for the German attackers to conquer. Heavily bombed by the Allies, Monte Cassino in Italy and Caen in Normandy served the Germans in a similar fashion in 1944.

Once the Soviet counterattack launched on November 19, 1942, had led, on November 23, to the encirclement of the German Sixth Army, nearly a third of a million men, in and close to Stalingrad, the Germans sought to provide sufficient supplies by air. This proved impossible: the Sixth Army needed 750 tons of supplies a day, Göring said the Luftwaffe could deliver 300, but on most days the army received fewer than 90, although on one day 262 tons were landed. Aside from lacking the resources, the Luftwaffe had no contingency plans for such an operation. Protests from the local Luftwaffe commander about the lack of necessary transport assets and infrastructure were overruled by Göring. During the operation, substantial units from Luftflotte 4 were withdrawn to deal with the Anglo-American Torch landings in North Africa. This did not help the airlift, although the very attempt to mount a large-scale airlift testified to the advances made by air power, while what was transported helped keep the Sixth Army alive, albeit at the loss of 495 transport aircraft. The failure of ground troops to break through the Soviet encirclement, which instead became stronger, led to the surrender of the army on January 31 to February 2, 1943.[14]

Air-power effectiveness, meanwhile, increased in the Mediterranean war. Blamey reported to the Australian prime minister in September 1941 that air support had become a priority for Allied forces planning to attack the Germans and Italians in North Africa:

> Great advance in this in last two months. Attitude Air Force here most co-operative. . . . All suitable air squadrons to be trained in army co-operation and joint control organization for field co-operation being set up. During operations specific air units to be allotted to military organizations under control army commander with air controller on his staff.[15]

The RAF in North Africa focused on unrelenting offensive action against German supply and communication lines. This, in turn, drew German fighters into attritional battles for air superiority that they could not win. The increased provision of air support for British forces from July 1942 proved highly significant for a recovery of morale by the British Eighth Army and also hit German and Italian morale.[16]

The range of air-power operations expanded in 1942 with the stepping up of the Allied bombing of Germany and occupied Europe. This bombing was designed to have a direct impact on the Germans and to meet Soviet pressure for action. Churchill insisted to the Soviets that the bomber offensive constituted a "Second Front" against Germany. A British strategic review of August 1941 had noted the consequences of British forces being unable to compete with the Germans in Continental Europe. The response of Britain, at that stage the weaker power, was to seek strategic advantage from indirect attack, in the shape of bombing, blockade, and subversion, each of which was designed to hit the German economy and German morale:

> Bombing on a vast scale is the weapon upon which we principally depend for the destruction of German economic life and morale. To achieve its object the bombing offensive must be on the heaviest possible scale and we aim at a force limited in size only by operational difficulties in the UK. After meeting the needs of our own security we give to the heavy bomber first priority in production.
>
> Our policy at present is to concentrate upon targets which affect both the German transportation system and morale. As our forces increase we intend to pass to a planned attack on civilian morale with the intensity and continuity which are essential for success. We believe that by these methods applied on a vast scale the whole structure on which the German forces are based can be destroyed. As a result these forces will suffer such a decline in fighting power and mobility that direct [British] action will once more become possible.

It was even mistakenly believed that these methods might be enough to make Germany sue for peace.[17]

On the night of May 30–31, 1942, the British launched over 1,050 bombers at the German city of Cologne; 40 were lost. Although the raid, which killed over 460 people, did not achieve all its objectives in terms of the destruction of industry and morale, it indicated the ability of the Allies to make a major attack on a German city and was seen as a way to persuade the British public that the Germans could be hit hard. Arthur Harris, appointed commander in chief of Bomber Command on February 23, 1942, was determined to show the viability of RAF attacks and to stop talk of ending bombing and allocating the bombers to help the navy and the army. The raid saw the use of the bomber-stream tactic, with bombers gathered in one stream in order to use mass to counteract the power of the defenses.

However, for attacks to be sustained, it would be necessary to have a major buildup in air power, in terms of not only the number of aircraft but also their quality, including their payload. The small bombers, such as the Hampden I and the Blenheim, were not fast enough and had poor defensive capabilities. Indeed, the concept of the small bomber was not fully thought out. These aircraft were withdrawn from bombing in 1942 and 1943, respectively. Britain lacked an effective bomber until the advent of the Lancaster, with its bomb load of twenty-two thousand pounds, into operational service in March 1942.

As a sign of what was to come, most of the casualties in Cologne were civilian. In attacking Germany, the RAF was supplemented by the Americans (flying from British bases) from July 1942. The Cologne attack, however, was an exception, as most of the raids in 1942 were fairly small scale. The cities of the Ruhr industrial region, notably Essen and Dortmund, were the main targets. The raids were important to the development of an effective ground-support system to support a bombing offensive, as well as in the gaining of operational experience, a process necessary for the American and British armies and navies as well as for the air forces. The Germans, in turn, continued to bomb British cities, especially in the Baedecker raids, devastating, for example, the city of Exeter.

AIR WAR IN 1943: EASTERN FRONT AND MEDITERRANEAN

In 1943, there were again contrasts between the significance of air warfare on different fronts, however intense it might be. On the Eastern Front, there was this intensity, but not an accompanying strategic significance. Thus, the successful German counteroffensive under Manstein in March 1943 benefited from the ability to defeat the Soviets in the air, albeit at the cost of many aircraft, but this ability was not the key element. So also with the German Kursk offensive in July, which showed how, despite inflicting more losses on its opponents, the struggle in the air had moved against the Luftwaffe. Large numbers of Soviet fighters prevented it from gaining control of the skies, and, although German ground-attack aircraft inflicted much damage on Soviet forces, the same was true of their opponents. Moreover, there were improvements in Soviet aircraft, with the YAK-9U fighter, the LA-7 fighters, and the TU-2 bomber entering squadron service in 1943. At the same time, the Soviet focus on close air support ensured that there was no systematic attempt to destroy the Luftwaffe and obtain, as a result, broader air superiority.[18]

Air power also played a major role in the Mediterranean in 1943, although without being decisive. The Anglo-American invasion of Sicily on July 10 had been preceded by a thorough air assault during June, which had neutralized the Axis airfields and gained the Allies control of the air over the invasion zone. However, the use of airborne troops for the invasion proved difficult: due to strong winds, many of the gliders landed in the sea. Inexperienced and undertrained pilots were a problem, as was a lack of coordination with Allied naval forces who fired on the airborne armada, causing significant casualties and breaking up the cohesion of the transports and glider tugs. On Sicily, the airborne troops were scattered and without heavy weapons support. Moreover, the provision of effective air support for land operations proved hard to secure, both there and in continental Italy when it was invaded later in the year.[19]

Allied land control over southern Italy provided air bases, notably near Bari and Foggia, both captured in September 1943, extending the Allied air assault on the German Empire, notably in the Balkans. In contrast, the British inability to secure local air superiority over the Germans led to a serious

British failure in the Dodecanese Islands campaign in the Aegean in September–November 1943. The establishment of garrisons on Leros, Cos, and the other islands was ill conceived, poorly resourced, and badly executed. This failure indicated the continued importance of air power, which in this case the Germans were able to deploy effectively, in part because of the greater flexibility brought by land-based air power. Operating at extreme range, the RAF, which lost 113 aircraft, was outclassed, and the army units, lacking effective air cover, suffered accordingly, while the British warships tended to keep to the dark.[20] British failure formed a striking contrast with American successes in the Pacific where island targets were isolated before attack.

AIR WAR IN 1943: PACIFIC

The American "twin drives" across the Pacific were a great military operational feat, and air power was central in them. Carriers played a major role, but so also did the creation and securing of airfields. They were important not only for their attack role but also as part of the far-flung American command-and-control and supply systems. American and Australian operations in New Guinea depended heavily on air support, not least in the successful raids on the Japanese airfield at Wewak on August 17–18, 1943, after which Allied ground operations were rarely threatened.[21]

Whereas the Japanese had not introduced new classes of aircraft, the Americans had done so, and then produced the aircraft and their munitions in large numbers and trained pilots accordingly. This process enabled the Americans to challenge the Zero, which had made such an impact in the initial Japanese advances. Now the Americans had the Corsair (which entered operations in February 1943) and the Hellcat (which entered operations that August), each of which outperformed the Zero. So also did the Lightning, a twin-engined aircraft in service from 1941. The Corsair and the Hellcat had powerful Pratt and Whitney air-cooled radial engines. In addition, their specifications included better protection, which enabled them to take more punishment than Japanese aircraft. The Japanese had designed the Zero with insufficient protection, in part because its light weight increased range and maneuverability, but also because the safety of their pilots was a low priority. The pilots themselves wanted the range and maneuverability over the protection: they were good samurai, and the samurai never used shields. When combined with the growing disparity in quality between pilots, a matter of numbers, training, and flying experience, it was clear that the Japanese could not compensate for growing numerical weakness in the air, though, with their emphasis on willpower, they were apt to believe they could.

Masters in aerial combat, American fighters were able to provide cover for their bombers, which, anyway, were better able than their counterparts in Europe to deal with opposition without heavy losses. In part, this was because, with far more territory to cover, the Japanese lacked a fighter defense system to match that of the Germans. The Japanese had a lower density of fighters and lacked the integrated nature of the German defense system, as well as its capacity to improve. Moreover, Japanese airfields were without protective radar, which weakened Wewak in 1943. It was easier to isolate island targets in the Pacific than in the Mediterranean: the American navy could concentrate force more effectively as a result.

THE AIR ATTACK ON GERMANY, 1943

Japan remained out of the range of regular and heavy American air attack, especially once the Chinese air bases initially used had been overrun by the Japanese in 1942 in an offensive deliberately launched for that purpose. In contrast, Germany was under heavy air attack by 1943. Wartime factors accentuated the use of bombing, not simply the determination to employ available forces but also the need to show domestic and international audiences that efforts were being made. A belief that the war being waged was a total one served to justify bombing, and, in turn, the latter was an instrumental demonstration that the war was indeed total. At the Casablanca Conference that January, the Americans and British agreed on what was termed the Combined Bomber Offensive, with the Americans attacking by daylight and the British by night. This was seen as a way to show Stalin that the Western Allies were doing their utmost to weaken Germany and thus to aid Soviet operations. Similarly, the commitment at Casablanca to unconditional surrender by the Axis powers as a war goal was designed to reassure Stalin.

At Casablanca, it was agreed that the bombing should serve to destroy the German economic system and so hit German popular morale that the capacity for armed resistance would be fatally weakened. As most German factories were in cities, these goals were linked. Until the opening of the Second Front, by invading German-held France in June 1944, this was the most effective way to hit at Germany. Although challenged by the strategic depth Germany enjoyed thanks to its conquests in 1940, strategic bombing was made more feasible by four-engined bombers, such as the British Lancaster, as well as by heavier bombs and thanks to developments in navigational aids and training.

The availability of large numbers of bombers reflected Allied industrial capacity, with American and British production of aircraft rising from over 70,000 in 1942 to over 120,000 in 1944. The Allies considerably outbuilt their opponents in the air. Numbers, however, were not the sole issue. The

Allies also developed the ability to organize production so that it could be retooled quickly for improved marks and to ensure the production of a range of aircraft with different capabilities.

The first American raids deep into Germany occurred in February 1943 when the major rail marshaling yard at Hamm was attacked, finally with success on March 2. The Americans focused on daytime high-altitude precision bombing to hit industrial targets, especially ball-bearing factories. This reflected the unsuitability of the B-17 bomber for night flying and American criticism of the value of British area bombing. The British wished to destroy industrial targets, but the Butt Report on night raids in June–July 1941 showed that they were not doing so. Accuracy was difficult with nighttime freefall bombing, and also, despite American bombsights, with daytime bombing, for there was no electronic navigation and target identification and no guided bombs. Instead, concerned about the daytime vulnerability of their bombers, the British focused, from March 1942, on nighttime area bombing. There was a similar contrast in the bombing of Italy by the Americans and the British.

Area bombing could lead to heavy civilian casualties, many factory workers, and this was seen by the protagonists of the policy, notably Harris, as likely to wreck German and Italian morale and thus the ability to continue the war. Cities were ranked on their economic importance as targets. About thirty-four to forty thousand people were killed in the British raids on Hamburg in July 1943, notably on July 28 as the result of a firestorm created by a combination of incendiary and high-explosive bombs. The impact was horrifying: those killed were either suffocated or burned to death. The raid, which followed the first firestorm, at Wuppertal on May 29/30, in which over 3,500 people were killed, badly affected German morale, leading to the partial evacuation of cities, including Hamburg and Berlin, and resulted in a marked increase in criticism of the Nazi regime.

Although the B-17 was a steady platform that could carry a large bomb load of up to 4,800 pounds (2,200 kg), precision bombing was not an easy alternative. Indeed, with bombs with lethal radii measured in a few tens of feet, a bombing tactic that involved bombardment squadrons all dropping simultaneously could not be accurately described as precision. Moreover, heavily armed bomber formations lacking fighter escorts proved far less effective, both in defending themselves and in destroying targets, than had been anticipated in interwar bombing doctrine. This conviction of the value of the bomber was partly responsible for a failure to push the development of long-range fighters sufficiently early. Prior to their introduction, bombers were very vulnerable to interceptors. German day fighters learned to attack head-on because the B-17's top turret could not fire forward. B-17s were supposed to fly in box formations of four to provide mutual fire support, but, once the box was broken, the aircraft became easy targets. Diving steeply onto the formations, or attacking from above and behind, gave the fighters the edge. As a result, in a classic instance of the action-reaction cycle, a forward-firing chin turret with two remotely operated .50-caliber Brownings, the most defensive machine guns of any model, was added with the B-17G, introduced in July 1943.

Cripplingly heavy casualty rates occurred in some raids, notably the American ones against the ball-bearing factory at Schweinfurt in August and October 1943. Nineteen percent of the aircraft on the August 17 raid were lost, mostly to German fighters, and the factory continued to operate. The Germans had developed a complex and wide-ranging system of radar warning, with long-range, early-warning radars, as well as short-range radars that guided night fighters (which also had their own radars) toward the bombers. Indeed, the strength of the German resistance was a major reason, alongside bombing inaccuracy, inadequate intelligence, and poor weather, for the failure of the bombing to match optimistic prewar expectations.

Each was a significant factor. For example, poor industrial research greatly reduced the effectiveness of both British and American bombing. Although the locations of the head offices and major plants of most leading German companies was known, there was little or no knowledge of precisely what was made and where. Further, when the right city was known, it all too often was not known which industrial location made the most critical components or processed the critical materials. The attack on Schweinfurt involved a failure to understand the structure of the target company. Moreover, Albert Speer quickly dispersed this manufacturing immediately on taking over direction of German industry. This intelligence failure was also to be seen in the bombing of Japan. In the postwar period, in contrast, both Soviet and NATO forces made industry structure a priority intelligence task in preparing for a possible conflict.

The air war over Europe became attritional in 1943. There were problems with identifying the target, even in daylight and without antiaircraft guns or enemy fighters, and accuracy remained heavily dependent on the skill of the pathfinder aircraft that preceded the bombers in order to identify targets. The technology to make precision bombing possible did not really exist. Despite improvements, the American Norden bombsight could not deliver the precision claimed. Indeed, until the advent of the smart bomb, which was used by the Americans from the Vietnam War, "precision bombing" is a largely misapplied term. There were some notable exceptions, such as the British bombing of Amiens prison on February 18, 1944, by Mosquitoes in order to free resistance leaders, but this was a very low-altitude attack by a small number of fast twin-engined bombers. So also with the successful attack by Mosquitoes and American Mustang fighters against the Gestapo headquarters in Copenhagen in March 1945.

The needs of air defense ensured that much German military production was devoted to aircraft and antiaircraft guns (about 60 percent in 1943),[22] while Luftwaffe strength was increasingly concentrated in Germany, to the detriment of ground support, although much of the Luftwaffe continued to be employed on the Eastern Front. The protection of Germany from air attack reflected the concern about the prestige of the Nazi regime and the morale of the German populace to which bombing gave rise. Joseph Goebbels, the Nazi propaganda chief, sought to maintain morale in the face of bombing, not least by ensuring that the civil relief program worked well. The availability of more air power on the Eastern Front would have been operationally useful to Germany, but, given Soviet resources, it would not have had strategic effect there. In this respect, the contribution of the Allied air offensive to Soviet campaigning was very valuable, but not decisive.

A long-term emphasis on bombers, as well as the consequences of heavy aircraft losses from 1940, and a failure to increase aircraft production significantly until 1943 meant that the German fighter arm was weak. There were serious problems with the management of German air power, in part due to a lack of necessary experience in the senior ranks and a gap between the High Command and the fighting component of the Luftwaffe.[23] Moreover, the Germans suffered from being the focus of Allied air power. However, in response to the Allied bombers, German fighter-bombers and medium bombers were adapted to act as night fighters. In addition, the Hamburg raid was followed by the development by the Germans of new night-fighting methods that were not dependent on radar. Radar-defense systems could be wrecked by the British use of "window": dropping strips of aluminum foil that appeared like bombers on radar screens. In response, the Germans relied on radar guidance to the general area of British air activity, which window contributed to, and on visual sightings thereafter. This caused British losses to mount from the late summer of 1943. Furthermore, that autumn, German radar was adapted so as to be able to circumvent the impact of window.

This action-reaction cycle was seen in other aspects of the air war. The British Lancaster bomber had a very advanced communications system for its time, being fitted with the R1155 receiver and T1154 transmitter, ensuring radio direction firing. However, its H2S ground-looking navigation radar system, fitted from 1943, was eventually homed in on by the German night fighters' NAXOS receiver and had to be used with discretion. In November 1943, the RAF formed 100 Group (Bomber Support) which flew electronics countermeasures aircraft. Moreover, with OBOE (a targeting system first used in December 1941) and Gee-H (a radio navigation device introduced in 1942), the British developed accurate radio navigation systems which ensured that weather, darkness, and smog were less of an obstacle to bombing. It was the Pathfinder aircraft, which used OBOE, target markers, and H2S, that made the big difference by 1944, providing a valuable combination of technology and tactics.

Meanwhile, Anglo-American bombing had had a heavy impact on Italy. About 60 percent of Italy's industrial capacity was wrecked. Around sixty thousand Italian civilians were killed in bombing during the war, which for Italy lasted from 1940 to 1945. Italian morale was badly affected, with the damaging attacks on the industrial centers of Genoa, Milan, and Turin in early 1943 leading to strikes and demonstrations for peace, neither of which would have been possible in Germany. There was anger about the government's inability to protect civilians. The Allies deliberately sought to encourage such attitudes through the bombing, and they underlined this message through extensive leafleting.[24] The deficiencies of antiaircraft defenses and civilian shelters contributed to this situation. The home front was close to collapse.[25] However, it was the Allied invasion of Sicily on July 10 that precipitated Mussolini's overthrow by senior members of the military and governmental leadership on July 25.

ALLIED GROUND SUPPORT, 1944

In 1944, it was again campaigning on land that was decisive in Europe, while carriers provided a more significant role for air power in the war against Japan, or, at least, in America's war. On the Eastern Front, both the Germans and the Soviets employed air power principally in ground support. Benefiting from a major rise in the production of aircraft, from about fifteen thousand in 1941 to about forty thousand in 1944, the Soviets had far more aircraft, while their tactical and operational effectiveness had improved. They were therefore better able to drive the Luftwaffe from the battlefield. The Soviets focused on ground support, complementing ground attack with close interdiction missions that hit German mobility, whether reinforcing or withdrawing from the zone of attack. The high German casualties that resulted from the integrated use of air power may be referred to as tactical, but this use had a strategic consequence.[26] Operation Bagration, the advance through Belarus that led to the destruction of Army Group Center, was supported at the outset, in June 1944, by over six thousand Soviet aircraft out of a frontline strength of thirteen thousand. The Germans, in contrast, had under two thousand aircraft for the entire Eastern Front.

In turn, the rapid Soviet advance further south across the Rivers Dniester and Prut led to the surrender of Romania on August 23. The loss of control over Romanian oil, the only significant source of nonsynthetic oil in the German-dominated section of Europe, affected the fuel that could be spared for the training of German pilots. The German shortage of fuel encouraged the process by which members of the Luftwaffe were switched to deployment for ground warfare. In 1943, Romania had produced 2,406,000 tons of petroleum products for Germany, a supply Hitler regarded as crucial. Italian-based American air attacks in April–August 1944 destroyed most of the refineries.

Air power proved important in support of Anglo-American operations in Western Europe. In Italy, air power backed amphibious landings at Salerno in September 1943 and Anzio in January 1944. German counteroffensives could be stopped by air attack, although the weather was a key element impacting its effectiveness. General Alexander wrote about Anzio, "Given reasonable weather we should be able to break up any large concentration [German] counter-attack by switching on the whole of the Mediterranean Air Force, as we did at Salerno."[27] However, the Germans were able rapidly to repair bombing damage to rail links in Italy and to lessen the Allied advantage over Anzio by bringing in aircraft from Germany, France, Greece, and northern Italy.[28]

If by the time of the Normandy landings the Germans had lost the air war, this was a hard-won success, and German aircraft production actually rose to a peak in 1944.[29] The contrast with the earlier situation, like that, from the spring of 1943, in the Battle of the Atlantic against German submarines, was one of the reasons why the Allies were wise to delay the opening of a Second Front by invading France until 1944. Only two Luftwaffe pilots fired shots in anger on June 6. German units treated aircraft as probably hostile, while Allied soldiers assumed that aircraft would be Allied. The contrast between the Luftwaffe's ability to threaten the British retreat from Dunkirk in 1940 and its failure to disrupt the Normandy landings was striking. In part, this was due to a failure of intelligence, with aircraft deployed to resist the invasion of the Calais area that was anticipated.

On D-day, much of the supporting firepower for the invasion force was provided by British and American warships. The bombers found it difficult to deliver the promised quantities of bombs on target on time. The targeting of the German Atlantic Wall fortifications by warships and bombers was not as good as it should have been, so that many of the casemates and bunkers were not hit, while the Allies overestimated how effective shells and bombs would be against concrete, notably in the American assault on Omaha Beach. Separately, air attacks on German coastal defenses in France inflicted relatively little damage. Steel-reinforced concrete, a composite material in which a three-dimensional lattice of steel has concrete poured over it, is very resistant to high explosives, and, on D-day, even direct hits by fifteen-inch shells and by one-thousand-pound bombs made very little impact on the structures, although the concussive effect of explosions was demoralizing to the occupants of the bunkers. Most gun emplacements that were put out of action by warships or bombers along the Atlantic Wall had their guns badly damaged rather than their concrete casements or bunkers destroyed in the action. Moreover, the defenders ran out of ammunition.

Intermediate-stage (between tactical and strategic) bombing had been developed by the British, using Wellingtons and Blenheims, and by the Americans, using B-25s and B-26s. This was seen in early 1944 in the bombing of Monte Cassino in Italy and of northern France.

Despite Allied air attacks, from February 1944 and continuing after D-day, especially on rail bridges and marshaling yards, attacks which Harris (although not the Air Staff) regarded as a distraction from his air war on the German heartland, the Germans were able to reinforce their units in Normandy. On D-day, the Germans were unable to challenge Allied command of the air over the combat zone and over the nearby communication routes, which therefore deprived them of reconnaissance, and the delays forced on them by air attacks ensured that the Allies gained time to deepen their beachhead and obliged the Germans to respond in an ad hoc fashion to Allied advances. When the German armor was eventually used in bulk, on June 29–30, it was stopped by Allied air attack. Allied ground-attack aircraft also played a role in wrecking the German tank counterattack launched through Mortain on August 7, 1944, although the defense by American ground forces, notably their artillery, was more important. The campaign saw the successful use of close air support for Allied land forces, particularly with the cab-rank system provided by the Second Tactical Air Force.[30]

The effectiveness of Allied ground support owed much to the long-term process of gaining air superiority over the Luftwaffe, but there had also been improvements in doctrine and organization, including the use of air liaison teams with the army, as well as the improvement in radio communications.[31] Allied aircraft were used in ground support, both against specific targets and for "carpet bombing." The latter was unsuccessful in the advance of British forces in Operation Goodwood, but more successful in the advance of American troops in the breakout from Normandy, Operation Cobra, in late July, although many of the bombs fell on American positions, killing numerous troops and delaying the start of the operation.

On the earlier pattern of the Stuka against Allied forces, the rocket-firing Typhoon had a serious impact on German morale. Germans who were captured in Normandy said that the two main differences between fighting in Normandy and on the Eastern Front were, first, the lack of night operations in Normandy and, second, the ever-present threat from "Jabos": British and American ground-attack fighter-bombers. However, these aircraft inflicted less damage in practice. The accurate targeting of unguided rockets was very difficult against tanks, indeed against anything smaller than a train.[32]

Despite failures in coordination, as in Operation Cobra and the bombing of Monte Cassino, the Allies had become far more skilled at integrating their forces. However, air support could not prevent heavy casualties in ground fighting. The British field commander in northwest Europe, Montgomery, was to write in December 1944,

> Present operations in Western Europe in all stages have been combined Army/Air operations . . . the overall contribution of the Air Forces to the successes gained has been immense. . . . The greatest asset of air power is its flexibility. . . . The moral effect of air action is very great and is out of proportion to the material damage inflicted. . . . It is necessary to win the air battle before embarking on the land battle. . . . Technical developments in the air weapon continue apace and their possibilities are bounded only by the imagination. It follows that land operations are likely to be influenced more and more by air action.[33]

Allied ground attack proved so significant that, in December 1944, Hitler launched the counterattack that led to the Battle of the Bulge only when bad weather promised protection. This was a major contrast with the German offensive in 1940 when the Germans had wanted good weather in order to ensure air support, as well as to use parachutists and glider-borne troops in Belgium and the Netherlands. In turn, once the weather had improved in the winter of 1944–45, ground-support air attacks helped the Allies regain the initiative and proved particularly important against concentrations of German tanks.[34]

GERMAN ROCKET ATTACKS, 1944

Just as in the First World War, bombing increased in the later stages of the conflict, so air attacks on the economic capability and civilian morale of opponents were stepped up in 1944. The biggest change in weapon systems occurred with the beginning of rocket attacks by Germany. Ground-to-ground V-1s were launched at Britain from June 13. However, the problems encountered in hitting German bombers during the Blitz had led to the Anglo-American development of the proximity fuse. Widely used in the Pacific in 1943, the proximity fuse was responsible for the vast majority of V-1s shot down. These were followed, from September 8, by V-2s, which traveled at up to three thousand miles per hour, could be fired from a considerable distance, and could not be destroyed by antiaircraft fire.

Large numbers of rockets were aimed at London, which was hit by 2,419 V-1s and 517 V-2s. Morale was badly affected. Other targets were also hit. More than 4,000 V-1s and 1,700 V-2s were fired at Greater Antwerp, reflecting the importance of its harbor for Allied operations, although the majority did not reach the port area, not least because of the bottleneck in the supply of rocket fuel as well as the limitations of the weapon. The casualties and damage inflicted by rockets led the British to devote particular effort to air raids on production facilities, as well as to capturing the launching pads in the advance from Normandy. This effort was an instance of the extent to which Allied bombing was devoted to far more than attacking German cities.[35]

The use of missiles reflected the inability of the Germans to sustain air attacks on Britain, as well as Hitler's fascination with new technology and the idea that it could bring a paradigm leap forward in military capability, as well as satisfy the prospect of retaliation for British bombing.[36] Missiles, in fact, lacked the multipurpose capacity of aircraft. Moreover, their explosive payload was small. Because the rocket had to reenter Earth's atmosphere, the nose cone heated up due to friction, which affected the payload that could be carried. Due to the lack of a reliable guidance system, the missiles could not be aimed accurately. The rush by the Germans to force the V-2 into service when the war was increasingly going very badly for them helped to lead to a high margin of error. The manufacture of missiles was symptomatic of the nature of the German war economy, with the harsh and murderous treatment of brutalized and malnourished foreign slave labor leading to high death rates.[37]

THE ALLIED AIR ATTACK ON GERMANY, 1944

Allied air attacks, meanwhile, had changed in intensity and method. Attacks on distant targets proved costly, reflecting the extent to which control and use of the air over Germany were difficult to gain. British night attacks on Berlin from November 18, 1943, until March 31, 1944, which Harris had promised would undermine German morale, led instead to the loss of 492 bombers, a rate of loss (5.2 percent overall; 9.1 percent on the final attack) that could not be sustained despite the major expansion in the production of aircraft and the training of pilots.[38] The British raid on Nuremberg on March 30–31, 1944, led to the loss of 106 out of the 782 bombers. There was only limited damage to the city, and few German fighters were shot down. This led to the end of the bomber-stream technique of approaching the target, a technique that had exposed the slow, vulnerable, and highly inflammable Lancasters to the cannons of more mobile German night fighters. The 20,224 British bomber sorties against German cities from November 1943 to March 1944 encountered formidable defenses, while the bad winter weather also caused serious problems.

However, the Allied air attack was stepped up that year as a result of the American introduction of long-range fighters. P-38s (twin-engined Lightnings), P-47s (Thunderbolts, which used drop fuel tanks), and P-51s (Mustangs, which also used these tanks) provided necessary escorts for the bombers and also enabled Allied fighters to seek out German fighters and thus to win the air war above Germany. This contrasted with the Luftwaffe's failed offensive on Britain in 1940–41: the Germans had lost the air war over Britain and had been unable to accompany serious devastation of Britain with the destruction or degradation of the British air force.

Whereas the Germans focused on a new technology in the shape of rockets, the Allies benefited more from developing an existing technology by equipping long-range fighters with drop fuel tanks. The superiority of American long-range fighters to German interceptors was demonstrated in late February and March 1944, when, especially in "Big Week," major American raids in clear weather on German sites producing aircraft and oil led to large-scale battles with German interceptors which could not avoid battle in these circumstances. Many American bombers were shot down, but the Luftwaffe also lost large numbers of aircraft and pilots as a result of the American policy of attrition. From 1944, the American fighters focused on seeking out the Luftwaffe rather than on close bomber support.[39] There had also been heavy Luftwaffe losses over combat zones, notably on the Eastern Front. Hitler insisted that the Luftwaffe retain an offensive capability.

Pilots were very difficult to replace, in large part because German training programs had not been increased in 1940–42, as was necessary given the scale of the war. This helped to ensure that, irrespective of aircraft construction figures, the Germans would be far weaker in the air. German aircraft construction was itself hit hard in these raids. Toward the end, the Germans, affected by the Allied bombing of synthetic oil plants, could not afford the fuel for training, while a lack of training time was also a consequence of the shortage of pilots. Fuel shortages had a similar impact on the Japanese. In mid-1944, Allied pilots received up to 400 hours of training, but their German counterparts only about 110. The net effect was a lack of trained pilots comparable in quality to those of the Allies, a lack that led to a high accident rate, killing pilots and wrecking aircraft, and that particularly lessened the effectiveness of the Luftwaffe's night fighters.

Benefiting, as with tanks and other arms, from major economies of scale, the Americans were able to build large numbers of fighters: fourteen thousand Mustangs were built. Drop fuel tanks increased the range of aircraft and, in 1944, increasingly large tanks were introduced. The P-47, which entered squadron service in 1944, was the largest, heaviest single-engined fighter of the Second World War, and it could take a huge amount of punishment, which was a characteristic of many American aircraft. Fighter escorts could go all the way to Germany and take part in dogfights once there. The American engagement with long-range fighters was, for long, not matched by the conceptually more conservative RAF leadership.[40] This was an instance of the way in which the range of available resources and policies, which had grown greatly with large-scale air capability, created particular demands on command-and-control skills and planning systems and therefore enhanced their role.

In 1944, the Allied emphasis over Germany was, again, not on precision attack, which had proven difficult to execute, but on area bombing, with its attendant goals of disrupting the war economy and destroying urban life in order to hit morale and the workforce. This was clearly the policy of the RAF, and, although the USAAF never officially switched to area bombing over Europe, its winter months' campaigns often became area bombing operations in practice, not least as a result of aiming through the clouds using radar targeting, which proved far from precise. By increasing the target area, area bombing also made the task of the defense more difficult. V raids, in which aircraft came in a succession of horizontal V formations to sweep a continuous path through the city, as employed against Darmstadt in 1944, proved devastating. The air force command, notably General Henry "Hap" Arnold, the commander of the USAAF, remained convinced of the strategic impact of bombing Germany and was less than supportive of other uses for heavy bombers.

The effectiveness, as well as the morality, of bombing has been the subject of considerable debate and, especially the former, were so at the time. There is the question whether British Bomber Command underrated early assessments that stressed the limited value of the area bombing of German cities and whether this attitude reduced the value of air attack and possibly led to a misuse of resources better devoted to ground or naval support. In January 1944, a group of scholars, asked by the USAAF to determine whether strategic bombing could force Germany out of the war by that spring, reported,

> Although the blockade and bombing have deranged Germany's economic structure, the German military economy has not been crippled at any vital point.... Although bombing has made a vital contribution to the ultimate defeat of Germany and although complete defeat cannot be achieved without an acceleration and intensification of bombing, it is improbable that bombing alone can bring about a German collapse by spring of 1944.[41]

These themes were also taken up for the public. J. F. C. Fuller, a supporter of a negotiated peace, argued in the American journal *Newsweek* on October 2, 1944, that the bombing of Germany had not ended the war and had not cracked the morale and will of the German forces, referring to the "ineffectiveness of the Douhet theory." A fortnight later, he added that bombing had failed to paralyze the German High Command.

Moral issues were raised by George Bell, bishop of Chichester, and by others, and have been pressed much more vigorously since.[42] The most frequently cited instance is that of "Dresden," a reference to the heavy casualties caused by the Anglo-American bombing of the city of Dresden on February 13–14, 1945, toward the close of the war, which is frequently mentioned as an Allied atrocity. However, the general consensus at the time was that the bombing campaign was a deserved return for earlier German air attacks (as well as current rocket attacks), and also was likely to disrupt the German war effort and hit morale.

During the war, most military leaders did not argue that bombing alone could win. Instead, it was generally accepted that bombing should be part of an integrated strategy. Nevertheless, it was claimed that area bombing would cause heavy casualties, which would terrorize the civilian population and hopefully put pressure on their governments, a revival of the British hopes of 1918. The extent to which civilian morale was broken is controversial, but it is possible that the impact of bombing on civilians has been underestimated by the habitual conclusion that the bombing did not end the war. There was more to German resilience than Hitler's determination, and the inability to stop bombing encouraged a sense that defeat was likely, indeed was already occurring. In Nuremberg, bombing was responsible for a serious decline in civilian morale from 1943, a process of social dissolution, and a matching crisis of confidence in the Nazi party.[43] Propaganda about the inability of Allied bombing to damage targets within Germany was totally discredited. These benefits came with heavy civilian casualties and a high level of losses among Allied aircrews, but, by 1944, total war was being pushed as precisely that, and was anyway being waged by Germany and Japan.

As a result, the concerns of contemporary military planners can best be addressed in instrumental terms, that is, with reference to the effectiveness of air attack and to possible alternative use of the resources devoted to it, including different possible targets for heavy bombers. As, however, there were serious practical and institutional restrictions to any reallocation of resources, and economic difficulties confronting the retooling of manufacturing, the feedback process of judging policy could not be expected to work even had information flows been accurate and speedy—as is rarely the case in war.

Bombing was also advocated for the damage it could do to particular targets, an approach that accords with modern doctrine. Despite the limited precision of bombing by high-flying aircraft dropping free-fall bombs, strategic bombing was crucial to the disruption of German communications and logistics, largely because it was eventually on such a massive scale and because they could not be attacked by any other means. Attacks on communications seriously affected the rest of the German economy, limiting the transfer of resources and the process of integration which is so significant for manufacturing. The reliance of European industry on rail was far greater than today, and that increased its vulnerability to attack, because rail systems lack the flexibility of their road counterparts, being less dense and therefore less able to switch routes. As critical points, bridges and marshaling yards proved particular targets for attack. Air attack brought the SNCF (the French rail system then under German control) to collapse, followed by the Reichsbahn (the German rail system). Damage was extensive enough to preclude effective repairs, which indicated the potential for increasing returns to scale in the air offensive. Its vulnerabilities ensured that the rail system was also prone to partisan attack in occupied areas.

In addition, the oil industry and aircraft production were savagely hit by Allied air attack. Such bombing directly benefited the Allied war effort. It acted as a brake on Germany's expanding production of weaponry, which had important consequences for operational strength. For example, thanks to bombing, the construction of a new, faster class of submarine—Type 21— was delayed, so that it did not become operational until April 1945. This was too late to challenge Allied command of the sea, although, even had it become operational earlier, it would not have been in sufficient numbers to determine the struggle.[44] In addition, British bombing hit V-1 launches.

Furthermore, from 1943, the Germans diverted massive resources to antiaircraft defense forces, as well as much of the Luftwaffe itself. By 1944, more German guns were devoted to antiaircraft defenses than to ground targets. These guns and aircraft, for example the 88 mm antiaircraft gun, which was also very effective against Allied tanks, might otherwise have made a major contribution on the Eastern and, later, the Western Front. This is a counterfactual (what-if)[45] that it is impossible to prove, not least because it assumes a ready response on the part of German decision makers, but it is not the less pertinent for that. Many of the military assets employed by the Germans in air defense were readily transferable—they were not fixed defenses—and, for that reason, their commitment to air defense and their nonavailability for transfer, whether permanently or even temporarily, was important. Far more German industrial capacity was used for aircraft and guns intended to oppose the Allied bomber offensive than for the manufacture of tanks.

Moreover, this was an aspect of a more widespread focus. For example, the success of the British Dambusters' raid in breaching German dams near the Ruhr on the night of May 16/17, 1943, and thus in hitting the production of the hydroelectric power that helped industrial production, led to a major commitment of antiaircraft guns, labor, concrete, and additional resources to enhancing the defenses of these, and other, dams. This commitment resulted in a reduction in the availability of concrete and workers to improve the defenses of the Atlantic Wall against Allied invasion of France.

The Allied air assault also played a role in the wider strategic equation. For example, once the Allies had invaded southern France on August 15, 1944, the holding of northern Italy was of dubious value to the Germans, as it committed troops to an extensive perimeter, rather than the shorter line that would have been gained from relying on the Alps, a line that would also have taken advantage of Swiss neutrality. However, aside from Hitler's disinclination to countenance retreat, and his particular wish not to abandon Mussolini, there was also a justified concern that an Allied presence in Lombardy would facilitate the aerial assault on Germany by permitting a major advance of Allied air bases. Northern Italy itself was heavily bombed, notably the industrial cities of Genoa, Milan, and Turin.

The impact of the Second Front on the air war provided a salutary lesson. Part of the German air-defense system was lost as the Allies advanced in France and the Low Countries in 1944, and the major lack of depth of defense that resulted from the advance compromised the remainder of the defense. Furthermore, Allied bombers and escort fighters were now moved forward into reconquered areas and were able to support the American and British heavy bombers based in eastern England. As a result, the bombing offensive on Germany that was launched from the autumn of 1944, as air support for the launching of the Second Front became less necessary, was far more intense and damaging than hitherto. Moreover, the destructiveness of the bombing offensive was further increased by the rise in the Allied number of aircraft.

More generally, the Allied air attack intensified economic disruption within Germany and speeded up defeat. It affected not only Germany, which was far harder hit in 1944–45 than hitherto, but also her allies. For example, heavy bombing attacks on Bulgaria began on November 19, 1943. The raids, especially that of March 30, 1944, on the capital, Sofia, indicated clearly the shift in fortunes and encouraged a decline in enthusiasm for continued support for Germany. Bulgaria abandoned Germany in September, although the Soviet advance into the Balkans was far more significant in this than the bombing.[46]

1945, EUROPE—JET AIRCRAFT

In 1945, total Allied control of the air in Europe reflected the extent to which the Luftwaffe had been outfought, while a lack of flying training and fuel had gravely compromised its capability. As at a smaller scale in the Battle of Britain in 1940, a key element was the ability to replace losses in aircraft and trained crew, and the Allies proved superior in this to the Germans.

Operation Bodenplatte (Baseplate) was the last large-scale strategic offensive mounted by the Luftwaffe during the war. The Luftwaffe intended to cripple Allied air forces in the Low Countries and gain air superiority in the region. The Battle of the Bulge had been stagnant for some time, and Bodenplatte was intended to facilitate an advance of German forces. Repeatedly delayed due to bad weather and launched on January 1, 1945, the attack benefited from Allied complacency and achieved some success, destroying

Allied aircraft on the ground, but could not win air superiority. In what proved a misconceived operation in which the flaws and problems of the Luftwaffe were fully revealed, the Germans lost many of their pilots. A lack of fuel and spares, as well as of skilled pilots, was apparent.

Thereafter, the Luftwaffe continued to shoot down Allied bombers, inflicting serious losses, but the size of the bombing force was so large that the percentage of casualties was relatively low. In contrast, the percentage for the Luftwaffe was less favorable. Attrition had helped wreck the latter.[47] After Bodenplatte, whatever was left of the Luftwaffe had had even more limited training. Bombing continued to inflict great damage on Germany, which went on fighting.

The jet fighter arrived in service in 1944, too late to affect the outcome of the war. With 1,430 German Me-262s built (only 564 in 1944), there were insufficient numbers to transform the course of the war, as well as a shortage of trained pilots and design faults with the aircraft, notably problems with the turbines and poor engine reliability. As a reminder that use, as well as technology, was an issue, the lead in jet-powered aircraft was, to a degree, squandered by Hitler. This was because of his preference that the Me-262 should not be used as an interceptor of Allied bombers, despite its effectiveness in the role, but rather as a high-speed bomber. Indeed, in June 1944, he ordered its name changed to Blitzbomber.[48] The tactics of the Me-262 posed serious problems. It could seize the initiative effectively, diving at high speed through the Allied fighter screen and continuing under the bombers, prior to climbing up in order to attack the bombers from behind. If, however, the Me-262 was involved in a dogfight, it was vulnerable, as it had a poor rate of turn. There were also efforts to catch it when even more vulnerable: on takeoff and particularly as it was coming in to land. The Me-262 had slow acceleration with low thrust at slow speeds. About 190 Me-262s were lost in aerial combat, while no more than 150 Allied aircraft were shot down by the Me-262, although there is no consensus on these figures.

1945, THE FALL OF JAPAN

Japan was too weak in the air to protect itself against the American air assault. Initially, the American raids were long distance and unsupported by fighter cover, as fighter range was less than that of bombers. This situation led to American bombing attacks from a high altitude, which reduced their effectiveness. The raids that were launched were hindered by poor weather, especially cloudy conditions; strong tailwinds; and difficulties with the B-29's reliability, as well as the general problems of precision bombing with the technology of the period.

From February 1945, there was a switch to low-altitude nighttime area bombing of Japanese cities. The impact was devastating, not least because many Japanese dwellings were made of timber and paper and burned readily when bombarded with incendiaries, and also because population density in the cities was high. Fighters based on the recently conquered island of Iwo Jima (three hours by air from Tokyo) from April 7, 1945, could provide cover for the B-29s, which had been bombing Japan from bases on the more distant island of Saipan since November 1944. The Marine Corps defended its costly conquests of Iwo Jima and of Pacific islands on the grounds that carriers could not provide a base for aircraft of this size and for launching and adequately supporting air attacks of this scale.

These attacks were designed to hit Japanese industrial production, in part by devastating the cities where much of it was based. The industrial working class was the target, alongside the attempt to mount precision attacks.

Weaknesses in Japanese antiaircraft defenses, both aircraft and guns, eased the American task and made it possible to increase the payload of the B-29s by removing their guns. Although the Japanese had developed some impressive interceptor fighters, especially the Mitsubishi A6M5 and the NIK2-J Shiden, they were unable to produce many due to the impact of Allied air raids and of submarine attacks on supply routes, and they were also very short of pilots. In 1944–45, American bombers destroyed over 30 percent of the buildings in Japan, including over half of the cities of Tokyo and Kobe. The deadliness of bombing was amply demonstrated. On March 9, 1945, 690,000 pounds of bombs were dropped on Tokyo in less than an hour, killing 87,793 people. The city smelled of burning flesh. An American invention (at Harvard in 1942), napalm, a thickened fuel, operated as a sticky gel that was used to deadly effect as an incendiary, destroying people and property.[49] Firebombing killed more Japanese than the atomic bombs.

The weakness of Japanese air power was apparent in all areas. Although the Japanese XIV Area Army on Luzon in the Philippines, where the Americans landed on January 9, had more than 250,000 troops, it had only about 150 operational combat aircraft to support it. These aircraft and their pilots could not match the Americans in quality, and most were destroyed by American carrier aircraft before the invasion. The Japanese army in Manchuria was also heavily outnumbered in the air when attacked by Soviet forces in August 1945, forces that benefited from airborne operations, for example at Harbin and Port Arthur, in advance of their ground units. The Soviets had about five thousand aircraft, the Japanese only fifty frontline ones.

ATOMIC BOMBS

The creation of the atomic bomb was indicative of the exceptional nature and scale of activity possible for an advanced industrial society. This was the product not only of the application of science, but also of the powerful industrial and technological capability of the United States and the willingness to spend about $2 billion in rapidly creating a large nuclear industry.

At the Potsdam Conference, the Allied leaders issued the Potsdam Declaration on July 26, 1945, demanding unconditional surrender, as well as the occupation of Japan, Japan's loss of its overseas possessions, and the establishment of democracy. The threatened alternative was "prompt and utter destruction," but, on July 27, the Japanese government decided to ignore the declaration, which they saw as a political ultimatum. President Harry Truman wrote, "My object is to save as many American lives as possible."[50]

The air assault on Japan culminated in the dropping of atomic bombs on August 6 and 9 on Hiroshima and Nagasaki, respectively, the bombs landing very close to the aim points. As a result, probably over 280,000 people died, either at once or eventually through radiation poisoning. This transformed the situation by demonstrating that Japanese forces could not protect the homeland. On August 14, Japan agreed to surrender unconditionally. The atomic bombs were particularly destructive products of industrial warfare. They were employed to achieve the total war goal of unconditional surrender without having to resort to the fight to the finish that would follow an American invasion.

The heavy Allied losses in capturing the islands of Iwo Jima and Okinawa earlier in the year suggested that the use of atom bombs was necessary in order both to overcome a suicidal determination to fight on, and to obtain unconditional surrender. The apparently inexorable process of devastation seen with the dropping of the second bomb, on Nagasaki, had a greater impact on the Japanese government than the use of the first. The combined shock of the two bombs led the Japanese to surrender, although the Soviet invasion of Manchuria was also a factor. The army had refused to believe what had happened and still wanted to fight after Hiroshima.[51] The limited American ability to deploy more bombs speedily was not appreciated: no other bomb was available on August 9, although one would have been about a week later. However, planning ahead, the Americans were already considering the use of atom bombs in tactical support of the envisaged landing on the island of Kyushu, which would have been the first of the main Japanese islands to be invaded.

Had the war continued, civilian casualties would have been immense. Aside from the direct and indirect consequences of air invasion, the continuation of the conventional bombing campaign would have been very costly, both directly and indirectly. Had the war lasted to 1946, the destruction of the

Japanese rail system by bombing would have led to famine, as it would have been impossible to move food supplies.

RANGE OF AIR POWER

The war demonstrated the range and variety of air power. At a strategic level, the transport capabilities of aircraft were seen in the Anglo-American delivery of nearly 650,000 tons of matériel from northeastern India over the "Hump," the eastern Himalayas, to the Nationalist forces fighting the Japanese in China from July 1942 to 1945. This achievement represented an enormous development in air transport, and in very difficult flying conditions, even though the individual load of aircraft was low by later standards.[52]

Airdropped supplies were important on many occasions, including to the defensibility of British positions against Japanese attack on the India-Burma border in 1944, to the advance of Australian forces in North Guinea the same year, and to the success of the Soviet invasion of Manchuria in 1945. The Germans and Japanese were not as well served by transport aircraft. Although the German Ju-52 did good service, it was not as good as the American C-47, which, cheaper and easier to manufacture than the Ju-52, was produced in vast numbers and used in every theater. Another key capability was provided by aerial intelligence, which became crucial to Anglo-American operational planning.[53]

Technological change was incessant. For example, unmanned flight brought together air power and artillery. Guided bombs and rockets were dramatic innovations but did not affect the course of the war. Accuracy was a major problem for the guided weapons developed by both sides,[54] but the Germans employed Fritz-X radio-guided bombs against ships in the Mediterranean in 1943. Some were sunk, notably the Italian battleship *Roma* on the way to surrender to the Allies, while others suffered severe damage. The Germans also used the Henschel Hs-293 radio-guided glider bomb with some success against shipping. The Germans employed these bombs against bridges in Normandy in August 1944, but less successfully. Taking air warfare in a different direction, the Japanese unsuccessfully sought to use incendiary balloons in order to set American forests alight.

More usefully, the air evacuation of the wounded and the ill developed, such that the Allies evacuated over one million casualties by air in 1943–45. This was an aspect of air power in which women took a direct role, with over 5,400 female flight nurses in the US Army Air Forces' Medical Air Evacuation Squadrons.[55]

CONCLUSION

The scale of air power was extraordinary. At the beginning of 1945, more men were employed in Britain in producing bombers than as British infantry in northwest Europe. The United States produced not only over two hundred thousand aircraft, as well as the largest number of, and most powerful, aero-engines,[56] but also eighteen fleet carriers and eighty-six light fleet or escort carriers. Very differently, but as a reminder of the varied use of air power, and of the extent to which high specifications were not necessarily a key characteristic of its use, the RAF used aircraft to overawe crowds threatening strategic railways during the anti-British Quit India campaign in 1942–44.[57]

There was a new range for air power. American air bases in Brazil were crucial to the movement of aircraft and shipment of arms to the Allies in the North African campaigns. Aircraft were flown from the United States (and shipped from Britain) to Takoradi in the Gold Coast (Ghana), and then, via Lagos and Khartoum, on to near Cairo. Similarly, the air base at Keflavik in Iceland was important to the American air bridge to the British Isles. American air bases in Latin America and elsewhere familiarized a range of states with the regular use of military air power. American support was important in the development of the air force of Brazil, America's leading Latin American ally.

An emphasis on the value of air power led to a stress on the acquisition and protection of air bases. This stress helped determine operational and strategic options. Thus, in 1944, with the Japanese overrunning bases in China that might otherwise have served the purpose, the United States emphasized gaining control of Pacific islands from which raids could be launched against Japan, notably Saipan. This was also an issue in Europe, Southwest Asia, and North Africa, with the occupation of Persia (Iran) in 1941 seen as the basis for British air attacks on the important Baku oil fields in Azerbaijan if the Germans seized them from the Soviet Union.[58] Similarly, the capture of southern Italy in 1943 provided a base for Allied strategic bombing, including, in 1944, heavy raids on the oil refineries in Ploesti, Romania, a key element in the "oil war" against the Axis, which intended to hit oil supplies and thus affect their mobility. This focus on air bases looked forward to American and British priorities in the first two decades of the Cold War.

So also with the repeated emphasis on oil, which included Italian raids in 1940 on the oil refineries in British-controlled Haifa and an unsuccessful attempt on two in the Gulf.[59] In turn, the Allied attack on fuel supplies and refining capacity was a major feature of the air assault on the Axis powers. Thus, on January 24 and 29, 1945, aircraft from four British carriers, their names redolent of British naval aspirations—*Illustrious*, *Indefatigable*, *Indomitable*, and *Victorious*—attacked Japanese oil refineries in Sumatra, as well as their supporting airfields. The aircraft had to overcome Japanese interceptors as well as heavy flak, each a testimony to the importance the Japanese placed on oil, and succeeded in cutting production of aviation fuel in Sumatra as well as in destroying many Japanese aircraft.

Combined operations faced significant difficulties. In particular, close air support proved more difficult than tactical interdiction, a difficulty that affected the debate over their respective merits. Problems of inaccurate targeting and the vulnerability of tactical bombers to ground fire and opposing fighters limited the ability of aircraft to kill tanks and hit combat formations. The effectiveness of the Soviet use of the IL-2, the Shturmovik, a specialized ground-attack aircraft, depended on massive numbers (about thirty-six thousand were built) and a willingness to take heavy losses. Britain and the United States had entered the war not only with an exaggeration of what they could then achieve by strategic bombing, but also with weak or misguided tactical air doctrines that scattered aircraft in small units subject to ground commanders' orders. This resulted in wasteful attacks on minor targets and in continuous air cover for advancing units that proved of limited value against ground opposition.

Unified tactical air command proved the solution, while the use of fighters as fighter-bombers provided aircraft that could defend themselves in dogfights and that were also fast and maneuverable enough to heighten their survival rate in ground support and for delivering more accurate bombing against tactical targets, such as bridges, than medium and heavy bombers flying at high altitude ever could. This was an instance of the more general innovatory use of air power during the war. The varied needs of the conflict drove the pace of innovation. However, the themes of combined air operations and ground support clashed with the idea of victory by air power alone through strategic bombing, and the latter dominated postwar American and British doctrine and procurement to a disproportionate extent.

Conclusions

> The business of the day proceeds—a vast business impossible to describe—as one travels from the base to the front and along behind the lines for a hundred miles or more, with the transport columns moving up with their usual supplies of rations for men and guns with labour companies working on the roads and digging new trenches, with battalions "in rest" training hard in the open fields, and battalions in support putting their new drafts through their paces, and all the activities of millions of men doing a hundred thousand jobs which have only one purpose and meaning, which is to perfect every part of that highly complicated machine known as an army in the field.
> —Philip Gibbs, *Daily Telegraph*, June 26, 1918

REASONS FOR VICTORY

The unprecedented nature of the two wars owed much to the demographic and industrial strength of the states involved and their ability and determination to mobilize resources. Yet the demands of the world wars also posed major difficulties, not simply in sustaining the struggle but also in conceiving of practical strategies and operational methods. Moreover, the difficulty of securing victory in a single battle or campaign forced participants to take part in learning processes in a competitive context. In this process, resources, skills, leadership, morale, and alliance cohesion all proved significant, albeit with a differing ratio for the particular levels of war.

The contexts, circumstances, and contingencies of specific campaigns were all relevant to their outcome. For example, in 1918, the Germans suffered from poor generalship on the Western Front, notably an emphasis on sequential attacks on different parts of the Western Front rather than a sustained drive in one sector. However, as a reminder of the difficulties of discussing policy and explaining events, the switching of the point of attack later in the year was also one of the crucial factors in Allied success, albeit within a context of continual pressure. Again, the range of elements at play was significant and challenges attempts at monocausal explanations, a point that is more generally true. Thus, the German failure in attacking on the Western Front in 1918 also owed much to the general limitations of the offensive during the war, as well as the superior Allied resources, the Allied conduct of the defensive, and the extent to which the German army suffered more seriously from the virulent influenza epidemic, the misnamed "Spanish flu," than its British and French opponents. Moreover, the delay in settling with the communists in Russia and in transferring sufficient troops from the Eastern Front was also highly pertinent to German failure. As a separate issue, strategic choices posed many difficult issues in both world wars, notably of prioritization, as in America's "Germany First" policy in the Second World War. These issues were voiced publicly in some states, but in Germany, the Soviet Union, and Japan there was no allowable criticism of government policy. Americans of an isolationist disposition sometimes ask me what would have happened had they decided not to follow Pearl Harbor by going to war with Germany; they have forgotten that it was Germany that declared war on the United States. Similarly, given the previous American stance, the German resumption of unrestricted submarine warfare in 1917 in effect was a declaration of war.

More generally, the resource-based explanation of success is clearly pertinent in both world wars. Aside from the substantial contributions from Britain, for example of coal to France and Italy during the First World War, American financial, industrial, agricultural, and energy resources were formidable and important to the Allies in each world war both before American entry into the war and once it had occurred. Indeed, this contribution explained the strategic centrality of the security of maritime routes. Aircraft production is a good instance. In 1939–45, the United States produced more than 300,000 aircraft, compared to 125,000 each for Britain and Germany, 99,000 for the Soviet Union, 65,000 for Japan, and 13,500 for Italy. Its strength enabled the United States in the Second World War to overcome the constraints posed by operating in a successful offensive fashion on many fronts and against two major opponents, Germany and Japan. More generally, the Allies were wedded to concepts of operations that were founded upon a significant advantage in resources and industrial capability. Manpower was far less important to them. Indeed, American war making, particularly with Japan, reflected a determination not to be limited to attritional methods, which posed significant consequences for manpower availability.

The Second World War was ultimately to see the successful deployment of American and Soviet resources in order to secure the crushing of Germany and Japan in 1944–45. The extent of these resources was already apparent earlier in the war. In 1940–41, the ability of Britain to continue trading with the United States was important to the survival of the country, although, per capita, Britain derived much more support during the war from the Canadians. Furthermore, in 1940 and early 1941, Soviet cooperation in providing resources was important in enabling the German economy to draw on raw materials. Conversely, in late 1941, the scale of Soviet resources and the impact of brutal state control[1] were indicated by the Soviet ability to continue fighting Germany and producing fresh forces. This was despite major losses of territory, manpower, and productive capability, albeit with the last lessened by the transfer of industrial plant eastward away from exposed areas. This Soviet ability to produce fresh forces and to sustain the campaigning, both on the defensive and in the attack, became even more apparent in 1942–43, let alone later.

Soviet resilience and American intervention were not dependent on German policies but were related to Hitler's multiple strategic failures. These failures helped to ensure that Germany would lose, a situation shared by Japan; but, allowing for these flaws, it remained necessary for the Allies to win. This reflected success at every level of war, and also in its crucial political and economic dimensions. Differing impressions are created if the emphasis is placed first on Axis deficiencies or Allied advantages, but the two were linked. Deficiencies become pertinent if they created opportunities for opponents, and within contexts created by pressures on resources and morale. Thus, in 1917, David Lloyd George, the British prime minister, pressed Field Marshal Douglas Haig on the impact of failure and casualties on Allied public opinion.

The key Axis failures were those of strategy, both military and political. In his radio address of December 9, 1941, Roosevelt decried a "joint plan" between Germany and Japan. He claimed that "all the continents of the world, and all the oceans, are now considered by the Axis strategists as one gigantic battlefield. . . . We must realize for example that Japanese successes against the United States in the Pacific are helpful to German operations in Libya." In practice, help through diverting opposing forces, as the Japanese certainly did with the Australians—from the Middle East to the southwest Pacific—was far more feasible than joint planning. Moreover, as the Allies took the initiative from late 1942, even this option disappeared. Toward the close of the war, Hitler was very keen to transfer advanced weapons technology to Japan in order to enable her to fight on, but this was not viable, and the two powers had common enemies (up to a point) rather than shared aims and objectives. Japan, like Italy, would have preferred that Hitler settle with the Soviet Union so that Germany could focus on their shared enemies, Britain and the United States, but this was not Hitler's priority, although Stalin feared that if he did not settle with Hitler, Britain and the United States might.

Moreover, the failure of the German and Japanese Empires in the Second World War as integrating systems capable of winning mass support in the areas conquered was also very serious and a key aspect of Axis deficiencies. German, Japanese, and Italian belief in race superiority and their brutality greatly hindered prospects for such cooperation. Neither Germany nor Japan wanted allies, but only associates who would do what they were told. Their attitudes and brutality not only undermined the chance of winning support but also encouraged opposition and resistance. Indeed, the degree to which the Second World War was a peoples' war was seen in resistance activities, which were far greater than in the First World War, although far more territory was occupied in the Second World War, so that the comparison is only of limited value. There were particularly heavy civilian casualties in some occupied territories. Among the sixteen million Soviet civilians who died were a quarter of the population of occupied Belarus, while about six million Poles, a quarter of the population, died.

When the Germans invaded the Soviet Union in 1941, Stalin ordered guerrilla activity and proclaimed a "patriotic war" against the Germans. This was a new version of the patriotic mobilization seen in Russia during the First World War.[2] Initially, however, there was little real partisan threat, as the Soviets were not adequately prepared. However, with time, partisan support became far more widespread. The German use of indiscriminate brutality reduced the options for the population and encouraged support for the partisans. The Soviet winter counteroffensives in 1941–42 also proved highly effective in rallying support for resistance, as it showed that German victory was not inevitable. This was a key instance of the importance of campaigns in signaling resolve as well as capability.

Partisan activity contributed to the Germans' sense of the alien character of the occupied territories, a sense that also had a strong ideological element at least in the form of racism. The same was true of Japanese forces in China. More specifically, a feeling of disorientation and alienation among ordinary soldiers contributed to their implementation of harsh policies and to the brutality and sadism they often displayed. The public execution of partisans by the Germans reflected the attempt to terrorize the population, while the photographing of the process underlined a macabre pride in it.

German methods, however, proved self-defeating. Both the ruthlessness of the occupation policy and the lack of adequate resources for security made it difficult to conduct an effective occupation policy, whether peaceful or warlike, and particularly jeopardized the chances of economic benefit from the conquest, while also throwing away the initial willingness of many to collaborate with the Germans, as in Ukraine. A lack of sufficient manpower for the extensive long-term occupation of areas susceptible to the partisans helped lead to a reliance on high-tempo brutality, including deterrent repression by vicious example, which was, to a considerable degree, a correlate of the nature of German war making at the front. Resistance to the Germans (as to the Japanese) was greatly affected by the detailed configuration of local geography, ethnicity, politics, religion, and society, as well as by the nature of occupation and the complex relationship of collaboration and opposition. The Germans and the Japanese proved unwilling to understand these processes.

The better-armed Germans were generally able to defeat partisans in open conflict. Resistance attacks, in contrast, were most useful when coordinated with Allied operations. Large numbers of troops had to be deployed by Germany and Japan in order to limit resistance operations or to prevent their possible outbreak. This was an aspect of the significant contribution of the resistance to the Allied war effort. Moreover, the need to adopt antipartisan policies affected the efficiency of German and Japanese rule and of economic and transport activities. Resistance also achieved the vital political goal of weakening collaboration and undermining coexistence. This isolated the German, Japanese, and allied militaries, increasing their sense of vulnerability and the violence they displayed, and, as a crucial aspect of the struggle for support, made their new orders appear transient and thus not worth supporting.

In contrast to the Axis deficiencies, there were Allied advantages. Despite major tensions, notably between the Soviet Union and Britain, especially over the postwar fate of Poland, the Allies were able to achieve a degree of cooperation, and, in the case of the Western Allies, a great degree at both the strategic and operational levels. This cooperation between Britain and the United States in 1941–45 matched that between Britain and France in 1914–18, although it was less easy than that had been. There were tensions, but also an ability to focus on problem solving and burden sharing. This was seen in the Second World War on land, at sea, in the air, and in key backup facets such as reconnaissance, logistics, and communications, as well as in industrial capability.

The situation was far less happy as far as the Soviet Union was concerned. There can be a danger in ignoring or underplaying the ideological centrality of Stalin's beliefs to Soviet strategy. It helped explain his alliance with Germany in 1939–41, a feature not seen with Russia in the First World War, as well as his willingness to consider peace feelers with Germany in 1942 and 1943. Moreover, Soviet espionage continued to be directed against British and American targets. Nevertheless, the major impact of Soviet land operations, operations significantly assisted by American and British supplies, on the Germans constituted a degree of strategic cooperation greater than that applied by Russian attacks on the Eastern Front during the First World War, important as those were in 1914 and 1916.

In the Second World War, moreover, the Allies outfought their opponents, repeating the major success of the Western Allies in late 1918. Resources were important, but so also was military skill. Like resources, skill was not a single factor but, instead, an interacting range of conception and execution, stretching from strategic insight and planning, via operational intensity, notably from the Soviets on land and the Western Allies in the air in 1944–45, to unit cohesion and tactical competence. In contrast, Hitler's deficiencies were part of a more general failure of German war making, not least an inability, more marked as the war developed, to set sensible military and political goals and to think of attainable fallback positions.

The Japanese equivalent in explaining failure in terms of Allied resources includes an overemphasis on American bombing, especially the dropping of the atom bombs. As with Germany, there is an unwillingness to address the issue of comparative fighting quality in the field in 1944–45. Against the Japanese, a major improvement in quality was seen with the Americans, Australians, and British, and in each case the Japanese did badly as a consequence. Against the Germans, this improvement was true of the Americans, British, and Soviets.

Alongside continued fighting determination,[3] German and Japanese planning became increasingly grandiose and divorced from reality as the war progressed, with wishful thinking replacing sober calculation, although both were readily apparent already in 1941, and disastrously so in the planning for, and conduct of, the invasion of the Soviet Union. Subsequently, as a product of sheer desperation, fanaticism, a self-serving leadership, and a focus on operational issues, the German army increasingly disregarded military reality, as in the Battle of the Bulge in December 1944 when Allied fighting quality and responsiveness were underestimated. More generally, losing the intelligence war, the Germans and Japanese were unable to outthink their opponents, while the Allies also proved superior in applied research.

The strategic dimension remained crucial as that set the tasks that defined operational needs. The Allied emphasis on unconditional surrender ended the option of a compromise peace and therefore ensured the need for a total outcome. On January 18, 1945, Churchill told the House of Commons, "I am clear that nothing should induce us to abandon the principle of unconditional surrender, or to enter into any form of negotiation with Germany or Japan, under whatever guise such suggestions may present themselves, until the act of unconditional surrender has been formally executed." The British had been determined not only to keep the Soviet Union in the war but also to ensure that the United States sustained the peace settlement, unlike after the First World War when it had refused to join the League of Nations. In turn, Roosevelt wanted to ensure that Stalin was committed, in the short term, to conflict with Japan and, in the long term, to the eventual peace settlement. It was unclear how far Soviet assistance would be required in order to defeat

Japan, which is another aspect of the combination of resources, fighting quality, and politics.

IMPACTS

The world wars sit within a longer period of the fall of empires, one that began with that of Spain to American attack in 1898 and culminated with that of the Soviet Union to internal opposition in 1991. The world wars were directly responsible for the collapse, in the first case, of the Habsburg, Hohenzollern, Ottoman, and Romanov Empires of Austro-Hungary, Germany, Turkey, and Russia, respectively, and, in the second, of the German, Italian, and Japanese Empires. Moreover, the Second World War was also followed by the weakening and, to a great extent, end of the European colonial empire, notably those of the British, Dutch, and French, all of which were, in effect, gone by 1964, with key losses by 1950, notably of Syria from the French Empire (1946), India from the British (1947), and Indonesia from that of the Netherlands (1949).

In practice, very different processes and causes were at play in these developments. Nevertheless, the exhausting consequences of the wars, and the way in which they helped lead to the fall of empires that resulted in the transfer of control over much of the world's population, were some of the most significant consequences of the struggle. Indeed, they help provide a linkage, although not coherence, to the idea of a "long war" from 1914 to 1945. This is not a linkage that automatically focuses, as so much of that discussion does, on Germany and the conflicts it launched.

Looked at differently from the imperial perspective, a common theme in both world wars became that of the fate of the British Empire, although that was not the central intention of Germany in 1914 and 1939, nor of Japan when it attacked China in 1937. However, with Britain playing a principal role, which German policy makers, predicting a short war and focusing on the army, had not anticipated, the First World War became a major challenge to the British Empire. This element was even more apparent in 1940 when Germany threatened an invasion of Britain itself, while Italy sought to conquer Egypt, the central place of Britain's Middle Eastern empire. Japan in 1941–42 compounded the crisis by overrunning Britain's Southeast Asian empire and threatening both India and Australia. In part, the war became one for the succession to the British Empire, a conflict that was in practice won by the United States.

Reference to Japan brings in another dimension of the long war, the struggle over control of East Asia. However, even if that issue is seen only in terms of Japanese expansionism, the key episodes fall not in 1914 to 1945 but in the period 1894 to 1945, with the Sino-Japanese (1894–95) and Russo-

Japanese (1904–5) wars playing a more significant role than the First World War. Conversely, if the broader question of regional dominance is considered, then the long war begins with the British intervention in China in the Opium War (1839–42) and closes with the conflict between China and Vietnam that began in 1979. The major participants in this long war were China, Japan, Russia/the Soviet Union, the United States, and Britain. The crucial turning point is 1944–45, which brought repeated and, eventually, total defeat for Japan and the establishment of the United States as the key oceanic balancer for East Asia.

Turning to the broader dimension, external conflict was crucial in the eventual fall of the German and Japanese Empires. In both world wars, a drive for a stronger position in the global hierarchy of power had been expressed through the seizure of territory by the states that launched the conflicts: Austria and Germany in 1914 and Japan and Germany in 1937–41. This seizure was the cutting edge of a process that also involved the development of a more potent industrial capability and military, the construction of a stronger alliance system, and the disruption of that of opponents. In turn, the decision of individual states to join alliances affected the balance of forces and helped define strategic parameters and operational possibilities for these states and others. No state wished to join an alliance that was collapsing, and all were encouraged by signs of success.

Neither the German nor the Japanese Empires in the Second World War was faced by revolution, as Germany and Austria were by late 1918, but the German situation in particular then owed much to military failure. In 1944–45, with domestic opposition weak and overcome by totalitarian means, the two empires had to be defeated and brought to surrender. This was done by alliances that overcame the initial advantages held by Germany and Japan.

The wars also saw profound changes in social, economic, and cultural structures and practices. These included the impacts of economic mobilization and social change on the position of women, and as a consequence of both wars. Women, by far the majority on the home front, did jobs hitherto only or largely done by men. Moreover, they faced the pervasive fear, and multiple anxieties and challenges, brought by the war, not least, but not only, as mothers and wives.[4]

In each world war, inflation and taxation greatly affected socioeconomic structures. The government direction of resources became normative and far more extensive, as did the process of planning. Much of the home front was militarized. There was an emphasis on collective solutions, and this moved some states in a leftward direction, most notably Britain, where Labour did better in general elections from 1918 and won the general election in 1945.[5] That was a very different course from the communist seizure of power in Russia in 1917.

The American development of the atomic bomb, a formidably expensive task that required much scientific, technological, industrial, and organizational capability, reflected the extent to which the war saw the mobilization of societies across the full range of their capabilities.

In the Second World War, targeting civilians was taken to far more brutal levels than in the First by the harsh occupation policies of Germany and Japan, policies that reflected a racism and racist sense of mission that were central to their attitudes and policies. The Holocaust was a totally one-sided German war on the Jews that led to the slaughter of over six million. They were not alone. There was also much German slaughter of non-Jews, notably of Russians. Overall deaths during the Second World War were twenty-two to twenty-five million military and thirty-eight to fifty-five million civilians, with the Soviet Union and China suffering the highest casualties. Brutality was deliberately encouraged, notably in the Japanese army, where in Nanjing in 1937 soldiers were forced to torture Chinese civilians and beaten hard if they refused. Later in the war, Japanese units used cannibalism to get food, as from captured Allied soldiers in Borneo.

Aside from the deliberate slaughter of civilians, harsh occupation policies, notably the seizure of food, could cause heavy casualties, as in the Netherlands in the winter of 1944–45 when tens of thousands of Dutch civilians died due to the Germans seizing all of the food. So also with German policy in northern Norway.

The very scale of the Second World War and the nature of operations, including air attack and submarine blockades, put unprecedented pressure on societies, although most military manpower remained in the armies. Scale interacted with other significant developments, and contemporaries were well aware of the process of change, even as they struggled to manage it. Writing in 1944, three retired senior British military figures argued that four factors had caused radical changes in Western civilization and, therefore, in twentieth-century warfare: the increasing necessity in war for political authority, national discipline, economic self-sufficiency, and mechanization.[6] The accumulation and use of information was also very important to the war efforts. They were seen in particular with the creation and growth of intelligence services.

The role of states increased at the same time that they faced major challenges in directing economies and in maintaining social cohesion and morale. This was not least for the Second World War in the face of unprecedented bombing, in particular on Germany and Japan. The impact of the war reached across life, animal as well as human. For example, in the first four days of Britain's participation in the Second World War, over four hundred thousand dogs and cats, as well as many other pets, were killed in London alone by a populace terrified by the onset of war and ready to embark on mass mercy killing.[7] A very different impact was provided by the official war artists who accompanied troops into action in both world wars.[8]

AFTERMATH

The Second World War left the United States and the Soviet Union as the dominant powers, and to a degree that would have been surprising in 1923. It also ensured that the resumed Cold War centered on their rivalry, rather than that of Britain and the Soviet Union, which had been the key rivalry in the earlier Cold War that had begun with the Russian Revolution.

Planning for a new hot war reflected the experience of the Second World War. Considering, in May 1945, the possibility of war between the Soviet Union and an Anglo-American alliance, the British Joint Planning Staff anticipated that Soviet resilience would prevent a speedy war and that the conflict could only be waged as a total war, entailing a fully mobilized American war economy, as well as German support.[9] Indeed, West German rearmament was pushed through in the mid-1950s as a consequence of concerns about the Soviet threat.

To look ahead from the two world wars to the resumed Cold War is, at least in part, to present the world wars as but part of a sequence, and, accordingly, to suggest that they settled relatively little, and certainly nothing comparable to the scale of the conflicts. That would not be an appropriate conclusion. The crises caused by German and Japanese expansionism, and the highly bellicose and aggressive nature of their regimes, were such that war at some time was the likely outcome, even if its exact timing and the full lineup of combatants were uncertain. To that extent, the avoidance of war was not really an option.

That these wars had to be fought does not answer the question about their long-term impact. With the British Empire gone within two decades of the end of the Second World War, and the Soviet Union within a half century, it is scarcely the case that it created a world dominated by the victors. Indeed, that was true of only one power, the United States. It had fought hard in both world wars but without having to face total war on the home front, not least because there was no foreign occupation. This helped ensure a contrast between subsequent American and European attitudes to war and to the experience of occupation.[10]

By 2000, and even more 2019, America's principal rival was China, a state that had faced repeated defeats at the hands of Japan in 1931–45 and therefore had benefited greatly from American and Soviet success in 1945. The world's third leading economy in 2019 was Japan, one of the defeated Axis powers. Germany was the dominant force in the European Union. The nonlinear character of history, already demonstrated in 1940–42, with

France, a key victor of the First World War, defeated and Britain, its counterpart, pummeled and newly vulnerable, was thus repeated after the Second World War.

This nonlinear character can be taken further in the case of the fighting. The two world wars suggested that war meant the large-scale clash of conventional forces operating across a full spectrum of effectiveness and with a determination to achieve total victory. That, indeed, was planned for during the Cold War that followed, but, although they did not appear so to many involved, the symmetrical conflicts that followed the Second World War were limited. There was no use of atomic or thermonuclear weaponry, and the leading states did not fight each other. China during the Korean War (1950–53) came the closest by attacking American forces, but it was not then, nor, indeed, until the 2000s, a leading military power.

The leading powers also dispensed with the model of conscription-fed mass armies that had fought the world wars, the United States doing so in the early 1970s. Instead, they established the new key model of a totally professional, all-volunteer force.

Moreover, both during the Cold War and more generally, asymmetrical conflict became more significant. Whether seen in Maoist terms as peoples' warfare, or referred to as "wars among the people," this process appeared to make the combat of the world wars as redundant as did the more nimble, professionalized, technologically cutting-edge forces of the so-called Revolution in Military Affairs of the 1990s.

This approach was, and is, limited. In practice, the world wars offer many lessons, notably on the importance of alliance politics to policy; the crucial significance, even for authoritarian societies, of popular support; the need to build pragmatism into strategy; the requirement for an effective operational dimension between strategy and tactics; the tactical value of combined-arms structures and practices; and the importance of continuous openness to learning lessons, innovation, and changing commanders. The nature and number of the weaponry change, and will continue to do so, as will the international alignments in play, but the key insights offered by the study of the world wars remain.

POSTSCRIPT: THE LONG WAR REVIEWED

Ideas date and, in doing so, can be better understood in the particular context of their genesis. So for such notions as the "Military Revolution" in the early-modern period, or the "End of History" and the "Revolution in Military Affairs," both in the 1990s. So also with the "long war." Linking together the two world wars, and focusing them on Germany and "the German Question," appeared understandable to commentators in the late twentieth century, such as Michael Howard, who had fought Germany and then experienced a Cold War where the front line appeared to run through Germany and where its most vivid symbol was the Berlin Wall. Marshal Foch, the Allied commander, warning in 1919 that the Versailles settlement would be only a twenty-year truce, provided a ready quote for question setters and commentators. He was expressing a view also voiced at the time by J. F. C. Fuller. Moreover, the idea of a long war served some political strategies, notably the idea, advanced within Germany in the 1960s, and also seen in British policy-making circles during the Second World War, that the Nazi regime was not an aberration but, instead, part of a continuous characteristic in modern German history, one requiring fundamental reform.

From the perspective, however, now, toward the end of the second decade of a new century, indeed millennium, where the focus, politically and economically, is far more on South and, particularly, East Asia, and their relationship with the United States, the situation looks very different. The idea of the long war appears highly Eurocentric, while the contrasts between the two world wars are greatly to the fore if the focus is on East Asia, and both for China and Japan. This is also the case in terms of the United States and Indonesia. India was in the front line in the Second World War, but not the First. Japan and, even more, China were not significantly involved in the First World War. Michael Howard, and others, really failed to engage with this point.

On the other hand, the two wars with time are increasingly run together for educational (and other) reasons. This can be readily seen in general textbooks as well as in accounts of military developments. The last is particularly so with the two world wars grouped as total wars, and also contrasted with conflict prior to 1914 and after 1945. This suggests that a contrast may open up within scholarly views, with this approach contrasted with those that share a greater engagement with the granulated character of the two world wars and a greater willingness to probe differences in the fighting between them. Thus, for example, to turn to the type of conflict, the Second World War saw an intensity in naval operations and amphibious attacks not seen in the First. While particularly true of the war in the Pacific, this was also the case of that with Germany. The use of air power as a strategic and operational weapon was also totally different. Indeed, the contrasts between the conflicts are worthy of attention precisely because of the insights they offer for both world wars as military struggles. It is for this reason that the idea of the long war deserves attention.

Notes

INTRODUCTION

1. Michael Howard, "A Thirty Years' War? The Two World Wars in Historical Perspective," *Transactions of the Royal Historical Society*, series 6, 3 (1993): 171–84.

1. CAUSES

1. Michael Paris, *Warrior Nation: Images of War in British Popular Culture, 1850–2000* (London: Reaktion, 2000).
2. Azar Gat, *A History of Military Thought from the Enlightenment to the Cold War* (Oxford: Oxford University Press, 2001), 343.
3. Paul Schroeder, "A.J.P. Taylor's International System," *International History Review* 23 (2001): 25.
4. John Röhl, *Wilhelm II: Into the Abyss of War and Exile, 1900–1941* (Cambridge: Cambridge University Press, 2014).
5. Michael Howard, *The Franco-Prussian War: The German Invasion of France, 1870–1871* (London: Methuen, 1961), 220–21.
6. D. N. Collins, "The Franco-Russian Alliance and Russia's Railways, 1891–1914," *Historical Journal* 16 (1973): 777–88.
7. Matthew Seligmann, "A View from Berlin: Colonel Frederick Trench and the Development of British Perceptions of German Aggressive Intent, 1906–1910," *Journal of Strategic Studies* 23 (2000), and *Spies in Uniform: British Military and Naval Intelligence on the Eve of the First World War* (Oxford: Oxford University Press, 2006).
8. Robert Foley, *Alfred von Schlieffen's Military Writings* (London, 2003).
9. Anika Mombauer, *Helmuth von Moltke and the Origins of the First World War* (Cambridge: Cambridge University Press, 2001).
10. Keith Armes, "French Intelligence on the Russian Army on the Eve of the First World War," *Journal of Military History* 82 (2018): 779.
11. W. D. Godsey, "Officers vs Diplomats: Bureaucracy and Foreign Policy in Austria-Hungary, 1906–1914," *Mitteilungen des Österreichischen Staatsarchiv* 46 (1998): 43–66.

12. Hans Ehlert, Michael Epkenhans, and Gerhard Gross, eds., *The Schlieffen Plan: International Perspectives on German Strategy for World War I* (Lawrence: University Press of Kansas, 2014).

13. C. Ahlund, ed., *Scandinavia in the First World War: Studies in the War Experience of the Northern Neutrals* (Lund, 2012).

14. Richard Hamilton and Holger Herwig, ed., *Decisions for War, 1914–1917* (Cambridge: Cambridge University Press, 2004); William Mulligan, *The Origins of the First World War* (Cambridge: Cambridge University Press, 2010).

15. Roderick McLean, *Royalty and Diplomacy, 1890–1914* (Cambridge: Cambridge University Press, 2001).

16. Jack Levy and William Mulligan, "Shifting Power, Preventive Logic, and the Response of the Target: Germany, Russia, and the First World War," *Journal of Strategic Studies* 40 (2017): 731–69.

17. Thomas Otte, "'The Method in Which We Were Schooled by Experience': British Strategy and a Continental Commitment before 1914." In *The British Way in Warfare: Power and the International System, 1856–1956*, ed. Keith Neilson and Greg Kennedy, 301–24 (Farnham: Ashgate, 2010), 318–19.

18. Thomas Otte, "Neo-Revisionism or the Emperor's New Clothes: Some Reflections on Niall Ferguson on the Origins of the First World War," *Diplomacy and Statecraft* 11 (2000): 285.

19. Dennis Showalter, "From Deterrence to Doomsday Machine: The German Way of War, 1890–1914," *Journal of Military History* 64 (2000): 708; Xu Qiyu, *Fragile Rise: Grand Strategy and the Fate of Imperial Germany, 1871–1914* (Cambridge, MA: MIT Press, 2017).

20. Avner Offer, "Going to War in 1914: A Matter of Honour?," *Politics and Society* 23 (1995): 213–41.

21. Antulio Echevarria, *Imaging Future War: The West's Technological Revolution and Visions of War to Come, 1880–1914* (Westport, CT: Greenwood, 2007).

22. BL Add., 50344, p. 3; Michael Howard, "Men against Fire: The Doctrine of the Offensive in 1914," in *Makers of Modern Strategy from Machiavelli to the Nuclear Age*, ed. Peter Paret et al., 510–26 (Princeton, NJ: Princeton University Press, 1986).

23. Lawrence Sondhaus, *Franz Conrad von Hötzendorf: Architect of the Apocalypse* (Boston, MA: Humanities Press, 2000); John Zametica, *Folly and Malice: The Habsburg Empire, the Balkans and the Start of World War One* (London: Shepheard-Walwyn, 2017).

24. "Forum on the Spread of War, 1914–1917: A Dialogue between Political Scientists and Historians," *Foreign Policy Analysis* 7 (2011): 139–216.

25. Lawrence Sondhaus, *German Submarine Warfare in World War I: The Onset of Total War at Sea* (Lanham, MD: Rowman & Littlefield, 2017).

26. Chad Fulwider, *German Propaganda and U.S. Neutrality in World War I* (Columbia: University of Missouri Press, 2016); Bill Mills, *Treacherous Passage: Germany's Secret Plot against the United States in Mexico during World War I* (Lincoln, NE: Potomac Books, 2017).

27. Roger MacGinty, "War Cause and Peace Aim? Small States and the First World War," *European History Quarterly* 27 (1997): 46–47.

28. Stefan Rinke, *Latin America and the First World War* (Cambridge: Cambridge University Press, 2017).

29. X. Guoqi, "The Great War and China's Military Expedition Plan," *Journal of Military History* 72 (2008): 124–38.

2. THE FIRST WORLD WAR, LAND WARFARE

1. Lieutenant Colonel Percy Worrall, British army on the defense against the German Lys offensive, Exeter, DRO, 5277M/F3/29.

2. James Lyon, *Serbia and the Balkan Front, 1914: The Outbreak of the Great War* (London: Bloomsbury, 2015).

3. Frank Buchholz, Janet Robinson, and Joe Robinson, *The Great War Dawning: Germany and Its Army at the Start of World War I* (Vienna: Verlag Militaria, 2013).

4. William Astore, "Loving the German War Machine: America's Infatuation with *Blitzkrieg*, Warfighters, and Militarism," in *Arms and the Man*, ed. Michael Neiberg, 5–30 (Leiden: Brill, 2011).

5. Anika Mombauer, *Helmuth von Moltke and the Origins of the First World War* (Cambridge: Cambridge University Press, 2001); Hans Ehlert, Michael Epkenhans, and Gerhard Gross, eds., *The Schlieffen Plan: International Perspectives on the German Strategy for World War I* (Lexington: University Press of Kentucky, 2014); Dennis Showalter, Joseph Robinson, and Janet Robinson, *The German Failure in Belgium, August 1914: How Faulty Reconnaissance Exposed the Weakness of the Schlieffen Plan* (Jefferson, NC: McFarland, 2018).

6. "Great War Stories," *RUSI Journal*, 162/3 (June–July 2017): 7.

7. Keith Jeffery, *1916: A Global History* (London: Bloomsbury, 2016).

8. Nick Lloyd, "'With Faith and without Fear': Sir Douglas Haig's Command of First Army during 1915," *Journal of Military History* 71 (2007): 1068–76.

9. Alistair Horne, *The Price of Glory: Verdun, 1916* (New York: St. Martin's, 1962); Robert Foley, *German Strategy and the Path to Verdun: Erich von Falkenhayn and the Development of Attrition, 1870–1916* (Cambridge: Cambridge University Press, 2005).

10. Hew Strachan, "The Battle of the Somme and British Strategy," *Journal of Strategic Studies* 21 (1998): 79.

11. Robert Foley, "Learning War's Lessons: The German Army on the Somme, 1916," *Journal of Military History* 75 (2011): 471–504; Fritz von Lossberg, *Lossberg's War: The World War I Memoirs of a German Chief of Staff*, ed. David Zabecki and Dieter Biedekarken (Lexington: University Press of Kentucky, 2017).

12. Mark Grotelueschen, *The AEF Way of War: The American Army and Combat in World War I* (New York: Cambridge University Press, 2007); Richard Faulkner, *The School of Hard Knocks: Combat Leadership in the American Expeditionary Forces* (College Station: Texas A&M University Press, 2012); David Woodward, *The American Army and the First World War* (Cambridge: Cambridge University Press, 2014).

13. Nicholas Hall, "The French 75 mm Modèle 1897 Field Gun," *Arms and Armour* 12, no. 1 (April 2015): 4–21.

14. George Cassar, *Trial by Gas: The British Army at the Second Battle of Ypres* (Lincoln, NE: Potomac Books, 2014); Jean Pascal Zanders, ed., *Innocence Slaughtered: Gas and the Transformation of Warfare and Society* (London: Uniform Press, 2016).

15. Roger Lee, *British Battle Planning in 1916 and the Battle of Fromelles: A Case Study of Evolving Skill* (Farnham: Ashgate, 2015).

16. Christopher Pugsley, *The Anzac Experience: New Zealand, Australia, and Empire in the First World War* (Aotearoa: Reed Publishing, 2004).

17. General Henry Horne, commander British First Army to his wife Kate, January 16, 1917, in *The First World War Letters of General Lord Horne*, ed. S. Roberts (Stroud: History Press, 2009), 205.

18. Sidney Rogerson, *Twelve Days on the Somme: A Memoir of the Trenches, 1916* (London: Greenhill, 2006).

19. Jonathan Krause, *Early Trench Tactics in the French Army: The Second Battle of Artois, May–June 1915* (Farnham: Ashgate, 2013).

20. Elizabeth Greenhalgh, *The French Army and the First World War* (Cambridge: Cambridge University Press, 2014).

21. May 30, 1915, AWM, 3DL/2316, 1/1, p. 72.

22. Nick Lloyd, *Passchendaele: The Lost Victory of World War I* (New York: Basic Books, 2017).

23. Richard DiNardo, *Invasion: The Conquest of Serbia, 1915* (Santa Barbara, CA: Praeger, 2015).

24. Michael Barrett, *Prelude to Blitzkrieg: The 1916 Austro-German Campaign in Romania* (Bloomington: Indiana University Press, 2013).

25. Geoffrey Wawro, *A Mad Catastrophe: The Outbreak of World War I and the Collapse of the Habsburg Empire* (New York: Basic Books, 2014).

26. Graydon Tunstall, *Written in Blood: The Battles for Fortress Przemyśl in WWE* (Bloomington: Indiana University Press, 2016), 301, 333.

27. Mark Thompson, *The White War: Life and Death on the Italian Front, 1915–1919* (London: Faber and Faber, 2008).

28. Neil Faulkner, *Lawrence of Arabia's War: The Arabs, the British, and the Remaking of the Middle East in WWI* (New Haven, CT: Yale University Press, 2010).

29. Edward Erickson, *Palestine: The Ottoman Campaigns of 1914–1918* (Barnsley: Pen and Sword, 2016); Metin Gürcan and Robert Johnson, eds., *The Gallipoli Campaign: The Turkish Perspective* (Farnham: Ashgate, 2016); Yiğit Akin, *When the War Came Home: The Ottomans' Great War and the Devastation of an Empire* (Stanford, CA: Stanford University Press, 2018).

30. Kristian Coates Ulrichsen, *The First World War in the Middle East* (London: Hurst, 2014); T. G. Fraser, ed., *The First World War and Its Aftermath: The Shaping of the Middle East* (Chicago, IL: University of Chicago Press, 2015); Jeffrey Grey, *The War with the Ottoman Empire* (Melbourne: Oxford University Press, 2015); Robert Johnson, *The Great War and the Middle East* (Oxford: Oxford University Press, 2016).

31. Bruce Gudmundsson, *Stormtroop Tactics: Innovation in the German Army, 1914–1918* (New York: Praeger, 1989); Martin Samuels, *Command or Control? Command, Training, and Tactics in the British and German Armies, 1888–1918* (London: Frank Cass, 1995).

32. London, Greater London Record Office, MS 9400.

33. Exeter, DRO, 5277M/F130, September 28, 1918.

34. David Zabecki, *The German 1918 Offensives: A Case Study in the Operational Level of War* (New York: Routledge, 2006); Stephen McGeorge and Mason Watson, *The Marne: 15 July–6 August 1918* (Washington, DC: US Government Publishing Office, 2018).

35. Peter Dennis and Jeffrey Grey, *1917: Tactics, Training and Technology* (Loftus: Australian Military History Publications, 2008).

36. Tim Cook, *Vimy: The Battle and the Legend* (London: Allen Lane, 2017), 67.

37. David Aubin and Catherine Goldstein, eds., *The War of Guns and Mathematics: Mathematical Practices and Communities in France and Its Western Allies around World War I* (Providence, RI: American Mathematical Society, 2014).

38. AWM, 3DRL/6643; Nick Lloyd, *Hundred Days: The Campaign that Ended World War I* (New York: Basic Books, 2014).

39. Paddy Griffith, ed., *British Fighting Methods in the Great War* (London: Frank Cass, 1996); Jonathan Boff, *Winning and Losing on the Western Front: The British Third Army and the Defeat of Germany in 1918* (Cambridge: Cambridge University Press, 2012).

40. Jean Bou, ed., *The AIF in Battle: How the Australian Imperial Force Fought, 1914–1918* (Melbourne: Melbourne University Publishing, 2016).

41. Patrick Dennis, *Reluctant Warriors: Canadian Conscripts and the Great War* (Vancouver: University of British Columbia Press, 2017).

42. Rodney Atwoods, *General Lord Rawlinson* (London: Bloomsbury, 2018), 193–200.

43. Alexander Nordlund, "'Done My Bit': British Soldiers, the 1918 Armistice, and Understanding the First World War," *Journal of Military History* 81 (2017): 425–46.

44. "Characteristics and Tactics of the Mark V, Mark V One Star and Medium 'A' Tanks," June 27, 1918, AWM, 3DRL/6643, 5/27, pp. 1–3; Wilson to Marshal Foch, July 20, 1918, in *The Military Papers and Correspondence of Major-General J. F. C. Fuller*, ed. Alaric Searle (Stroud: History Press, 2017), 128.

45. Tim Gale, *The French Army's Tank Force in the Great War: The "Artillerie Spéciale"* (Farnham: Ashgate, 2014).

46. Stephen Biddle, *Military Power: Explaining Victory and Defeat in Modern Battle* (Princeton, NJ: Princeton University Press, 2004).

47. Robert Stevenson, *To Win the Battle: The 1st Australian Division in the Great War, 1914–1918* (Cambridge: Cambridge University Press, 2013); Reginald Bacon, J. F. C. Fuller, and Patrick Playfair, *Warfare Today* (London: Odhams, 1944), 18.

48. Exeter, DRO, 5277M/F3/26.

49. Exeter, DRO, 5277M/F3/29.

50. *Daily Telegraph*, July 25, 1917.

51. Corey Reigel, *The Last Great Safari: East Africa in World War I* (Lanham, MD: Rowman & Littlefield, 2015).
52. Edward Gutiérrez, *Doughboys on the Great War: How American Soldiers Viewed Their Military Experience* (Lawrence: University of Kansas Press, 2014).
53. Joshua Sanborn, *Imperial Apocalypse: The Great War and the Destruction of the Russian Empire* (Oxford: Oxford University Press, 2014).

3. THE FIRST WORLD WAR AT SEA

1. Jonathan Winkler, *Nexus: Strategic Communications and American Security in World War I* (Cambridge, MA: Harvard University Press, 2008).
2. Phillip Pattee, *At War in Distant Waters: British Colonial Defence in the Great War* (Annapolis, MD: Naval Institute Press, 2013); John Reeve, "Maritime Strategy 1914: Some Observations on the Issues," in *Maritime Strategy 1914*, ed. Tom Frame (Canberra: Barton Books, 2015), 138–40.
3. Hervé Coutau-Bégarie, "French Naval Strategy: A Naval Power in a Continental Environment," in *Naval Power in the Twentieth Century*, ed. Nicholas Rodger (Annapolis, MD: Naval Institute Press, 1996), 59–64.
4. D. Morgan-Owen, "An 'Intermediate Blockade'? British North Sea Strategy, 1912–1914," *War in History* 22 (2015): 478–502.
5. Eric Osborne, *The Battle of Heligoland Bight* (Bloomington: Indiana University Press, 2006).
6. James Goldrick, *Before Jutland: The Naval War in Northern European Waters, August 1914–February 1915* (Annapolis, MD: Naval Institute Press, 2015).
7. Tobias Philbin, *Battle of Dogger Bank: The First Dreadnought Engagement, January 1915* (Bloomington: Indiana University Press, 2014).
8. George Nekrasov, *North of Gallipoli: The Black Sea Fleet at War, 1914–1917* (New York: Columbia University Press, 1992).
9. Alan to Edith Thomson, October 7, 1915, Thomson papers, privately owned.
10. Christopher Bell, *Churchill and Sea Power* (Oxford: Oxford University Press, 2013), 73–74.
11. Peter Hart, *Gallipoli* (New York: Oxford University Press, 2011).
12. Keith Neilson, "R. H. Brand, the Empire and Munitions from Canada," *English Historical Review* 126 (2011): 1430–55.
13. Gautam Mukunda, "We Cannot Go On: Disruptive Innovation and the First World War Royal Navy," *Security Studies* 19 (2010): 124–59; Greg Kennedy, ed., *The War They Thought, the War They Fought* (Farnham: Ashgate, 2016).
14. John Brooks, *Dreadnought Gunnery and the Battle of Jutland: The Question of Fire Control* (London: Routledge, 2005); Reinhard Scheer, *Germany's High Seas Fleet in the First World War* (Barnsley, South Yorkshire: Frontline Books, 2014).
15. BL Add., 49714, fol. 145; BL Add., 49715, fol. 210.
16. Dwight Messimer, *Find and Destroy: Antisubmarine Warfare in World War I* (Annapolis, MD: Naval Institute Press, 2001); Jan Breemer, *Defeating the U-boat: Inventing Antisubmarine Warfare* (Newport, RI: Naval War College Press, 2010).
17. Dennis Conrad, "Were They So Unprepared? Josephus Daniels and the United States Navy's Entry into World War I," *U.S. Military History Review* 3, no. 1 (2016): 5–19.
18. Peter Jackson, "French Security and a British 'Continental Commitment' after the First World War: A Reassessment," *English Historical Review* 126 (2011): 350.
19. David Redvaldsen, "The Role of Britain in Late Modern Norwegian History: A Longitudinal Study," *Britain and the World* 9 (2016): 16.
20. William Still, *Crisis at Sea: The United States Navy in European Waters in World War I* (Gainesville: University Press of Florida, 2007); Michael Simpson, ed., *Anglo-American Naval Relations, 1917–1919* (Aldershot: Naval Records Society, 1991).

21. Daniel Horn, *The German Naval Mutinies of World War One* (New Brunswick, NJ: Rutgers University Press, 1969).
22. BL Add., 49714, fol. 28.
23. Robert Feuilloy, Lucien Morareau, et al., *L'Aviation maritime française pendant la Grande Guerre* (Paris: Ardhan, 1999), 277–79.
24. Richard D. Layman, *Naval Aviation in the First World War: Its Impact and Influence* (Annapolis, MD: Naval Institute Press, 1996).
25. Nicholas Black, *The British Naval Staff in the First World War* (Woodbridge: Boydell, 2009); Mike Farquharson-Roberts, *A History of the Royal Navy: World War I* (London: I. B. Tauris, 2014); Lawrence Sondhaus, *The Great War at Sea: A Naval History of the First World War* (Cambridge: Cambridge University Press, 2014); Norman Friedman, *Fighting the Great War at Sea: Strategy, Tactics and Technology* (Annapolis, MD: Naval Institute Press, 2014).
26. Duncan Redford, *The Submarine: A Cultural History from the Great War to Nuclear Combat* (London: I. B. Tauris, 2010).
27. Jan Glete, "Naval Power and Warfare 1815–2000," in *War in the Modern World since 1815*, ed. Jeremy Black (London: Routledge, 2003), 228.

4. THE FIRST WORLD WAR IN THE AIR

1. *The Times*, March 20, 1917, 9.
2. Matthew Seligman, "A View from Berlin: Colonel Frederick Trench and the Development of British Perceptions of German Aggressive Intent, 1906–1910," *Journal of Strategic Studies* 23 (2000): 131.
3. Alec Brew, *The History of Black Country Aviation* (Stroud, UK: Sutton, 1993).
4. Susan R. Grayzel, "'The Souls of Soldiers': Civilians under Fire in First World War France," *Journal of Modern History* 78 (2006): 588–622, esp. 597–600, 621.
5. Alan to Edith Thomson, November 3, 1915, cf. September 24, 1915, Thomson papers, privately owned.
6. BL Add., 49703, fols. 184–89.
7. Georges Pagé, *L'Aviation française, 1914–1918* (Paris: Grancher, 2011), 88–93.
8. Michel Bénichou, *Un siècle d'aviation française* (Clichy: éditions Larivière, 2000), 28–29.
9. LMA, CLC/533/MS 09400.
10. Christopher Duffy, *Through German Eyes: The British and the Somme, 1916* (London: Weidenfeld and Nicolson, 2007).
11. LMA, CLC/533/MS 09400.
12. Dean Juniper, "Gothas over London," *RUSI Journal* 148, no. 4 (2003): 74–80.
13. Jonathan Bailey, *The First World War and the Birth of the Modern Style of Warfare*, Occasional Paper No. 22 (Camberley: Strategic and Combat Studies Institute, 1996).
14. August 31, 1918, DRO, 5277M/F3/30.
15. Gary Sheffield, *A Short History of the First World War* (London: Oneworld, 2014), 48.
16. Malcolm Cooper, *The Birth of Independent Air Power* (London: HarperCollins, 1986).
17. George K. Williams, *Biplanes and Bombsights: British Bombing in World War I* (Maxwell Air Force Base, AL: Air University Press, 1999); Craig Morris, *The Origins of American Strategic Bombing Theory* (Annapolis, MD: Naval Institute Press, 2017).
18. Child-Villiers to his mother, September 26, 1918, LMA, ACC/2839/D002.
19. Dean Juniper, "'Some Were Chosen': A Study of Aeroplane Procurement in the First World War," *RUSI Journal* 149, no. 6 (December 2004): 62–69.
20. Alan to Edith Thomson, November 11, 1918, Thomson papers, privately owned.
21. Jean-Baptiste Manchon, *Aéronautique militaire française outre-mer, 1911–1939* (Paris: PUPS, 2013), 149.
22. Monash to wife, July 18, 1916, AWM, 3DRL/23/6, 1/1, pp. 201–2.

23. Brett Holman, "Dreaming War: Airmindedness and the Australian Mystery Aeroplane Scare of 1918," *History Australia* 10 (2013): 180–201; Margaret McClure, *Fighting Spirit: 75 Years of the RNZAF* (Auckland: Random House NZ, 2012).

24. Margam Philpott, *Air and Sea Power in World War I: Combat Experience in the Royal Flying Corps and the Royal Navy* (London: I. B. Tauris, 2013).

5. THE INTERWAR YEARS, LAND WARFARE

1. Robert Citino, *The Path to Blitzkrieg: Doctrine and Training in the German Army, 1920–1939* (Boulder, CO: Lynne Rienner, 1999).

2. LH, Liddell Hart papers, 7/1920/167.

3. Jochem Boehler, *Civil War in Central Europe, 1918–1921: The Reconstruction of Poland* (Oxford: Oxford University Press, 2018).

4. Peter Whitewood, *The Red Army and the Great Terror: Stalin's Purge of the Soviet Military* (Lawrence: University Press of Kansas, 2015).

5. Roger Reese, *Stalin's Reluctant Soldiers: A Social History of the Red Army, 1925–1941* (Lawrence: University Press of Kansas, 1996).

6. Laura Engelstein, *Russia in Flames: War, Revolution, Civil War, 1914–1921* (Oxford: Oxford University Press, 2017).

7. A. G. Park, *Bolshevism in Turkestan, 1917–1927* (New York: Columbia University Press, 1957).

8. Jonathan Smele, *The "Russian" Civil Wars, 1916–1926: Ten Years That Shook the World* (New York: Oxford University Press, 2015); focusing on 1928–32: Lynne Viola, *Peasant Rebels under Stalin: Collectivisation and the Culture of Peasant Resistance* (Oxford: Oxford University Press, 1996).

9. Michael Malet, *Nestor Makhno in the Russian Civil War* (London: Palgrave, 1982).

10. Geoffrey Best, *Humanity in Warfare: The Modern History of the International Law of Armed Conflicts* (London: Weidenfeld and Nicolson, 1990).

11. Robert Gerwarth and John Horne, eds., *War in Peace: Paramilitary Violence in Europe after the Great War* (Oxford: Oxford University Press, 2013).

12. Michael Neiberg, *The Treaty of Versailles: A Concise History* (New York: Oxford University Press, 2017), 9–10.

13. Robert Gerwarth, *The Vanquished: Why the First World War Failed to End, 1917–1923* (London: Allen Lane, 2016); Jochen Böhler, Włodimierz Borodziej, and Joachim von Puttkamer, eds., *Legacies of Violence: Eastern Europe's First War* (Munich: Oldenbourg, 2014).

14. Matthew Butler, *Popular Piety and Political Identity in Mexico's Cristero Rebellion: Michoacán, 1927–1929* (Oxford: Oxford University Press, 2004).

15. Nick Lloyd, "Colonial Counter-insurgency in Southern India: The Malabar Rebellion, 1921–1922," *Contemporary British History* 29 (2015): 297–317.

16. Michael Russ, "The Marine Air-Ground Task Force in Nicaragua, 1927–33: A Campaign against Sandino's Counterinsurgency," *Marine Corps History* 2 (2016): 55–64.

17. Gyanesh Kudaisya, "'In Aid of Civil Power': The Colonial Army in Northern India, c. 1919–42," *Journal of Imperial and Commonwealth History* 32 (2004): 41–68.

18. Adam Zamoyski, *Warsaw 1920: Lenin's Failed Conquest of Europe* (London: Harper Press, 2008).

19. Amin Banani, *The Modernization of Iran, 1921–1941* (Stanford, CA: Stanford University Press, 1961).

20. Peter Hart, *The IRA and Its Enemies: Violence and Community in Cork, 1916–1923* (Oxford: Oxford University Press, 1998).

21. William Sheehan, *A Hard Local War: The British Army and the Guerrilla War in Cork, 1919–1921* (Staplehurst: Spellmount, 2011).

22. Gerry White, "Free State *versus* Republic: The Opposing Armed Forces in the Civil War," in *Atlas of the Irish Revolution*, ed. John Crowley, Donal Ó Drisceoil, and Mike Murphy (Cork: Cork University Press, 2017), 692.

23. Arthur Waldron, "The Warlord: Twentieth Century Chinese Understandings of Violence, Militarism, and Imperialism," *American Historical Review* 96 (1991): 1073–110.

24. Arthur Waldron, *From War to Nationalism: China's Turning Point, 1924–1925* (Cambridge: Cambridge University Press, 1995).

25. Donald Jordan, *The Northern Expedition: China's National Revolution of 1926–1928* (Honolulu: University of Hawaii Press, 1976).

26. Peter Worthing, "Continuity and Change: Chinese Nationalist Army Tactics, 1925–1938," *Journal of Military History* 78 (2014): 995–1016.

27. Peter Harmsen, *Shanghai 1937: Stalingrad on the Yangtze* (Havertown, PA: Casemate, 2013).

28. Hans van de Ven, *War and Nationalism in China, 1925–1945* (London: Routledge, 2003), and *The Battle for China: Essays on the Military History of the Sino-Japanese War of 1937–1945* (Stanford, CA: Stanford University Press, 2011); Rana Mitter, *China's War with Japan, 1937–1945: The Struggle for Survival* (London: Penguin, 2013).

29. "The Present Sino-Japanese Military Situation," report by Chiefs of Staff, December 9, 1939, NA CAB, 66/4/2, pp. 16–19.

30. Enno Kraehe, "The Motives behind the Maginot Line," *Military Affairs* 8 (1944): 109–22; Joseph E. Kaufmann et al., *The Maginot Line: History and Guide* (Barnsley: Pen and Sword, 2011); Anthony Kemp, *The Maginot Line: Myth and Reality* (London: Frederick Warne, 1981).

31. Montgomery-Massingberd to Viscount Halifax, secretary of state for war, August 17, 1935, LH, Montgomery-Massingberd papers, 10/4/1.

32. LH, Montgomery-Massingberd papers, 10/6.

33. David Stone, "Tukhachevsky in Leningrad: Military Politics and Exile, 1928–31," *Europe-Asia Studies* 48 (1996): 1382.

34. Joe Maiolo, *Cry Havoc: The Arms Race and the Second World War, 1931–1941* (London: John Murray, 2010).

35. Mark Calhoun, *General Lesley J. McNair: Unsung Architect of the U.S. Army* (Lexington: University Press of Kansas, 2015).

6. THE INTERWAR YEARS AT SEA

1. Evan Mawdsley, *The Russian Revolution and the Baltic Fleet: War and Politics, February 1917–April 1918* (London: Macmillan, 1978), 154; Norman Saul, *Sailors in Revolt: The Russian Baltic Fleet in 1917* (Lawrence: Regents Press of Kansas, 1978), 219.

2. John Ferris, "The Symbol and Substance of Seapower: Britain, the United States and the One-Power Standard, 1919–1921," in *Anglo-American Relations in the 1920s: The Struggle for Supremacy*, ed. Brian McKercher (Edmonton: University of Alberta Press, 1990), 55–80.

3. Donald Lisio, *British Naval Supremacy and Anglo-American Antagonisms, 1914–1930* (Cambridge: Cambridge University Press, 2014).

4. Albert Nofi, "An Overlooked Angle on the Naval Arms Limitation Treaties," Combat Information Center, Strategy page, no. 451, http://www.strategypage.com/cic/docs/cic124b.asp, accessed April 28, 2016.

5. NA CAB, 29/117, fol. 78.

6. Thomas Wildenberg, *Billy Mitchell's War: The Army Air Corps and the Challenge to Seapower* (Annapolis, MD: Naval Institute Press, 2013).

7. Robert Stern, *The Battleship Holiday: The Naval Treaties and Capital Ship Design* (Annapolis, MD: Naval Institute Press, 2017).

8. William Trimble, *Admiral William A. Moffett: Architect of Naval Aviation* (Washington, DC: Smithsonian Institution Press, 1994).

9. BL Add., 49045, fols. 1–2.

10. James Goldrick, "Buying Time: British Submarine Capability in the Far East, 1919–1940," *Global War Studies* 11, no. 3 (2014): 33–50.

11. Louis Morton, *Strategy and Command: The First Two Years* (Washington, DC: Office of the Chief of Military History, US Army, 1962), 27.
12. Report by the Chiefs of Staff, January 11, 1927, NA CAB, 24/184, fols. 42–43.
13. Edward Miller, *War Plan Orange: The U.S. Strategy to Defeat Japan, 1897–1945* (Annapolis, MD: Naval Institute Press, 1991).
14. Jon Kuehn, "The U.S. Navy General Board and Naval Arms Limitation: 1922–1937," *Journal of Military History* 74 (2010): 1159–60.
15. Thomas Wildenberg, "In Support of the Battle Line: Gunnery's Influence on the Development of Carrier Aviation in the U.S. Navy," *Journal of Military History* 65 (2001): 709.
16. Craig Felker, *Testing American Sea Power: US Navy Strategic Exercises, 1923–1940* (College Station: Texas A&M University Press, 2007); Albert Nofi, *To Train the Fleet for War: The US Navy Fleet Problems, 1923–1940* (Newport, RI: Naval War College Press, 2010); John Lillard, *Playing War: Wargaming and U.S. Navy Preparations for World War II* (Lincoln, NE: Potomac Books, 2016).
17. Garry Weir, *Building American Submarines, 1914–1940* (Washington, DC: Naval Historical Center, 1991).
18. Douglas Ford, "A Statement of Hopes? The Effectiveness of US and British Naval War Plans against Japan, 1920–1941," *Mariner's Mirror* 101 (2015): 63–80; William Braisted, *Diplomats in Blue: U.S. Naval Officers in China, 1922–1933* (Gainesville: University Press of Florida, 2009).
19. David Ulbrich, *Preparing for Victory: Thomas Holcomb and the Making of the Modern Marine Corps, 1936–1943* (Annapolis, MD: Naval Institute Press, 2011).
20. Trent Hone, "The Evolution of Fleet Tactical Doctrine in the U.S. Navy, 1922–1941," *Journal of Military History* 67 (2003): 1146.
21. John Kuehn, *Agents of Innovation: The General Board and the Design of the Fleet That Defeated the Japanese Navy* (Annapolis, MD: Naval Institute Press, 2008).
22. Keith Neilson, "The Defence Requirements Sub-Committee, British Strategic Foreign Policy, Neville Chamberlain and the Path to Appeasement," *English Historical Review* 118 (2003): 675.
23. Charles Eade, ed., *Winston Churchill's Secret Session Speeches* (London: Cassell, 1946), 47.
24. David Evans and Mark Peattie, *Kaigun: Strategy, Tactics and Technology in the Imperial Japanese Navy, 1887–1941* (Annapolis, MD: Naval Institute Press, 1997).
25. Geoffrey Till, *Air Power and the Royal Navy, 1914–1945: A Historical Survey* (London: Macdonald and James, 1979).
26. Thomas Hone, Norman Friedman, and Mark Mandeles, *American and British Aircraft Carrier Development, 1919–1941* (Annapolis, MD: Naval Institute Press, 1999); Thomas Wildenberg, *Destined for Glory: Dive Bombing, Midway, and the Evolution of Carrier Airpower* (Annapolis, MD: Naval Institute Press, 1998).
27. Geoffrey Till, "Maritime Airpower in the Interwar Period: The Information Dimension," *Journal of Strategic Studies* 27 (2004): 298–323.
28. Jon Sumida, "'The Best Laid Plans': The Development of British Battle-Fleet Tactics, 1919–1942," *International History Review* 14 (1992): 682–700.
29. Gerhard Koop and Klaus-Peter Schmolke, *Battleships of the Bismarck Class* (Annapolis, MD: Naval Institute Press, 1998).
30. Timothy Mulligan, "Ship of the Line or Atlantic Raider? Battleship *Bismarck* between Design Limitations and Naval Strategy," *Journal of Military History* 69 (2005): 1013–44.
31. Joseph Maiolo, *The Royal Navy and Nazi Germany, 1933–39: A Study in Appeasement and the Origins of the Second World War* (Basingstoke, UK: Palgrave Macmillan, 1998).
32. George Franklin, *Britain's Anti-Submarine Capability, 1919–1939* (London: Routledge, 2003).
33. David Massam, *British Maritime Strategy and Amphibious Capability, 1900–40* (PhD diss., Oxford, 1995).
34. BL Add., 74806.

35. Lennart Samuelson, "Mikhail Tukhachevsky and War-Economic Planning: Reconsiderations on the Pre-war Soviet Military Build-up," *Journal of Slavic Military Studies* 9 (1996): 804–47.

36. Peter Whitewood, *The Red Army and the Great Terror: Stalin's Purge of the Soviet Military* (Lawrence: University Press of Kansas, 2015).

37. Jürgen Rohwer and Mikhail Monakov, *Stalin's Ocean-going Fleet: Soviet Naval Strategy and Shipbuilding Programmes, 1935–1953* (London: Frank Cass, 2001).

38. William Garzke and Robert Dulin, *Battleships: United States Battleships, 1935–1992* (Annapolis, MD: Naval Institute Press, 1995).

7. THE INTERWAR YEARS IN THE AIR

1. Thomas Faith, *Behind the Gas Mask: The U.S. Chemical Warfare Service in Peace and War* (Urbana: University of Illinois Press, 2014).

2. Andrew Barros, "Razing Babel and the Problems of Constructing Peace: France, Great Britain, and Air Power, 1916–28," *English Historical Review* 126 (2011): 75–115, esp. 75–77, 114.

3. Neville Parton, *The Evolution and Impact of Royal Air Force Doctrine, 1919–1939* (London: Continuum, 2011).

4. Richard Overy, *The Bombing War: Europe, 1939–1945* (London: Penguin, 2013), 25–26.

5. John Ferris, "The Theory of a French 'Air Menace': Anglo-French Relations and the British Home Defence Air Force Programmes of 1921–25," *Journal of Strategic Studies* 10 (1987): 62–83.

6. David Killingray, "A Swift Agent of Government: Air Power in British Colonial Africa, 1916–39," *Journal of African History* 25 (1984): 429–44; Jafna L. Cox, "A Splendid Training Ground: The Importance to the RAF of Iraq, 1913–32," *Journal of Imperial and Commonwealth History* 13 (1985): 157–84.

7. Robin Higham, *Britain's Imperial Air Routes, 1918–1939* (Hamden, CT: Shoe String Press, 1960); Robert L. McCormack, "Imperialism, Air Transport and Colonial Development: Kenya 1920–1946," *Journal of Imperial and Commonwealth History* 17 (1989): 374–95.

8. Thomas Hippler, *Bombing the People: Giulio Douhet and the Foundations of Air-Power Strategy, 1884–1939* (Cambridge: Cambridge University Press, 2013).

9. Galen Perras and Katrina Kellner, "'A Perfectly Logical and Sensible Thing': Billy Mitchell Advocates a Canadian-American Aerial Alliance against Japan," *Journal of Military History* 72 (2008): 786.

10. Colin Sinnott, *The RAF and Aircraft Design, 1923–1939: Air Staff Operational Requirements* (London: Frank Cass, 2001).

11. Richard Overy, "Air Power and the Origins of Deterrence Theory before 1939," *Journal of Strategic Studies* 15 (1992): 73–101.

12. Roger E. Bilstein, "Airplanes," in *A Companion to American Technology*, ed. Carroll Pursell (Oxford: Blackwell, 2005), 263.

13. Bernd Jürgen Fischer, *Albania at War, 1939–1945* (London: C. Hurst & Co., 1999), 24.

14. Dirk Starink, *De Jonge Jaren Van de Luchtmacht. Het luchtwapen in het Nederlandse leger 1913–1939* (Amsterdam: Boom, 2013), 377, 380–81.

15. Ministerial Committee, July 16, 1934, NA CAB, 24/250, fol. 119.

16. Sebastian Ritchie, *Industry and Air Power: The Expansion of British Aircraft Production, 1935–1941* (London: Frank Cass, 1997); John Buckley, *Air Power in the Age of Total War* (London: UCL Press, 1999), 109–10.

17. Steven Weinberg, "What Price Glory?," *New York Review of Books*, November 6, 2003, 59.

18. Peter Fritzsche, *A Nation of Flyers: German Aviation and the Popular Imagination* (Cambridge, MA: Harvard University Press, 1992).

19. Richard Overy, "From 'Uralbomber' to 'Amerikabomber': The *Luftwaffe* and Strategic Bombing," *Journal of Strategic Studies* 1 (1978): 154–78.

20. Edward L. Homze, *Arming the Luftwaffe: The Reich Air Ministry and the German Aircraft Industry, 1919–39* (Lincoln: University of Nebraska Press, 1976); Klaus A. Maier, "Total War and Operational Air Warfare," in *Germany and the Second World War II*, ed. Klaus A. Maier et al. (Oxford: Oxford University Press, 1991), 31–59; James Corum, *The Luftwaffe: Creating the Operational Air War, 1918–1940* (Lawrence: University of Kansas Press, 1997); James Corum and Richard R. Muller, *The Luftwaffe's Way of War: German Air Force Doctrine, 1911–1945* (Baltimore, MD: Nautical & Aviation Publishing, 1998).

21. James Corum, *Wolfram von Richthofen: Master of the German Air War* (Lawrence: University of Kansas Press, 2008).

22. Jason Warren to Jeremy Black, emails March 5, 2015.

23. Joel Hayward, "The Luftwaffe's Agility: An Assessment of Relevant Concepts and Practices," in *Air Power: The Agile Air Force*, ed. Neville Parton (Shrivenham: Royal Air Force Centre for Air Power Studies, 2008), 40–49.

24. Diego Navarro Bonilla and Guillermo Vincente Caro, "Photographic Air Reconnaissance during the Spanish Civil War, 1936–1939: Doctrine and Operations," *War in History* 20 (2013): 345–80.

25. Lionel Evelyn Oswald Charlton, *War from the Air: Past, Present, Future* (London: Nelson, 1935).

26. Scot Robertson, *The Development of RAF Bombing Doctrine, 1919–1929* (Westport, CT: Praeger, 1995); Philip Meilinger, "Trenchard and 'Morale Bombing': The Evolution of Royal Air Force Doctrine before World War II," *Journal of Military History* 60 (1996): 243–70.

27. November 10, 1932, Hansard, House of Commons Debates, vol. 270, col. 632.

28. James Corum, "The Spanish Civil War: Lessons Learned and Not Learned by the Great Powers," *Journal of Military History* 62 (1998): 313–34.

29. Robert Young, "The Strategic Dream: French Air Doctrine in the Inter-War Period, 1919–1939," *Journal of Contemporary History* 9 (1974): 56–76; Lucien Robineau, "French Air Policy in the Interwar Period and the Conduct of the Air War against Germany from September 1939 to June 1940," in *The Conduct of the Air War in the Second World War*, ed. Horst Boog (Oxford: Oxford University Press, 1992), 85–107.

30. Scott W. Palmer, *Dictatorship of the Air: Aviation Culture and the Fate of Modern Russia* (Cambridge: Cambridge University Press, 2006).

31. Uri Bialer, *Shadow of the Bomber: The Fear of Air Attack and British Politics, 1932–1939* (London: Royal Historical Society, 1980), 132; G. G. Lee, "'I See Dead People': Air-Raid Phobia and Britain's Behavior in the Munich Crisis," *Security Studies* 13 (2003–4): 230–72.

32. Arnold D. Harvey, "The Bomber Offensive That Never Took Off: Italy's Regia Aeronautica in 1940," *RUSI Journal* 154, no. 6 (December 2009): 96–97.

33. George C. Peden, *British Rearmament and the Treasury, 1932–1939* (Edinburgh: Scottish Academic Press, 1979), 183.

34. David Edgerton, *England and the Aeroplane: An Essay on a Militant and Technological Nation* (Basingstoke: Palgrave Macmillan, 1991).

35. Peter Flint, *Dowding and Headquarters Fighter Command* (London: Airlife, 1996), 11–12.

36. Milne, "The Role of the Air Force in Relation to the Army," LH, Milne papers, Box 3; Tami Davis Biddle, *Rhetoric and Reality in Air Warfare: The Evolution of British and American Ideas about Strategic Bombing, 1914–1945* (Princeton, NJ: Princeton University Press, 2002).

37. Philip Meilinger, "Clipping the Bomber's Wings: The Geneva Disarmament Conference and the Royal Air Force, 1932–1934," *War in History* 6 (1999): 306–30; Waqar Zaidi, "'Aviation Will Either Destroy or Save Our Civilization': Proposal for the International Control of Aviation, 1920–45," *Journal of Contemporary History* 46 (2011): 150–78.

38. David Edgerton, *Britain's War Machine: Weapons, Resources and Experts in the Second World War* (London: Allen Lane, 2011), 37–39.

39. Martin J. Bollinger, *Warriors and Wizards: The Development and Defeat of Radio-Controlled Glide Bombs of the Third Reich* (Annapolis, MD: Naval Institution Press, 2010).
40. David Zimmerman, *Britain's Shield: Radar and the Defeat of the Luftwaffe* (Stroud: Sutton, 2001).
41. Michael Budden, "Defending the Indefensible? The Air Defence of Malta," *War in History* 6 (1999): 453.
42. Wesley K. Wark, *The Ultimate Enemy: British Intelligence and Nazi Germany, 1933–1939* (Ithaca, NY: Cornell University Press, 1985); Gerald Lee, "'I See Dead People': Air-Raid Phobia and Britain's Behaviour in the Munich Crisis," *Security Studies* 13 (2003–4): 230–72, esp. 245, 251, 254.
43. Brett Holman, *The Next War in the Air: Britain's Fear of the Bomber, 1908–1941* (Farnham: Ashgate, 2014).
44. Annual Review, November 1933, NA CAB, 24/244, fol. 138.
45. Arnold Harvey, "The Royal Air Force and Close Support, 1918–1940," *War in History* 15 (2008): 482–84, and "How Ill-Equipped Was the Fleet Air Arm in 1939?" *RUSI Journal* 155, no. 3 (June/July 2010): 67.

8. CAUSES

1. NA CAB, 24/228, fol. 66.
2. Michael Walker, *The 1929 Sino-Soviet War: The War Nobody Knew* (Lawrence: University Press of Kansas, 2017).
3. B. Shillony, *Revolt in Japan: The Young Officers and the February 26, 1936 Incident* (Princeton, NJ: Princeton University Press, 1973); Sandra Wilson, *The Manchurian Crisis and Japanese Society, 1931–1933* (London: Routledge, 2002); Ian Nish, *Japanese Foreign Policy in the Interwar Period* (Westport, CT: Praeger, 2002).
4. Louise Young, *Japan's Total Empire: Manchuria and the Culture of Wartime Imperialism* (Berkeley: University of California Press, 1998).
5. Richard Smethurst, *A Social Basis for Prewar Japanese Militarism: The Army and the Rural Community* (Berkeley: University of California Press, 1974).
6. Walter Skya, *Japan's Holy War: The Ideology of Radical Shintō Ultranationalism* (Durham, NC: Duke University Press, 2009).
7. Brian Victoria, *Zen at War* (New York: Weatherhill, 1997; 2nd ed., Lanham, MD: Rowman & Littlefield, 2006).
8. Richard Evans, *The Third Reich in Power* (London: Allen Lane, 2005).
9. Jeffrey Record, "The Use and Abuse of History: Munich, Vietnam and Iraq," *Survival* 49 (2007): 163–80; *Washington Post*, March 19, 2013.
10. Sally Marks, "Mistakes and Myths: The Allies, Germany, and the Versailles Treaty, 1918–1921," *Journal of Modern History* 85 (2013): 632–59.
11. Eugenia Kiesling, *Arming against Hitler: France and the Limits of Military Planning* (Lawrence: University of Kansas Press, 1996).
12. Joe Maiolo, *Cry Havoc: The Arms Race and the Second World War, 1931–1941* (London: Penguin, 2010).
13. Keith Neilson, *Britain, Soviet Russia, and the Collapse of the Versailles Order, 1919–1939* (Cambridge: Cambridge University Press, 2006); Joe Maiolo, "Anglo-Soviet Naval Armaments Diplomacy before the Second World War," *English Historical Review* 123 (2008): 352.
14. Richard Overy, *1939: Countdown to War* (London: Penguin, 2009); Roger Moorhouse, *The Devils' Alliance: Hitler's Pact with Stalin, 1939–1941* (New York: Basic Books, 2014).
15. Adam Tooze, *The Wages of Destruction: The Making and Breaking of the Nazi Economy* (London: Penguin, 2006), 665.
16. Talbot Imlay, *Facing the Second World War: Strategy, Politics, and Economics in Britain and France, 1938–40* (Oxford: Oxford University Press, 2003); David Edgerton, *Brit-

ain's War Machine: Weapons, Resources, and Experts in the Second World War (Oxford: Oxford University Press, 2011).

17. Adam Claasen, "Blood and Iron, and 'der Geist des Atlantiks': Assessing Hitler's Decision to Invade Norway," *Journal of Strategic Studies* 20 (1997): 71–96.

18. Jeffery Gunsburg, "*La Grande Illusion*: Belgian and Dutch Strategy Facing Germany, 1919–May 1940 (Part I)," *Journal of Military History* 78 (2014): 101–58, esp. 141–54.

19. Churchill to Hoare, September 18, 1940, Churchill Papers, Cambridge, Churchill College.

20. Macgregor Knox, *Common Destiny: Dictatorship, Foreign Policy, and War in Fascist Italy and Nazi Germany* (Cambridge: Cambridge University Press, 2000); Robert Mallett, *Mussolini and the Origins of the Second World War, 1933–1940* (Basingstoke: Palgrave, 2003).

21. Galeazzo Ciano, *Diario 1937–39* (Milan, 1980), 209.

22. Ciano, *Diario*, 140.

23. Galeazzo Ciano, *L'Europa verso la catastrophe* (Verona: Mondadori, 1948), 373–78.

24. Ciro Paoletti, "The International Motivations and Politics of Italy behind the Greek Campaign of 1941—the Italian Side" (paper presented to the Seventy-Ninth SMH Annual Conference, Arlington, Virginia, May 10, 2012).

25. Richard Raack, *Stalin's Drive to the West: 1938–1945* (Stanford, CA: Stanford University Press, 1995); Evan Mawdsley, "Crossing the Rubicon: Soviet Plans for Offensive War in 1940–1941," *International History Review* 25 (2003).

26. Oscar Pinkus, *The War Aims and Strategies of Adolf Hitler* (Jefferson, NC: McFarland, 2005).

27. Jeffrey Herf, *The Jewish Enemy: Nazi Propaganda during World War II and the Holocaust* (Cambridge, MA: Harvard University Press, 2006); Lorna Waddington, *Hitler's Crusade: Bolshevism and the Myth of the International Jewish Conspiracy* (London: I. B. Tauris, 2007).

28. Gabriel Gorodetsky, *Grand Delusion: Stalin and the German Invasion of Russia* (New Haven, CT: Yale University Press, 1999); David Murphy, *What Stalin Knew: The Enigma of Barbarossa* (New Haven, CT: Yale University Press, 2005).

29. Robert Citino, *Death of the Wehrmacht: The German Campaigns of 1942* (Lawrence: University of Kansas Press, 2007).

30. Paul Hanebrink, *In Defense of Christian Hungary: Religion, Nationalism and Anti-Semitism, 1890–1944* (Ithaca, NY: Cornell University Press, 2006).

31. Marius Turda, "In Pursuit of Great Hungary: Eugenic Ideas of Social and Biological Improvement, 1940–1941," *Journal of Modern History* 85 (2013): 588–91.

32. Dennis Deletant, *Hitler's Forgotten Ally: Ion Antonescu and His Regime, Romania 1940–1944* (Basingstoke: Palgrave, 2006).

33. James Herzog, "The Influence of the United States Navy in the Embargo of Oil to Japan, 1940–1941," *Pacific Historical Review* 35 (1966): 317–28.

34. Jay Taylor, *The Generalissimo: Chiang Kai-shek and the Struggle for Modern China* (Cambridge, MA: Harvard University Press, 2009), 172.

35. E. Kinmonth, "The Mouse that Roared: Saitō Takao, Conservative Critic of Japan's 'Holy War' in China," *Journal of Japanese Studies* 25 (1999): 331–60.

36. Mark Peattie, Edward Drea, and Hans van de Ven, eds., *The Battle for China: Essays on the Military History of the Sino-Japanese War of 1937–1945* (Stanford, CA: Stanford University Press, 2010).

37. David Kaiser, *No End Save Victory: How FDR Led the Nation Into War* (New York: Basic Books, 2014), 15.

38. Waldo Heinrichs, *Threshold of War: Franklin B. Roosevelt and American Entry into World War II* (Oxford: Oxford University Press, 1988); James Schneider, *Should America Go to War? The Debate over Foreign Policy in Chicago, 1939–1941* (Chapel Hill: University of North Carolina Press, 1989).

39. D. F. Harrington, "A Careless Hope: American Air Power and Japan, 1941," *Pacific Historical Review* 43 (1979): 217–38.

40. Akira Iriye, *The Origins of the Second World War in Asia and the Pacific* (London: Longman, 1987); Donald Goldstein and Katherine Dillon, eds., *The Pearl Harbor Papers: Inside the Japanese Plans* (McLean, VA: Brasseys, 1993).
41. Emily Rosenberg, *A Date Which Will Live: Pearl Harbor in American Memory* (Durham, NC: Duke University Press, 2003).
42. William Johnsen, *The Origins of the Grand Alliance: Anglo-American Military Collaboration from the Panay Incident to Pearl Harbor* (Lexington: University Press of Kentucky, 2016).
43. Ian Kershaw, *Fateful Choices: Ten Decisions That Changed the World, 1940–1941* (London: Penguin, 2007), 382–430.
44. Neill Lochery, *Brazil: The Fortunes of War; World War II and the Making of Modern Brazil* (New York: Basic Books, 2014).
45. Frank McCann, *The Brazilian-American Alliance, 1937–1945* (Princeton, NJ: Princeton University Press, 1973); Michael Francis, *The Limits of Hegemony: United States Relations with Argentina and Chile during World War II* (Notre Dame, IN: University of Notre Dame Press, 1977); Thomas Leonard and John Bratzel, eds., *Latin America during World War II* (Lanham, MD: Rowman & Littlefield, 2006); S. I. Schwab, "The Role of the Mexican Expeditionary Air Force in World War II: Late, Limited, but Symbolically Significant," *Journal of Military History* 66 (2002): 1115–40.

9. THE SECOND WORLD WAR, LAND WARFARE

1. NA PREM, 3/328/5, pp. 23–26.
2. John Kiszely, *Anatomy of a Campaign: The British Fiasco in Norway, 1940* (Cambridge: Cambridge University Press, 2017), 293.
3. William Bartsch, *Victory Fever on Guadalcanal: Japan's First Land Defeat of WWII* (College Station: Texas A&M University Press, 2014).
4. Alfred Rieber, *Stalin and the Struggle for Supremacy in Eurasia* (New York: Cambridge University Press, 2015).
5. James Corum, "Myths of *Blitzkrieg*," *Historically Speaking* 6 (2005): 11–13.
6. Reginald Bacon, J. F. C. Fuller, and Patrick Playfair, *Warfare Today* (London: Odhams, 1944), 21.
7. Philippe Ricalens and Jacques Poyer, eds., *L'armistice de juin 1940: faute ou nécessité* (Paris: Economica, 2011).
8. Andrew Stewart, *The First Victory: The Second World War and the East Africa Campaign* (New Haven, CT: Yale University Press, 2016).
9. S. Anglim, *Orde Wingate and the British Army, 1922–1944* (London: Pickering and Chatto, 2010).
10. John Gooch, *Mussolini and His Generals: The Italian Armed Forces and Fascist Foreign Policy, 1922–1940* (Cambridge: Cambridge University Press, 2007).
11. Craig Stockings, *Bardia* (Sydney: University of New South Wales Press, 2009), and, ed., *Zombie Myths of Australian Military History* (Sydney: University of New South Wales Press, 2010).
12. Craig Stockings and Eleanor Hancock, *Swastika over the Acropolis: Re-interpreting the Nazi Invasion of Greece in World War II* (Brill: Leiden, 2013); David Horner, "Britain and the Campaigns in Greece and Crete in 1941," *Proceedings of the NIDS International Forum on War History*, 2014, 40–41.
13. Callum MacDonald, *The Lost Battle: Crete 1941* (New York: Free Press, 1993).
14. Roger Reese, "Lessons of the Winter War: A Study in the Military Effectiveness of the Red Army," *Journal of Military History* 72 (2008): 825–52.
15. David Glantz, *Stumbling Colossus: The Red Army on the Eve of World War II* (Lawrence: University of Kansas Press, 1998).
16. David Stahel, *Operation Barbarossa and Germany's Defeat in the East* (Cambridge: Cambridge University Press, 2009).

17. Larry Addington, *The Blitzkrieg Era and the German General Staff, 1865–1941* (New Brunswick, NJ: Rutgers University Press, 1971), xi, 216–17.

18. Frank Ellis, *Barbarossa 1941: Reframing Hitler's Invasion of Stalin's Soviet Empire* (Lawrence: University Press of Kansas, 2016).

19. David Stahel, *Kiev 1941: Hitler's Battle for Supremacy in the East* (Cambridge: Cambridge University Press, 2012).

20. David Stahel, *Operation Typhoon: Hitler's March on Moscow, October 1941* (Cambridge: Cambridge University Press, 2013).

21. David Stahel, *The Battle for Moscow* (Cambridge: Cambridge University Press, 2015).

22. Evan Mawdsley, *Thunder in the East: The Nazi-Soviet War 1941–1945*, 2nd ed. (New York: Bloomsbury Academic, 2016).

23. J. A. English, *Marching through Chaos: The Descent of Armies in Theory and Practice* (Westport, CT: Praeger, 1996), 105.

24. Christian Hartmann, *Operation Barbarossa: Nazi Germany's War in the East, 1941–1945* (Oxford: Oxford University Press, 2013).

25. Glyn Harper, *The Battle for North Africa: El Alamein and the Turning Point for World War II* (Bloomington: Indiana University Press, 2017).

26. Vincent O'Hara, *Torch: North Africa and the Allied Path to Victory* (Annapolis, MD: Naval Institute Press, 2015).

27. Mungo Melvin, *Manstein: Hitler's Greatest General* (London: Weidenfeld and Nicolson, 2010).

28. Steven Newton, ed., *Kursk: The German View* (Boston, MA: Da Capo, 2002); Martijn Lak, "The Death Ride of the Panzers? Recent Historiography on the Battle of Kursk," *Journal of Military History* 82 (2018): 917–18.

29. Noburo Tajima, "The Japanese Perspective on Germany's War," *Proceedings of the NIDS International Forum on War History*, 2011, 62–63.

30. Christian Tripodi, "Strategy, Theory, and History: Operation Husky, 1943," *Journal of Strategic Studies* 40 (2017): 990–1015.

31. Raymond Callahan, *Triumph at Imphal-Kohima: How the Indian Army Finally Stopped the Japanese Juggernaut* (Lawrence: University Press of Kansas, 2017), 126–17.

32. John McManus, *The Dead and Those about to Die: D-Day, the Big Red One at Omaha Beach* (New York: NAL Caliber, 2014).

33. Andrew Holborn, *The D-Day Landing on Gold Beach* (London: Bloomsbury, 2015).

34. John Buckley, ed., *The Normandy Campaign 1944: Sixty Years On* (London: Routledge, 2006); Stephen Napier, *The Armored Campaign in Normandy: June–August 1944* (Havertown, PA: Casemate, 2015).

35. Walter Dunn, *Stalin's Keys to Victory: The Rebirth of the Red Army* (Westport, CT: Praeger, 2006).

36. Shimon Naveh, *In Pursuit of Military Excellence: The Evolution of Operational Theory* (London: Frank Cass, 1997).

37. Bastiaan Willems, "Defiant Breakwaters or Desperate Blunders? A Revision of the German Late-War Fortress Strategy," *Journal of Slavic Military Studies* 28 (2015): 353–78.

38. C. J. Dick, *From Defeat to Victory: The Eastern Front, Summer 1944* (Lawrence: University Press of Kansas, 2016).

39. A. Searle, *Armoured Warfare* (London: Bloomsbury, 2017), 91.

40. David Glantz, *Red Storm over the Balkans: The Failed Soviet Invasion of Romania, Spring 1944* (Lawrence: University Press of Kansas, 2007).

41. Nicholas Stargardt, *The German War: A Nation under Arms, 1937–1945* (London: Bodley Head, 2015).

42. C. J. Dick, *From Victory to Stalemate: The Western Front, Summer 1944* (Lawrence: University Press of Kansas, 2016).

43. Anthony Beevor, *The Battle of Arnhem* (New York: Viking, 2018).

44. Douglas Nash, *Victory Was beyond Their Grasp: With the 272nd Volks-Grenadier Division from the Hürtgen Forest to the Heart of the Reich* (Bedford, PA: Casemate, 2008).

45. Peter Schrijvers, *Those Who Hold Bastogne: The True Story of the Soldiers and Civilians Who Fought in the Biggest Battle of the Bulge* (New Haven, CT: Yale University Press, 2014).

46. Douglas Nash, "Kesternich: The Battle that Saved the Bulge," *Army History* 109 (Autumn 2018): 34–50.

47. Jeremy Crang, "The British Soldier on the Home Front: Army Morale Reports, 1940–45," in *Time to Kill: The Soldier's Experience of War in the West, 1939–1945*, ed. Paul Addison and Angus Calder (London: Pimlico, 1997), 74.

48. Rick Atkinson, "Projecting American Power in the Second World War," *Journal of Military History* 80 (2016): 349.

49. Manchester, John Rylands Library, Special Collections, GOW, 1/2/2/2, pp. 33, 54, 1/2/1, p. 6.

50. O'Connor to Major General Allan Adair, July 24, 1944, LH, O'Connor papers, 5/3/22.

51. John Buckley, *Monty's Men: The British Army and the Liberation of Europe* (New Haven, CT: Yale University Press, 2013).

52. A. D. Harvey, "The Bayonet on the Battlefield," *RUSI Journal* 150, no. 2 (April 2005): 62–63.

53. Benjamin Coombs, *British Tank Production and the War Economy, 1934–1945* (London: Bloomsbury Academic, 2013).

54. Peter Caddick-Adams, *Show and Steel: The Battle of the Bulge, 1944–45* (Oxford: Oxford University Press, 2017), 527.

55. Russell Weighley, *History of the United States Army* (New York: Macmillan, 1967), 467–69.

56. O'Connor to Major General Sir Percy Hobart, August 24, 1944, LH, O'Connor papers, 5/3/41.

57. J. M. Vernet, "The Army of the Armistice 1940–1942: A Small Army for a Great Revenge," in *Proceedings of the 1982 International Military History Symposium: The Impact of Unsuccessful Military Campaigns on Military Institutions, 1860–1980*, ed. C. R. Shrader (Washington, DC: US Army Center of Military History, 1984), 241–42, 246–47.

58. Mark Wilson, *Destructive Creation: American Business and the Winning of World War II* (Philadelphia: University of Pennsylvania Press, 2016).

59. Steven Barry, *Battalion Commanders at War: U.S. Army Tactical Leadership in the Mediterranean Theater, 1942–1943* (Lawrence: University Press of Kansas, 2013).

60. Douglas Nash, "Army Boots on Volcanic Sands: The 147th Infantry Regiment at Iwo Jima," *Army History* 105 (Fall 2017): 10.

61. Hugh Rockoff, *America's Economic Way of War: War and the US economy from the Spanish-American War to the Persian Gulf War* (Cambridge: Cambridge University Press, 2012).

62. K. Jones, "A Curb on Ambition: Intelligence and the Planning of Eighth Army's Liri Valley Offensive, May 1944," *Intelligence and National Security* 22 (2007): 745–66.

63. Stephen Hart, *Montgomery and "Colossal Cracks": The 21st Army Group in Northwest Europe, 1944–45* (Westport, CT: Praeger, 2000).

64. Charles Forrester, "Field Marshal Montgomery's Role in the Creation of the British 21st Army Group's Combined Arms Doctrine for the Final Assault on Germany," *Journal of Military History* 78 (2014): 1319–20.

65. LH, Alanbrooke papers, 6/2/37.

66. See, impressively, Isaak Kobylyanskiy, *From Stalingrad to Pillau: A Red Army Artillery Officer Remembers the Great Patriotic War* (Lawrence: University Press of Kansas, 2014).

67. H. Nelson, "Kokada: And Two National Histories," *Journal of Pacific History* 42 (2007).

68. AWM, 3DRL/6643, 3/9, p. 1.

69. For an example from the close of the war, K. Ungváry, *Battle for Budapest: One Hundred Days in World War II* (London: I. B. Tauris, 2004).

70. Niall Barr, *Eisenhower's Armies: The American-British Alliance during World War II* (New York: Pegasus, 2015).

10. THE SECOND WORLD WAR AT SEA

1. Kalevi Keskinen and Jorma Mäntykoshi, *Suomen laivasto sodassa 1939–1945: The Finnish Navy at War in 1939–1945* (Tietotoes: Espoo Finland, 1991).
2. Chiefs of Staff Subcommittee, report, February 9, 1937, NA CAB, 24/268, fol. 104.
3. Patrick Salmon, *Deadlock and Diversion: Scandinavia in British Strategy during the Twilight War, 1939–1940* (Bremerhaven: German Maritime Museum, 2012).
4. Adam Claasen, "Blood and Iron, and 'der Geist des Atlantiks': Assessing Hitler's Decision to Invade Norway," *Journal of Strategic Studies* 20 (1997): 71–96.
5. Adam Claasen, "The German Invasion of Norway, 1940: The Operational Intelligence Dimension," *Journal of Strategic Studies* 27 (2004): 114–35.
6. Geirr Haarr, *The German Invasion of Norway: April 1940* (Annapolis, MD: Naval Institute Press, 2009).
7. Pound to Admiral Cunningham, May 20, 1940, BL Add., 52560, fol. 120.
8. Anthony Cumming, *The Royal Navy and the Battle of Britain* (Annapolis, MD: Naval Institute Press, 2010); Garry Campion, *The Battle of Britain, 1945–1965: The Air Ministry and the Few* (Basingstoke, UK: Palgrave, 2015).
9. Philippe Lasterle, "Could Admiral Gensoul Have Averted the Tragedy of Mers-el-Kébir?," *Journal of Modern History* 67 (2003): 835–44.
10. James Sadkovich, "Understanding Defeat: Reappraising Italy's Role in World War II," *Journal of Contemporary History* 24 (1989): 38.
11. Ben Jones, ed., *The Fleet Air Arm in the Second World War*, vol. 1, *1939–1941* (Farnham: Ashgate, 2012).
12. Cunningham to Pound, May 28, 1941, BL Add., 52567, fol. 117.
13. Blamey to Minister for Army, August 15, 1941, AWM, 3DRL/6643, 1/2. See, for same, August 2, 1941.
14. Vincent O'Hara, *In Passage Perilous: Malta and the Convoy Battles of June 1942* (Bloomington: Indiana University Press, 2013); James Sadkovich, "Re-evaluating Who Won the Italo-British Naval Conflict, 1940–2," *European History Quarterly* 18 (1988): 455–71.
15. Robert J. Winklareth, *The Battle of the Denmark Strait* (Havertown, PA: Casemate, 2012).
16. Christopher Bell, "Air Power and the Battle of the Atlantic: Very Long Range Aircraft and the Delay in Closing the Atlantic 'Air Gap,'" *Journal of Military History* 79 (2015): 691–719.
17. William Casto, "Advising Presidents: Robert Jackson and the Destroyers-for-Bases Deal," *American Journal of Legal History* 52 (2012): 1–135.
18. Joel Hayward, "A Case Study in Early Joint Warfare: An Analysis of the *Wehrmacht*'s Crimean Campaign of 1942," *Journal of Strategic Studies* 22 (1999): 122–26.
19. Hedley Paul Willmott, *Pearl Harbor* (London: Orion, 2001); Mitsui Fuchida, *For That One Day: The Memoirs of Mitsuo Fuchida, Commander of the Attack on Pearl Harbor* (Kamuela, HI: Experience, 2011); Alan Zimm, *Attack on Pearl Harbor: Strategy, Combat, Myths, Deceptions* (Havertown, PA: Casemate, 2011), and "A Strategy Has to Be Able to Work to Be Masterful," *Naval War College Review* 68 (2015): 128–35.
20. Derek Howse, *Radar at Sea: The Royal Navy in World War 2* (Basingstoke, UK: Palgrave, 1993), 123–24.
21. Christopher Bell, "The 'Singapore Strategy' and the Deterrence of Japan: Winston Churchill, the Admiralty and the Dispatch of Force Z," *English Historical Review* 116 (2001): 604–34.
22. Andrew Stewart, *A Very British Experience: Coalition, Defence and Strategy in the Second World War* (Brighton, Sussex: Academic Press, 2012).
23. Edward Harrison, "British Subversion in French East Africa, 1941–42: SOE's Todd Mission," *English Historical Review* 114 (1999): 358–60.
24. Milan Vego, "The Port Moresby-Solomons Operation and the Allied Reaction, 27 April–11 May 1942," *Naval War College Review* 65, no. 1 (Winter 2012): 93–151.

25. Tom Lewis, "The Japanese Airmen Who Attacked Australia's North," *Quadrant* 62, no. 6 (June 2018): 54–57.

26. Mitsuo Fuchida and Masatake Okumiya, *Midway: The Battle That Doomed Japan; The Japanese Navy's Story* (Annapolis, MD: Naval Institute Press, 1992); Alvin Kernan, *The Unknown Battle of Midway* (New Haven, CT: Yale University Press, 2005); Thomas Hone, ed., *The Battle of Midway* (Annapolis, MD: Naval Institute Press, 2013).

27. Dallas Isom, *Midway Inquest: Why the Japanese Lost the Battle of Midway* (Bloomington: Indiana University Press, 2007); James Levy, "Was There Something Unique to the Japanese That Lost Them the Battle of Midway?," *Naval War College Review* 67 (2014): 119–24; Carl Hodge, "The Key to Midway: Coral Sea and a Culture of Learning," *Naval War College Review* 68, no. 1 (2015): 119–27.

28. James Smith, "Admiral William Pye's 1943 Evaluation of the Naval Battle of Guadalcanal, November 13–15, 1942," *U.S. Military History Review* 1, no. 1 (2014): 48–51.

29. War Cabinet Minutes, July 29, 1942, NAA, p. 1404.

30. John Wukovits, *Tin Can Titans: The Heroic Men and Ships of World War II's Most Decorated Navy Destroyer Squadron* (Boston: Da Capo, 2017).

31. Reg Newell, *The Battle for Vella Lavella: The Allied Recapture of Solomon Islands Territory, August 15–September 9, 1943* (Jefferson, NC: McFarland, 2015); Ronnie Day, *New Georgia: The Second Battle for the Solomons* (Bloomington: Indiana University Press, 2016).

32. Carl Boyd and Akihiko Yoshida, *The Japanese Submarine Force and World War II* (Annapolis, MD: Naval Institute Press, 1995).

33. For the valuable individual experience, see Craig McDonald, *The USS Puffer in World War II: A History of the Submarine and Its Wartime Crew* (Jefferson, NC: McFarland, 2008), and James Scott, *The War Below: The Story of Three Submarines That Battled Japan* (New York: Simon and Schuster, 2013).

34. Joel Holwitt, *Execute against Japan: The U.S. Decision to Conduct Unrestricted Submarine Warfare* (College Station: Texas A&M University Press, 2009).

35. David Bercuson and Holger Herwig, *Long Night of the Tankers: Hitler's War against Caribbean Oil* (Calgary: University of Calgary Press, 2014).

36. David Syrett, "The Infrastructure of Communications Intelligence: The Allied D/F Network and the Battle of the Atlantic," *Intelligence and National Security* 17 (2002): 163–72; David Kahn, *Seizing the Enigma: The Race to Break German U-boat Codes 1939–1943*, 2nd ed. (Barnsley, South Yorkshire: Frontline Books, 2012).

37. Richard Doherty, *Churchill's Greatest Fear: The Battle of the Atlantic* (Barnsley, South Yorkshire: Pen and Sword, 2015), 176–79.

38. Marcus Jones, "Innovation for Its Own Sake," *Naval War College Review* 67, no. 2 (Spring 2014): 215–17.

39. Michael Dobbs, "Homeland Security Implications from the Battle of the Atlantic," *RUSI Journal* 148, no. 5 (October 2003): 38.

40. Peter Nash, *The Development of Mobile Logistic Support in Anglo-American Naval Policy, 1900–1953* (Gainesville: University Press of Florida, 2009).

41. Mark Peattie, *Sunburst: The Rise of Japanese Naval Air Power, 1909–1941* (Annapolis, MD: Naval Institute Press, 2002).

42. T. C. Hone, "Replacing Battleships with Aircraft Carriers in the Pacific in World War II," *Naval War College Review* 66 (2013): 72–73.

43. Hedley Paul Willmott, *The Battle of Leyte Gulf: The Last Fleet Action* (Bloomington: Indiana University Press, 2005), 57; Anthony Tully, *Battle of Surigao Strait* (Bloomington: Indiana University Press, 2014).

44. Barbara Tomblin, *With Utmost Spirit: Allied Naval Operations in the Mediterranean, 1942–1945* (Lexington: University Press of Kentucky, 2004); Robert Stern, *The US Navy and the War in Europe* (Barnsley, South Yorkshire: Seaforth Publishing, 2012).

45. Simon Ball, *The Bitter Sea: The Struggle for Mastery in the Mediterranean, 1935–1949* (London: Harper Perennial, 2009).

46. Craig Symonds, *Neptune: The Allied Invasion of Europe and the D-Day Landings* (New York: Oxford University Press, 2014).

47. Howard Grier, *Hitler, Dönitz and the Baltic Sea: The Third Reich's Last Hope, 1944–5* (Annapolis, MD: Naval Institute Press, 2007).

48. William Rawling, "The Challenge of Modernization: The Royal Canadian Navy and Antisubmarine Weapons, 1944–1945," *Journal of Military History* 63 (1999): 377–78.

49. D. M. Giangreco, *Hell to Pay: Downfall and the Invasion of Japan, 1945–1947* (Annapolis, MD: Naval Institute Press, 2018).

50. Ismay to Churchill, March 16, 1944, LH, Alanbrooke papers, 6/3/8.

51. Peter Elphick, *Liberty-Ships That Won the War* (Annapolis, MD: Naval Institute Press, 2006), 91; Frederick Lane, *Ships for Victory: A History of Shipbuilding under the U.S. Maritime Commission in World War II* (Baltimore, MD: Johns Hopkins University Press, 1951), 252–59.

52. Richard Mayne, *Betrayed: Scandal, Politics, and Canadian Naval Leadership* (Vancouver: UBC Press, 2007); James Pritchard, *A Bridge of Ships: Canadian Shipbuilding during the Second World War* (Montreal: McGill-Queen's University Press).

53. Malcolm Murfett, *Naval Warfare, 1919–1945: An Operational History of the Volatile War at Sea* (New York: Routledge, 2009).

54. Pound to Admiral Layton, February 9, 1943, BL Add., 74796.

55. Phillips Payson O'Brien, *How the War Was Won: Air-Sea Power and Allied Victory in World War II* (Cambridge: Cambridge University Press, 2015).

56. Hal Friedman, "Blue versus Orange: The United States Naval War College, Japan, and the Old Enemy in the Pacific, 1945–1946," *Journal of Military History* 78 (2014): 231.

57. Nachman Ben-Yehuda, *Atrocity, Deviance, and Submarine Warfare: Norms and Practices during the World Wars* (Ann Arbor: University of Michigan Press, 2013).

58. Angus Mansfield, *"I Wish I Had Your Wings": A Spitfire Pilot and Operation Pedestal, Malta 1942* (Stroud: History Press, 2016), 100.

11. THE SECOND WORLD WAR IN THE AIR

1. Harry Truman, *Year of Decisions, 1945* (London: Hodder and Stoughton, 1955), 352–53.

2. Robert Doughty, *The Breaking Point: Sedan and the Fall of Paris, 1940* (Hamden, CT: Archon, 1990).

3. Robert Doughty, "Winning and Losing: France on the Marne and on the Meuse," in *Arms and the Man: Military History Essays in Honor of Dennis Showalter*, ed. Michael S. Neiberg (Leiden: Brill, 2011), 183–84.

4. Brian Burridge, "Technical Development and Effects Based Operations," *RUSI Journal* 149, no. 5 (October 2004), 27.

5. Richard Overy, *The Battle of Britain* (London: Penguin, 2000), 116–17.

6. Gavin Bailey, "The Narrow Margin of Criticality: The Question of the Supply of 100-Octane Fuel in the Battle of Britain," *English Historical Review* 123 (2008): 351–78.

7. Anthony J. Cumming, *The Royal Navy and the Battle of Britain* (Annapolis, MD: Naval Institute Press, 2010).

8. Garry Campion, *The Good Fight: Battle of Britain Propaganda and the Few* (Basingstoke: Palgrave Macmillan, 2009).

9. War Cabinet, Chiefs of Staff Committee, Weekly Résumé, no. 56, Churchill Papers, Churchill College, Cambridge.

10. Helen Jones, *British Civilians in the Front Line: Air Raids, Productivity and Wartime Culture, 1939–1945* (Manchester: Manchester University Press, 2006); Susan R. Grayzel, *At Home and Under Fire: Air Raids and the Culture in Britain from the Great War to the Blitz* (Cambridge: Cambridge University Press, 2012).

11. Rolf-Dieter Müller, *Enemy in the East: Hitler's Secret Plans to Invade the Soviet Union* (London: I. B. Tauris, 2015), 232–33.

12. The YAKs did not enter service in ascending model number.

13. Andrew Brookes, *Air War over Russia* (Hersham, Surrey: Ian Allan, 2003).

14. Joel Hayward, *Stopped at Stalingrad: The Luftwaffe and Hitler's Defeat in the East, 1942–1943* (Lawrence: University Press of Kansas, 1998).

15. Blamey to Curtin, September 27, 1941, AWM, 3DRL/6643, 1/2.

16. Jonathan Fennell, "Air Power and Morale in the North African Campaign of the Second World War," *Air Power Review* 15, no. 2 (Summer 2012): 1–15.

17. Strategic review for regional commanders, August 16, 1941, AWM, 3DRL/6643, 1/27.

18. Von Hardesty and Ilya Grinberg, *Red Phoenix Rising: The Soviet Air Force in World War II* (Lawrence: University Press of Kansas, 2012).

19. Robert Ehlers, *The Mediterranean Air War: Airpower and Allied Victory in World War II* (Lawrence: University of Kansas Press, 2015).

20. Anthony Rogers, *Churchill's Folly: Leros and the Aegean—The Last Great British Defeat of World War Two* (London: Weidenfeld and Nicholson, 2003).

21. Report by General Thomas Blamey, commander in chief of the Australian army, July 1943, and report by General Stanley Savige, AWM, 3DRL/6643, 3/10, p. 12.

22. Phillips Payson O'Brien, *How the War Was Won: Air-Sea Power and Allied Victory in World War II* (Cambridge: Cambridge University Press, 2015), 484.

23. With a striking account of air combat in June–July 1943, J. Steinhoff, *Messerschmitts over Sicily: A Luftwaffe Ace Fighting the Allies and Göring* (Barnsley: Pen and Sword, 2004).

24. Claudia Baldoli and Marco Fincardi, "Italian Society under Anglo-American Bombs: Propaganda, Experience, and Legend, 1940–1945," *Historical Journal* 52 (2009): 1022–25.

25. Baldoli and Fincardi, "Italian Society under Anglo-American Bombs," 1026–28.

26. James Sterrett, *Soviet Air Force Theory, 1918–1945* (Abingdon: Routledge, 2009); Joel Hayward, "Air Power: The Quest to Remove Battle from War," in *The Ashgate Research Companion to Modern Warfare*, ed. George Kassimeris and John Buckley (Farnham: Ashgate, 2010), 58.

27. Alexander to Brooke, January 26, 1944, LH, Alanbrooke papers, 6/2/19.

28. Milan Vego, "The Allied Landing at Anzio-Nettuno," *Naval War College Review* 67 (2014): 114–15, 129–30.

29. Richard Overy, *The Air War, 1939–1945* (London: Europa, 1980); Stephen McFarland and Wesley Newton, *To Command the Sky: The Battle for Air Superiority, 1942–4* (Washington, DC: Smithsonian Institution Press, 1991); Horst Boog, ed., *The Conduct of the Air War in the Second World War: An International Comparison* (Oxford: Berg, 1992); Eric Hammel, *The Road to Big Week: The Struggle for Daylight Air Supremacy over Western Europe: July 1942–February 1944* (Pacifica, CA: Pacifica, 2009).

30. Ian Gooderson, *Air Power at the Battlefront: Allied Close Air Support in Europe, 1943–1945* (London: Routledge 1998); Michael Bechtold, "'The Development of an Unbeatable Combination': U.S. Close Air Support in Normandy," *Canadian Military History* 8 (1999): 7–20.

31. David I. Hall, "From Khaki and Light Blue to Purple: The Long and Troubled Development of Army/Air Co-operation in Britain, 1914–1945," *RUSI Journal* 147, no. 5 (October 2002): 82, and "The Birth of the Tactical Air Force: British Theory and Practice of Air Support in the West, 1939–1943" (PhD diss., Oxford, 1996), esp. 165, 177, 287.

32. Romedio Thun-Hohenstein, "Response to 'How Effective Were Tank-Busting Aircraft in the Second World War?,'" *RUSI Journal* 154, no. 1 (February 2009): 92–93.

33. Montgomery, "Some Notes on the Use of Air Power in Support of Land Operations and Direct Air Support," December 1944, LH, Alanbrooke papers, 6/2/35, pp. 1, 5, 9, 29; John Buckley, *Monty's Men: The British Army and the Liberation of Europe, 1944–5* (New Haven, CT: Yale University Press, 2013).

34. Antony Beevor, *Ardennes 1944: Hitler's Last Gamble* (London: Viking, 2015).

35. Richard Overy, "Identity, Politics and Technology in the RAF's History," *RUSI Journal* 153, no. 6 (December 2008): 77.

36. Ralf Blank, "The Battle of the Ruhr, 1943: Aerial Warfare against an Industrial Region," *Labour History Review* 77 (2012): 45.

37. Tracy Dungan, *V-2: A Combat History of the First Ballistic Missile* (Yardley, PA: Westholme Publishers, 2005). For the role of the rockets in driving Anglo-American leaders to increase the scale of their strategic bombing campaign, Tami Davis Biddle, "On the Crest of

Fear: V-Weapons, the Battle of the Bulge, and the Last Stages of World War II in Europe," *Journal of Military History* 83 (2019): 157–94.

38. Sebastian Ritchie, *Industry and Air Power: The Expansion of British Aircraft Production, 1935–1941* (London: Routledge, 1997).

39. Stephen McFarland, "The Evolution of the American Strategic Fighter in Europe, 1942–44," *Journal of Strategic Studies* 10 (1987): 189–208.

40. David Stubbs, "A Blind Spot? The Royal Air Force (RAF) and Long-Range Fighters, 1936–1944," *Journal of Military History* 78 (2014): 673–702.

41. Gian Gentile, "General Arnold and the Historians," *Journal of Military History* 64 (2000), 179.

42. Ronald Schaffer, *Wings of Judgment: American Bombing in World War II* (Oxford: Oxford University Press, 1985); Stephen Garrett, *Ethics and Airpower in World War Two* (New York: Palgrave Macmillan, 1993).

43. Neil Gregor, "A *Schicksalsgemeinschaft*? Allied Bombing, Civilian Morale, and Social Dissolution in Nuremberg, 1942–1945," *Historical Journal* 43 (2000): 1051–70.

44. Alfred Mierzejewski, *The Collapse of the German War Economy, 1944–1945* (Chapel Hill: University of North Carolina Press, 1998).

45. For this approach, see Jeremy Black, *Other Pasts, Different Presents, Alternative Futures* (Bloomington: Indiana University Press, 2015).

46. The best general account of the subject is Richard Overy, *The Bombers and the Bombed: Allied Air War over Europe, 1940–1945* (New York: Viking, 2014), and, for a longer text, notably on the war in Eastern Europe, the English edition (London: Penguin, 2014).

47. Philip Sabin, "Why the Allies Won the Air War, 1939–45," in *Rethinking History, Dictatorship and War*, ed. Claus-Christian W. Szejnmann (London: Continuum, 2009), 158.

48. Mike Pavelec, *The Jet Race and the Second World War* (Westport, CT: Naval Institute Press, 2007).

49. Kenneth Werrell, *Blankets of Fire: U.S. Bombers over Japan during World War II* (Washington, DC: Smithsonian Institution Press, 1996); Herman Wolk, *Cataclysm: General Hap Arnold and the Defeat of Japan* (Denton: University of North Texas Press, 2010).

50. Michael Neiberg, *Potsdam: The End of World War II and the Remaking of Europe* (New York: Basic Books, 2015), 239–46; David McCullough, *Truman* (New York: Simon and Schuster, 1992), 458.

51. Sado Asada, "The Shock of the Atomic Bomb and Japan's Decision to Surrender—A Reconsideration," *Pacific Historical Review* 67 (November 1995): 99–115.

52. John Plating, *The Hump: America's Strategy for Keeping China in World War II* (College Station: Texas A&M Press, 2011).

53. Taylor Downing, *Spies in the Sky: The Secret Battle for Aerial Intelligence during World War II* (London: Little, Brown, 2011).

54. Donald Hanle, *Near Miss: The Army Air Forces' Guided Bomb Program in World War II* (Lanham, MD: Scarecrow Press, 2007).

55. Judith Barger, *Beyond the Call of Duty: Army Flight Nursing in World War II* (Kent, OH: Kent State University Press, 2013).

56. David Edgerton, "Brains at War: Invention and Experts," in *The Oxford Illustrated History of World War II*, ed. Richard Overy (Oxford: Oxford University Press, 2015), 358–60.

57. Robert Johnson, "The Army in India and Responses to Low-Intensity Conflict, 1936–1946," *Journal of the Society for Army Historical Research* 89 (2011): 174.

58. Blamey to Minister for Army, September 1, 1941, AWM, 3DRL/6643, 1/2.

59. Arnold Harvey, "The Bomber Offensive That Never Took Off: Italy's Regia Aeronautica in 1940," *RUSI Journal* 154, no. 6 (December 2009): 99–100.

CONCLUSIONS

1. Catherine Merridale, *Ivan's War: The Red Army, 1939–1945* (London: Faber, 2006).

2. Peter Gatrell, *Russia's First World War: A Social and Economic History* (Harlow: Longman, 2005); M. Stockdale, *Mobilizing the Russian Nation: Patriotism and Citizenship in the First World War* (Cambridge: Cambridge University Press, 2016).

3. Robert Citino, *The Wehrmacht's Last Stand: The German Campaigns of 1944–1945* (Lawrence: University Press of Kansas, 2017).

4. Susan Grayzel and Tammy Proctor, eds., *Gender and the Great War* (Oxford: Oxford University Press, 2017); Patricia Fara, *A Lab of One's Own: Science and Suffrage in the First World War* (Oxford: Oxford University Press, 2018); Denise Kiernan, *The Girls of Atomic City: The Untold Story of the Women Who Helped Win World War II* (New York: Simon and Schuster, 2013).

5. Edward Bujak, *English Landed Society in the Great War: Defending the Realm* (London, Bloomsbury, 2019).

6. Reginald Bacon, J. F. C. Fuller, and Patrick Playfair, *Warfare Today* (London: Odhams, 1944), 21.

7. Hilda Kean, *The Great Cat and Dog Massacre: The Real Story of World War Two's Unknown Tragedy* (Chicago: University of Chicago Press, 2017).

8. Sarah G. Forgey, ed., *The Great War: U.S. Army Art* (Washington, DC: US Army Center of Military History, 2018).

9. Julian Lewis, *Changing Direction: British Military Planning for Post-War Strategic Defence, 1942–47*, 2nd ed. (London: Frank Cass, 2001).

10. Hew Strachan, "The War to End All Wars?," *Foreign Affairs* 82 (2003): 155.

Index

Admiralty memorandum, 121
aerial reconnaissance: antiaircraft guns against, 82; against artillery, 86; Britain leading in, 74–75; against trench systems, 30; value of, 90
Africa, 91. *See also* North Africa; *specific countries*
air bases, 301
airborne troops: Germany using, 195–196; in Mediterranean, 281; in Normandy invasion, 207, 208; rising interest in, 146
aircraft: Allies production of, 283–284; antiaircraft guns for, 82, 89, 295; arming of, 82; CC gear for, 84–85; Douhet on potential of, 142; German production of, 286; ideology regarding, 144; Luftwaffe lacking, 277–278; mass production of, 90; submarines over, 76; Turkey using, 83; United States upgrading, 282. *See also specific aircraft*
aircraft carriers: Battle of Midway regarding, 245–247; battleships compared to, 119, 130; improvements in, 127, 128–129; lack of interest for, 129
air power/warfare: in Africa, 91; air base locations crucial to, 301; Allies ground-support, 287–290; atomic bomb, 275–299; in Battle of Britain, 273–274; at Battle of the Somme, 83–84; at Battle of Verdun, 83; battleships resistance to, 120; Blitz conflict, 275–277; blitzkrieg attacks, 270–273; Britain increasing, 152–153; for deterrence, 108; on Eastern Front, 281; in Europe 1942, 278–281; in First World War 1914, 79–80; in First World War 1915, 81–83; in First World War 1916, 83–84; in First World War 1917, 84–86; in First World War 1918, 86–89; flexibility with, 79; against France, 272; German offensives, 277–278; on Germany in 1943, 283–287; on Germany in 1944, 291–297; against Greece, 277; hope and expectations of, 156; in insurrectionary warfare, 141; international concerns regarding, 140; Japan fall by, 297–298; jet fighters and, 296–297; land warfare compared to, 91; limitations of, 90–91; in Mediterranean, 281–282; Nazi regime propaganda, 147; in Netherlands, 271–272; in Pacific War, 282–283; poison gas and, 139; against Poland, 270–271; radar for defense of, 154; rocket attacks, 290–291; Second World War range of, 300; Spanish Civil War and, 149–150; technology changing, 270, 300; unification of air command for, 302; Winter War and,

337

271. *See also* Luftwaffe; naval air power/warfare; Royal Air Force; strategic bombing
air power/warfare, interwar period: debates on, 142–144; in Far East, 155–156; of Germany, 146–149; innovations of 1930s, 144–146, 154; planning for, 140–141, 154–155
airships: vulnerability of, 144; zeppelin, 80, 81
air travel, 141
El Alamein battle, 201, 224–225
Albania, 193–194
alliances: deterrence and, 108–109; of Germany in Second World War, 178–179; against Hitler, 170; of Hitler and Mussolini, 174–175; interwar period, 102; Jiang Jieshi on, 180; naval, 62; world wars impacted by, 22, 186, 310
Allied Maritime Transport Council, 71
Allies: aircraft production of, 283–284; air power/warfare on Germany in 1944, 291–297; air power/warfare success on Western Front, 87–88; artillery dominance of, 219; cooperation among, 307; on Germany, advance of, 212; ground-support air attacks, 287–290; Italy bombed by, 287; Italy invaded by, 204–205; keys to success of, 265–266; Mediterranean controlled by, 260; naval power/warfare success of, 59–60; Normandy invaded by, 205–209; oil production bombed by, 292; oil production dominated by, 200; resource superiority of, 222–223; shipping strategies of, 254–255, 256; strategic enhancement of, 35; superiority over Luftwaffe, 206; trade protection convoy by, 70–72; trench systems overcome by, 30; on unconditional surrender, 308; underestimation of opponents, 189; United States industrial contribution to, 39–40, 64; Western Front campaign of, 50–51. *See also specific countries*
American Civil War (1861-1865), 2, 22
American Naval War College, 115, 266
American navy: amphibious operations of, 249–250; Guadalcanal success for, 247–248; Iowa-class battleships of, 240–241; Japanese navy compared to, 257; Japanese navy threat to, 122, 124–125; Japanese trade attacked by, 250–251; kamikaze attacks against, 213, 262–263; large-scale movements of, 123–124; naval power/warfare superiority of, 248–249; war games, 124
amphibious operations: of American navy, 249–250; in Europe, 259–261; First World War lacking, 75–76; against Japan, 264; by Japan, 137
Anglo-German Naval Treaty (1935), 132
antiaircraft guns: against aerial reconnaissance, 82; Germany producing, 295; improvement in 1918, 89
antisubmarine warfare: in Battle of the Atlantic, 254; mine laying for, 72–73; United States using, 71
appeasement: as call for action, 164; Chamberlain issues regarding, 165; expansionism response as, 169; Second World War and, 163–168
armistice: First World War ending with, 51; regarding Vichy France, 193
armored warfare: of Britain, 216–217; mechanization, 109
arms race: of interwar period, 111–112; of Second World War, 167
artillery: aerial reconnaissance against, 86; Allies dominance in, 219; Britain improving, 50; lethality of, 40–41; modernization of, 86–87
the Atlantic: Battle of, 205, 253–256; St. Nazaire attack in, 252; Second World War struggle for, 236–237; shipping targeted in, 237–239; United States expansion in, 239
Atlantic trading system, 63–64
Atlantic Wall fortifications, 288–289
atomic bombs: mobilization regarding, 311; Second World War and, 299–300; Truman speech regarding, 269
Australia: Japan isolating, 245; naval air power/warfare of, 75; trench warfare perspectives of, 45

Austria: Germany relations with, 9–10, 11; Italy declaring war on, 25; nationalism rising in, 11; Serbia relations with, 16–17

Axis powers: failure to confront prewar, 163; intelligence war lost by, 308; lack of civilian support, 306; North Africa retreat of, 259; oil war against, 301–302; in Second World War 1942, 200–202; strategic failures of, 305. *See also* Germany; Italy; Japan; Nazi regime

B-17 bombers, 284–285
B-29 bombers, 297–298
Balkans: anxiety regarding, 9; Mussolini ambitions toward, 176; Soviet Union advancing into, 211
Balkan Wars, 7, 11, 21
Baltic: Royal Navy views on, 62–63; Russia emphasis on, 62
banditry, 102
Battle of Arras, 45–46
Battle of Britain, 273–274
Battle of Cambrai, 52, 85
Battle of Dogger Bank, 61–62
Battle of Heligoland Bight, 60–61
Battle of Jutland, 66–68
Battle of Kursk, 202–203
Battle of Leyte Gulf, 259
Battle of Loos, 36
Battle of Midway, 245–247
Battle of Passchendaele: horrors of, 41; strategic consequences of, 45
Battle of Tassafaronga, 248
Battle of the Atlantic: antisubmarine warfare in, 254; Normandy preparations from, 205; in Second World War, 253–256
Battle of the Barents, 253, 254
Battle of the Bulge: Ardennes offensive in, 214; Operation Bodenplatte in, 296–297
Battle of the Coral Sea, 245
Battle of the Ebro, 149
Battle of the Java Sea, 243–244
Battle of the Kasserine Pass, 204
Battle of the Marne, 33–34
Battle of the Philippine Sea, 258

Battle of the Somme: air power/warfare at, 83–84; Battle of Verdun in relation to, 38

Battle of Verdun: air power/warfare at, 83; Battle of the Somme in relation to, 38; defensive positions and, 38; strategy for, 37–38

battleships: air power/warfare resistance of, 120; Bismarck, 236–237; carriers compared to, 119, 130; Deutschland class, 132; emphasis on, 118–119; firepower of, 119–120; Hitler's fascination with, 132–133; Iowa-class, 240–241; Second World War effectiveness of, 121; Washington Naval Treaty and, 115–116

Beatty, David, 62, 66
Belarus, 225, 287
Belgium: air power/warfare in, 269; fortifications, 32–33; Germany invading, 19–20, 190; neutrality violation, 14–15, 18
bellicosity: encouragement of, 9–10; of Japan, 160
Bismarck, Otto von: France relations with, 10; Wilhelm II compared to, 10–11
Bismarck battleships, 236–237
Black Hand, 16
Blitz conflict, 275–277
blitzkrieg attacks: air power/warfare, 270–273; as Blitz conflict, 275–277; exaggeration of, 191–192; strategic bombing by, 148
Bolsheviks ideology, 98
bombers: B-17, 284–285; B-29, 297–298; Cologne attacked by, 280; Combined Bomber Offensive, 283; Geneva Disarmament Conference (1932-1934) discussing, 153; improvement of, 143; RAF innovation of, 145; Soviet Union innovation of, 146; torpedo, 130; United States developing long-range, 144–145. *See also* strategic bombing
Brazil: air bases in, 301; First World War entrance of, 27; Second World War entrance of, 185
Britain: aerial reconnaissance led by, 74–75; air power/warfare increase of, 152–153; armored warfare of, 216–217;

artillery improvements of, 50; Atlantic trading system and, 63–64; Battle of, 273–274; Blitz conflict against, 275–277; in Burma conflict, 213–214; Combined Bomber Offensive and, 283; Dominions of, 168; economic warfare by, 58; in Ethiopia, 194; France relations with, 20; German morale attacked by, 279–280; German naval ambition concerns of, 14–15; Germany bombed by, 284–285; Gotha aircraft attacking, 85–86; infiltration tactics developed by, 48–49; IRA at war with, 104–105; Luftwaffe concerns of, 151–152; naval power/warfare during interwar period, 133–134; Nazi regime negotiations from, 167–168; Nazi regime security threat to, 164–165; North Sea controlled by, 58; Operation Sealion for invading, 231–232, 273; signals intelligence used by, 67–68; trade reliance of, 59; Turkey fighting against, 47–48; Washington Naval Treaty impacting, 114–115; Wilhelm II hostility toward, 9; zeppelin airship attacking, 81. *See also* Royal Air Force; Royal Navy

British Committee of Imperial Defence, 20, 81

British Royal Aircraft Factory, 80

Bulgaria: First World War entrance of, 25; Germany abandoned by, 296

Bureau of Aeronautics, U.S. Navy, 120, 130

Burma, 213–214

carriers. *See* aircraft carriers
Casablanca Conference, 283
CC gear, 84–85
Chamberlain, Neville, 165
Champagne offensive, 82–83
chemical weapons, 41
China: First World War entrance of, 27; during interwar period, 106–108; Japan invading, 107–108, 160–162; Jiang Jieshi strengthening nationalism of, 162; in Sino-Japanese War, 156
Churchill, Winston, 62–63; on Indian Ocean vulnerability, 126; on unconditional surrender, 308; on Vichy France, 174

civil wars/warfare: American Civil War, 2, 22; First World War and, 31; Russian Civil War, 98, 99; Spanish Civil War, 149–150, 162–163

COIN. *See* counterinsurgency

Cold War, 97; naval power/warfare and, 266; world wars in relation to, 312, 313

Cologne bombing, 280

combined-arms tactics: mobilization for, 54–55; tanks for, 53

Combined Bomber Offensive, 283

communism: Hitler clash with, 177; ideology, 96–97; Stalin advancing, 189–190

counterinsurgency (COIN), 99, 141

cruisers: London Naval Conference (1930) regarding, 118; Madden on, 117

Dardanelles, 63
Darwinian theory, 8
defensive positions: Battle of Verdun and, 38; danger of advancing against, 36; fortifications for, 42–44; naval power/warfare and, 77; Russian Civil War vulnerability of, 99
degeneration, 8
democracy: Hitler contempt for, 167; Roosevelt on arsenal of, 221; Spanish Civil War and, 162; Stalin opposition to, 170
Depression, 163
deterrence, 108–109
Deutschland class battleships, 132
Dimmer, John, 34
Dönitz, Karl, 133
Dorman-Smith, Eric, 216
Douhet, Giulio, 142
Douhet theory, 293
dreadnoughts, 74

Eastern Front: air power/warfare on, 281; Battle of Kursk on, 202–203; First World War and, 46; naval power/warfare regarding, 240; Second World War and, 202–203; Western Front compared to, 38–39 economic warfare: Casablanca Conference regarding, 283; against Germany, 58

Ethiopia: Britain in, 194; Italy invading, 131

Europe: air power/warfare in 1942, 278–281; amphibious operations in, 259–261; interwar period naval power/warfare challenges in, 130–133; jet fighters in, 296–297; Second World War beginning in, 169–173. *See also specific countries*

expansionism: appeasement response to, 169; rise of, 8–9; of Soviet Union, 176–177

Falkenhayn, Erick von, 37, 38
Far East, 155–156
Fashoda Crisis (1898), 10
fighters: jet, 296–297; long-range, 291–292; Me-262, 297
Finland, 190, 197, 271
First World War: aerial reconnaissance value in, 90; air power/warfare in 1914, 79–80; air power/warfare in 1915, 81–83; air power/warfare in 1916, 83–84; air power/warfare in 1917, 84–86; air power/warfare in 1918, 86–89; amphibious operations lacking in, 75–76; armistice ending, 51; Brazil entering, 27; Bulgaria entering, 25; casualties of, 42; China entering, 27; civil warfare and, 31; complexity of, 30; conflicts immediately following, 96; Eastern Front and, 46; face of battle in, 40–42; fortifications role in, 42–44; German declaration of war, 19; German policy pushing for, 13; German strategic mistakes in, 22, 31–32; Italy entering, 25; Italy role in, 47; key element leading to, 18; maps used in, 54; Middle East role in, 47–48; mobilization of resources for, 54–55; national pride contributing to, 21; naval air power/warfare development in, 74–75; naval power/warfare in 1914, 57–61; naval power/warfare in 1915, 61–63; naval power/warfare in 1916, 66–68; naval power/warfare in 1917, 68–73; naval power/warfare in 1918, 73–74; peoples' wars development and, 100; poison gas used in, 41; Romania entering, 25; strategies used in, 31–35; submarine warfare and, 63–66; tank development in, 52–53; trench warfare in, 44–46; trench warfare myths of, 29; United States entering, 26–27; wars preceding, 7, 23–24; Western Front and, 35–40; Western Front in 1917-18, 48–52. *See also specific battles*

Fischer, Fritz, 1–2
"Flying Men: The Chivalry of the Air," 79
Foch, Ferdinand: leadership of, 51; on poison gas, 139
fog of war, 32
Fokker Eindecker aircraft, 82, 83
force structures, 117–121
fortifications: Atlantic Wall, 288–289; Belgium, 32–33; First World War role of, 42–44; interwar period strengthening of, 109–111; Maginot Line, 109–110, 190–191; of Poland, 110–111; trench systems as, 42–43
France: air power/warfare against, 272; army spending increase of, 15; Battle of the Marne in, 33–34; Bismarck relations with, 10; Britain relations with, 20; defeat probability of, 13; German conquest of, 173–174, 192; Germany declaring war on, 19; infiltration tactics developed by, 48–49; Maginot Line of, 109–110, 190–191; naval power/warfare during interwar period, 134–135; naval power/warfare of Second World War in, 231; regarding North Africa, 193; Royal Navy help from, 60; strategic bombing views of, 150–151; Vichy, 174, 193, 232

Franco-Prussian War (1870-1871), 31
Fuller, J. F. C., 53, 191, 293

Gallipoli campaign, 47
Geneva Disarmament Conference (1932-1934), 153
Geneva Naval Conference (1927), 118
Germany: aircraft production of, 286; air power/warfare during interwar period, 146–149; air power/warfare in 1943 on,

283–287; air power/warfare in 1944 on, 291–297; air power/warfare offensives of, 277–278; alliances in Second World War, 178–179; Allies advance on, 212; Allies bombing oil production of, 292; antiaircraft gun production of, 295; Atlantic Wall fortifications of, 288–289; Austria relations with, 9–10, 11; in Battle of Dogger Bank, 61–62; in Battle of Heligoland Bight, 60–61; in Battle of Jutland, 66–68; Battle of Kursk defeat of, 202–203; Battle of the Marne defeat of, 33–34; Belgium fortifications captured by, 32–33; Belgium invaded by, 19–20, 190; Bismarck battleship of, 236–237; blitzkrieg attacks by, 148, 191–192, 270–273, 275–277; Bulgaria abandoning, 296; Eastern Front success of, 46; economic warfare against, 58; encirclement paranoia of, 15, 17; First World War entrance of, 19; France conquered by, 173–174, 192; Greece attacked by, 195–196, 234; infiltration tactics against, 50; Italy declaring war on, 25; Japan relations with, 180; Latin America policy of, 185; Mexico connections with, 27; militarism for unified, 10; mobilization of, 17–18; morale attack on, 279–280; naval power/warfare ambitions of, 14–15; naval power/warfare with, 252–253, 261–262; North Africa trouble for, 279; Norway invaded by, 173, 189; Norway significance to, 252–253; occupation policy of, 306–307; over-ambitiousness in world wars, 14; Peace of Versailles impacting, 113–114; Phony War and, 217; policy pushing for war, 13; radar warning systems of, 285; reconnaissance photography used by, 54; remilitarization of Rhineland, 166–167; rocket attacks by, 290–291; Romania relations with, 179; Russia concerns of, 11–12, 13; shipping targeted by, 65–66, 70, 237–239; Soviet Union deep operations against, 210; Soviet Union invaded by, 177–178, 196–199; Spanish Civil War and, 149–150; storm-trooper techniques of, 48; strategic mistakes of, 22, 31–32; submarine warfare used by, 26; underestimation of opponents, 20–21; United States at war with, 184–186; Western Front failure of, 303–304; Western Front strategy of, 48; Yugoslavia invaded by, 173, 195

Gibbs, Philip, 36, 303
Gilbert Islands, 249
Gotha aircraft, 85–86
Greece: air power/warfare against, 277; Germany attacking, 195–196, 234; Italy attacking, 193–194
Greek-Turkish War, 102–103
ground-support air attacks, 287–290
Guadalcanal, 247–248
guerrilla warfare, 99

Hart, Basil Liddell, 95
Hindenburg Line, 39, 43
Hitler, Adolf: alliances against, 170; battleship fascination of, 132–133; on communism, 177; contempt for democracy, 167; declaration of war by, 184; empire building of, 169; on Jews, 177, 178; Munich Agreement broken by, 169; Mussolini ally of, 174–175; naval power/warfare ignorance of, 252; oil fields pursued by, 223; Peace of Versailles revenge by, 147; Poland invaded by, 171–172, 188–189; racial ideology of, 163–164; Stalingrad defeat of, 200, 201; strategic failures of, 305; suicide, 215
Holocaust, 311
Hötzendorf, Franz Conrad von, 16–17
Howard, Michael, 1
Hungary, 178–179

ideology: regarding aircraft capabilities, 144; Bolsheviks, 98; communism, 96–97; Hitler's racial, 163–164; of insurrectionary warfare, 100; of masculinity, 8; nationalism and, 101; of total war, 26
Indian Ocean: Churchill on vulnerability of, 126; Japanese success in, 244
industrialization, warfare, 22–23

industrial mobilization, 2
infantry: mobility as theme for, 95; motorization of United States, 220–221
infantry tactics: evolution of, 44; against Japan, 222
infiltration tactics: Britain and France developing, 48–49; against Germany, 50; against Italy, 47; storm-trooper techniques as, 48
insurrectionary warfare: air power/warfare in, 141; ideology of, 100; in Latin America, 101–102
intelligence: Axis powers losing war on, 308; Pearl Harbor deficiency in, 241; signals, 67–68; against submarine warfare, 72
interwar period: alliances, 102; armored warfare mechanization in, 109; arms race of, 111–112; banditry fought in, 102; China during, 106–108; definition of, 95–96; deterrence and, 108–109; fortification strengthening in, 109–111; guerrilla warfare during, 99; Ireland during, 104–105; mechanization from, 95; Middle East volatility during, 97; nationalism rising in, 104; naval air power/warfare improvements during, 127–130; the Pacific planning in, 121–127; peacemaker failure during, 99–100; Peace of Versailles influencing, 96; Spanish Civil War during, 149–150; strategic bombing issues of, 150–154; technology shifts in, 113
interwar period air power/warfare: debates on, 142–144; in Far East, 155–156; of Germany, 146–149; innovations of 1930s, 144–146, 154; planning in, 140–141, 154–155
interwar period naval power/warfare: of Britain, 133–134; Europe challenges with, 130–133; force structures of, 117–121; of France, 134–135; limitations of, 113–116; in 1930s, 137; in the Pacific, planning for, 121–127; of Soviet Union, 135–137
Iowa-class battleships, 240–241
IRA. *See* Irish Republican Army
Ireland, 104–105

Irish Republican Army (IRA), 104–105
Ismay, Hastings, 264
isolationism, 165–166
Italy: Allies bombing of, 287; Allies invading, 204–205; Anzio, attack on, 288; Ethiopia invaded by, 131; First World War entrance of, 25; First World War role of, 47; Greece attacked by, 193–194; Libya challenges for, 194–195; Mediterranean defeat of, 232–234; Second World War entrance of, 174–176; Spanish Civil War and, 149–150; Treaty of London and, 24–25

Japan: amphibious operations against, 264; amphibious operations by, 137; atomic bombs used on, 275–299; Australia isolated by, 245; bellicosity of, 160; in Burma conflict, 213–214; China invaded by, 107–108, 160–162; economic weaknesses of, 180; German relations with, 180; Indian Ocean success of, 244; infantry tactics against, 222; Jiang Jieshi accommodating, 161; kamikaze attacks from, 213, 262–263; land warfare of, 199; League of Nations left by, 160; Malaya invaded by, 199, 243; naval power/warfare collapse of, 262–264; Pearl Harbor attacked by, 183, 241–242; Philippines invaded by, 242; racial discrimination toward, 182; Russia at war with, 23–24; Second World War advance of, 242–244; Second World War fall of, 297–298; in Sino-Japanese War, 156; Soviet Union declaring war on, 211; submarine warfare against trade of, 250–251; Truman speech to, 269; United States invading, 263–264; United States policy impacting, 181; United States seizing islands of, 213; Washington Naval Treaty impacting, 116, 126–127
Japanese navy: American navy compared to, 257; American navy threat from, 122, 124–125; Guadalcanal defeat for, 247–248; Marusan Program of, 126; naval aviation development of, 127–128; Operation Sho-Go, 259; Royal Navy threat from, 121–122,

125–126; torpedo launching improvements of, 127
Jellicoe, John, 66–67, 68
jet fighters, 296–297
Jews: Hitler on, 177, 178; Holocaust of, 311; Nazi regime blaming, 164
Jiang Jieshi: on alliances, 180; Chinese nationalism strengthened by, 162; Guomindang under, 107; Japan accommodated by, 161

kamikaze attacks, 213, 262–263

land warfare: air power/warfare compared to, 91; changes in, 225; German doctrine based on, 197; of Japan, 199; tanks for, 52–53, 53, 202–203, 218; world wars dominated by, 187–188. *See also* trench warfare
Latin America: German policy on, 185; insurrectionary warfare in, 101–102; Second World War entrance of, 185–186
League of Nations: Ethiopia invasion condemned by, 131; Geneva Disarmament Conference (1932-1934) and, 153; Japan leaving, 160
Lenin, 46, 104
Liberty ships, 265
Libya, 194–195
London Naval Conference (1930): regarding cruisers, 118; preparations for, 117
long-range fighters, 291–292
long war concept, 313–314
Luftwaffe: aircraft production lacking for, 277–278; Allies superiority over, 206; Battle of Britain defeat of, 273–274; Britain concerns over, 151–152; creation of, 147; long-range fighters against, 291–292; Me-262 fighter of, 297; Operation Bodenplatte of, 296–297; Royal Navy threat from, 231–232; in Stalingrad, 279; strategic bombing deficiency of, 148

Madden, Charles, 117
Maginot Line (France): failure of, 190–191; strength of, 109–110

Malaya, 199, 243
Malta: RAF and vulnerability of, 155; strategic importance of, 234–235
maps, 54
Mariana Islands, 258
Marusan Program, of shipbuilding, 126
masculinity ideology, 8
Me-262 fighter, 297
mechanization: armored warfare, 109; from interwar period, 95; lack of, 107; modernization in relation to, 52; results of, 224
Mediterranean: air power/warfare in, 281–282; Allies control in, 260; Mussolini focusing on, 130–131, 175; naval power/warfare in, 232–235; Second World War in wider, 193–196
meteorology, 50
Mexico: German connections with, 27; Second World War entrance of, 253
Middle East: First World War role of, 47–48; Soviet Union threat to, 140; volatility in, 97
militarism: for German unity, 10; against modernization, 9
military styles, 215–218
Milne, George, 153
mine laying, 72–73
Mitchell, Billy: battleship tests by, 120; on strategic bombing, 142
mobility: as infantry theme, 95; in Second World War, 220–222
mobilization: regarding atomic bombs, 311; for combined-arms tactics, 54–55; of Germany, 17–18; submarine warfare toward, 73; trade in relation to, 63–64
modernization: of artillery, 86–87; mechanization in relation to, 52; threat of, 9
Moltke, Helmuth von: anxiety of, 12, 13; strategic offensive skepticism of, 23
Monash, John, 45, 91
Montgomery, Bernard, 216, 222–223, 223, 289–290
morale: Blitz conflict impacting, 275, 276; controversy regarding civilian, 294; of Germany, attack on, 279–280; importance of, 51–52
Munich Agreement, 169

Mussolini, Benito: Balkan ambitions of, 176; declaration of war by, 184; First World War support from, 25; Hitler ally of, 174–175; Mediterranean as focus of, 130–131, 175; naval power/warfare expansion by, 130–131, 131; overthrow of, 204

nationalism: Austria rise in, 11; ideology and, 101; interwar period rise in, 104; Jiang Jieshi strengthening Chinese, 162
naval air power/warfare: of Australia, 75; in Battle of Midway, 245–247; First World War development of, 74–75; interwar period improvements in, 127–130
naval alliance, 62
naval power/warfare: Allies success with, 59–60; American navy superiority in, 248–249; in Battle of the Atlantic, 253–256; Cold War and, 266; defensive positions and, 77; regarding Eastern Front, 240; in First World War 1914, 57–61; in First World War 1915, 61–63; in First World War 1916, 66–68; in First World War 1917, 68–73; in First World War 1918, 73–74; German ambitions for, 14–15; with Germany, 252–253, 261–262; in Guadalcanal, 247–248; Hitler ignorance of, 252; importance of, 57; Japan's collapsing, 262–264; in Mediterranean, 232–235; Mussolini expansion of, 130–131, 131; in 1930s, 137; recognition failure of, 138. *See also* American navy; amphibious operations; Japanese navy; Pacific War; Royal Navy; submarine warfare; *specific ship types*
naval power/warfare, interwar period: of Britain, 133–134; Europe challenges with, 130–133; force structures of, 117–121; of France, 134–135; limitations of, 113–116; in the Pacific, planning for, 121–127; of Soviet Union, 135–137
naval power/warfare, Second World War: in France, 231; with Germany, 252–253, 261–262; Japan's collapse of, 262–264; in Mediterranean, 232–235; in Norway, 229–230; politics of, 239; summary of, 227–228
Navy Act (1916), 69
Nazi regime: air power/warfare propaganda of, 147; Britain negotiations with, 167–168; Britain security threat as, 164–165; Deutschland class battleships of, 132; German criticism toward, 284; Jews blamed by, 164; violence as heart of, 169–170; wonder weapons of, 262. *See also* Germany; Hitler, Adolf; Luftwaffe
Netherlands, 271–272
neutrality, 14–15, 18
Normandy: Atlantic Wall fortifications in, 288–289; battle for, 209–210; Battle of the Atlantic preparations for, 205; Operation Neptune in, 260–261; Operation Overlord in, 205–209
North Africa: El Alamein battle in, 201, 224–225; Axis powers retreat from, 259; Battle of the Kasserine Pass in, 204; France fearing for, 193; Germany attacked in, 279; Operation Torch in, 186, 201–202
North Sea: Battle of Dogger Bank in, 61–62; Battle of Heligoland Bight in, 60–61; Britain control of, 58
Norway: German significance of, 252–253; Germany invading, 173, 189; naval power/warfare in, 229–230; shipping protection for, 71

occupation policy, 306–307
oil fields, 223
oil production: Allies bombing German, 292; Allies dominating, 200; of Romania, 287–288
oil tankers, 264
oil war, 301–302
Operation Bagration, 225, 287
Operation Barbarossa, 277–278
Operation Blue, 200
Operation Bodenplatte, 296–297
Operation Cobra, 289
Operation Dragoon, 208–209
Operation Neptune, 260–261
Operation Overlord, 205–209

Operation Sealion, 231–232, 273
Operation Sho-Go, 259
Operation Torch, 186, 201–202
Operation Typhoon, 198
Operation Zitadelle, 202–203

the Pacific: interwar period planning for, 121–127; Pearl Harbor's strategic value in, 122–123; United States losing islands in, 242–243
Pacific War: air power/warfare in, 282–283; Battle of Leyte Gulf, 259; Battle of Midway, 245–247; Battle of the Coral Sea, 245; Battle of the Java Sea, 243–244; Battle of the Philippine Sea, 258; end of, 263–264; in Second World War 1942, 245–247; in Second World War 1943, 248–250; in Second World War 1944, 256–259; Second World War outbreak of, 179–183; submarine warfare in, 250–251
Pact of Steel, 174–175
paramilitary forces, 101
peacemakers, 99–100
Peace of Brest-Litovsk, 46
Peace of Versailles (1919): Deutschland class battleships and, 132; Germany impacted by, 113–114; Hitler's revenge on, 147; interwar period influenced by, 96
Pearl Harbor: Japan attacking, 183, 241–242; the Pacific strategic value of, 122–123
peoples' wars, 100
Philippines: Japan invading, 242; United States invading, 212–213
Phony War, 217
poison gas: Ferdinand on, 139; First World War use of, 41
Poland: air power/warfare against, 270–271; fortifications of, 110–111; Hitler invading, 171–172, 188–189; railway construction in, 12; in Russo-Polish War, 103–104; Second World War in, 188–190; Soviet Union relations with, 170–171
Portugal, 166
Potsdam Declaration, 299
Pound, Dudley, 230, 265–266

proximity fuse, 293

Q-ships, 65

racial ideology, 163–164
radar: for air-defense system, 154; RAF support from, 274; warning systems, 285
Raeder, Erich, 132–133
RAF. *See* Royal Air Force
railways: construction in Poland, 12; strategic bombing of, 294–295
reconnaissance photography, 54
resources: for success, 304–305; superiority of, 222–223; targeting of, 223
rocket attacks, 290–291
Romania: First World War entrance of, 25; German relations with, 179; oil production of, 287–288
Roosevelt, Franklin Delano: on arsenal of democracy, 221; isolationism regarding, 165–166
Royal Air Force (RAF): Battle of Britain victory for, 273–274; bomber innovation by, 145; concerns of, 129; establishment of, 88; Malta vulnerability and, 155
Royal Navy: Baltic views from, 62–63; in Battle of Dogger Bank, 61–62; in Battle of Heligoland Bight, 60–61; in Battle of Jutland, 66–68; France helping, 60; Japanese navy threat to, 121–122, 125–126; Luftwaffe as threat to, 231–232; Norway defeat of, 230; Singapore Strategy of, 121, 125–126; strength of, 57
Russia: Baltic emphasis from, 62; Eastern Front defeat of, 46; Germany concerned with, 11–12, 13; Germany declaring war on, 19; Japan at war with, 23–24; mobilization of, 17; Serbia relations with, 16. *See also* Soviet Union
Russian Civil War: civilian enemies in, 98; defensive position vulnerability in, 99
Russo-Polish War, 103–104

St. Nazaire, 252
Scandinavia, 188–190

Second World War: Allies ground-support air attacks in, 287–290; Allies keys to success in, 265–266; amphibious operations in Europe, 259–261; appeasement and, 163–168; arms race of, 167; the Atlantic in, struggle for, 236–237; atomic bombs and, 299–300; Axis powers in 1942, 200–202; Battle of Britain, 273–274; Battle of the Atlantic in, 253–256; battleship effectiveness during, 121; beginning in Europe, 169–173; Blitz conflict of, 275–277; Brazil entering, 185; close of, 212–215; combatants in 1940, 173–174; Eastern Front and, 202–203; German alliances in, 178–179; German rocket attacks in, 290–291; Germany and United States conflict during, 184–186; Guadalcanal in, 247–248; Italy entering, 174–176; Italy invaded in, 204–205; Japan advancing in, 242–244; Japan and China conflict preceding, 160–162; Japanese land warfare in, 199; Japan in, fall of, 297–298; jet fighters and, 296–297; Latin America entering, 185–186; in Mediterranean area, 193–196; Mexico entering, 253; military styles in, 215–218; mobility in, 220–222; Normandy battle of, 209–210; Normandy Operation Overlord in, 205–209; origins of, 159; Pacific War 1942 in, 245–247; Pacific War 1943 in, 248–250; Pacific War 1944 in, 256–259; Pacific War outbreak in, 179–183; Pearl Harbor attacked in, 183, 241–242; in Poland and Scandinavia, 188–190; resources for success in, 304–305; resource superiority in, 222–223; resource targeting in, 223; Soviet Union expansionism in, 176–177; Soviet Union invaded in, 177–178, 196–199; Soviet Union offensives in, 210–211; Spanish Civil War and, 162–163; submarine warfare in, 237–239; tank developments in, 218; training for, 217–218; Truman speech during, 269; Vichy France established in, 174; weaponry in, 218–220; Western Front collapse in, 190–193. *See also specific battles*

Second World War air power/warfare: blitzkrieg attacks of, 270–273; Eastern Front, 281; in Europe 1942, 278–281; German offensives in, 277–278; on Germany in 1943, 283–287; on Germany in 1944, 291–297; Mediterranean, 281–282; of Pacific War, 282–283; range of, 300; technological change in, 270, 300

Second World War naval power/warfare: in France, 231; with Germany, 252–253, 261–262; Japan's collapse of, 262–264; in Mediterranean, 232–235; in Norway, 229–230; politics of, 239; summary of, 227–228

Serbia: Austria relations with, 16–17; Russia relations with, 16

shipbuilding programs: increase in, 69; Marusan Program, 126; of United States, 184, 264–265

shipping: Allies strategies with, 254–255, 256; for army resupply, 256–257; Germany targeting, 65–66, 70, 237–239; for Norway, protection of, 71; raids on, 236

signals intelligence, 67–68

Singapore Strategy, 121, 125–126

Sino-Japanese War, 156

Solomon Islands, 249

Soviet Union: in Balkans, advance by, 211; Battle of Kursk victory for, 202–203; bomber innovation by, 146; declaration of war on Japan, 211; deep operations of, 210; expansionism in Second World War, 176–177; Germany invading, 177–178, 196–199; Hungary declaring war on, 178–179; Middle East threat from, 140; naval power/warfare during interwar period, 135–137; offensives in Second World War, 210–211; Operation Barbarossa against, 277–278; Poland relations with, 170–171; revolutionary ideas abandoned by, 97; in Russo-Polish War, 103–104; Stalingrad victory for, 200, 201; strategic bombing interests of, 151; in Winter War, 190, 197, 271; Young

School of, 135–136
Spanish Civil War (1936-1939): during interwar period, 149–150; Second World War and, 162–163
Spee, Maximilian Graf von, 59
Stalin, Josef: communism advanced with, 189–190; democracy opposition from, 170; patriotic war of, 306; purges by, 97–98, 135–136
Stalingrad: Hitler defeat at, 200, 201; Luftwaffe in, 279
storm-trooper techniques, 48
strategic bombing: Casablanca Conference regarding, 283; effectiveness of, 293; ethics regarding, 150–153; exaggeration of, 302; France's view on, 150–151; interwar period issues of, 150–154; Luftwaffe deficiency in, 148; Mitchell on, 142; of railways, 294–295; Soviet Union interests in, 151; against zeppelin airships, 80
submarines: over aircraft, 76; antisubmarine warfare for, 71, 72–73, 254; deficiency of, 64, 124; improvement of, 65; stealth capability of, 117
submarine warfare: in Battle of the Atlantic, 253–256; First World War and, 63–66; as future, 76; Germany using, 26; intelligence against, 72; against Japanese trade, 250–251; toward mobilization, 73; in Pacific War, 250–251; prize rules for, 65; in Second World War, 237–239; shipping target of, 65–66, 70, 237–239; Washington Naval Treaty and, 116
surrender, unconditional: Allies emphasis on, 308; atomic bombs and, 299

tanks: for combined-arms tactics, 53; First World War development of, 52–53; Operation Zitadelle using, 202–203; Second World War development of, 218
technology: air power/warfare change in, 270, 300; interwar period shifts in, 113; over strategy, 34–35
torpedo bombers, 130

total war: air power/warfare impacting, 81; ideology of, 26
trade: Allie convoys for protecting, 70–72; Atlantic trading system for, 63–64; Britain reliance on, 59; economic warfare impacting German, 58; mobilization in relation to, 63–64; shipping for, 65–66, 70; submarine warfare against Japanese, 250–251
training: from Phony War, 217; for Second World War, 217–218
Treaty of London, 19, 24–25
trench systems: aerial reconnaissance against, 30; as fortifications, 42–43; Hindenburg Line, 39, 43; maps for, 54
trench warfare: in First World War, 44–46; myths of First World War, 29; tanks impacting, 53; Western Front and, 30
Truman, Harry S.: Potsdam Declaration and, 299; speech to Japan, 269
Turkey: aircraft use by, 83; Britain fighting against, 47–48; Dardanelles controlled by, 63; in Greek-Turkish War, 102–103; Italy declaring war on, 25
Two-Ocean Naval Expansion Act (1940), 181, 240

U-boats. *See* submarine warfare
umbrella wars, 1
United States: aircraft upgrades of, 282; air-to-sea doctrine, 130; Allies industrial contribution from, 39–40, 64; American Civil War, 2, 22; antisubmarine warfare used by, 71; the Atlantic expansion of, 239; Bureau of Aeronautics, 120, 130; Combined Bomber Offensive and, 283; declaration of war by, 185; dreadnoughts, 74; First World War entrance of, 26–27; Germany at war with, 184–186; Germany bombed by, 284–285; infantry motorization of, 220–221; infantry tactics against Japan, 222; isolationism of, 165–166; Japanese islands seized by, 213; Japan invaded by, 263–264; long-range bombers developed by, 144–145; long-range fighters, 291–292; manufacturing capabilities of, 221; oil tankers, 264;

Pacific islands lost by, 242–243; Philippines invaded by, 212–213; policy impacting Japan, 181; rearmament delay of, 166; shipbuilding programs of, 184, 264–265; Vietnam concerns of, 182; weaponry production of, 255; on Western Front, 49–50

United States Navy. *See* American navy

Vichy France: armistice regarding, 193; establishment of, 174; in Mediterranean, 232

Vietnam, 182

warlord era, 106–107

Washington Naval Treaty: battleships and, 115–116; Britain impacted by, 114–115; Japan impacted by, 116, 126–127; submarine warfare and, 116

weaponry: industrial scale of manufacturing, 55; Nazi regime wonder, 262; in Second World War, 218–220; United States production of, 255. *See also specific weapons*

Western Front: Allies campaign on, 50–51; Allies success with air power/warfare, 87–88; Battle of Arras on, 45–46; Battle of Loos on, 36; Eastern Front compared to, 38–39; First World War and, 35–40; German failure on, 303–304; German strategy on, 48; 1917-18 on, 48–52; Second World War collapse of, 190–193; trench warfare and, 30; United States on, 49–50; world war comparisons on, 191–192

Wilhelm II (emperor): ambition of, 18–19; Bismarck compared to, 10–11; hostility toward Britain, 9

Winged Victory (Yeates), 91

Winter War (1939-1940), 190, 197, 271

women: flight nurses, 300; shipbuilding by, 265; world wars impacting, 310

wonder weapons, 262

world wars: aftermath of, 312–313; alliances impacting, 22, 186, 310; common narrative between, 1–2; German over-ambitiousness in, 14; impacts of, 309–312; land warfare dominance in, 187–188; reasons for victory in, 303–309; as umbrella wars, 1; Western Front comparisons in, 191–192. *See also* First World War; Second World War

Yamamoto Isoroku, 183, 245

Yeates, Victor Maslin, 91

Young School, 135–136

Yugoslavia: air power/warfare against, 277; Germany invading, 173, 195; nationalist coup in, 176

zeppelin airships: Britain attacked by, 81; strategic bombing against, 80; vulnerability of, 81

Zero aircraft, 282

Zhili-Fengtian Wars, 106–107

About the Author

Jeremy Black graduated from Cambridge University with a starred First and did graduate work at Oxford University before teaching at the University of Durham and then at the University of Exeter, where he is professor of history. He has held visiting chairs at the United States Military Academy at West Point, Texas Christian University, and Stillman College. He is a senior fellow of the Foreign Policy Research Institute. Black received the Samuel Eliot Morison Prize from the Society for Military History in 2008. His recent books include *Air Power: A Global History*, *War and Technology*, *Naval Power: A History of Warfare and the Sea from 1500 Onwards*, *Rethinking World War Two: The Conflict and Its Legacy*, *Fortifications and Siegecraft: Defense and Attack through the Ages*, and *War and Its Causes*.